Party Games

Party Games

Getting, Keeping, and Using
Power in Gilded Age Politics

MARK WAHLGREN SUMMERS

The University of North Carolina Press

Chapel Hill and London

Designed by April Leidig-Higgins
Set in Monotype Bulmer by Copperline Book Services, Inc.

The paper in this book meets the guidelines for permanence
and durability of the Committee on Production Guidelines
for Book Longevity of the Council on Library Resources.

Library of Congress Cataloging-in-Publication Data
Summers, Mark W. (Mark Wahlgren), 1951–
Party games: getting, keeping, and using power in Gilded
Age politics / Mark Wahlgren Summers.
p. cm. Includes bibliographical references and index.
ISBN 0-8078-2862-9 (cloth: alk. paper)
ISBN 0-8078-5537-5 (pbk.: alk. paper)
1. United States — Politics and government — 1865 – 1900.
2. Political culture — United States — History — 19th
century.   3. Political parties — United States — History —
19th century.   4. Power (Social sciences) — United States —
History — 19th century.   5. Political corruption — United
States — History — 19th century.   I. Title.
E661.S965 2004
324'.0973'09034 — dc22   2003021554

cloth   08 07 06 05 04   5 4 3 2 1
paper   08 07 06 05 04   5 4 3 2 1

CONTENTS

III. Policy—The Golden Rule?

IV. Rounding off the Two and a Half Party System

ILLUSTRATIONS

The Dog That Didn't Bark at Night

The Campaign is simply disgusting. We shall win, but what a victory!
—Edwin L. Godkin to a friend, 1896

Edwin L. Godkin, editor of the *Nation*, was right on both counts. For the 1896 election was the year when the Populists, greatest third party since the Civil War, allied with Democrats of South and West, mounted their challenge against the cities and business interests of the East. For Godkin and so many other liberal reformers, the sides could not have been clearer. Favoring a gold standard were all the forces of order, property, public responsibility, and financial sanity. Demagogues and madmen rallied their hosts on the other side. On election day, justice triumphed. The Populists were broken. Never again would they put the two-party system at serious risk. Indeed, though Godkin could not know it, never again would any third party mount quite such a challenge to the Republican and Democratic hold on America's political process.

Historians like Lawrence Goodwyn and Leon Fink tempt us to see how it could have turned out differently. From 1848 to the century's end, robust third and fourth parties were the norm. In the 1860s and 1870s, level-headed prophets foresaw a day when new parties would replace the old. It had happened before, more than once, as enemies became allies and allies sundered on the new, pressing issues. Parties based on issues like slavery and the Civil War must perish when the last fetter was broken, the last banner furled.[1] Greenbackers, Labor Party men, and Populists looked to the breakthrough to come. But that moment never came.

It was, in fact, less a possibility than we might imagine from the many excellent books dedicated to third-party fortunes—among which Goodwyn's, Fink's, Peter Argersinger's, and Robert McMath's hold the very highest rank. By 1896, the breakthrough was very like a news story that a small-town weekly is said to have carried on a slow day:

> As our reporter sat upon a street corner to-day he saw what might have been one of the most horrible accidents ever recorded. A hackman came very near running over a nurse and two children and killing them outright. Had it not been for the good judgment of the nurse, who, before she came out, left the children at home and herself had gone to the drug store to get some medicine, and the cabman before he reached the corner having turned down a by-street, there might have been a great accident in that locality.[2]

The horrible accident never happened to Democratic or Republican organizations. Third parties flared, flickered, and guttered out. That was the voters' choice in part; but, as this book suggests, it was also *the system*'s choice—the system, as it had been shaped by its owners, the politicians themselves. No extraordinary means were used to wreck the outsiders; the means were all too ordinary, used for thirty years by one major party against the other, and by both against any intruder into the system. The 1896 campaign may have been "disgusting," as Godkin described it, but he would have been first to admit that it was also politics-as-usual.

Politics-as-usual. We know some aspects so well that we run the risk of hardly knowing the system as a whole at all. On the one hand, popular historians like Matthew Josephson and Ray Ginger round up the usual suspects: corrupt city bosses buying elections with payoffs, patronage, and protection to urban low life, industrial robber barons trafficking in shares and congressmen, and tycoons buying themselves Senate seats until the upper house became the "millionaires' club." On the other, scholars like Jean Baker, Joel H. Silbey, John F. Reynolds, and Michael McGerr have stressed the vitality, even the romance of popular politics, and, in explaining its demise, have shown the hidden costs and self-interested aims behind such elementary reforms as a professionalized civil service, the secret ballot, and "campaigns of education," where tracts on abstruse issues blanketed the ground like snow and turned the campaign yell into the election-day yawn.[3]

Both schools of thought have plenty of evidence to prove their case. But both may obscure another point. It was the everyday workings of the system, not the big-money men, that gave the two major parties advantage. Nobody could own it—not the railroad monopolists or the sugar kings or the "goo-goo" reformers. In the last analysis, it was the politicians who owned it, shaped it to serve their own party needs, and did what they could to keep trespassers off. The evils that

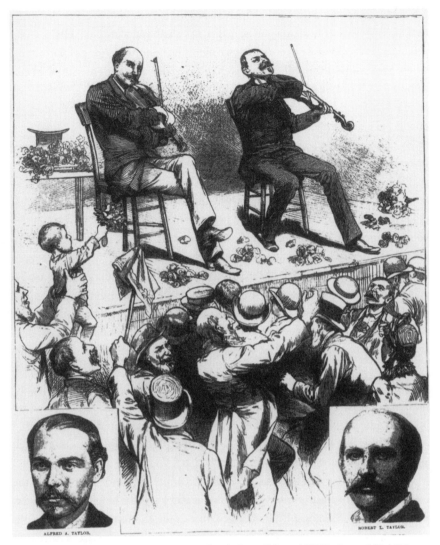

"Novel political campaign in Tennessee — the rival candidates, 'Alf' Taylor and 'Bob' Taylor, fiddling for votes" (*Frank Leslie's Illustrated Newspaper*, October 2, 1886). When the two major parties ran brothers for governor against each other, joint campaign appearances turned into a "war of roses." Those cherishing the exuberance of Gilded Age politics and skeptics, convinced of the emptiness of the whole spectacle, both might find grounds in the Taylors' campaign appearances.

reformers pointed to were real, palpable, and morally destructive, but the worst of them may have come from partisanship, not a panting after pelf. The popular politics of the Gilded Age, more than we might imagine, was a *guided* popularity, where great work behind the scenes went into driving as many voters to the polls as possible. That was the politicians' job. How they did that job, and how that affected the shape of Gilded Age politics and set limits on the possibilities for change, is what *Party Games* is all about.[4]

By no means am I suggesting that political contests were meaningless, a con-game, or an outright thwarting of the people's will. Public opinion could be shaped and tempered, but a major party would not have suppressed it and, as long as there were third-party alternatives, could not have afforded to do so. Even minus-cule challenges could undo one party's control in any state where the two parties were competitive, and many of the challenges were far from minuscule. Main-stream politicians made politics fun, and many of them gave good service, even if some of them did so solely for their own advantage. Self-interest made politi-cians with any expectation of a long career respond to demands from organized groups, and not just those clustered around boardroom tables. Without that flex-ibility, without a broad range of principles that the parties could apply to allow them to take up new issues and accede to demands put upon them, the third-party challenges would have had a much easier time of it.[5] But, as several schol-ars have shown, there also is another important part to the story, where public participation was channeled, if not thwarted, for Democratic and Republican benefit.[6] The proofs are strongest after 1890, and especially in the methods used to wreck the Populists. As I hope to show, the practice, and the culture that spawned it, had been around ever since the Civil War.

Cynics may treat this book as an owner's manual, far more interested in the mechanical problems to winning and holding office and the little tricks of the fix-it boys than of the larger spirit that, to give one example, motivated voters to con-nect the kingdom of Heaven with the reign of the "party of moral ideas" on earth. They may say it leaves out the politics of the disenfranchised and the power of the apparently powerless, to which the best new scholarship has devoted its at-tentions. This is entirely true. Politics is so much more than what has been writ-ten here; and for the Gilded Age, any political historian could put together a colossal un-bibliography, full of the titles of worthy books not yet penned, by scholars yet unborn. Arguably, politics spreads as wide as the struggle for power. The relationships between those with more power and those with less extends far beyond laws and government institutions. Familial relations, the authority to make decisions in churches or community groups—all might be seen as an extended form of politics; and, as one congressman put it, war was just politics with bayonets.[7]

Still, within its limits, this book aims to cast new, often harsh light, on politics as most Gilded Age observers would have grasped it, the kind worked out through elections and the doings of those striving to hold office. If in some things, it gives the mainstream parties a more generous appreciation for flexibility in policy and sincerity in intentions than popular historians have given, it may also give us more appreciation for the Godkins.

A century's perspective certainly shows us the narrowness of outlook, if not the outright bigotry of "liberal reformers," those genteel gray pundits in the pulpits and behind the editor's desk at big-city magazines. We may not see them as "man-milliners" and "Miss Nancys," as partisans referred to them in the Gilded Age, but terms like "elitist" or "Social Darwinist" work just as well to discredit their indictment of a system gone sour.[8] In our own jaded age, the politics of spectacle—banners, parades, marching clubs, and pole-raisings—seem as appealing as they are remote. We can hardly help feeling for those who saw to it that eight eligible voters in every ten showed up at the polls, year in, year out, or deploring those "reformers" who tried to take the political showmanship out of making policy.

Yet I hope that for those not blinded by the torchlight the defects in politics-as-usual should stand out the clearer. It was not from the wild imagination that paranoia and the cloistered life of a ritzy city neighborhood alone that the outsiders' call for reforms would come. With much justice, Populists, Greenbackers, labor agitators, Mugwumps, and "goo-goos" could have written a compelling *disowner's* manual, repudiating the whole idea of a politician-run democracy actually being able to register the people's will. That their skepticism spread and strengthened was certainly not all their own doing. To steal the words of President Grover Cleveland, it was not a theory they faced, but a condition.

So many people have helped turn this manuscript from a theory into a condition that I should be thanking them in blocks of five. I am beholden to the *Journal of American History* for permitting me to republish in considerably altered form my article "Party Games: The Art of Stealing Elections in the Late-Nineteenth-Century United States," in the September 2001 issue; and I am grateful for the permission from the *Journal of Policy History* to do the same with those portions that filled out part of the article "To Make the Wheels Revolve We Must Have Grease & Barrel Politics in the Gilden Age," from volume 14, number 1 (2002).

Archive on archive has spread their dusty troves before me with courtesy and occasional zeal. The buoyancy and eagerness to help at the New Hampshire Historical Society quite made up for its truncated hours, and Bowdoin's staff endured much. If I could move into the Minnesota Historical Society, I certainly would, though for efficiency mixed with great consideration, I would just as lief settle in the excellent James J. Hill Library down the hill from it. Department colleagues, especially Karen Petrone, Joanne Melish, Bill Freehling, and Ronald Formisano, wrangled over more than one chapter in brown-bag colloquium and asked many useful questions, only some of which have been answered, and not all of which, alas, may have been answered correctly. Ed Blum, a graduate student of singular perception and unrivaled goodwill, critiqued, considered, and conjectured. David Hamilton, Philip Harling, and Tracy Campbell read the work through from end to end with their usual sagacity. An encyclopedic source on vote fraud in American history, Tracy mixed helpfulness with horse sense. If I ever steal an election, I shall certainly call on his know-how, and if I ever am caught, it will be because somebody else consulted him about how exactly I did it. For all his fine criticisms, R. Hal Williams did me too much kindness in his reflections on the manuscript, and John F. Reynolds may have done simple justice in helping me to fry the fat from it. What grammatical and syntactical mistakes could possibly be prevented, Mary Caviness took care of in copyediting, and again am I grateful for her endeavors. Because the work never mentioned Godzilla, Galen gave it no help at all, but I am beholden for his exuberance and the small intergalactic clay penguins that he made to cheer me up at low points in the revising. And finally, to the first and best critics, my parents, Clyde W. and Evelyn Summers, my last and best thanks.

To Susan, shimmering pearl of the Cuyahoga, of course, the book is dedicated.

Party Games

Our Friend the Enemy

A Typical Year

Bring the good old frying-pan, we're going to fry some fat;
Bring a peck of anthracite in grandpa's old white hat,
Put the "Protects" in the pan, then we'll know "where they're at"
While we are frying for Bennie.
—*New York World*, August 19, 1892

Particulars aside, the 1888 campaign was one like any other.[1]

Every election differs from every other, of course. There was no mistaking blunt, bulky Grover Cleveland for any other president, his rough edges softened by a White House marriage, his great frame stirred only by a sense of duty and a passion for hard work. "We love him . . . for the enemies he has made," an admirer had declared, and in four years of vetoing private pension grabs and scowling down office beggars, Cleveland should have increased that love tenfold. Not since 1840 had a Democratic incumbent president sought a second term. Contemporaries couldn't help remembering it: the winner, William Henry Harrison, was grandfather to Republicans' current nominee, former senator Benjamin Harrison. Political old-timers compared the parades and gimmickry to that first "log cabin and hard cider" campaign, and Democratic cartoonists drew Harrison as a half-pint, dwarfed under his grandfather's hat.[2] Read the tracts, hear the marching masses' cries, and 1888 might seem the election of elections, settling the nation's destinies for the next quarter century. "Vote out Republican disease," the *New York Sun* exhorted,

Vote out the nation's lasting hurt;
Vote out four years of bloody shirt,
Vote in four years of thorough peace.[3]

Armageddon with brass bands: that was the 1888 campaign.

And every other. If any partisan had paused to flip through newspapers' back files, he would have discovered that the country, by its votes in 1868, apparently chose bayonet rule over revolution and anarchy, just as it selected empire and robbery over free love and treason in 1872, fraud in vote-counting over fraud in vote-casting in 1876, political degeneracy over economic ruin in 1880, and sexual depravity over a saturnalia of corruption in 1884.[4] The republic was always at stake. This heightened, apocalyptic sense was one by-product of the political carnival.

In truth, just about everything about 1888 was new except the basic pattern: the methods, wiles, and arts of the politician. The 1888 campaign, therefore, becomes a fitting showcase not just for the pleasures of partisan politics but for its perils. Hoopla, hype, trickery, bribery, and fraud were as natural to the process as a torchlight parade. Not just in its best but in its worst and most manipulative, not just in its most public attractions but in its most private rascalities, this was a typical election year in the so-called party period.

The brighter side of partisan display was plain to see. Politics could be savored in buttons, campaign clubs, and parades, and in the contributions of an intensely partisan press. "The whole face of the country is plastered with politics," a visitor to the Indiana farm country reported. "Seen from a train, the whole country might be thought the camp of some great army with the flags marking regimental headquarters."[5] Every town had one mass meeting, and most cities had more. Just before the election, Republicans and Democrats shared the same night and paraded down different streets in New York. Each spectacle had its own attractions, of course. Democrats put the mother of Irish patriot Charles Stewart Parnell on their reviewing stand and Wild West showman "Buffalo Bill" Cody in a yellow dogcart. Onlookers could see banners of blue and gold, and scarlet pennants ornamented with golden legends, canes with flags waving from the handle, brass bands tramping under the guerdon of a stuffed rooster, platoons wielding brooms, jewelers carrying life-size portraits of the president, and endless mottoes. For the first time, campaign buttons became the fashion, including one for Cleveland that looked like the pin that members of the Grand Army of the Republic wore—which, since most GAR members were Republican, put many Union veterans in a rage. Consciously cultivated to give politics a more moral tone, women were enlisted in campaign clubs, displayed on floats as symbols of liberty and the purity of the republic, and provided with a whole array of badges that combined partisan identification with that tastefulness and discretion that a male electorate expected of ladies—whose involvement in politics, of course, was preeminently to protect home, family, and morality and unsullied by a sordid desire for offices or power. Something new called a "kazoo" allowed partisans to project a tune "with a lugubrious, whining intensity of dolor," and since these sold for twenty dollars per hundred, there was no escaping them. Songsters issued "rot of an offensively partisan character," and canvassers passed out cigars that may have been even more offensive than they were partisan. "I am so glad this damn campaign is over," labor leader Terence V. Powderly sighed as election day approached; "if it lasted another month, I believe every man, woman and child in the country would be stark, staring mad."[6]

Likely enough, Powderly was not contemplating the kazoos. Republicans were incensed at the smear campaign of faked quotations from Benjamin Harrison. Not that they should have felt surprised; the spirit of intense partisanship that set parades in motion inevitably breached the rules of courtesy and biased each party's press to keep lies alive. Indianapolis residents knew that during the great railroad strike of 1877, Harrison never drilled a private company and marched them to the depot threatening to start "them trains running by force." They were not likely to believe that he ever said "a dollar a day was enough for any workingman" and "any amount was too much for a striker." But the quotations spread, and all Harrison's own denials could not stop them.[7]

Even more sinister was the undercurrent of ugly gossip about Grover Cleveland's marriage, the inescapable result of campaigns so committed to selling a candidate's personality and the recognition of women's particular interest in upholding the highest personal morality in public life. High-placed Republicans carried on a whispering campaign, alleging that Cleveland beat his wife and went on drunken sprees. Confronted with his role in fostering the stories, Senator John J. Ingalls offered a curious defense. The very fact that the president's friends felt called upon to deny the charges was all but a confirmation that they were true, he declared. In West Virginia, the stories were traced back to the wives of Republican leaders, though far less delicate versions regaled the smoking rooms.[8]

Whereas Cleveland's domestic life was whispered, of course, the tariff issue was shouted. In explaining policy issues in detail, the Gilded Age party system showed itself at its best, and the tariff certainly was one about which the voters, whether as consumers or producers, had every right to care. Workers knew that changes in rates would affect their own wages or general prosperity, though the parties differed on exactly how. In an age when women's attention to politics seemed to be quickening, and certain causes like the restraint of the liquor traffic had turned growing numbers of them into activists at election time, talk about the tariff was sure to appeal to mothers and wives worried about what the family's breadwinner earned and how much a week's wage could buy, and to temperance advocates aware that the liquor traffic throve in part because the government needed excise taxes to make ends meet. Raise tariff rates and the government could afford to shut down saloons without reckoning the cost. Women could vote just about nowhere, but both parties counted on their support to make men vote right and to soften what might seem a matter of crass advantage into a question of virtue and protecting the home. For that, Republicans warned, was just what was at stake. Did husbands want to see their wives "unsex themselves in their struggle for bread" like free-trade England's? Did they want to see "the pregnant mother" sent into the factory and the brothels filled by women unable to make a decent living on the starvation wages that foreign competition were sure to bring?[9]

But amid the many arguments intricate and subtle that both sides retailed, the issue also was used to prove one party patriotic and the other one un-American, even treasonable, or to show that legislation was bought and sold like meat in a butcher's shop. What Republicans were aiming for was not that catchphrase of the late 1880s, the ideal of genteel reformers, a "campaign of education," but a feeling of alarm, even panic. In close northeastern industrial states, even a modest defection would shift the balance, and any issue appealing to class and ethnic loyalties at the same time was doubly useful. Party managers were bidding for the Irish American vote especially. Any enemy of England was Ireland's friend, and so Republicans gave the British lion's tail a twist whenever they could. John Bull–baiting fitted well with the protective tariff issue; England was America's greatest rival for industrial goods and, protectionists warned, would expand into American markets the moment tariff walls fell. Irish Americans were reminded that "free trade ruined Ireland" and by it was ruined still.[10] Throughout the campaign, Republicans spotted Cleveland badges of the finest silk that English mills could spin — as fine, indeed, as the English-made Harrison badges proclaiming, "No Free Trade, but Protection for America."[11]

Finding quotations proving the Republican case was as easy as lying. It took only a typewriter and some imagination. Who, for example, in reading a damning confession from the *English Iron Era*, would check to see whether any such magazine existed? Republicans passed out tens of thousands of cards with the Union Jack on one side and quotes from English newspapers on the other, all assuring readers that a vote for Grover was a vote for England. "It need hardly be said that these quotations from the London papers are of exclusively American manufacture," the *St. James Gazette* commented.[12]

Democrats played the patriot game, too. On the West Coast especially, they tried to tie a Chinese pigtail to the protectionists. How could a tariff raise wages, when Republicans glutted the labor market with immigrants who came without families to support or appetites requiring more than "rat pie"? Republicans had put through the Burlingame Treaty, opening America to Chinese coolies by the thousands; two Republican presidents had vetoed laws excluding the immigrants permanently, and the 1882 law had passed with Republican opposition, Harrison's included.[13] Whites in Chinese masks and outfits paraded as a "Hallison Band," beating tin pans and clashing cymbals. "HALLISON'S FLENDS," the *New York Herald* shrieked:

CHICAGO'S MONGOLIAN REPUBLICANS RAISE A CAMPAIGN FUND.
THEY HOPE TO VOTE SOME DAY.
WORKING FOR HARRISON BECAUSE THEY CONSIDER HIM THEIR FRIEND.

Democrats proved their good intentions more concretely. In the closing hours of Congress, free-trade congressman William L. Scott of Pennsylvania offered a bill canceling the return permits of some 12,000 Chinese laborers who had returned home. A panicked House stampeded it through, and only three senators dared vote against it. "Cleveland and Scott / Made the Chinese trot," paraders chanted.[14]

At the same time, Democrats took their own twist of the British lion's tail, though compared to their rivals, they looked like amateurs. Responding to the opposition's emphasis on Harrison's pedigree, one newspaper traced his ancestors back to an English general among Oliver Cromwell's Roundheads, who, it alleged, took part in the massacre of 3,000 Irish prisoners at Drogheda.[15] Under political pressure from leading party operatives at national committee headquarters, President Cleveland sent in a message to Congress demanding retaliatory legislation against Canada for its refusal to extend landing privileges to American fishing fleets. Everyone knew that the real purpose of Cleveland's sudden militancy was political. "The President has done just what I expected him to do," Senator John Spooner of Wisconsin wrote disgustedly. "He has run up the American flag."[16] From Irish Americans, a flood of telegrams of approval poured into the White House. Catholic newspapers applauded. "Instead of a campaign of dreary statistics," a New York lawyer rejoiced, "it gave us a sentimental issue."[17]

It did, indeed, but only on temporary loan. To the British minister in Washington, Lionel Sackville-West, came a letter, apparently from one Charles F. Murchison, asking advice. Murchison was English-born and at heart still English, and the campaign troubled him. With all the president's posturing, he was no longer sure which presidential candidate would serve British interests best; could Sackville-West help him? Too much of a gentleman or a fool to suspect a trick, the British minister wrote back, assuring Murchison that Cleveland's call for retaliation was all a campaign ruse and advising a vote for Cleveland. But there was no Murchison. A citrus grower from southern California, George Osgoodby, had imposed on Sackville-West to smoke out England's true sentiments. Republican chairman Matthew Quay ran off "millions of copies" of the letter. Quickly, the president sent the minister packing in time for paraders to greet him with,

> Sack! Sack! Sackville West!
> Cleveland's in the White House—
> YOU KNOW THE REST!

But the damage had been done. "They have given Sir Sackville the shake," Senator John Sherman told one audience, "and now all that remains for you to do is to give Mr. Cleveland the sack."[18]

The Irish vote took more than sensations to peel it from its traditional Democratic loyalties. A sizable chunk would go where its leaders drove it, and the leaders with whom the party chose to deal were men cultivated and financed by Republican Party managers. "Nothing is required but careful and immediate organization," a Pennsylvania industrialist wrote the vice presidential nominee. "I have spent large sums in helping these men perfect their organization and I have increased since my last letter to you my personal expenditures to an amount all told in excess of $29,000."[19]

Money, indeed, was everywhere. A campaign could not get along without it, and that of 1888 showed how far the need for it defined the major parties' leadership and the way managers chose to direct public debate. Observers noted that the Democratic National Committee looked like a railroad board of directors, and there were plenty of representatives of coal interests, too. Tariff reform meant money in the purse for some firms, as well as financial risks for others. But the general rule was that a party in power always had less to offer its contributors than one out of power: fewer offices available to be filled, fewer commitments already made to follow a certain policy, and less of a chance of letting supporters' minds run wild with all the possible benefits that could come from a new lease on power. By contrast, Republican businessmen like John Wanamaker of Philadelphia raised money all the more willingly, having a reasonably certain commitment of recognition—in his case, as it proved, with his appointment as postmaster general. Different groups, each wanting a share of the credit and the rewards, vied with each other to produce the funds that would carry the big states.

Just such an aspiration inspired James P. Foster, head of a fresh-made federation of protectionist clubs. His so-called Republican League of the United States had no political track record, no bloc of votes to deliver. Unable to get funds from the national committee, which thought it a mere "Sunday-school political organization," Foster turned elsewhere. He issued a circular to league members, urging them to start a scare campaign on the tariff issue, one that would "put the manufacturers of Pennsylvania under the fire and fry all the fat out of them." The letter became public, much to the Republican National Committee's embarrassment, but Foster had no part in the frying. Chairman Matt Quay handled that. All told, Republicans extracted half a million dollars from the Keystone State, about four dollars in every ten that the national campaign raised. Some of it came from politicians in business, who hoped to advance their own political fortunes, but there was no question that others were buying a seat at the table when the winners met to discuss the specifics of tariff revision and that the agenda of the next Congress, whoever won, would treat contributors' desires with particular respect.[20]

A like ambition fired low-level politicians, who gave their time and money to buy themselves a better chance at a government job. State and local organizations turned to their friends for funds and knew that they could depend on generous contributions from the employees on the public payroll, in spite of a federal ban on forced assessments. "It reminds me of a custom that prevails in Jackson, Mississippi," Congressman "Private John" Allen told a reporter. "On the morning of each election day, the white Democrats fire a gun off. That is to notify the negroes that there is going to be a fair election that day. And if the one gun in the morning is not sufficient, the signal is repeated at intervals during the day. The opening of this office in a similar way will notify the Democratic officeholders that there are going to be voluntary contributions taken up."[21]

Money raised was as good as spent. Needs almost always outstripped supply. Working together or at cross-purposes, crowds of party committees fought to get out the high-tariff word to voters. There was plenty of money for scare campaigns and for buying up Democratic factions in New York City, though some ward bosses never delivered the goods. Just before the polls opened, it was later reported, the Republican National Committee bought out three political movements that claimed to command at least 40,000 votes—claims that proved 30,000 too high. Republican ward boss "Johnny" O'Brien took a hefty sum for delivering his regulars, and did so—but only for the nominees of his local machine. State leaders were so incensed that they kicked him out of the organization.[22]

Quay had better uses for the party's money. He concentrated 40 percent of the campaign funds on swinging New York. One hundred thousand dollars could bring around organizers of the ethnic vote and give them resources to work with. Another $150,000 could put on a spectacular state campaign and would give

Thomas Platt, the Republican boss, an added incentive for doing his utmost to carry the governorship and the legislature (Platt already had a pretty good incentive; he thought that he had been promised the Treasury Department in repayment for swinging New York's delegates behind Benjamin Harrison. A rude wakening awaited him—after the election, naturally). Most of all, $100,000 would give Quay the wherewithal to set up effective defenses against Democratic vote-tampering.

By offering a reward for uncovering any fraudulent registration and vote, Quay turned every partisan into a poll watcher and deputy. At the same time, he put John Davenport to work compiling a "city directory." Davenport had had long experience with Democratic "colonization" of voters. Now he hired hundreds of employees to make a census of New York. Hundreds of maps detailed the residents of each house, apartment, and saloon. Checked against the list of registered voters, Davenport's census could prove phony registrations. Alongside a separate tally of vacant apartments and hotel rooms, it could show exactly where last-minute "residents" who showed up at the polls had come from. The secret of success, though, lay in Democrats knowing exactly what Quay had, and how thoroughly he had covered the city. Publicly informed of the real purpose of Davenport's directory, Democrats were furious, especially those who thought they were calling Quay's bluff about having them arrested and then saw the jail door close on them. In that respect, at least, New York City had an unusually honest election, thanks to Quay's having "fried the fat."[23]

Beyond John Davenport's scrutiny, that same "fat" could turn an election into a shopping expedition. It was well known that legal voters could be bought, and many of these so-called floaters expected compensation, even for voting their consciences. Indiana was a particularly close state, with a long record of vote-buying on both sides.[24] As rival Republicans vied for leadership of the campaign and exclusive authority to receive and disburse the national committee's funds, they grew less discreet about how the money should be raised and for what. Former pension commissioner W. W. Dudley, whose vote-buying notoriety in the past had earned him the Democratic sobriquet, "Two-Dollar Dudley," decided to make an end run around the state committee. On his own authority, he issued a letter to county chairmen, assuring them of the funds they needed for their election-day efforts. What those efforts were, Dudley made entirely plain: it was to buy the floating vote. When the merchandise had been purchased, Republican organizers must not let it out of their sight. "Divide the floaters into blocks of five and put a trusted man with necessary funds in charge of these five and make them responsible that none get away and that all vote our ticket." A Democratic mail clerk got suspicious of the letters sent from Republican headquarters and opened one of Dudley's. On Halloween, the *Indianapolis Sentinel* published it on the front page with screaming headlines. As a roorback—a campaign allegation thrown before the public too late for the other side to undo the damage —"blocks of five" was a model of its kind.

In vain Dudley protested the letter a forgery, or at any rate an imprecise copy. If anything, Dudley's letter did what Davenport's city directory had done. It raised such a tumult that many more floaters than usual may have decided to avoid the fuss and let their consciences be their guide. (Not all, however. In Bloomington, Indiana, the Democratic newspaper reported that "the fight was for the 'floats,' and although the Republicans had loads of 'boodle,' the Democrats got a good share of them." Later, after they lost the state, Democrats would remember their opponents' enormities and forget about their own.) Reportedly, Republicans also made an unfortunate slip. Chris Magee, the Pittsburgh boss, was alleged to have raised a $40,000 fund for Indianapolis election-day expenses and given it to two light-fingered emissaries. They arrived at state party headquarters; the money didn't.[25]

Indiana Democrats had half expected to lose, but those in Delaware reeled at their losses. There, far more than in Indiana, Republican money seems to have been a decisive factor. Both parties bought voters. But there was a pretty considerable disproportion between party war chests. Republicans were so cocky in one town that when the polls were about to close and they found three hundren left in the kitty, they reputedly offered, "as by public auction," twenty-five dollars for any stray voter lingering around.[26]

Delaware was all the more precious for Republicans for being on the borders of the South, a vast area where Democratic margins could always be relied on, and denial of a full, free count became more legal every year. Vote-buying was a fact of Gilded Age political life, as inevitable as the campaign lie, the "scare," the fat frying, and the manipulation of public policy for immediate party ends. But no floating vote could do Republicans good in states where the laws had been written to rule out serious competition. However much chance the Republican Party might have in the Border South and locally along the Appalachian range, it had no chance of carrying the cotton kingdom. Far more than in the North, members of the dominant party ran the elections to suit themselves.

West Virginia showed what odds even a well-organized Republican campaign faced in one of the most open southern political systems. For resource, both financial and tactical, Stephen B. Elkins had hardly an equal, and in gubernatorial nominee Nathan W. Goff, he was backing a proven vote-getter. With Elkins's coal and railroad fortune thrown into the race against them, Democrats waged the most desperate fight in a generation. There were threats of violence and allegations of slush funds for buying voters. Twelve thousand more West Virginians voted than the eligible voters. Democrats blamed it on Republicans in the mining counties and on hordes of imported blacks from out of state. The real increase, though, came in backwoods Democratic strongholds, where election judges winked at fraud. Apparently, Grover Cleveland had carried the state by 500 votes out of 159,000 cast, but even then, Democrats could not quite count Goff out, too. With the legislature so closely divided, it took three months of pettifogging and political trickery to cheat Republicans of their due.[27]

Matters proceeded in a much uglier fashion in Louisiana. There, not just Republicans but Democrats chafed under the squalid, thievish administration of Samuel D. McEnery. "Reform Democrats," mostly upcountry farmers, wanted a new deal, one free from the domination of New Orleans bosses and the lubricating money of the Louisiana Lottery. Their best hope was onetime governor Francis T. Nicholls. Pretty rough methods preceded the state convention. In one case, local campaign managers met on the streets of Farmerville and shot each other to death.

Then a near-miracle seemed in the making. When Nicholls won the nomination, McEnery proved a more depraved man than Democrats had expected. Sore with defeat, he vowed to see that Louisiana got a "fair count" in the general election. Any such count, Nicholls's supporters knew, would permit blacks to vote freely, and a free vote meant a Republican victory. "Reform Democrats" rushed to buy the governor's cooperation. Louisiana was saved from self-government in the nick of time. Five thousand Republican ballots made it to East Feliciana parish for distribution; just five were counted for the Republican ticket. Republicans lost the state by nearly three to one, and when Nicholls came in, he put McEnery on the state supreme court.[28]

Republicanism had been smothered in Louisiana. Brutal means suppressed another opposition movement in Arkansas that summer. The radical Union Labor Party, backed by the farmers' Wheel movement and what remained of the Republican organization, nominated a former Democrat for governor. With considerable white support, Union Laborites fooled themselves into believing that Democratic authorities would never dare try the kind of methods they used on blacks. Election day taught them a brutal lesson. Out of the ashes of stolen and burned poll books in the state capital, the Democratic county ticket rose triumphant. Elsewhere, presses were smashed, visiting reporters were driven away, merchants were burned out of their businesses, and opposition voters were counted out by exclusively Democratic election officials. "There will be no opposition to Democracy in Union County for some years to come," the Democratic *Sentinel* crowed. "Old scores are all settled, and we now take a new start, with peace and brotherly love as our watchword."[29]

Mississippi and South Carolina carried on quiet campaigns, but theirs were the stillness of political death. Blacks outnumbered whites, and most of them, given the chance, would have voted Republican, but Democratic leaders never meant to give them that chance. "Private John" Allen's reference to the "custom" on a Jackson election day was blunt fact, dressed up as a joke. "The niggers can vote if they want to, and we're not doing anything to hinder them," a white in Meridian, Mississippi, told a northern reporter, "but we don't propose to let them run our local government. We *count* the votes, and you can just bet your bottom dollar that the white men are going to stay on top." At one box, Republicans outpolled Democrats two to one; but when the hundred votes were counted, they gave the Democratic congressman a majority of 280.[30] One Republican squib quoted a patriotic Mississippian vowing war to the death against any new tariff taxing shotguns: "Why, dang it all, it costs too blamed much to carry an honest election in this country!"[31]

If Mississippi represented the violent heritage, South Carolina foreshadowed the orderly prospect of a solid South to come. As the lieutenant governor pointed out, reporters would find no violence, intimidation, or "shuffling of boxes" in South Carolina any more. Since the "eight-box ballot law" of 1882 wiped out most of the black vote by creating a confusing array of separate boxes in which to deposit ballots for different offices and an army of all-powerful elections officers were able to disqualify a ballot on any technicality, there was hardly anyone left for Democrats to intimidate. Republicans who tried to register found the registration boards stacked against them. In any case, what was there to vote for? Congressional districts had been nicely gerrymandered to give blacks just one seat in seven, a geographical design of shreds, patches, and squiggles, and Democrats, by omitting to open polling places where the black majority could reach them, captured that district, too.[32] When Republicans asked the governor to give them a fair deal—at least one Republican commissioner in each county and a manager for each precinct—they were told that bipartisanship would only risk a return to "disgraceful scenes and unscrupulous manipulations of elections, so confessedly prevalent during the days of Republican rule."[33]

Plainly, partisan politics relied on much more than brass bands and bandanas, ribbons and roorbacks. South and North, it used every legal and illegal means to shape the popular will to its own ends. From a foreign policy tempered to serve domestic political ends to a count of the votes tampered with for Democratic purposes, Americans would have had good reason to feel troubled by the price that partisanship demanded for putting on so enthralling a show, and to feel suspicious of the legitimacy of the outcome—as, indeed, the losers almost always did.

This November, the Democrats came out 100,000 votes ahead and two states short. Results came in slowly, but from the first, Harrison led. By midnight, all doubts had vanished and Republicans turned their attention to thwarting a supposed effort by Democrats to "steal" the House by counting in enough of their candidates in close districts.[34]

On the face of the returns, Cleveland ran a strong second. More people voted for him than for Harrison. But the close result was an artificial one, just as Cleveland's popular plurality was. It came about by the systematic suppression of a Republican turnout down south and the usual distortions that a winner-take-all system in the Electoral College gave him. Where the elections were freest, in the North, Cleveland met a decisive defeat, and those southern ones with the least bulldozing, like Maryland, Delaware, and Kentucky, showed Republican gains. A free vote and a fair count might have given Harrison North Carolina and the two Virginias as well. The most one could say for the Democrats was that they had not quite been able to cheat the people out of the presidential candidate who most of them favored.[35]

Yet it was Democrats who felt cheated. The Sackville-West trick, the "blocks of five," and "treachery" in New York all gave them reasons for complaint. It was certainly not true that Governor David Bennett Hill had worked out a swap with Republican managers to win another term in Albany, but Cleveland's friends believed it.[36] Stories, some plausible, told of black voters demanding a payoff of five dollars instead of the customary two, and getting it, of Indiana Republicans packing floaters into the GAR hall and the party newspaper office keeping them above temptation until they could be marched to the polls. Civil service reformer Lucius B. Swift put the two-party spending in Indiana at a quarter of a million dollars, for buying 25,000 purchasables. "You see what boodle can do," Republicans told their Democratic friends gleefully, regaling them with tales of New York precincts helped along with quarters and five-dollar bills. No one could calculate how many votes that lies about Cleveland's domestic life cost the president, though it seemed reasonable to guess the number in the thousands and to speculate that they changed the result in several close states.[37]

The more sober observers among them knew well that this was not the whole story. The real culprit in Cleveland's defeat up north was the tariff issue and his failure, once he had made the issue with his message, of not leaping in to defend it aggressively. The public had been educated, informed, aroused — and, in the end, convinced that Democratic tariff tinkering carried too high a risk to permit.[38] Here, too, though, the Democrats could argue that there had been no fair referenda. Their followers had been misled and spooked, their leaders smeared. Money beat Cleveland, money used for all the legitimate needs, but with plenty left over to hoodwink some voters and capture others.

Nor was Cleveland the only victim. For those who suspected that the two-party system, for all its appeals to labor before the election, tilted toward the "monopolists," the congressional elections gave serious confirmation. To credit their reading of events, in California "the wine and fruit trusts" picked off the one antimonopoly Democrat in the state delegation; in Wisconsin, the Pacific Railroad rings submerged the Labor Party congressman in vote-buying boodle to punish his defense of homesteaders against railroad grabs of the public domain. In St. Louis, two of the foremost battlers against contract and pauper immigrant labor were beaten by interests that profited from hiring newcomers at penurious rates. Iowa railroads successfully targeted two independent voices for producers' rights, including Greenback congressman James B. Weaver. In every case, the results were the best public will that money could buy.[39]

From a century's perspective, many of the obvious questions were ones that Americans then asked: was *this* the necessary fruit of democracy? was this a political system that represented the people or that worked as the founders or even the high-flown cant of later generations boasted? But the last thing contemporaries would have felt was incredulity. Like it or not, this *was* how Gilded Age politics worked. It combined spirit and a free exercise of the electorate's will between choices that the politicians and institutions had limited and defined, with a constant readiness to thwart that public will for the sake of party success.

Examples abound. It was unnecessary to point to the most extreme of them. The presidential election of 1876 really did stand alone. It had been stolen twice over — once by Democratic fraud, bullying, killing, and manipulation of the election laws down south, and once by Republican "returning boards" in three southern states counting the votes to give their nominee a majority in the Electoral College of precisely one. Gentle, honest Rutherford B. Hayes was still remembered by Democrats as "His Fraudulency," the one White House occupant without legitimate title. So, too, any southerner of middle age could remember the 1870s, when two governments, each claiming to be legal, ran Louisiana and private armies overthrew the Republican governor until federal troops imposed him again. There were rival governments in Louisiana again two years later, and in South Carolina and Florida. Earlier, the same thing had happened in Alabama and Texas. In Arkansas, the self-proclaimed governors mustered troops and went to war. Political impeachments had deposed governors in Mississippi, Louisiana, Florida, and North Carolina, and governors had bought their acquittals in Arkansas and South Carolina.[40] But these incidents, Gilded Age observers would insist, did not reflect the normal workings of the system. They were the residue of the Civil War and the attempted revolution that Republicans in Washington tried to bring about in the postwar South.

Rather, the typicality of 1888 showed itself most clearly in what happened every time there was a presidential race, and in many of the off years as well. It had distinct resemblances to the campaign of 1880. In South Carolina, Democrats used the most blatant frauds, from repeaters to "tissue ballots" (on paper thin enough to allow one folded slip to contain a dozen more inside it) and the destruction of ballot boxes from Republican precincts to win most of the House seats. Then, as in 1888, a roorback had roiled politics at the last minute and, thanks to credulous voters, had cost the Republicans Nevada, California, and very nearly the presidency; memory of it, in 1888, helped Republicans persuade themselves that Dudley's "blocks of five" missive was one more wile of the enemy.[41]

If anything, the partisan tricks that carried Indiana had been more blatant in 1880. Both sides strained every resource to win the state, though Republicans had more resources to strain. The more one national committeeman, privy to the clamor for funds, heard, the more alarmed he grew. Some "of our worst men are in the lead," he wrote onetime committee secretary William E. Chandler, "and God only knows what they will do. If they do not cover the party with disgrace I shall be thankful." What they did was cover the state's precincts with "soap," as the vote-buying money was called. Five thousand residents were "hired" to "work" for the ticket, at twenty to seventy-five dollars apiece. Warning that federal deputy marshals would bar legitimate Democratic voters from the polls, the *Evansville Courier* announced that the party had set up a defense fund for any citizen "who shoots down Marshal Dudley's deputies who dare to prevent them, by the forms of law, from voting the Democratic ticket." The *Indianapolis Journal* was shocked at such an incitement to violence, but not all that surprised, and advised Republicans that gunpowder made "a good disinfectant" for Democratic fraud. Republicans won narrowly, and four months later, the vice president elect immortalized Dudley's role at a swank dinner at Delmonico's. "Indiana was really, I suppose, a Democratic state," he allowed. "It had been put down on the books always as a State that might be carried by close and perfect organization and a great deal of —." Spying reporters in the banquet hall, Chester Alan Arthur stopped before the fatal word, but his audience, far less discreet laughed and supplied it for him: "Soap!"[42] That soap had cost Republicans dearly. Garfield needed campaign funds and all but promised to give railroad tycoon Jay Gould a veto power over Supreme Court nominees. Indeed, his first nomination, Stanley Matthews, had a reputation for doing Gould's bidding in the Senate and for having shared in the dirty work of stealing three southern states for Hayes in the 1876 election.[43]

The list of manipulations could have gone on, year after year: shoestring districts to keep one party in control of the state's delegation in the House, moguls elected to Congress on the basis of the "bar'l" of cash they could open, conventions rigged or carried by voting forged proxies, newspaper editors pensioned with foreign consulates and post office appointments, and coalitions between mainstream parties and their minor rivals for a share of the offices and, less commonly, a share of the political agenda. Much of the behavior was perfectly legal, much of it was part of the acceptable privileges of those in power, and all of it was customary. But it highlighted a crucial point about the Gilded Age political system. For all the popular participation, it was on the terms that politicians set and was channeled in directions that suited their ends most. Grassroots movements were ones well-watered, fertilized, and nurtured by those to whom such movements would be of advantage, and those most capable of doing the encouraging were those most experienced in the rules and bounds of politics.

The system was not run *for* the people, and not, in the largest sense, *by* them, even when they voted in record numbers. It was a system of the politicians, created by the politicians and for the politicians, and, generally speaking, for the politicians in the two mainstream parties. It was one that survived because it heeded organized demands from the public. No politician could afford not to heed them. But it did not just heed but headed off and deflected those demands, and the politician's highest goal, quite naturally, was not the best representation of the people's will. It was to keep and hold office, and to keep the other fellow out.

The one purpose of the professionals involved in politics was power: power to spread favors, power to reward friends, power to serve the public interest, power to put guiding principles into law. Government works that way, by definition. Even the true, ideal democracy of town meetings and fullest participation works that way. The only differences are in the limitation those governments put on choices and the ways of expressing authority; on those differences depend all the variety of political systems, from absolute freedom to totalitarianism. For that reason, it is all the more necessary to gauge how far American "democracy" restricted the openness and the flexibility of government by and for the people.

What Else Could He Have Put into H--l?

Thou shalt have one God only; who
Would be at the expense of having two?
—Arthur Hugh Clough, "The Latest Decalogue"

Death Loves a Shining Mark—That's Why the Democratic Party Has Lived So Long.
—Republican banner, Freeport, Illinois, 1888

In an age when Republican and Democrat clashed and clamored, a western traveling man offered an isothermal explanation for differing party allegiance. "Politics," he told a reporter, "depends wholly on the mean annual temperature. I've just been up to Dakota, where the air is cool and bracing, and there the people are nearly all republicans." Iowa, slightly warmer, raised a few more Democrats; Missouri, warmer still, had a Democratic majority; in Texas, "where it's blasted hot, the people are nine-tenths Democrats. And in hell it's unanimous! I tell you, sir, it's all in the climate."[1]

He was right, but not in the way he meant. Partisanship in the Gilded Age did not spring up, fully matured, at birth. It was nurtured by family and by neighborhood and tradition. In some states, to be a Democrat was the only "respectable" course a man could profess; in Vermont or Iowa, to be a Democrat was to become suspect. "Ten miles from Kansas City the Confederate can still be smelled," a Republican orator told Kansans, but, then, as his listeners had heard over and over again, treason naturally prospered in Missouri. "A Democrat has no business in Kansas."[2] In some areas, belonging to the wrong party could be physically dangerous, and the danger increased when poverty or skin color deprived one of the power to call on influential friends for aid. Church doctrines helped train the communicants of one faith that personal behavior must remain a matter of individual conscience and the responsibility of priests, while they convinced others that the law must be used to do the Lord's work and lay America on a more moral foundation. Irish Catholics, if they inclined to the former doctrine, were likely to vote Democratic, while evangelical Protestants, leaning the other way, voted Republican. Whatever his religion, a Welsh Democrat was almost unheard of. "If that city down the river [the very Irish and German St. Paul] had as many Scandinavians as you have," Congressman Knute Nelson told a Minneapolis crowd, "it would be a Republican city instead of being, as it always has been, a Democratic city."[3]

Partisanship was something constantly drilled into followers of the rival organizations. They were reminded of the party's traditions and the menaces they fought. A friend of his wondered why the Lord had made the Democratic Party, Senator Henry W. Blair told one Republican gathering: "What on earth else could He have put into H--l?" "How can anyone be anything else but a Democrat?" Charles B. Aycock quizzed North Carolina listeners: "It is to this party that we owe our liberty—and all that is desirable in government and life."[4]

That begged the question of who we were—who shared in that liberty—and how far other things would be sacrificed for that liberty's sake. Here, matters of personal advantage and injury came into play. The liberty Aycock spoke of was so precious a thing that his white southern listeners kept it just scarce enough to supply their own needs. The value they placed on such liberty was shaped by much not related to politics at all, including the way one saw blacks and women in God's design. It might come from inclinations shaped from so many directions that no one could point to all the sources. As one critic defined it, the Democracy was never simply "an organized 'no.'" Still, there was something to be said of the *Nation*'s description of Democrats as driven more by temperament than ideas. "Its members desire nothing so much as to be let alone."[5]

How Americans thought or felt alike went to the heart of partisanship, and any study of the ways in which the major parties shaped the system to crimp each other and eliminate all rivals must begin there. Only by understanding their worldview can we explain why partisanship went so deeply with those it touched —and consequently why reformers would find its effects so difficult to uproot and its forms so hard to supplant. What did partisans believe and how deeply? And what consequence did their beliefs' intensity have?

Loyalty to party was more than a matter of clubs, spoils, and parades, and, far from losing its relevance as the issues changed, it found touchstones in the past for problems of the present. The two major parties had spent a generation framing their messages to appeal to that combination of interest, inclination, and impulse that made up partisanship, and as far as they addressed America's problems, they addressed those problems in terms of each other. Ask Republicans, and they would tell you that the Democracy was the party of "ignorance and crime," the "cherished old party of the bare-foots and moss backs." The slum-dwelling immigrants, the Catholic bog trotters from Ireland, the day laborers with a penchant for bad language and good liquor, the brewers, bartenders, distillers, and dram sellers — the uncultivated farmers on poorly cultivated land — the rowdies with one eye on an alderman's seat and the other on a yawning jail-house door — the draft dodger from the North and untamed traitor from the South: all these the Democrats claimed as their own. Newspapers conjectured that the reason Democrats so rarely read leaders out of the party was that reading was a rare skill among them. When Yankees decried the way that combs, brushes, and soap had slipped into a legislative expense account, an editor was quick to note that the graft was peculiarly Republican—"no body of Democrats ever quarreled over the same articles."[6]

In defining Democrats, Republicans defined themselves. From the first, they had been the party of moral ideas, committed to the idea that government power could be used to make people behave better and that the Protestant morality of so many of the party followers could be written into law, whether in protecting equality under the law or in closing down the gin mills and keeping shopkeepers and postal employees from desecrating the Sabbath by carrying on their trade. Theirs was the party that called a halt to slavery's expansion and then outlawed it, the party that harnessed the untapped powers of the Constitution to wage war to save the Union. The same authority that could make men good could make them wealthy and wise; it could provide for taxpayer-supported schools, a protective tariff, pensions for the disabled veteran, his widow, and his children, and laws protecting free, fair elections.[7]

Republicanism saw itself as the party of ordered progress, and, as strikes and social tensions grew, the stress on order intensified, but it also highlighted the commitment of Democrats to the ideal of white men's complete liberty, at least in the abstract. "Whenever a saloon keeper claims the right to sell liquid fire and distilled damnation in spite of legal and constitutional Prohibition, you have one of the fruits of Democracy," an Iowa newspaper warned readers. "Whenever strikes and mobs and riots of labor against capital occur you have another." The very words "law and order" were enough "to throw a Democrat into convulsions," the governor of Kansas told one cheering crowd. Republicans defined themselves as the respectables, whether that meant professionals, up-to-date farmers, or the kind of laborer honored in the strive-and-succeed literature of the day. Respectability did not require wealth, only a readiness to make the most of one's opportunities and talents, which, in the America of full opportunity and free labor that Republicanism envisioned, meant persons on their way up, not just economically, but socially.[8]

Democrats, naturally, cast themselves in a different role. They allowed that their foes were more likely to be the party of the propertied, usually with an assist from the government: the coupon-clippers, prospering on tax-free bonds, the national bankers given exclusive privileges to circulate their paper, the iron-mongers and lords of the loom, able to gouge the consumer in what they sold because a Republican tariff cut out cheap foreign competition. If the Republicans cast themselves as the party of the Union, Democrats declared themselves the party of reunion, and if the terms were those most satisfactory to white southerners, that was only right in a nation formed by and for white men. Over the years, the language tempered, especially in northern states where the Democrats sought black and former Republican votes; by the 1880s, the rhetoric may have defined America more as a government formed by whites for the good of all. But the racial message remained, and well into the 1870s, if not beyond, white Democrats probably outnumbered Republicans nationwide.[9]

Democracy appealed to liberty rather than to progress. That liberty, certainly, was of a truncated sort. It was the liberty of wives to be mothers, unsoiled by the proffered right of voting, the liberty of Utah's Mormons to have one wife or many as they pleased, and the liberty of white men to run elections to suit themselves and to keep blacks in their place. But restricting the full measure of American freedom to white males fit what Democrats saw as the republicanism of the founders. The price of a more egalitarian society would be more government action and, like as not, at the federal level, remote from the people. Democrats were not anarchists, but the Civil War had given them proofs enough of how power could be abused, even for patriotic ends: profiteering and pardon-brokering, arbitrary arrests, disfranchisements, and loyalty oaths directed at winnowing the Democratic side of the House. Reconstruction afforded enduring lessons to white southerners that the party of positive government would negate their liberty and empty their treasuries.[10]

Parties, plainly, were defined not just by what they were but by what they were not. Later scholars would describe this as "negative-referencing": one voted Republican not because Protestants did but because the Irish Catholics stood on the other side. Partisans in the Gilded Age knew well enough that *what* the other side was indicated what it would do with power when given the chance. Not by chance, the last states to outlaw dueling and prizefights were Democratic ones;

the first to institute the convict chain gang, the last to abolish capital punishment for crimes other than murder, were Democratic states. If one were a Republican in 1879, one voted against the Rebels, not just because they had spilled loyal soldiers' blood in the war for the Union, but because they were spilling it now, and wanted control of the federal government so that they could spill it in greater safety. "I suppose the Democratic party is our Evil," novelist John Hay sighed, "—our virtue is developed by fighting it."[11]

To those within the mainstream political culture, partisanship seemed as natural as the seasons, though nowhere near as variable. "Gentlemen of the Democratic convention," a Missourian announced, "if the Democrats of this deestrict would nominate a yaller dog for Congress I'd vote for him"—and "yaller dog Democrats" the nominee's supporters were known from then on. To many a partisan, no death could be nobler than Daniel Gildersleeve's. Eighty-six years old in 1884, he rose from a sickbed to go to the polls in Brooklyn over his son's protests. Ticket in hand, he fell within reach of the ballot box, and his remains were borne home. A robust political belief was treated as manliness itself, a token of those aggressive energies by which masculinity was defined. Scornfully, Senator John J. Ingalls of Kansas likened the independents unable to form a lasting love with one party to the "third sex . . . possessing the vices of both and the virtues of neither, effeminate without being masculine or feminine; unable either to beget or to bear; possessing neither fecundity nor virility endowed with the contempt of men and the derision of women, and doomed to sterility, isolation and extinction."[12]

Party loyalties could fade or change. Even so, converts from one major party to the other were a minority, and conversions possibly occurred among active politicians more than among the rank and file. The prospect of preferment by switching sides or the certainty of oblivion by staying where one was were powerful incentives for a change of allegiance. Below the office seeking and office-holding levels, the conversions seem to have been less likely, and the lasting conversions rarer still. A disgruntled partisan might disapprove of some of the ticket and "scratch" (that is, cross out) names on it, and in local contests might even vote a split ticket, if one was available, but his likeliest way of showing disaffection was to refrain from voting at all. Even most deserters kept the faith in a presidential election year: off years seem to have acted as an outlet for grumpy partisans to send a message to the high command without doing it lasting damage. Disaffections rose, but the bad tempers of July usually eased off by November. With Republican newspapers teeming with reports of unhappy Democrats in

THE DAY THEY CELEBRATE.

ANNUAL POULTRY ERUPTION OF THE AVERAGE COUNTRY PAPER ON
THE VILLAGE ELECTION.

"The day they celebrate. Annual poultry eruption of the average country paper on the village election" (Frederick Opper, *Puck*, October 24, 1883). Very likely a Democratic country paper: the rooster was a party symbol from the 1840s on and appeared abundantly at the moment of victory. Republicans preferred the eagle.

two Ohio congressional districts, the *Cincinnati Enquirer* sent its crack political reporter for confirmation. He found none. Just about every alleged "blood-boil of fearful proportions" proved "nothing but a pimple in the end."[13]

Still, party managers worried about that rare case. As recent scholars rightly have emphasized, while partisanship shaped public life, its sway was never complete. Indiana might be the exception. There, an observer suspected, the adult who failed to neglect his business for politics in the month before election was as rare as a German who knew nothing of soldiery. "Its male population consists of politicians," a visiting correspondent wrote. "It goes mad on politics once a year. Its margin of uncertain votes is so small that the fight for them is like two bites at a cherry." Elsewhere, even among those who voted a partisan ticket, organizers occasionally spotted an unsettling apathy or cynicism. In every election, editors urged their readers to vote the whole party ticket and not to "scratch" off a single name, a request implying that, without a lot of coaching, some of them might pick and choose freely. Worried Philadelphia politicians, hearing that independent-minded Republicans might paste stickers over some of the names on the GOP ballot, issued the party ticket on oiled paper one year. Stickers would not stick, and the oil repelled pencil marks. A Cincinnati insider guessed that the "scratchers" and unaligned voters amounted to 11.64 percent, only one-fourth of them buyable. Especially in off years, the numbers probably went up. Disgruntled regulars were likeliest to take a nonpartisan holiday when control of the national government did not seem to be at stake. They were not the only reason why Republicans lost control of the House in a landslide in 1874, 1882, and 1890, but they helped.[14]

Whatever partisanship had done, it had not tamed the American voter to politicians' satisfaction. From the press and pulpit, bookstalls and business journals, citizens could hear a rising chorus of critics challenging the mainstream parties' right to define policy. One might even mistake it for an antagonism to the whole notion of party itself.[15]

Partisanship itself provided much of the ammunition for an assault on politics as a way of making policy. For all the vigorous praise that the party press lavished on its own candidates, the picture it drew of the rest of them reinforced a vision of politics as a pretty shabby business. Newspapers were not demure about making clear that the lust to win mattered more than anything else . . . for the other side's politicians. Office to them was a fat job, rewards to their friends were gravy, their office seekers were cormorants. Indeed, the very impurity of the system became one of the strongest arguments for excluding women from any part in it beyond ornament and adding a certain moral tone: the scramble for power was not simply unladylike but corrupting. One might as well send the graduates of finishing schools into brothels to raise their character as to send women to the polls to clean up politics. So every campaign against giving women the vote predicated itself on saving the home and protecting the family. That reflected not just the assumed fragility of women's virtue but the ineradicable depravity of politics-as-usual and its essential irrelevance as a way of furthering moral principles.[16]

Praise their own party though they did, politicians could not praise their profession into respectability. Newspapers, novels, and jokes all held up the generic politician as something of a rascal, a bounder, and a thief. "The politician is my shepherd," one Georgia burlesque ran, "I shall not want. He leadeth me into the saloon for my vote's sake. He filleth my pockets with five-cent cigars and my beer-glass runneth over. He inquireth concerning the health of my family even unto the fourth generation. Yea, though I walk thro' the mud and rain to vote for him, and shout myself hoarse, when he is elected he straightaway forgetteth me. Yea, though I meet him in his own office he knoweth me not. Surely the wool has been pulled over my eyes all the days of my life."[17]

Politicians like those worked for themselves first and last, critics warned. Candidates were chosen for the availability and personal popularity, not their capacity. Since winning was all that mattered, politicians turned parties into machines to carry an election, not to carry out principles. They defined political debate, smothering the real issues that were inconvenient to them and replacing them with phony ones. Trifling matters and incidents arousing a visceral response in the voters replaced sober discussions of complicated topics. Instead of expressing the popular will, the owners of the political system set the electorate chasing after will-o'-the-wisps.

Great issues, for example, should have stirred the two parties in Ohio in 1886. Strikes, lockouts, and an assertive labor movement had brought to the fore the issue of what worker's fair share was and how far a privileged few ran government for their benefit. Instead, the issue of an ill-used class narrowed down to a collection of horror stories. Alleging maltreatment of inmates in public institutions during Democratic rule, Ohio Republicans circulated tales of dead convicts skinned and turned into the casing for walking sticks. One of these, with all the ethnic balance of a state ticket, had been made of the skin of two prisoners, one Irish and one black. Democrats, thoroughly disgusted by such bad taste, replied in kind.[18]

Among the loudest critics were the liberal reformers, who were disenchanted as the early crusaders of the Republican Party gave way to the organization men, for whom victory at the polls seemed to matter more than victory for the principles for which the party had stood and for whom a division of the spoils once the election was over occupied more of their energies than the passage of much-needed legislation. Detractors pinned the term "Mugwump" upon them, which jokesters would later ascribe to their place on the fence, with their mugs on one side and wumps on the other. As great men often will, they looked down with distaste from their pulpits and city office windows on the political mob scene spread before them—and the economic mob scene where getting and spending were all that seemed to matter, too. They were more likely to speak of gentlemanly behavior than the ordinary run of politicians, and far more likely to point to England as a model for what America should be doing in revenue and civil service reform. And, naturally, they were far more inclined to belong to the one "respectable" party, the Republicans.[19]

But that did not make their outlook mistaken. As they saw so clearly, there was nothing respectable in the partisanship of the 1880s. Party newspapers gave the clearest evidence that partisanship survived not just on issues but on the suborning of individual conscience and the intimidation of those who dared to think independently. The defection of Congressman John Anderson, who was once lauded as a bold paladin of Iowa Republicanism, transformed him into a "dissembling political hunchback," "Farmers' Alliance, office-for-revenue-only, anything-to-get-there candidate." A Democrat might be exemplary in person and principles, but let a Republican vote for him, and Republican editors would suggest that the renegade "go out and kill a hog and get some new brains."[20] Party loyalty, then, rested not just on blindness but on a fear that the political disciplinarians only too readily justified.

To commit oneself to a party was to surrender one's freedom, and yet this was what Americans had done by the 1880s. "The ideas which make a party strong and aggressive in our times are always ideas which spring up by a kind of spontaneous generation among the voters themselves," the *Nation* insisted. Politicians had reversed the natural order. They defined the issues and by their sway over the press, podium, and primary, forced the voters to accept it. Even when the issues fit events of the day, partisanship turned their expression into cant.[21]

Principles, traditions, and party heritage, in the age of machine politics, were a gilded lure, reformers protested, nothing more. As Republicans unfurled the bloody shirt one more time in 1880, critics caught one outburst at the national convention that seemed to sum up all the real passion that the politicians had. Appalled that the platform might commit the party to civil service reform, the Texas spoilsman Webster Flanagan burst out, "What are we here for?" Democrats supplied the answer:

"We are here" said the patriot Texan,
"To get into place if we can again,
And what do we think we are after?
Why, nothing but office," said Flanagan.

. . . .

Though bleached is the shirt that was bloody,
The party must try the old plan again,
For that is the curtain that covers
The excellent platform of Flanagan.[22]

Not all of the liberal reformers would have agreed. Many of the Mugwumps of a later day knew that Republicanism meant more than the "high moral doctrine of Flanagan," much as they deplored the party's backtracking on its pledge to a merit system. Still, every year, more dissidents came to see partisan differences in just such empty terms, and that gradual transformation highlights a point that historians may overlook. For all the criticism Mugwumps leveled at the two parties' sincerity, their anger was not really directed at partisanship itself. Indeed, even their anger at the parties was something of a lover's quarrel. Most of them had been true believers themselves once, in the days when Democrat and Republican meant something. They believed that with change, the parties could be returned to their original purpose, the promotion of great and important causes. What was needed, instead, was a refined partisanship, true to Republican or Democratic gospel, but able to pick and choose. Conscience must restore the place that partisan fealty had usurped in guiding a citizen's choice. Until the voting process could be changed to allow a really secret ballot, that meant taking the party tickets that each side gave out and crossing out the names of offending candidates. "Scratch, brothers, scratch with caire," the *Indianapolis News* sang,

Scratch in the face of the poll-keepaire,
A big black scratch for a Legislataire,
Another one to make it a pair,
Scratch, brothers, scratch with caire.[23]

Quite a different challenge to Gilded Age partisanship came from the third parties. There was not, in fact, a two-party system between the Civil War and the turn of the century. It was more like a two-and-a-half party system. Parties arose, some locally, some regionally, and some with strength enough to run presidential candidates. Riled over railroad exactions and exasperated at officeholders fattened on their perquisites, the Grangers ran tickets in the Midwest in the mid-

1870s. New England workers and farmers fielded Labor Reform candidates, and in 1876 exponents of a reflated money supply, wrested from the control of national bankers, set up the Greenback Party and kept it alive in some states for more than a decade. Republicans and Democrats had to turn back a serious threat in 1878 from the newborn Workingmen's Party of California (WPC). There were antimonopoly parties in New York and Nebraska, and in the late 1880s a whole spate of rival workingmen's parties, two of which—the Union Labor Party and United Labor Party—ran presidential candidates in 1888. Arkansas insurgents joined the Wheel, and farmer-labor parties elected legislators in Illinois and Minnesota.[24] "Independent" and "Readjuster" movements in the South won congressional seats and, in Virginia, control of the state government. Finally, wherever the temperance issue flared in the 1880s, the Prohibition Party ran a ticket pledged to go beyond the mainstream parties' halfway measures and outlaw the sale or manufacture of strong drink. Given visible and active support by the Women's Christian Temperance Union and church groups, it was, not surprisingly, a strong supporter of woman suffrage and of renewing the emphasis on government as a force for moral reform.

"Sideshow" parties, as the mainstream editors called them, never got more than a small share of the vote, but that share could throw one party out of power in a state and ease the other one in. That was because so many of the members were old Republicans or Democrats, breaking ranks. Again and again, their programs asserted that the old political system had outlived its usefulness; again and again, they asserted that the two major parties were ducking the real issues of the day. The national Greenback platform in 1876 put it plainly. Theirs was the cause "of INTEGRITY against CORRUPTION—the cause of the PEOPLE against the OFFICE-HOLDERS—the cause of true Democracy against the false." But an attack on party *managers* and parties grown irrelevant was not the same as a repudiation of government by party, any more than a protest against politicians was a renunciation of political organization and political action.[25] Greenbackers and Prohibitionists would have liked nothing better than a party system based on true principles, and many of them remembered the days when one had existed. Their war was not so much on party itself as on the parties as they had come to be, not on partisanship so much as a *bi*partisanship, a mutual hostility or apathy on the issues that counted.[26]

Mugwumps and minor party spokesmen saw the cynicism. Indeed, they saw quite a bit more than there really was. Underlying the assumptions of all the outsiders was that the real issues were being cast aside and that the party leaders were mouthing slogans that no longer had resonance to anyone but themselves.

Parties put on a show "because there was really nothing to discuss."[27] As any examination of political correspondence would show, this was just not so.

Time changed issues, of course, and it was always convenient for parties to stand still, where they knew the ground best. "The gentleman from Pennsylvania takes a gentle refuge in the past—that home of Democracy—the place where they live and from which they never go," Maine congressman Thomas Brackett Reed jeered. His own party, stressing its wartime service, was open to similar charges, though spokesmen put it more appealingly.[28]

Yet the reformers' charge of irrelevance did not hold up very well. Causes might change, but the past served as a touchstone. Over and over, party spokesmen insisted that the mission of thirty years ago was that of today, applied in fresh ways. Protection for the laborer had always been a Republican doctrine, its defenders insisted, from the days when it gave three million of them their freedom to the time when English trade goods threatened to drive wage earners into conditions of near slavery. As long as a single enemy lived, the time for a change in allegiances had not come.[29]

The best test of issues' relevance was whether the party directed its attention to a pressing wrong, one with serious effects on individuals' lives. Did it? "Waving the bloody shirt" by talking about the suppression of the black vote was the chief of the phony issues that Mugwumps used as their example of the meaninglessness of Gilded Age politics.[30] It may have seemed so to Edwin L. Godkin, editor of the *Nation*, staring out on a Manhattan ill-run and rogue-ridden. To a Greenbacker, the evidence of the great issue of a currency big enough to serve a country's need was as plain as the silent forges and shootings in coalfields and railroad yards. But the black militiamen of Hamburg, South Carolina, besieged, captured, and then shot in cold blood might have seen greater relevance in the GOP's choice of issues. Republicans of all races, cheated and bullied out of their ballots, could have said the same.

Indeed, the bloody shirt illustrates quite a different point than the Mugwumps thought—though it was one of which they were perfectly aware. The real problem with partisanship may not have been its cynicism but its sincerity and the extent to which it would go. Partisanship made men hesitate to denounce wrong, if their own friends were involved, and quick to look for ways to blame it on the opposition. It muzzled reformers and encouraged them to wait for better times rather than to desert. Partisanship deafened the ears of other true believers to argument. Running for Congress in the eastern end of Connecticut, revenue reformer David A. Wells knew he had more brains, more experience, and more ideas than his opponent. All availed him nothing in "a district in which, if the Democrats were to nominate George Washington & the Republicans, Benedict Arnold, the latter would get the most votes."[31]

Partisan ruthlessness was at its worst where differences of class or race marked party lines. Against "demagogues," the spokesmen for the "mob," the mainstream parties up north discarded most of the rules. Southern partisanship was harsher still. There it involved the fear that a Republican win might create a biracial coalition and upset what white supremacists saw as the natural order of society. Politics there, more than anywhere else, were a man's sport, and manliness, as Democrats defined it, meant white male control. "It is a struggle for existence, for civilization, for the very hearthstones of the people," the *Charleston News & Courier* cried in 1880. "There are not in Charleston City to-day one hundred colored men who are not dependent upon the prosperity of Democratic citizens for their food, their raiment, and their homes. Should this ignorant class, wrought up into a pitch of political fanaticism," be left to vote "for a set of Vandals" likely to ruin their own employers? "We say decidedly No!"[32]

Hecklers might disrupt a northern rally, and political paraders had to dodge an occasional stone, but there were no northern equivalents for the southern custom of "dividing time." The very phrase sounded like fairness itself. In practice, it meant the appearance of Democrats in armed force at largely black Republican gatherings and the forcible seizure of the platform. They could do it because they had the guns and any black resisting risked a race riot. Given the excuse, whites would do the killing and blacks by the dozens do the dying. There was no such dividing of time at Democratic gatherings. Dividing time silenced Republican speakers, forced their mass meetings to shut down or to be held discreetly, with small audiences, and provoked a melee. It also reminded their listeners, too clearly to miss, just where the power lay and which side had the manly virtues that, come what may, were surest to triumph.[33]

In the face of such a mixture of race prejudice and partisanship, southern Republicans found themselves helpless. That was explanation enough for the cold-blooded suggestion of Albion W. Tourgee. Tourgee knew the South well. As the popular novelist of *A Fool's Errand*, he had drawn an indictment of halfhearted and cowardly northern Republicans' failure to back up their southern allies during Reconstruction; as a North Carolina judge, he learned all too well the brutal methods by which the white South would "redeem" itself from a competitive party system.[34] So his passion was understandable when he wrote presidential candidate Benjamin Harrison, urging him to win the election by sending campaigners southward, "to go and conquer Mississippi, Louisiana and South Carolina — in all of which there is an average of 60 percent black Republicans — and to help the Republicans in North Carolina." Party faithful certainly would be killed or injured. But that, Tourgee insisted, was just the point. As Democrats threw off the mask, the lives lost down south would gain votes for Republicans up north. Onlookers would "learn southern methods and southern spirit." A solid North would emerge. "Of course it is not pleasant to contemplate such a result," Tourgee admitted; "but men were killed at Resaca [in the Civil War] and yet you still commanded, 'Forward!' This is only a *much more important part* of the same conflict."[35]

There was nothing cynical in Tourgee's proposal, but its ruthlessness in imperiling lives to awaken northern consciences was as much an expression of the true believer's instinct as of any white partisan who "divided time" in the Carolinas or stole a ballot box for the "Grand Old Party." Because partisanship rooted itself in a sense of greater purposes than political success, much more was permissible than a dispassionate onlooker would have considered fair or even legal. The critics may not have gone far enough. It was not the parties themselves, nor the politicians, that did the damage. It was partisanship. In that sense, the way of thought that no new party system could efface, the evils of Gilded Age politics, were indeed "all in the climate."

Politics Is Only War without the Bayonets

They tell us that we chose them,
And bank on that, you bet—
Though more than half the voters
Wanted quite a different set.
In districts corked and herded,
Gerrymandered, too, in style,
No chance for able, honest men,
If the corporations smile.
—Alfred Denton Cridge from *Arena* 10 (November 1894)

Years after his death, admirers used to tell a story of Ohio congressman Clement Vallandigham. Coming upon a boy reading Jomini's *Art of War*, he beamed. "That's a good book to study, if you intend to be either a soldier or a politician," he assured the youngster. Seeing puzzlement, he explained, "Well, war is only politics with bayonets, and politics is only war without the bayonets."[1]

Any observer would have been justified to think so. Postwar political discourse mustered legions of military analogies. A campaign was "the fight" or "the smoke and dust of battle." "Wherever we can find one guard standing on the battlements of the old Democratic party, carrying aloft her flags and her banners, let us rally there and fight the battle out under the old flag, and beside those rusty old guns which have so often led us to victory," one partisan begged his followers. No parade was complete without battalions in uniform: White Boys in Blue, Wide-Awakes, or Plumed Knights. (That martial style, it might be added, only underscored that politics was predominantly a man's game. War was no place for women, and the link between soldiering and party service just reinforced the old argument that those unable to defend America with bullets ought not to control it with ballots. "It is the part of women to-day, as it has always been, to send forth their men to battle for the right," a Wisconsin newspaper explained. "Men are only half men without the inspiration and advice of women, in politics as everywhere else." The martial tone also gave added point to the stress laid on the "manly" courage of a candidate and to the attack on the Mugwumps as a kid-gloved, effete, and sexless, crowd of "political flirts, / The delicate, dainty few." "A simpering, heartless, beardless man," one Republican congressman sneered,

> He never since the world began,
> For right or justice, truth or law,
> Was ever known a sword to draw,
> And when the land was wild with war
> He snuffed its battles from afar.)[2]

Vallandigham, though, had a more specific point. Politics, like war, depended on the three leading principles that armies needed for winning: organization, discipline, and aggression. Observers might well lose sight of these facts amid the spectacular display that every campaign provided, but the political foot soldiers, even on parade, were soldiers for all that; the processions just softened politics' image for a public wary of being driven anywhere and quick to resent the suggestion that they were being guided there, even by the subtlest of drillmasters.

In outward form and in design, of course, politics had two unmistakable qualities, closely related. It was America's most popular participatory sport and an expression of the people's will. Thanks to the federal character of American politics, regular elections came at irregular times. As late as the 1870s, several southern states and all of the New England ones elected state officers in odd-numbered years. In even-numbered ones, the political calendar might begin with New Hampshire's election in mid-March and Connecticut's early in April. Then came some municipal races like Albany's and Cincinnati's. In early August, North Carolina, Kentucky, and Iowa voted. September opened with Vermont and Arkansas voters heading to the polls. Two weeks more and Maine cast its ballots. Then came the "October states," Pennsylvania, Ohio, and Indiana, and on election day in November, just about everybody else. Anyone with an unslaked appetite for political news could wait a few more weeks for the Boston mayoral race in early December.[3] The real story here, though, is more than a constant barrage of political news. Scattered as they were across the calendar, elections were a constant reminder that Americans had a government—somewhere at least—fresh from the people. (New England had the freshest: well into the 1870s, governors and legislatures had to renew their mandates yearly.) Again and again, the message was driven home: the politicians might appeal, but the voters did the deciding. It was their government, after all.

A Gilded Age political campaign built itself on the pretense that the people's will decided every part of the final result. Half a century before, political conventions had seemed like dangerous innovations over the caucus of party worthies. Southern governors chose justices of the peace to run local government, and in Connecticut no less than the Carolinas, the "long-tailed families" had preference when the offices were to be handed out. Now all that had changed. At least on paper every candidate won his place after a full consultation of the consent of the governed — assuming that governed was adult, male, and able to meet the voting requirements. Early in a presidential year, the party's national committee would schedule the time and place for a convention and authorize the selection of delegates. In most states, these would be chosen locally. Neighborhood party committees would hold primary elections, open to all party members — and, on occasion, to those whose support might be expected in the future; the delegates elected would attend county conventions, where delegates to a state convention were chosen, and, usually, delegates to the national convention as well. The state convention would do as its elected majority dictated in choosing the at-large delegates to the national convention, usually pledged to one particular nominee, but those few were a small minority of the whole delegation sent. Except where the state convention bound the whole delegation by instructions, the so-called unit rule, it would be every county's national delegate for himself. The national convention, itself the end point of a series of expressions of what was reputedly the rank and file's will, negotiated and ratified the decision of the state conventions.[4]

Then came the campaign itself. Here the parties put on a tremendous show, one calculated to draw as many voters into the process as possible. Partisan newspapers reminded voters daily of the reasons why their side should win and, until the 1890s, usually printed the ticket at the editorial page's masthead. Party workers fanned out, making sure that their supporters were registered, their poll taxes paid, and their levels of enthusiasm known, so that it could be bolstered, if need be, in the time remaining before election day. The intricacies of the law that might keep prospective Democrats off the books, the perplexities of filling out a ballot that might discourage the unlettered elector from showing up at the polls, could be eased by expert help, and the parties were there to give it. Where women could not vote, their influence over the males in the house made them worth cultivating, and, by the end of the 1880s, politicians were shaping their arguments to appeal to the voter as a member of the family, rather than as a citizen of the republic, with that in mind. "Republican wives!" an Ohio editor appealed. "Get your husbands and sons off to the polls before breakfast tomorrow morning and after they have voted the straight, clean republican ticket, from end to end, give them a royal spread, rich and red-hot."[5]

By that time, literate voters had been given a spread of quite a different sort, in reading matter, some of it red-hot, indeed. Party managers sent it to known opponents, to break their confidence, and to sure loyalists, to bolster their beliefs, as well as to potential converts. The national committees printed leaflets, booklets, and handbills, which were sent out by the tens of thousands for local committees to distribute. A newspaper might issue a special campaign edition and drum up subscribers until election day, or draw on party funds to broadcast it on a regular basis for nothing. Campaign committees encouraged the creation of subscription clubs for party newspapers and set up reading rooms where callers could get a full set of the latest partisan information. Sometimes, especially in presidential years, the parties set up special newspapers to spread the word. Thanks to the franking privilege, congressmen could send speeches, including undelivered philippics, by the thousands without cost. Political almanacs gave comparative lists of how states, counties, even cities had voted in past elections and reprinted the party platforms for easy reference. And no presidential year would be complete without the issuing of authorized campaign biographies, usually blending proofs of the candidate's humble origins with tokens of his present dignity, solemnity, and statesmanship. (General Ulysses Grant's father wrote one, which, an editor protested, was the most terrible attempt on a child's life since Abraham tried to sacrifice Isaac.) Election-year biographies, as the *New York Times* quipped, had "the accuracy, discrimination and impartiality of a tombstone inscription."[6]

Partisans could paper the country not just because they had the will but because they had devised the way. All through the Gilded Age, presses improved their quality and the speed of their output. New techniques for making paper cheaply from wood pulp allowed handouts and brochures to be made in quantity for a lower price. Improvements in technique allowed full play for rascality such as never before. There had always been forged letters and lying affidavits broadcast on parties' behalf, but never, the *Philadelphia Public Ledger* claimed, had there been so many as in 1880, or so little compunction about extracting a politician's private and personal letters from the mail and printing them to expose him. The *New York Tribune* decoded telegrams documenting Democrats' attempt to buy electoral votes down south and plastered the "cipher" dispatches across the front pages for a month before the off-year elections. A Pennsylvania congressman's private letter grumbling about southern unfriendliness to pension legislation for northerners was used to prove, quite against the evidence, that he acted as Rebels' willing accomplice. Worst of all were the forged letters, and the readiness of party papers to insist that no denial by the author constituted proof on his behalf, unless he assembled concrete evidence that he was not lying.[7]

Politics fit for perusing in the parlor was all very well, but the mainstream parties supplemented it with a politics of the streets, with events to spur public interest. They put on barbecues and raised liberty poles and party flags, plastered the sides of barns with posters, and put candidates' portraits in shop windows. Among the temperance-minded farmers in Pennsylvania's Quaker counties, candidates set out picnic spreads with doughnuts, sandwiches, and pumpkin pies, but they knew that other constituents would expect stronger fare. A smart politician made the rounds of every saloon, setting up for the whole house. One Kentucky congressman, Asher Caruth, sent out boxes of cigars, specially labeled, "The 'Ash' Caruth Cigar: a square cigar and a square man," not to mention printed flags, portraits of himself framed in ash sticks, and ash canes. While the orators thundered, crowds might nod, but they woke up for the brass band. Nobody cared that it had played the very same tunes for the opposition's rally the night before — not even those who attended both performances.[8]

Thanks to mass-production techniques, the number of ways that partisans could flaunt their fealty grew tremendously in the 1880s. The great innovation for 1888 was the campaign button. In everything from watch charms to ladies' jewelry, there were endless variations for discriminating tastes: a broom and dustpan design, a horseshoe or a ram's head with the candidate's face beneath (signifying "Free wool" to Democrats and "Protection" to wool interests to Republicans), and modest flag pins in red, white, and blue.[9]

Participatory politics, though, showed itself most splendidly in the parades and mass meetings, designed to draw out the rank and file, both to ratify the nominations by their presence at public events and to stir up a sense of connection with the candidate and the party. The bigger the event, the more it would convince onlookers that those hosting it were likely to win, and that mattered almost as much as what the speakers talked about. "Men will go to that side where they think the power and brains are," an upstate New York editor explained. "Nothing, sir, like humbug and a good, stiff outside appearance nowadays."[10]

Typically, the high point in a local campaign came with the visit of some famous representative of the party. Campaign committees would welcome him at the station with flowers and the music of a brass band; there would be a carefully prepared impromptu parade to the hotel or private home where he was staying and some equally impromptu remarks. Later, crowds would gather to watch a parade of the party's campaign clubs. Houses would be illuminated, banners with mottoes and cartoons on them would be carried, marchers would carry coal-oil-fired torchlights or paper lanterns, and the procession might include soloists, glee clubs, or people chanting catchword slogans and couplets.[11]

Parades were both entertainment and distilled ideology. They included brass bands playing martial airs; floats with symbolic representations of the nation or of various crafts; traveling exhibits advertising local industries and fraternal and ethnic societies; and a scattering of printed and painted statements of what the party stood for. Always there were mottoes fit for the occasion: "Down with Rings," "We want honest government," and, when it suited partisan purposes, "The patriotic citizen rises above partisanship." But parades were also a way around argument. "When a man puts on a uniform, or carries a torch in procession," the radical theorist Henry George pointed out, "his self-pride is enlisted in the success of the party, and all appeals to his reason are vain."[12]

A good parade usually ended at the speaker's stand at the courthouse or in the public park. There, on a platform festooned with flags and patriotic symbols, or overlaid in evergreen boughs, a collection of worthies would address the crowd. There would be a warm-up speech, a formal address of an hour or more, and perhaps other talks as well. Afterward, there might be fireworks, refreshments, and another parade.

The speech was not just the price to be paid for all this enjoyment. It was the centerpiece. Here, under flickering lantern or gaslight, the parties tried to tie their present mission to the past, recited the injuries and accomplishments of a generation, explained the party's position on key issues, and inspired their followers for the fight ahead. The occasion was meant partly to convince, partly to hearten. Under the spell of dramatic language, listeners would go home convinced, even if only for a night, that their side deserved to win and, indeed, stood every probability of winning.

Handled correctly, campaign speaking became an art form. At his best, the speaker could cope with any emergency, switching topics if the one he had chosen failed to take, expanding a point if his audience proved unusually appreciative. His remarks were delivered, not read. Audiences appreciated the quick thinking of a William Jennings Bryan, who, standing on a manure spreader, declared it the first time he had spoken from a Republican platform. They also expected a ready response to hecklers, assuming that any showed up. One of the best in that line was Thomas Brackett Reed, later Speaker of the House. He deliberately lured pests into the open. "If a photographic snapshot could be taken of the Democracy at any time or any place, it would reveal them in the act of doing some mean, low-lived, and contemptible thing," he told one Maine audience. Democrats hissed. "There," said Reed cheerfully, "I told you so."[13]

Platform rhetoric was meant to rouse rather than to last for the ages, and even statesmen whose quotes became celebrated rarely delivered their gems on the campaign trail. Ohio congressman Robert "King Bob" Kennedy worked up a speech that was more than polished; it was positively embalmed, for constant use. Scraps of the address embroidered an impromptu funeral oration and talks at Sunday-school conventions, county fairs, and even the summing-up in a murder case. Talking every day, a politician could hardly help driveling, and some took stimulants to drivel more beautifully. In 1872, alcohol inspired vice presidential candidate B. Gratz Brown to butter a piece of watermelon at a political banquet. Perhaps what friendly reporters usually explained away as exhaustion or illness explains how one orator could liken a movement to "a little spark that rolled and rolled until it became a great wave." "Plunder us and oppress us," the *St. Louis Globe-Democrat* begged Democratic stumpers, "but do not add insult to injury by inflicting on us your damnable rhetoric."[14]

Given a certain minimum standard of competence, however, audiences really did not attend mass meetings for literary exaltation. They came to see their leaders in the flesh and to feel the sympathy of hundreds or thousands of other listeners with views in common with themselves. It followed that a bigger name could draw a bigger crowd and inspire those who came with a greater confidence that theirs was a faith widely shared. A crowd wanted to see party statesmen, not unknowns, though its definition of statesman was broad enough to include local heroes, celebrated veterans, and those with a statewide reputation. The longer a campaigner had been in the business, the more his appearance alone was sufficient to bring a crowd, no matter what he was likely to say. Time made him a living reminder of the listeners' partisan heritage, in which he had played his part.[15]

A campaigner's was no easy living. "Poor meals—poor beds," a veteran of the hustings, Friedrich W. Holls, grumbled, "—the same 'President of the Club' and 'Chairman of the Ex. Com.' to receive me everywhere and carrying my trunk & carpetbag to the hotel—the same 'What's the matter with Holls? HE's, etc., etc.' The same torches, windbroken bands, and nervous presiding officer, whose different versions of my name would fill a 'Dictionary of Pseudonyms.'" In an age before microphones, many an address had to be given at a shout, just to be heard above the murmur of the crowd. When the wind howled strongly enough to make the torches gutter, a speaker could hardly hear himself. Exercised two or three times a day, voices strained from overuse. Experienced speakers all had their panaceas, most of which involved a mixture of liquor and raw egg. (Prohibitionists got the same result from lemon juice, sugar, egg, milk, and seltzer, which, a reporter asserted, made its devotees "very gentle and kindly" and cleared the voice magnificently for singing temperance hymns.)[16]

Yet the rewards were worth the pains, and there were always plenty of would-be speakers ready to serve the parties' needs. For aspiring young politicians, there was no better training than a stump campaign for someone else. For those with little money of their own, it was the surest way to push oneself on the party leaders' attention and to be treated seriously. Years before making the run for Congress, apt orators covered the districts where later they announced their candidacy. It was the perfect means of building up name recognition and allowing the rank and file to associate what would otherwise be a name of mere local importance with some large, pleasant event. It built up political IOUs among those the stump speaker helped out, and it also trained the guest of honor for one of the most important duties expected of a congressman, a ready ability to bloviate.[17]

Speakers did not always come cheaply. Partisans never liked to admit it. Love of party should have been enough to motivate their speakers, and no charge was more effective than that an enemy orator was a hessian, a hireling expounding his principles strictly on a cash basis. The plain truth, though, was that most politicians had business careers to look after. Only the independently wealthy could pay for their own travel and lodging, or leave behind a paying legal practice for three months to gallivant around among strangers. So local party treasuries would foot the bill for food and lodging, and partisans would arrange travel expenses and a little something on the side. There was no question about Jonathan P. Dolliver's devotion to Republicanism, but Iowa's "boy orator" asked for, and got, $300 above expenses from the state committee, and the members felt themselves the gainers by the investment.[18]

Second only to the orator in importance, the campaign clubs and marching societies swelled the length of political parades and gave a theatrical touch to events. Most of the clubs sprang into being just for the campaign. They took on names and uniforms of their own design. There were Italian, Irish, and German clubs, organizations open only to members of the Wall Street business community and to Manhattan jewelers, and even groups dedicated to young men not yet of voting age. Candidates for governor always had a few clubs named in their honor—especially if they contributed to their upkeep. When Republicans in Amsterdam, New York, nominated a carpet manufacturer, John Sanford, the town blossomed with political pseudomilitaries. "The Sanford Legion, the Sanford Continentals, the Sanford Protectives, the Sanford Hussars, the Sanford Republicans, the Sanford First Voters, the Sanford Veterans, the Sanford Guards, the Sanford Recruits, the Sanford Squadron, the Sanford Vigilants, the Sanford Light Brigade, the Sanford Sharpshooters, [and] Sanford Lancers are camped upon a thousand hills, and the Sanford Terrors would have been among them but for some slight misunderstanding about the terms on which they would take the field as mercenaries," a hostile reporter commented.[19]

Club members usually created a marching society to show off their qualities on parade. They took pride in their military discipline and their acrobatics. It was not uncommon to have dozens of clubs pass in review and 4,000 torches decorating the line.[20] All through the 1880s, club life expanded. Party strategists spoke of turning them into permanent agencies, assembling regularly throughout the four years between presidential elections and keeping awareness of the issues alive. One could hardly educate people to the full meaning of a protective tariff or election reform in just a few meetings. Full understanding of Republicanism needed attendance as regular as churchgoing. Properly formed and directed from the top, the Republican League of Clubs could become an organizational tool to bring out the vote. Not to be outdone, Democrats set up the Association of Clubs.[21]

Taken at face value, all the clubs, parades, and banners seem like tokens of the public support for party politics. "To hear a girl of seventeen sit down and discuss majorities, caucuses, and the entire history of party rule, reeling dates off the end of her tongue with suavity and ease is an astonishing experience, even in America," a visitor to Wilmington, Delaware, admitted in 1888. But he could have found other levels of commitment no less impressive. Until the 1880s, women had been, by and large, ornamental more than useful, especially among the Democrats, who preferred women as a cheering section or in their usual role, sewing silken banners for political clubs and, like the sweethearts blessing their loved one's sword before he marched to the fray, showing up for their formal presentation and dedication. Now, under the pressure of closely contested elections, the activism found mostly in the Midwest had gone national and bipartisan: Frances Folsom Cleveland Clubs and Carrie Harrison Clubs, women as organizers and marchers, and the first Democratic women's glee clubs. If this was how deeply the nonvoters shared in the process, what could one say about the electorate itself? On election day, the turnouts seemed to confirm that the will of the parties was an uprising of the people. Just about every adult male eligible under the laws showed up to vote. A turnout of 80 percent was common in some northern states, and over 90 percent not unheard of—and, significantly, much bigger than in elections run on nonpartisan lines.[22]

Yet it is vital to see that all of this popular upwelling was not spontaneous but induced, shaped, and created by the institutions of the parties themselves. The willingness to take part in politics was not artificial. The depth of public involvement may have been. Even good Republicans needed a prod to do their duty at times. "Garfield's life is a romance—it is typical of the possibilities of the poor American boy," an insider wrote his congressman as the 1880 campaign began. "But if our folks go to talking about the scandals with which Garfield's name has been linked it will be hard to arouse enthusiasm."[23]

Behind everything lay the force of political machinery, decentralized and poorly coordinated but present and influential. A federated system of committees coordinated the parties' actions from the Capitol to the precinct. Usually each town would have its committee, and if it were a place of any size, neighborhoods would be organized as well. Ideally, there would be vigilance committees in every school district.[24]

Most of the day-to-day tasks that parties performed rested with their local equivalents. Only they could make the door-to-door canvass of the potential vote and enter the names of trusty electors into the poll books. A list of doubtful voters would need to be kept and, if the local organization knew its business, the price tag of those voters in the market. The ward or district leader had to know which political tracts would do the most service and which men could be counted on to deliver more than his own vote. Local and county committees decided on the best time for a mass meeting and the right speaker to sway that particular audience, and they sometimes advertised him before inviting him to appear. They spent the money and probably raised most of it. From there, the chain of command and communication led upward. With 3,000 precincts to cover in Ohio, a state committee of a dozen men and a dozen clerks had to leave most decisions to politicians on the spot, but it could coordinate county efforts, hear complaints, raise funds for special needs in areas that could not pay their own way, and set the tone and the issues for the campaign as a whole.[25] In even-numbered years, a congressional committee sent out speakers, handled the distribution of franked documents, and, when it could get away with it, dunned federal officeholders to pay for operations. National committees awakened only in presidential years. They worked out larger strategy, assigned speakers of national reputation, collected funds, and handled press releases related to the national ticket.[26]

Party management could not afford to leave public interest to chance. It was not enough to announce an address. The organization must actively encourage attendance. For a respectable mass meeting, one editor guessed, managers must pass out about three handbills for each adult in town and start spreading the word two weeks ahead of time. That amounted to some two to seven thousand leaflets in every county. Mark the alternative! Asher Caruth, a Democratic presidential elector in 1880, came to a little Kentucky town where the party had advertised him to speak at the courthouse. Not a single person was there except the jailer. He brought in the judge, who brought in the clerk and the sheriff. The judge summoned the grand and petit juries who were sitting in the hotels to the hall to listen—twenty-four petit and sixteen grand jurors brought by the sheriff and jailer, respectively—and to make sure that they gave the speaker a full hearing, locked them in.[27]

Inducing a good turnout may have been one more reason for the paraphernalia of a hoopla campaign, the banners, processions, torches, spectacle, food and drink. All of these may have meant that attending the speeches themselves was simply the price that many in the audience paid for the other, more hedonistic pleasures of a campaign event and for the comforts of partisan identification.

One ought not to take the numbers on parades and campaign clubs too seriously, then, as a token of a public spontaneously stirred. Parties swelled processions with outlanders, strangers, hirelings, and beardless youths. Scornfully, a La Crosse Democrat noted one such parade in 1876. Republican newspapers counted 500 to 1,000 torches in line, all borne by supposed "Boys in Blue," the battle-hardened heroes of the Civil War. If the number was correct, this was impressive, the speaker remarked, since by actual count, the marchers numbered 125. A hundred of them *were* boys. But perhaps the bibs that the older ones wore during the war had been blue, he added. Democrats did not make a precise count of how many eggs were thrown at the paraders, but they were willing to give Republicans the credit for throwing every one of them, and for having bought them at the grocery store of the local Republican candidate for presidential elector.[28]

That some marchers paraded for pay and that, in any case, the number of clubs depended on the amount of outside money available to help partisans keep up their habit was a fact widely known, though not so often admitted.[29] The purpose was not simply to put on a show but to bolster the morale of onlookers and inspire them to do their part for the party, especially at the polls. Through district leaders and leading articles, the same message was repeated until election day: the key to success was not public spirit but discipline among the ranks of the true believers. Again and again, the parties called on their members to march to the polls or to drop work to attend. They must assemble as an unofficial posse

"A paying business for gentlemen out of employment during the campaign" (Frederick Opper, *Puck*, July 30, 1884).

to keep an eye on their neighbors, who might go wrong, or on the enemy, which was sure to try some trick.

Organization counted most on election day itself. It was a day freighted with meaning, at once the people's assertion of their right to govern themselves and the managers' final proof of whether discipline and morale had done their work. An election could not take place without party action. Parties printed up the ballots, or tickets, as they were called, and distributed them. There was nothing particularly secret about the ballots; while a few citizens might prepare their votes at home, "vest-pocket voters" were few. Most people gave away their preference by approaching the party agents peddling tickets to any comers and sometimes calling over those on whose vote they counted. Sometimes voters marched to the polls in brigade formation, under ward leaders, and now and then managers provided a brass band, a barbecue, or refreshments. Election judges were chosen by the parties, and so were the poll watchers, who scrutinized the lists and challenged suspicious-looking voters.[30]

Ballots were designed to make maverick voting difficult, though not impossible. A party ticket might have its symbol at the top, to help along illiterates; Republicans preferred the eagle, Democrats the rooster, though everything from Abraham Lincoln's portrait to a Chinaman being given the boot adorned local variants. All the names down to dogcatcher would be listed, and most voters had neither the time nor inclination to "scratch" names off, much less write other names on. Local party organizations might save them the trouble, especially those that had worked out a swap with the opposition to divvy up the offices. They would print up tickets freshly concocted, or they might issue two sets of tickets bunched together, one for local offices and the other for some national slate, either their own party's or the one with which they had made arrangements on the sly. Even "independent" voting, then, was something that good organization could enhance. The printed ballot helped poll watchers calculate precisely how the voting was going from one hour to the next. If they found too great a swell of the opposition, there was yet time to redouble their own efforts to turn the tide by nightfall.[31]

Panoply and organization alike put the minor parties at a disadvantage. For the Prohibitionists, whose support depended heavily on church parishioners and women's groups, the problems may have been less severe. With an emphasis on reforms that could be implemented at the township or state level, they could raise the needed funds a little more easily. The hoopla that mainstream politics required was not just unnecessary but a little dubious: moral movements looked for conversions, and the saving of souls was a little too serious for brass bands and firecrackers. But even for them, a national campaign was a burden far beyond their means—at least without cutting a deal on the quiet with one of the mainstream parties and mortgaging their political souls. Even the simplest needs cost money that came readily to organizations with a serious chance of winning but far less so to hopeless causes. Standing right with God did Massachusetts Prohibitionists little good in 1883, if they had nowhere to stand on election day. But the party had only enough money to print ballots for one town in seven. Covering the whole state required 50,000 packages of tickets; Boston and Lynn alone needed 80,000 ballots distributed, not to mention flyers explaining how to stick some 50,000 gummed "pasters" on top of particular names on the Republican ballot. This was not one of those cases where the Lord would provide. "There is evidently something rotten somewhere," an organizer for the People's Party complained after a paltry rally in Brooklyn's Irving Music Hall. With a week to stir up interest, "*no advertisement* or notice appeared *in any paper* and there was neither music or fireworks. . . . It is true, however, that a few circulars were thrown in dooryards on a windy day."[32]

All of this suggested the puzzle of politics, of a public consent that, to some extent, was artificially induced and shaped in certain directions. People who might not otherwise do so were encouraged, even bullied, into voting for candidates whom they might not have chosen, even if the party itself had their support. It was not a distortion of the individual public will, necessarily; but of the collective public will—the wish of a majority of those ready and willing to back a certain set of nominees—it turned portrait into caricature. Popular input was controlled and channeled in ways that party committees chose. It might be the committees' responsibility to define the basis of representation in conventions and locate the convention site, to set the terms for participation in the primary and certify the winner, to select the officers that brought delegates into session and appoint the committees that would examine contesting members' credentials, and to determine what would go into the party platform. The actual wording of the planks rested with committees chosen within the party leadership, not from outside, and while a convention could amend the platform from the floor or strengthen the language of wishy-washy resolutions, and often did take the minority report over the majority, the advantage lay with the backstage managers, who had on their side not only partisans who thought as they did but also those wary about risking party harmony by joining a floor fight.

That assumed that the conventions would speak for the rank and file of the party. Given a fully open, fair system, perhaps they would. But observers could see that victory in primary elections depended not just on the people's will but on the willingness of party managers to heed it. Ward bosses and professional politicians were able to put together a network of organizers to get out the voters they wanted. Those whose position of influence permitted them to extend favors had forces to draw on, bought with past gratitude and the promise of future service. Since many primaries were held as meetings, where the majority was registered by a show of hands or a roar of voices, local bigwigs had plenty of leeway to announce a result suiting themselves. They could schedule "snap" primaries, giving the opposition little time to mobilize, or pick days for local caucuses when harvest season was at its height and farmers hard put to attend. They could also call on nonmembers of their party or nonresidents, without fear of legal penalties. "Two years ago, I found eight hundred names to strike off our registration lists, and this autumn, one thousand six hundred and seventeen," a Baltimore reformer complained; "and this is a clean ward."[33]

The wider the area a convention covered, the less susceptible to grassroots pressure it was, and the more the layers of management showed. Those elected delegate were likelier to have the name recognition that went along with past political service. They came as politicians, perfectly prepared to deal in ways suiting their own future interests. How successfully they did so would depend on the county and district committees' influence. Whoever ran convention machinery had tremendous power to recognize or ignore as he saw fit, to permit or refuse the right to vote on particular matters, and to use parliamentary rulings to stifle opposing factions. Politicians did not come to a convention to do their local constituents' will alone but to choose a candidate likely to win the county, the district, or the country. The two aims might clash. As a result, any convention was a distillation of the people's will, carefully culled and quite possibly transformed to suit the politicians' needs.[34]

Bosses could be beaten. Often they were, and the more arrogantly they held themselves the likelier a revolt would undo them, as the managers of rival machines made common cause with reformers. But nobody had to be told that the professional politicians had the edge in every set-to with outsiders and that any fight would be a hard one. With some exaggeration, insurgents declared theirs a government not of the people but of the "office-brokers. . . . They do the dictating, the people the voting."[35]

Leaving aside the issue of organization, however, the very character of the hurrah campaign came under ever louder attack. It may have instilled and reinforced partisanship, but to nonpartisans on the outskirts of the party system, the concentration on hoopla and coal oil showed why Gilded Age politics was mostly tinsel.

There was no question about it; part of the appeal in politics was that it made itself interesting, often hilariously so. A successful campaigner knew any number of tricks, and, when the election was over, these entered the political folklore. "Pump-handle Politicians" played "the social dodge" by holding open house at a hotel and giving cordial handshakes to commoners. A candidate might buy tickets to every place of amusement, to please the owners, and subscribe to every benevolent society, though, as one New York congressman did, he might draw the line at paying for a ticket to a clambake that had taken place three months earlier.[36] In many city districts, candidates followed the custom of showing up at bars a few days before the election and setting up drinks for all. A crafty Ohio

Democrat was reported to have hired an impostor who looked like his rival, had him call at every saloon a week before the election, make a boilerplate Republican speech—and then order himself a five-cent beer and walk out. By the time the Democrat showed up a few minutes later, the crowd around the bar was seething at its ill treatment and all the thirstier for the drinks it had been expecting. Wards where the trick was pulled gave the Democratic nominee just enough votes to win.

Yet to those who thought of governance as a science, operating by easily understood rules, and for those who wanted policy to be worked out in businesslike ways, the very artfulness to politics became one more reason for uneasiness. The age of eloquence was not past, "and we are right sorry for it," an editor complained. Barren of thought, flabby in logic, tired in expression, such eloquence was "a pretense, a sham, a fraud, which has long since wearied and disgusted all sensible men."[37]

Year by year, the cant of politics wore phrases smooth. "A weak invention of the enemy" entered the vocabulary of politics until its Shakespearian origin was forgotten (except by one irreverent newspaper's inquiry as to whether the invention had been patented). Wearily, the *San Francisco Daily Alta California* listed phrases so overused that they glided by listeners without leaving an impression: "the people don't enthuse," "it fell like a wet blanket," "the millions are moving," "the ballot-stuffers, shoulder-hitters, and sloggers are out in force," "the slogan of battle," "the cowardly, sneaking opposition," "the bloated bondholder," "the demands of the business interest," and that varicose favorite, "the great heart of the people." What were "God-given rights," anyhow? "We are marching to the music of the Union" was nonsensical, even in literal terms, "for the Union makes no music and very few of us march."[38]

If the words were hollow, then what did that say about the people that politics brought to the fore, with those words at their command? What did it say about the system itself? Serious issues certainly were at stake. Yet newspapers could not help admitting, every so often, that their application in a campaign setting had all the qualities of a game, where the pleasure came in the playing of it, almost as much as in the winning. It was well not to take it too seriously. "Four-fifths of politics is humbug," a reporter covering the parties' national committees wrote in 1892. "The other fifth is self—pure and simple." And, really, was that such a bad thing? "The game of politics played without humbug would be as uninteresting as a game of baseball without rules or umpire. . . . The more artistically it is done the better we like it."[39]

But if humbug defined the soul of politics, as a campaign practiced it, how could any party make a mandate for any meaningful change? To politicians, a party platform was like a railroad depot's: not so much to stand on as to get in by. It followed, then, that politicians, so good at winning office, would be a terrible failure at using it. Their sight extending no further than the next election, they could not legislate, and their partisan loyalties stood in the way of a joint, statesmanlike solution. Election by humbuggery did not promise well for effective government. It only invited more of the same, with congressmen making speeches for campaign handouts and scoring cheap points on their opponents.

It also invited a politics that was both negative and irresponsible, where cheap attacks and personal abuse served as well as reasoned discussion of the issues. Those who followed the 1880 campaign closely could have learned a great deal about the dangers of too powerful a South and too divided a Democratic Party. But partisanship also threw loads of claptrap into the contest. Partisan editors proved to their own satisfaction that the Democratic nominee, General Winfield Scott Hancock, had not really been much use at the battle of Gettysburg and that he was known for cruelty to his soldiers. Republican editors asserted that the general wore a corset, with all that implied. He was, they jeered, a "self-maid man" with "pretty-man ideas in dress."[40]

Let both parties speak of the "campaign of education"; the more the *Indianapolis News* learned in 1888, the more appalled it grew. For three months the party hucksters had labeled each other liars and forgers, even as they tried "corruption in every form, from buying a drunken voter to bribing a Legislature; filling the papers every day with countless repetitions of every variation of the imputation of falsehood, 'liar,' 'infamous lie,' 'scandalous lie,' 'willful liar,' 'malicious liar,' till positively there has been hardly anything else discernable except an occasional police item, and that was a record of theft or violence or prostitution."[41] The fault lay not in a few irresponsible political managers but in the whole culture of partisanship itself, and in the concentration on hoopla politics.

Negative campaigning usually worked, and especially among people for whom the risks of change mattered more than the possibilities for improvement. As campaigning was practiced, it was much safer to defend what was already in place than to propose something new, with all of its potential for bad consequences. To maintain, to sustain, and to restore—each party set these at the heart of its appeal in the Gilded Age.[42] Even at their most crusading, reformers hearkened back to a bygone culture of selfless public servants that, they assured readers, once had existed. Yet as the stakes diminished between the two major parties, the same apocalyptic rhetoric, the same invocation to battle, persisted. When a general wounded in the service of the Union could be accused of acting as the front man for traitors and a reforming New York governor pilloried as a thief-master general, reformers were right to think that there was something unhealthy, certainly out of place, in Gilded Age partisanship.[43]

Hoopla had consequences for how Americans saw the issues, saw the legitimacy of the opposition, and what they actually did. That was the *Philadelphia Public Ledger*'s point when the 1880 returns were in and little boys celebrated with bonfires of tar-boxes and ash-barrels. The "bigger boys of the country, especially in committee chairs, for months past, have set their tar-barrels ablaze with any material that came to hand." But the fires, the editor noted, had spread beyond rhetorical ones. When Republicans in New York City tried to prevent Democrats from electing a mayor by making much of his Catholicism and screaming that the public school system was in danger, they awakened a bigotry that no election returns would allay. If they accused southern Democrats of plotting treason long enough, northern voters would believe it was so, and reasonable politicians would find themselves confined in what they could do, once in power. And, the *Public Ledger* suspected, between the Democrats' waving the Chinese bogeyman and a riot in Denver, where several Chinese were murdered and many others beaten just before the elections, there was a clear connection. Party operatives "lit their fuses in those directions where popular fury kindles easiest, and in the direction of religious prejudice and caste hatred. Once fired, who is responsible for the explosion,— the tools at the havoc end, or the wily hands that set the match?"[44]

A party flag pole-raising anywhere could turn into a melee with shots being fired, and when one Republican procession met a Democratic one in New York City, a grappling for the Stars and Stripes ended in a shindy that the police joined only to crack as many black heads as possible. A future governor of Ohio left a Republican mass meeting only to meet with a Democratic shower of stones and a crowd of roughs, who knocked out his teeth, beat him, and fled.[45] Still, the hidden cost of popular politics was worst in the South. Even in Kentucky, where Democrats played down the race issue and where too strong a flaunting of the Lost Cause could cost many Union veterans' votes, a "quiet" election day was defined as one with less than five killings. The violence was so common that newspapers thought it worth only a passing mention. Farther south, Republicans who mounted a hoopla campaign were sure to be threatened, beaten, or killed. Nothing inflamed more than the race issue, and Democrats awakened the most terrible passions where they thought there was a chance of losing control. The effect

"Colorado—The anti-Chinese riot in Denver on October 31st" (*Frank Leslie's Illustrated Newspaper*, November 20, 1880).

might be an increase in lynchings, and often a race riot, which, after a suitable number of blacks had been killed, could be blamed on them for "incendiary" remarks.[46]

Concern over the passions let loose explained why some towns went out of their way to regulate partisan parades, to make sure that they marched nowhere close to each other. Instead of greeting each other as rivals, members of the procession very likely would maul each other. In villages where courtesy ruled, political clubs might divide the nights between them, but in other places, like Chester County, Pennsylvania, they deliberately chose to take to the streets on whatever night the opposition had scheduled. "This is the bummers' end of the campaign," the *Indianapolis News* reported three weeks before the 1888 election. It belonged to "the strikers and heelers; the waiters on two-dollar bills and whatever else may come to them." It was too late to win voters with torchlight processions, but not too late to create mischief. Officials must suppress them, if they became a nuisance. Some cities did, passing ordinances forbidding parades after dark.[47]

But might there not have been a different message in the regulation of parades: that instead of being an outpouring of the people, the collective *us*, the partisan marchers increasingly were becoming an entity distinct and distinctly less, an irritating *them*? For another problem was developing with hoopla as a way of rousting turnout in the last fifteen years of the century: it no longer seemed to be working as well. Politicians detected an increasing weariness with the political process — or, perchance, wariness. One observer suspected that the change in turnout and in enthusiasm had something to do with a change in temperature. Party feelings cooled as the weather did. Reporting from Wisconsin, a reporter in 1876 saw chilling effects as October advanced. Partisans had to meet inside, in churches and schoolhouses. Beyond city limits, no building could accommodate a big audience, and it was widely agreed that the larger the gathering, the more intensely an audience could be fired up. No campaign could be carried on at fever heat with small meetings only.[48]

The reasons went deeper. Indeed, the establishment of the Republican League and the Democratic Association of Clubs may not have been proof that partisanship was at its zenith in 1888 but that it was in decline. The parties were not able to wait for members to come, as in the old days. Especially among the young, the clubs had to go out recruiting. The gaudiness of the campaign clubs had been part of their appeal; politics was no longer enough. But the new kind of societies that Republicans were talking about founding in 1888 were meant as schools to indoctrinate party members on the issues, a function that had never seemed so necessary before. Was spectacle no longer enough, either?[49]

Later historians would blame the Mugwumps, in their attack on blind partisanship and their clamor for campaigns of education, for the decline in political interest. But that decline seemed to happen even where no liberal reformer trod, and every year, party organizers reported that the old methods were not taking the way they used to. How many tracts were issued was really beside the point, if the recipients only used them to light the stove. Onlookers admired the clubs' regalia as they paraded, and, a reporter suspected, then went home none the more convinced by the "pretty show." The very professionalism of the clubs and their demonstrations set them off from the audience. "It is altogether too much a matter of uniform and drill," the *Boston Herald* protested. "We doubt if it lasts into another presidential campaign to any extent."[50]

— Property = Right = shareholder

The Demon Lovers

With an economy just emerging from a depression in 1880 and two candidates for president, one of them simple and the other slightly soiled, one might have thought that the two parties would have found plenty to talk about without fantasizing. Yet fantastical shapes troubled both parties.

Blame some of the chimeras on General Ulysses Grant. Having retired after two terms as president and taken a round-the-world cruise, he had not resisted Republicans' call for his renomination. As so often in the past, the general let political tides carry him where they would, and among his old supporters, disturbed at the weakness of his successor in the White House, the tide seemed to be setting in the war hero's direction. All that spring the press teemed with reports of the third-term sentiment and predictions of the perils that the nation faced by Grant's willingness to let his friends return him to power. Some of the predictions fit past experience pretty well: incompetence, muddle, corruption, and rewards for unworthy favorites. But beyond it all was the cry that this stolid, plodding man would show an emperor's ambitions at last. Not content with one more term, far more eager to assume power than he implied, Grant would topple free institutions by making himself sovereign for life.[1]

So when, after a grim struggle and long deadlock, Grant was beaten at the national convention by the comparatively insignificant James A. Garfield of Ohio, Democrats read profound significance into the result. Farewell to Ulysses the First! His rejection signaled "the end of imperialism in America," a Kentucky newspaper declared. "It dissipates the dream of empire and awakens the country to a sense of security."[2]

Democrats were not really breathing a sigh of relief; they were catching their breath for a fresh panic attack. They would need that breath, for their enemies were shouting with alarm on their own. Those passions deserve a closer look, both as a cause of the heightened interest of the American people in politics and as an illustration of how the partisan temperament and a party press misled the people and nourished a worldview at once plausible and paranoid.

Echoing the charges of twenty years of campaigns, Republicans insisted that the Democratic Party had committed itself not just to states' rights but to state "supremacy," where the states had a right to break the national compact. It hardly mattered that the Democrats' platform commitment to states' rights was not a whit stronger than that of the Republicans' two decades before nor, indeed, that all Democrats protested their belief in the Constitution as the supreme law of the land.[3]

The proofs that Democrats would cheat their way to victory already had reached a mountainous height. Bulldozing of Republican voters and tissue ballots down south made elections there a sham. Without midnight raids, arson, and assassination, not one of 138 southern electoral votes could be assured to the Democracy. A minority ran the South, and that section, itself a minority in the nation as a whole, ran the national Democratic Party, and through it the House and Senate. The *Albany Evening Journal* considerately noted the typographical error in a Democratic song published in the *Argus*: "Then rally with shot and song / And waving banner, help the boom along." Surely the line *really* read, "Then rally round with shot-*gun* and song."[4]

Come November 1880, Republicans warned, the results of the war would be reversed. As soon as they had a president, southerners would pack the Supreme Court. They would create new states, Democratic rotten boroughs. Texas would divide itself into four new states, making ten senators where there had been two before. Out of the desert Southwest, still more rotten boroughs could be formed. Federal election laws would be instantly repealed, assuring that the House would continue to return Democratic majorities through fraud down south and in northern cities. Already a bill lingered in committee to expand the Supreme Court from nine to twenty-one justices. The purpose was plain, and the result, the interpreting of the Reconstruction amendments into meaninglessness, could hardly be missed. Under the right direction, the high court would uphold every state court decision legitimating the collection of Rebel war claims, no matter what the Fourteenth Amendment actually said. And what of that other measure that Democrats had drawn up, abolishing the Court of Claims and setting up a new superior court to handle the same jurisdiction? All five of the new judges would be Democrats, naturally. Let a now-loyal master come with a demand for recompense for slaves emancipated, or property damaged by Union troops, and the Treasury would open on well-oiled hinges. Confederate soldiers could collect veterans' pensions. The tax burden that these new obligations imposed would fall equally on all Americans, from Maine to Minnesota. But not down south; Democrats would get rid of the Internal Revenue System, which southerners complained of most loudly.[5]

Democrats replied that it was Republicans who really threatened liberty. One newspaper quoted the Fond du Lac *Chronicle*'s sardonic mock advice to party members: "Every Republican in Wisconsin should go armed to the polls on next election day. The grain stacks, houses and barns of all active Democrats should be burned, their children killed and their wives outraged, and that they may understand the Republican party is bound to rule and the one they should vote for or keep their carcasses away from the polls." What clearly was an ironic reflection on Democratic methods down south was taken literally as "Republican Principles." With their constant denunciation of states' rights, their long record of federal intervention in local disorders, and this year's clamor for a "strong man" in the presidency, Republicans had turned centralization into their guiding principle, "and centralization means the destruction of the Union of States, the destruction of the republic."[6]

Just how the threat would manifest itself, publicists could not agree, though all the possibilities were dreadful ones: monarchism and rule by the army, eradication of state lines, and the abolition of national elections. "What do we want with a strong government?" asked the *Raleigh News and Observer*. "Is it to enable a minority of 264,000 to foist again upon the people a fraudulent President?"[7] More pervasive was the assumption that Republican reelection meant the reimposition of military rule on the South. Having whipped their supporters into a frenzy of hysteria against the South, Republican leaders would have no trouble convincing them that Reconstruction must begin anew. Read carefully, Senator Roscoe Conkling's speeches could be interpreted to mean that the Reconstruction constitutional amendments had not been adopted and that not a single southern state government was lawful. Every southern senator and congressman could be kept out of the next Congress. What could bloody-shirt talk mean, if not that "a new crusade is preached and a new invasion is to follow." Negroes and carpetbaggers would be installed in state capitals and upheld with federal bayonets.[8]

At the least, the South must not be permitted to make a president. From the *Chicago Inter Ocean* came warnings, widely echoed in other Republican newspapers, that any Democratic victory in South Carolina would be a sham. With three in every five inhabitants black, and with blacks overwhelmingly Republican, the fraud would be plain on the face of it. What if South Carolina's electors made the difference between Republicans losing the White House and retaining it? Such an outrage would not be accepted. Democrats seized on statements like those to show a widespread Republican design to overturn the results, when the South voted en masse for General Winfield Scott Hancock. This was "Mexicanization . . . lawlessness . . . disunionism . . . Republicanism."[9]

Grant didn't help matters late in September when he chatted with a gabby clergyman, who immediately passed on what purported to be the general's candid thoughts to the press. Allegedly, Grant had declared that if Hancock were elected and "things began to go wrong," every "Northern legislature would be convened and compel their representatives to resign or resist the Solid South." That sounded suspiciously like a call for disunion or civil war. (Hancock was one of the few Democrats with common sense enough to doubt that Grant said or meant any such thing.) Alarmists reported that the administration had been passing out muskets to the Grand Army of the Republic, the largest veterans' organization in the country, and that the ultimate aim was for Garfield to preside — and Ulysses to rule until 1884, when he could don imperial purple outright.[10]

Against this conspiracy, there would be little that the people could do. Republicans had all the money necessary to buy voters with. Nine-tenths "of the monied patriots are enemies to the government," a Kentucky newspaper charged (meaning, of course, democratic government), "and the time is not far distant when the fact will become so apparent that he who runs may read." Fraudulent voting, of course, would count the opposition in. Four months before the election, California conspirators were preparing piles of "tape-worm tickets," ballots five inches long and half an inch wide, immediately recognizable. Employers would force them on their employees. That way, even from a distance, they could make sure that workers voted Republican and mete out dismissal to those voting any other kind of ballot. Officials would change the results, if they proved inconvenient. Desperate measures required drastic remedies. "If a fraudulent negro attempts to vote at your precinct tomorrow week spot him on the snoot," a reporter advised Indianans. "The harder you hit him the better it will be." Let Republicans be warned that "if they are caught stealing any electoral votes this year they will be shot on the spot," the *Louisville Courier-Journal* thundered. Perfectly aware that southern states would "count" the Democrats in, the *Albany Evening Journal* made a reasoned argument for how free institutions could be saved. What the governors of the eighteen Republican-run states could do would be to have the legislature choose the presidential electors, rather than leaving it to a popular vote. That way, the would-be traitors of the South would find their plans thwarted even before election day; a majority of the Electoral College would have elected Garfield. On the Democratic side, a state committeeman suggested that

Indiana's governor could counter Republican cheating by simply refusing to certify their presidential electors as legal.[11]

"The outlook is gloomy," a North Carolina correspondent commented at the election's close. "The tendency toward empire, Grant, consolidation and villainy is as palpable as it is startling and ominous. I doubt if the Democratic party can ever sufficiently recover from this defeat to make a national fight again."[12]

Seemingly, presidential campaigns made men run mad. Common though it was, historians generally dismiss the fevered rhetoric to concentrate on more plausible arguments. Yet Gilded Age politics cannot be understood without seeing the use of the campaign "scare," which was as constant and regular as the change of season.

For one thing, usually sensible people actually believed in what they heard. Privately, Republicans predicted a "horrible orgie" once southerners took power, and "legal glorification of the infernal rebellion." Democrats spoke of their readiness to defend the plot against their southern brethren's rights "in any and every emergency."[13] The cry about "Southern claims" always forced Democratic presidential candidates to issue letters slamming a door already barred and locked by constitutional amendment, and even then, Republicans found some way of insisting that it was as ajar as ever. Could a man who had been willing to use the army to overthrow Reconstruction in 1868 or to force Tilden into the presidency at the point of a bayonet in 1877 be trusted to keep his word now? (Probably not; but since Hancock was innocent of both allegations, the question was at best academic.) All the same, Democrats admitted privately, accusations like those told against them.[14]

For another, the fevers of 1880 were typical and, indeed, essential to the parties' ideological messages. Their success lay less in positive programs than in emphasizing a negative role, to protect America from change too awful to contemplate. Parties fed on fears, and those terrors had been reinforced by the Civil War experience, where liberty and the republic really *had* been in danger. "It is the work of freemen to-day," the *Poughkeepsie Daily Eagle* urged its readers. "Let us clinch to-day by the ballot the bloody victory of the bullet. The South will to-day vote as Lee and Jackson fought. Let us to-day vote as Grant and Sherman fought. Vote for humanity! Vote for continued prosperity! Vote for plenty of work and good wages! *Vote for a tariff*! Come out! Come out!"[15]

For Republicans, the enemy changed. The Solid South took the place of the Rebels, exchanging would-be traitors for selfish sectionalists, bit by bit, even though the South was never entirely solid and the Democrats there disagreed on a number of issues. Indeed, the Solid South would continue to do good service well into the Progressive Era and beyond. But the issues took a different packaging, more in line with current realities. Republicans accused "Rebel brigadiers" of dominating the opposition's counsels in Congress and of acting on behalf of southern interests. Those interests were incompatible with a North dependent on active federal encouragements to industry, bounties, tariffs, and subsidies for the overseas carrying trade. The brigadiers were downright hostile to pensions for Union veterans and at best conflicted about the national banking system. They stifled a fair two-party system in the South, the better to enhance the South's own control over the nation. Add to this recognizable picture of political realities an outlandish fantasy: that white southerners favored cheap government and states' rights mainly as an act of revenge. When they backed tariff reform, their main aim was to ruin those who had brought down the Confederacy. Nothing could please them more than the sight of jobless men and shuttered workshops across the North.[16]

Even as the warning of a Confederacy reborn tempered into an indictment of a malicious and undemocratic Democratic South, Republicans found a new bugaboo, or, rather, a very old one, hearkening back to the traditions of the first party system: England.

A mixture of emotions characterized Americans' response to England. Admiration for some of its traditions and certainly for a few of its politicians was as common as the avidity that the American upper crust showed for English customs and titled husbands from the penurious nobility. English authors like Oscar Wilde, theorists like Herbert Spencer, and actors like Henry Irving could fill a hall and do box-office business anywhere in the United States. Gilbert and Sullivan's operettas could set Americans to song as easily as they did Englanders —perhaps even more readily, before an international copyright law discouraged pirated editions.

But along with the appreciation and a certain masculine contempt for a society often stereotyped as effete and stifling, Americans continued to hold the vision of Britain as an oppressive empire, bent on the conquest of the earth. In England they also recognized their greatest industrial rival, with fleets that covered the globe and entered every market. With the suppression of disorders in Ireland a regular news story and with a vocal, influential Irish American community in most eastern cities to give voice to the worst suspicions of "perfidious Albion," it was easy enough to imagine British designs on the United States. Where once they had feared military conquest, now Anglophobes spoke of an economic sway, with London bankers controlling American bond markets, alien landlords holding immense tracts of western land, and mills in Manchester and Leeds driving down the wages of American workers with their production of cheap goods. They noted with alarm the liberal reformers, so devoted to English notions of a professional civil service with its permanent officeholding aristocracy. Irish American editor Patrick Ford even spotted "a small but wealthy party of conspirators" plotting a coup d'état to overthrow the republic, install a monarchy, and endow their wives with titles and themselves with seats in a House of Lords. Allied to them were "philosophic Anglo-maniacs," "saturated with English notions" and willing to read nothing but English books. "The free-traders generally belong to this category."[17]

By the late 1880s, John Bull–baiting had become a common stock-in-trade for Republican politicians, though not for them alone. England would do its all to prevent James G. Blaine from entering the White House, shipbuilder John Roach wrote the candidate in 1884. Losing the presidency, they would lose their South American trade. To hear propagandists tell it, English money and influence induced white southerners to break up the Union in 1860. Secession, a few orators explained, had not been proposed to protect slavery, or even to preserve states' rights. It was of English make, to create a nation without tariff barriers to which England could sell its goods. Americans needed reminding that a tremendous British slush fund elected James Knox Polk in 1844, repaid many times over by the "free-trade" Walker tariff of 1846. With jobless workers in England's mining and manufacturing districts "drifting into helpless pauperism," Tories—and to polemicists, the Tories were always in charge at Westminster—had every reason to invest in American politics again. There was always someone who knew someone else who had spoken with an Englishman in, say, Bradford, who was "understood to be" head of a local committee that had helped raised $350,000 for Hancock's presidential campaign and would spend two million to elect a free-trade president.[18]

Freighted with Anglophobic terrors, the tariff issue became all the more emotionally charged, and the revision of rates an affair of apocalyptic significance. A vote for Democrats, the *Lewiston Journal* warned readers, gave the winning party permission to bring British manufactures in on an equal footing and to hand the American market "to our chief competitors, with all that implies." It would stop every American mill until domestic wages were "reduced to the British standard," 62 percent below present levels.[19]

It followed that those who supported the Democrats were unpatriotic, if not purchased. Mugwump reformer Carl Schurz was accused of writing the party's *allegedly* free-trade plank in 1884, and of acting as the "agent" for "British free-traders." (The plank actually squinted toward protection, and Schurz had no hand in writing it, and if he was in Her Majesty's service, he must have been a double-agent; other credulous insiders declared him in the pay of the Second Reich.) "Great Britain hates Blaine; it hated George Washington," the *Auburn Daily Advertiser* cried. "It loves Cleveland; it loved Benedict Arnold. Voters don't forget it. The campaign is Great Britain against the United States; Cleveland against Blaine." Democrats were forced to reply in kind, accusing Republicans of being the best friends of England. It was their platforms that shut out the cheap building materials that American shipbuilders needed. As a result, twenty years of Republican rule had scoured the nation's carrying trade from the seas as effectively as Her Majesty's fleet ever could have done.[20]

John Bull–baiting was strong enough to drive the Democrats in ways that otherwise they might not have gone. It was not just as an appeal to the Irish voters that they embraced home rule for Ireland, but to distance themselves from England. Certainly President Cleveland's pugnacity in issuing warnings to Great Britain in the boundary dispute over Venezuela in 1895 was a reaction to the way the Democratic Party had been depicted, as the English free-trade party.

Scare politics did more than stir listeners' blood. It turned every election victory into an end in itself. Instead of having a program of positive changes, the winners achieved their goal simply by winning: they had checked the schemes of an insatiable lot of rascals. Each election thus became an exercise in "vindicationist" politics, to send a message, nothing more than that, to the other side. It became all the less necessary to do anything with one's mandate. Indeed, from the way the mandate could be misinterpreted, it became all the riskier for a party in power to do anything. For its actions would not be taken as an evil in themselves so much as an evil yet to be, the down payment on something far more dangerous and far less likely for the opposition to admit.

The harm in the Mills tariff bill in 1888 could hardly have been called all that alarming. As Democrats pointed out, a 7 percent cut in protective rates was no more free trade than washing one's face was drowning oneself. Leading industries got off especially lightly, particularly those with southern constituencies. Yet from the strident tone of the Republican press, one would have assumed that the American family was about to sup full on horrors. Take the first timid step and the nation could not help treading all the way down the path to an everlasting bonfire, with the immolation of all American industry. "The Confederate economists have set out to kill the protective system by 'girdling' it," the *Hartford Courant* warned. "The Mills bill is only the first gash."[21]

It was that "free trade scare" far more than the Mills bill itself that sent Dem-

"The political excitement in New York City—A 'rush' during the passage of a procession on Broadway. Harrison chorus: 'Trade, trade, no free trade.' Cleveland chorus—'Don't, don't be afraid; only low tariff, so don't be afraid'" (Matt Morgan, *Frank Leslie's Illustrated Newspaper*, November 10, 1888).

ocrats running for cover in 1888. Paraders chanted, "Don't be afraid! Don't be afraid! / Tariff reform is no free trade!" But who, except their own voters, were afraid? Newspapers cheerfully put the best face on conditions; there *had* been a real panic among workers, a month ago, a week ago, two days back, but a heartening change in feeling had set in. In fact, as Democrats admitted postelection, free-trade heebie-jeebies never actually diminished.[22]

Election results correspondingly were interpreted in ways far out of proportion to their actual meaning. "We must give such a final answer to Southern assumption as will settle its boasts, its claims, its domineering for the future," a Republican newspaper exhorted voters in 1880. A 50,000 majority in New York would let the "Chivs" (short for "Southern Chivalry") know who was master. This alone, and not new legislation, would end the unfair count down south. Those wanting to challenge Bourbon domination would take heart. States would cast off "the shackles of slavery." Sectional issues would end forever. And so, with the election over, Republican newspapers exulted that their goal had been achieved, even before Garfield came into power. Victories like that always gleamed like gold; and they were always a fool's gold. The other side never really learned, and the fight had to be made all over again four years hence.[23]

Demonizing political conflict did more than weaken the link between politics and policy. It also fostered an outlook toward politics that encouraged voters to imagine the control of policy by gray eminences and powers behind the scene. The villains differed. They might be the Money Power, or Jay Gould, whose money was apparently everywhere. They might be brewers' organizations or the "boss." But there was *always* a "true inwardness" in politics, as the phrase went. Sensible men fretted about the plans of the "Whiskey Ring . . . the silver-coinage Ring, the Cattle Ring, and whatsoever other Rings there may be" making an alliance in Congress.[24]

Conspiratorial thinking did more. It reflected but also helped foster an America that saw the political system as rigged, outside of those islands of honesty and decency in which the observer stood. It permitted all radicalism to be seen as conspiracy, nightmarish, terroristic, and remarkably competent. It turned the city boss from a boodler and broker into a mortal threat to liberty, watching like Caesar over the arena in which the Tammany Hall tiger clawed the republic and shattered the ballot box. It allowed unions and strikes to be seen as something alien but orchestrated from the top. And within the parties, it made plausible every charge of a sellout or a boss "knifing" the ticket.

Finally, conspiratorial thinking bred an attitude that one's enemies were always up to something dark and sinister, something that could only be countered by breaking the traditional rules of political competition. From Indiana in 1876, Republican national chairman Edwin D. Morgan heard that Democrats had bought his party's inspectors to make the count go their way in October, and, having seen how well it worked, were going to do the same in New York in November. "The Tilden managers have arranged for a number of expert ballot box stuffers from Baltimore and Philadelphia who are now traveling over this State visiting Democratic counties instructing the election officers how to commit frauds upon the ballot box," the Indianapolis postmaster wrote party headquarters. "We are doing all we can to expose this design of these men, but they are desperate and will stop at nothing."[25]

It was only natural for each party to think that the other one was far cleverer, far more unscrupulous and, in any close election, that sinister, underhanded means supplied "the true inwardness" of the outcome. Ask Democrats, and they would swear that they had won every national election since 1876. Republicans had counted them out in the Electoral College then and had stolen the 1880 election by buying votes with soap in Indiana in 1880 and with "blocks of five" in Indiana in 1888. Ask Republicans, and they would claim that at worst their party managers in 1876 simply recaptured stolen property when they used the government machinery to certify a Republican majority in three states where intimidation, fraud, and violence had prevented the people's will from asserting itself. There would have been no need for soap in 1880 or Dudley's floaters in 1888 if Democrats had allowed a fair election down south. In 1884, Republican gospel had it, Democratic rigging of the votes down south had the additional aid of imaginative vote-counting in New York City. There partisan officers counted third-party votes for Ben Butler as just so many more votes for Grover Cleveland, and by their ingenuity gave him the thousand-vote margin by which he won the state and the presidency.[26]

All of the charges were self-serving, and a few of them were outlandish; no evidence ever surfaced that a single Butler vote was counted for Cleveland, and Republicans' national chairman, Benjamin F. Jones, made the mistake of naming the specific places where fraud was alleged to have occurred, only to have local Republican leaders prove the contrary. Still, what mattered was not the strict truth of either party's account but that each believed it and acted accordingly.

What was one party to do to let the majority's true will succeed? They must cheat, too. "Our opponents resorted to the most infamous means to carry the election," Pennsylvania congressman "Honest John" Covode once remarked, "but d—n them we beat them at their own game." At least one Republican insider remembered those words in 1880, when the outlook seemed doubtful, and applied them to present events for William E. Chandler, who, for ways that were dark, could have given anybody lessons.[27]

As in so much else, the invocation of menaces and the harsh response showed itself worst in the South. There the terror, ever since the war, had been "Negro rule," which Republicans were accused of bringing. Republican governments collapsed or were overthrown, disowned and abandoned by their northern sponsors. Even so, the panicked cries continued. Elect Union Labor candidates to the legislature, Arkansas Democrats warned in 1888, and they would send Powell Clayton, onetime Republican governor, to the Senate. Had voters forgotten his tyranny? Just before election, newspapers discovered "race war" in backcountry settlements, imported black voters, "troubles," "threatenings," and clear proofs of a "well-planned scheme" to "stir up strife and bloodshed on the day of the election."[28]

Against third parties it was the constant refrain, and often effective. Outside of the Democratic Party, there was no safety. Any alliance with Republicans would mean Negro domination. "The Independents and Greenbackers in Copiah have built themselves into a fence for the rads to climb on," the *Crystal Springs Monitor* warned Mississippians in 1882, and the first to climb would be "saffron Jim" Hill, the black Republican leader in Copiah who had been nominated for Congress. "Can you vote it, or does it vomit you?" the editor demanded of dissidents. But the issue was not put just in terms of degradation. "The republicans in this district, led by Jim Hill, having declared war against us, we say let them have it as long as there is one of them left." As usual, Democrats insisted that it was not they but blacks who were drawing the color line; in vain Hill pointed out that, having a white Democratic father, it would be hard for him to draw the color line without being on both sides at once. "Intelligence—respectability— decency—democracy," the *Monitor* summed up for its side—and its side only. Voters knew their duty. "Bulldoze them with democratic votes."[29]

All it took to turn such a general fear into mob violence was an incident, and the Democratic press knew all about grasping at straws and turning them into political gold. On a regular basis, they would issue quotations from blacks endorsing intermarriage or threatening to set the torch to white houses. Every few years, a Negro uprising would be reported, in all its terrifying array. True, it never got any further than the planning stage. But the news that followed would always be the same, of whites leaping to arms to defend themselves by overthrowing a lawfully elected government.

Crittenden County stood twelve miles north and west of Memphis, across the Mississippi. Blacks outnumbered whites twenty to one. When Democrats regained the state, however, Republicans knew that they could not protect their voters, not even with a twelve-hundred-vote majority, and to assure themselves of some share of the offices, they worked out a bipartisan coalition ticket, "dividing the plunder with the men who rob them," as one Republican complained. Blacks had continued to serve on the bench and as assessors and clerks. No one accused officers of corruption, and a county debt of $60,000 was reduced to a tenth as much. There had been no trouble.

Until 1888. Then a grand jury indicted the black judge of the probate court, D. W. Lewis, and the black county clerk, David Furgeson, for drunkenness and neglect of duty. A private committee of "citizens" raised funds and hired counsel to push prosecution. As the trial date neared, tensions rose. In early July, the press announced that prominent whites had been sent anonymous threatening letters. Nobody ever produced one of the notices, much less the author. No one tried to arraign the offenders before the circuit judge. On the contrary, Furgeson and Lewis went into court to deny any knowledge of the incidents and to petition for a court order requiring the grand jury to investigate fully. The judge declined to act. But Democratic headlines accused Furgeson of penning the letters. The press set up the usual cry: "Turbulent Negroes threaten to Precipitate a War of Races in Crittenden County—Prominent White Citizens Ordered to Leave—Arming for Defense." In fact, the article had evidence only of whites coming into Memphis to buy Winchester rifles to arm for an attack on blacks. Later, Democrats offered as proof of Furgeson's complicity that he had recently attended the Republican National Convention. Undoubtedly the bloody-shirt element there had put him up to writing threatening letters himself. This was part of its scheme to enrage whites into overthrowing Negro rule and giving northern Republicans an issue.

"York Byers and Jim Beaver, two of the most reckless of the colored agitators," were said to have organized "a military company of 280 negroes and may endeavor to force a clash," the *Little Rock Gazette* announced on July 13. "This, however, will hardly occur." (Indeed not; nobody ever found any evidence of such a company.) "Crittenden county asks aid of us to quell negro uprising," the deputy sheriff in a nearby county wired the governor. From Woodruff County, local authorities called for 2,000 "needle-gun cartridges" to arm a company heading for Crittenden County that evening.

Even before outside militias could act, local whites with reinforcements from beyond the county line had engineered a coup d'état. The probate judge fled the state, the circuit judge absented himself in Memphis, and the sheriff, who owed his place to black votes, picked up a rifle and headed the mob. White militia took over the streets in Marion and manned the roads into town. On the morning of July 12, some 300 well-armed men stormed the courthouse in Marion and forced their way into the clerk's office. Summoning all the deputies, a country doctor issued the crowd's ultimatum. "Gentlemen," he told them, "this county is too small for you and for us. One must leave. We have decided it shall be you, and if you do not go we hope you'll get to heaven." Amid cocked guns, the clerk and his deputies signed a prepared letter of resignation, and, without even being given the chance to put on their coats, they were escorted to the jailhouse and held as prisoners. Vigilante squadrons carried on a full search for arms through the town. They broke into a Masonic lodge and broke up a concert band and a children's gathering, took more prisoners, and led them all out of town. A mile beyond Marion, a wagon was waiting to load the blacks into and carry them away under a guard of horsemen to the river. The mob handed them steamboat tickets and saw them out of the state. In all, at least nineteen black leaders were expelled and told not to return. They included a teacher, a doctor, some farmers, the editor of the *Headlight*, the county's only black newspaper, the county assessor, and the pastor of the local black Baptist church. "William Yancey, a respected white citizen of the county was elected as [Furgeson's] successor" that same day—by what process and by whom press reports did not say. The absent circuit judge was back that afternoon to accept the clerk's "resignation" and to certify the election winner, "an old and highly respected citizen," as the new clerk. Discovering his duties at last, he charged the grand jury to return indictments against members of the mob, if it saw fit. It did not see fit.

The exiles appealed to the governor for redress, but they were not so foolish as to expect anything more than a few sympathetic words. The governor chose Democrats to fill the offices "vacated" by black officials, and, Democrats declared, blacks in Crittenden should have considered themselves lucky. The "negro-dominated whites of Crittenden" showed "admirable display of self-control" in removing only leaders; they were prepared "against any contingency." Indeed, whites had done no more than what Mississippi and Louisiana had done state-wide twelve years before, and what Phillips County had done with rifles and artillery in 1878.

Terror-inspired terrorism had several obvious effects. In Crittenden County, it wiped out regular Republican majorities in presidential elections. Elsewhere, it created a strong enough fear to make blacks absent themselves from the polls. In heavily black counties, it increased the pressure on Republicans to avoid any election competition at all, and a fate like Furgeson's. They were all the likelier to sue for terms with Democrats in black counties, dividing up the ticket between the two parties, simply to keep the peace. It sounded like the highest degree of nonpartisanship; it was, in fact, nothing less than ransom, "giving away one-half of the county offices to get a title to the other half," as Justice John McClure put it. But what else could they do?[30]

As long as there was the fear of "Negro Domination," Republicans could not carry the cotton South, not with all their majorities. So the fear had another effect. It stimulated party managers to schemes to bleach the party. At all costs, blacks must not be nominated for office, for fear of raising white terrors. Some leaders even talked of creating a "lily-white" Republican organization, run by and for whites alone.[31]

The force of fear in politics did not simply distort political debate in the nation and cripple full participatory democracy in the South. It helped create a more conservative party system, one in which leaders were more chary about taking risks and more aware of the dangers of being depicted as enemies of liberty or of the state. It encouraged guarded, even empty, language in party platforms and campaigns that focused less on what one's own side could do and more on what the opposition might be up to. It narrowed mandates and limited the major parties' choice for candidates; Democrats might dare consider a Delaware senator for their presidential nominee, but to take someone from the ex-Confederate South was just committing suicide. It also almost assured that any third-party alternative would be depicted in the most bloodcurdling terms, as a threat to a republic that, from all Democrats and Republicans let listeners infer, was terribly fragile and within an election of being ruined forever. The outsiders would be seen either as the guileful tool of the Real Enemy or as anarchs, out to wreck the party bulwarks that preserved and protected American government. Even if they had not been inclined toward the waving of bogeymen themselves, third-party activists would have had no choice but to counter unreason and fear by raising fears of their own, just as potent or even more thrilling. And, as they found, the fears that struck deepest were those that the major parties had educated their followers into believing already.

Finally, historians might wonder how far the record turnouts of the 1870s and 1880s were fostered not just by deeply felt partisanship but by the scaremongering that the two parties engaged in so zealously. Americans voted partly from fear, not just from hope. What if the terrors evaporated?

For that is what happened in much of the country in 1892. For the first time ever, two presidents ran against each other; for the first time in many years, two men, well known from their performance in high national office, vied for the White House. In 1884, Grover Cleveland had been a comparative stranger. Republicans found it easy to portray him as a drunkard and debauchee or the weak tool of Rebels. After twenty-four years out of power, Democrats were unknowns. But only a prodigious gowk would believe any such fears about former president Cleveland in 1892. Blacks had continued to vote; the president even had appointed some to office. Whatever his defects, no one could accuse Cleveland of lacking courage. The South may have sent wild currency inflationists to Congress, but anyone who thought that they would push through dangerous legislation over that man's indomitable will was living on weaker fantasies than usual. The terrors that Republicans waved that fall were a particularly wan lot, and those that northern Democrats waved were not much better. Four years in power, frosty Benjamin Harrison was known too well and despised too widely to inspire fear in anyone. A campaign without fear was something new: a dignified bore. If the country was safe enough, no matter who won, what was the point of turning out? A listless electorate absented itself from the mass meetings. Some of them even failed to show up on election day. Just possibly, the party system had nothing greater to fear than the lack of fear itself.

Party Tricks

The Press of Public Business

Bear not false witness; let the lie
Have time on its own wings to fly.
—Arthur Hugh Clough, "The Latest Decalogue"

To credit the newspapers' own claims by 1890s, one would have imagined that truth was ringed round with guardians against the wiles of politicians and the claptrap of the two major parties. Time and again, editors pointed to their own independence or lauded the contrast between the papers of their own generation and those of an age gone by, when anything went in distorted news coverage.

Proof they had in plenty, for journalism, like politicking, was always making itself anew and, like the two major parties, basked in the warm glow of self-appreciation. Between the Civil War and the turn of the century, the number of Washington correspondents grew. Penny-a-liners and fly-by-nights gave way to professionals with a code of conduct. Insisting on complete reports of the nation's business, a score of newspapers stationed two to four reporters in Washington, and the listing of gentlemen of the press in the *Congressional Directory*, extensive though it was, represented only the chief of staff. In most great cities, newspapers directed their choicest appeals beyond party loyalists to the news-hungry crowd. Many of the leading editors in the country professed no partisan loyalty. From one campaign to another, they shifted their support, depending on which presidential candidate best suited their principles. City journals might not know it, one rural Minnesota editor wrote, "but in Minnesota, at this time, there is not a more independent class of men than the editors of local papers."[1]

The 1884 campaign made "independence" more respectable than ever, and even the partisan newspapers were becoming comprehensively less partisan. Some, like the *St. Louis Globe-Democrat* stood by the Republican ticket in presidential years but gloried in warring on the local nominees that the party's machine put forth, just as its Democratic rival the *Post-Dispatch* did on the opposite side of the fence. Other papers gave their partisanship a more tolerant flavor, reminding voters that, in fact, the republic was not in all that much danger, no matter which side won, and that patriotism knew no party lines. Editors even expressed boredom with the election—once it was over, and usually with more heartfelt emotion if their own particular candidate had lost.[2]

Finally, to stay in business, newspapers in major cities had to dish up far more than politically charged topics. There must be thorough news coverage, dispatches from the wire services, features of human interest, and sports coverage. Under the pressure of public demand and the lure of profit, more newspapers added Sunday editions, and these were likelier to entertain rather than pound political points home.[3] By the 1880s, more newspapers had added woodcuts and sketches to their columns. What began as modest islands in a sea of type soon turned into archipelagoes, or full-sized continents, taking up a quarter to a third of a page. Where most journals began with the faces of candidates, many of which "might have been hewn out of a cigar-box cover with a dull jack-knife," the art staff gradually expanded to produce street scenes, political cartoons, comic strips, fashion portraits, and sketches of high society. An agent of political instruction had turned into one of public amusement, or, in the rougher language of the *Minneapolis Tribune*, "to raise h--l and make money."[4]

As that happened, so, too, the news coverage of political events dwindled or lost its savor. Long the irrepressible voice of Ohio Democracy, the *Cincinnati Enquirer* reflected the change. In 1880, a student of politics might find a complete discussion of each congressional district—its past partisan habits, its prospective nominees, the intrigues of the ambitious, the jealousies of various factions, the persnickety habits of each county, the business interests most needing attention, and, when the campaign really got under way, a thorough examination of the foibles and unimaginable follies of the other side's candidate. Nothing so comprehensive graced its pages in 1892. Instead of a reporter's column and a half of commentary, a two-line mention appeared on page one that X had been nominated in the convention at Y and that great enthusiasm prevailed. Indeed, there were days during the campaign when one might not even know that such a campaign within the state was going on.

Clearly, the press coverage of politics was changing, and with it much of the excitement was removed. This would happen more every year, and for partisan organizers wanting to bring their voters to the polls or assure their support for one party's candidate over another, it posed an increasingly serious problem.

Until around 1890, though, none of these caveats amounted to as much as it seems. Challenged from without and changing within, the party press lasted and throve. Outside of the South, most towns had two organs, one Democratic, one Republican; every major city had them both, along with other papers of varying degrees of independence. There was room enough inside the Republican Party in towns like Lancaster or Reading, Pennsylvania, for two Republican papers to sell party nostrums in a variety of flavors.[5]

Those editors who expressed independence the loudest still supported one party or the other. What nonalignment may have done, in fact, was to raise the value as well as the price of their allegiance and to induce politicians to work harder for their support. And prating about "independence" did not make a journal so. The real test came in the coverage of conventions and parties, and there, no reader had to go beyond the front page to see which way a particular "independent" would go when the time came for endorsing candidates. What the city desk thought was news depended in part on what served one party's agenda. Reporters for the most important "independent" in the nation, the *New York Herald*, were typical in 1888 when they sent back a constant stream of heartening news from upstate about how the "tariff scare" was failing to take hold — until the election returns proved their claims no more than the journalistic equivalent of the Democratic headquarters' "rainbow-chasing."[6]

Press competition did not undermine partisanship; often it reinforced it. With roughly equivalent news coverage, the biggest newspapers had to find grounds for attracting readers, and they were almost instinctively at war with every news-gathering competitor in any case. "As an editor he is a dismal failure," Waco's William C. Brann snarled at a New York editor, who allegedly had "the physique of a bull elephant and the brains of a doodlebug," "but he would be a dazzling success as ballast for a canal boat." More economically, another editor responded to an Alabama journalist's inquiry about when he would pay the "debt of nature" by replying that when the questioner paid his, it would be by "execution."[7] In such a state of rivalry, partisanship paid. Given relatively equal access to news sources, Republicans preferred one with a Republican bias, and Democrats one with a Democratic inclination.

The question of whether to concentrate on news gathering at the expense of partisanship was far more easily answered for less well endowed papers. Technological change was all very well for those that could afford it. Deploring the old-fashioned manner of the local Democratic organ carrying its locked-in pages of type through the streets to a printing firm's steam printing press to be run off, solicitous Iowa partisans asked the editor why he did not buy a power press. "Why don't we buy the Bardman House, Woodbury block, and the public square?" the editor exploded. "Why don't we raise h--l on $4.50?" If he ever did more than break even, that would be the biggest news story of the year. "Printing Democratic papers in Iowa is like peddling peanuts in a grave-yard." Special features and illustrations might attract a different crowd for the journals with extra cash to spend, but outside the city, most newspapers could not afford it, and inside city limits, many chose not to until the 1890s. Most metropolitan newspapers had not embarked on what a critic called "the eyesore business," and few had the talent to put in more than a couple of small "revolting wood-cuts," most of them such poor likenesses as to deserve a Georgia newspaper's title, "The Slaughter of the Innocents."[8]

For those unable to pay for the fullest news coverage, partisanship continued to be the one way to keep an audience. It also was the one way to supplement a skimpy subscription list with the funding that county and state printing contracts or a postmastership provided, not to mention the party's outright subsidies and wholesale subscriptions to "campaign editions" in election year. Even when Joseph Pulitzer's "new journalism" had set the pattern for big-city dailies, there were plenty of "one-horse, pap-fed bureau edited sheets" in the hinterland.[9]

Plenty of newspapers needed patronage to survive, and civil service reform never kept them from getting it. From the 1870s on, the federal government had fewer favors to grant and relied on the public printing office, not individual pressmen, to publish its documents. But no such inhibition on bestowing printing contracts where friends were to be kept and made forestalled state and local governments. A small-town newspaper could live or die on the boon of printing laws at the end of a legislative session or the government advertisements; most southern Republican journals lived *and* died—lived while the support sustained them and perished when it was removed. Even at the federal level, though, there were plenty of offices available for friendly newspapers. Control of a post office in any small town meant regular pay. It permitted party materials to pass through the mails with little scrutiny and the other side's leaflets to vanish or be delayed unaccountably on their way to recipients, until the elections were over. Generally, the likeliest pick for a postmaster was the local editor. Listing all the weeklies edited by postmasters, one observer calculated, would run into hundreds of names, just in Iowa alone. In other cases, the parties subsidized flagging newspapers, funded campaign editions, or created new papers for the moment of need.[10]

Nor was partisanship inconsistent with news gathering or news reporting. Even in the cities, most people continued to read partisan papers, not only because they mirrored their own views, but because of their overall excellence. For all its technical innovations, there were few more intensely partisan papers than

Joseph Pulitzer's *World*, but even readers who might take umbrage would take it on a daily basis, as a price well worth paying. When it came to the latest about an ax murder, prizefight, or exclusive, Pulitzer gave his clientele all the news fit to print—and quite a good deal beyond it. Whitelaw Reid's *Tribune* exasperated Democratic readers. Partisan bias colored every leading article and spilled out of the editorials even into the foreign correspondence from Ireland. Still, the "Pooh Bah of Republicanism" kept a wide readership. That it provided stellar coverage for Washington affairs and foreign tangles was one big reason why.[11]

Innovations, indeed, could work to partisan journalism's advantage. Political cartoons showed that most plainly. Sporadically, comic-illustrated weeklies had broken with the custom of party-distributed cartoons provided as a presidential campaign broadside. Indeed, the partisan commentary turned into a broad-ranging discussion of issues and events, many of which did not advance one candidate or party over another. They were short-lived exceptions and money losers. Even as the cartoon art improved and the number of practitioners grew, in almost every case, a presidential race gave artists their real start and main purpose. Joseph Keppler's frothy humor magazine, *Puck*, seemed to signal a sharper break with tradition, if only because it lasted and prospered. Social and public events became its main focus, and its targets ranged from monopolists to Mormon polygamists. *Puck* trained the artists who made the Sunday funnies and may have softened the malice of political cartooning. Yet the old pattern held for most dailies well into the 1890s. On the whole, they stuck to commentary not on world events but on politics in the narrowest sense: not policies or laws but candidates and parties. Indeed, not until after the 1896 campaign did newspapers treat cartoons as a regular feature at all. Until then, when the election returns were in, the cartoons stopped.[12]

The Gilded Age party system could not have thrived without the journalists' skills. In a country where so many people changed residence and so many foreigners came to stay, the partisan press needed to reaffirm the political message constantly; that was how partisans were made. Politicians with a keen eye to their own future cultivated publishers, editors, and reporters and gave them a lead on how to handle issues during election campaigns. A rally was all very well, but without newspaper publicity, the organization could schedule an affair, and no one come. When speakers made their campaign tours, the partisan press was needed to publish their appointments so that audiences would show up. More than ever, the front page found room to celebrate a lawmaker's accomplishments and to familiarize readers with the intimate details of his private life. "Congressman Morrow has returned to San Francisco and the Government at Washington still lives!" a Democratic paper remarked sourly—perhaps because it was the only daily in town denied an exclusive interview.[13]

A partisan press mattered not just as the voice of the party but as its eyes and ears. Journalists had the closest connections with grass-roots public opinion. Instead of simply making it, they reflected it or tempered their own arguments to deal with it in the most acceptable way. To political leaders, journalists sent regular reports of local conditions and the inner workings of politics. Their acquaintance, necessarily, was a broad one. They made ideal go-betweens in negotiations with local machines, business leaders, and even across party lines. Their influence over coverage gave them a power that opened politicians' doors and gave them favors worth trading. Senatorial aspirants counted how well they were doing by the number of presses supporting them, and an *Oroville Mercury* mattered every bit as much as a *Los Angeles Herald*.[14]

Consequently, ambitious partisans cultivated the press and helped pay its bills. Naturally, those with the most money to spend were able to make the most steadfast friends. Politicians rich from coal, steel, and railroad investments usually extended their personal domain by buying either a newspaper or its editor, however indirectly. In West Virginia, the two Democratic magnates, Senators Johnson Camden and Henry G. Davis, sealed a friendly relationship with Lewis Baker, the editor of the party's top newspaper, with favors. "A very ordinary little man, with a large presumption of unbounded ambition," one enemy called Baker, but that ambition in the 1870s and early 1880s allowed ready access to loans, sought with bright predictions of an early repayment and later supplemented with threats that money already tendered would be irretrievably lost. When Baker turned on Davis in the 1884 campaign, the coal-mine magnate, having helped endow him with state printing contracts and endless political confidences, lost patience at last, foreclosed, and forced him to sell out and leave the state.[15]

Party organs therefore were most beholden to those able to unlock the cash box. They had to be. Outside of the cities, journalism rarely paid well. A politician able to raise the wherewithal could expect favorable coverage and a ready ally in factional quarrels. Often, party organs aligned with one faction or another, which, in states where one party had only a few newspapers, could skew the political debate considerably. Politics would have gone more smoothly for Senator Mitchell if Oregon's leading Republican newspaper had had an editor other than Harvey Scott. Republicans could pick whomever they chose for office, the *Salem Daily Statesman* growled, but they must put up with the *Portland Oregonian's* tantrums. To suit Scott, a governor had to be like himself, "a son-of-a-gun on wheels . . . , a ring-tail snorter, . . . the double distilled quintessence of egotism, cynicism and diabolism."[16]

Partisanship could transform any affair by packaging the event in biased analysis of its meaning. It may not have been literally true that in joint debate between two rivals for Nevada's House seat the Republican did his opponent "up, picked the meat off his bones and threw the bones out the window," or that the Democrat responded with "a bully's attack" that "turned out to be nothing but fuss and feathers," but the *Reno Evening Gazette* knew better than to feed readers with actual quotes; they actually might dare judge for themselves. With a protective tariff deeply unpopular in Minnesota, Republican newspapers tried to shift attention from their senior senator's vote for the rate hikes in the McKinley bill to his battle on behalf of duty-free binding twine. Around "his panting form the party artists are throwing a halo brighter than that which circles Aeneas emerging from smoking Troy with his father on his back," the *St. Paul Globe* commented disgustedly.[17]

Partisan journalism also created a politics of outrages, victims, and swindlers. It was the custom of editors to find the worst, the most appalling facts, about the opposition and to publish these without scruple. Habitually, editors warned that the campaign about to begin would be full of partisan lying and billingsgate and then went on to prove it by their own outbursts. Candidates would discover for the first time the enormity of their own crimes; for partisanship would etch their personal histories in venom, and "if it were possible their bodies would be consumed by the cannibals of the press."[18]

All of these biases might have been classed as matters of opinion, though the distinction between outright lying and interpretive reporting was a fine one, when crowds were estimated at numbers far beyond the physical capacity of the hall in which they assembled or when candidates were described with the pallor of death to suit the prognoses of doctors that they would not live past election day. All the details of a campaign could be modified to build up partisan enthusiasm. Even in the 1880s, when they prided themselves on their professionalism, reporters still cleaned up language and popped speeches into the candidates' mouths, converting "wormy chestnuts into apples of gold" and "ghastly and oft-repeated yarns into Websterian logic." Booms materialized out of nothing and were spread full-scale by reporters interviewing supporters, usually nameless. "Mr. Woodard [of the *Cincinnati Enquirer*] is supposed to be the only man in America who can sit on the arid plains of Kansas and get his imagination worked up to such a pitch that the cactuses look to him like so many Democratic voters, all howling for Henry B. Payne," the *Chicago Daily News* jeered. "He will probably keep clear of

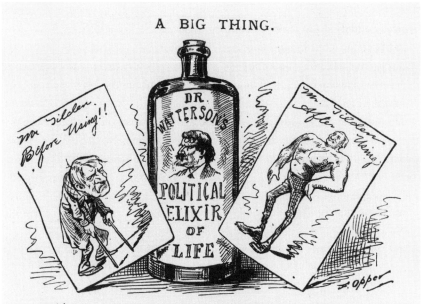

A BIG THING.

PRINCIPAL DEPÔT FOR THIS WONDERFUL MEDICINE AT THE OFFICE OF THE "LOUISVILLE COURIER-JOURNAL."

"A big thing. Principal depot for this wonderful medicine at the office of the Louisville 'Courier-Journal'" (Frederick Opper, *Puck*, July 25, 1883). Henry Watterson's *Courier-Journal* was former governor Samuel Tilden's most energetic booster and the most enthusiastic purveyor of fantasy about the robust state of the candidate's physical condition.

the Kaw River district. There is no Payne boom along the Kaw. On the contrary, the Kaw is solid for [Justice] Stephen J. Field, because the Kansas City *Times* has said so."[19]

For the sake of party, the press could make up a story, foster a forgery, and carry it on as long as necessary. One of the worst such incidents took place during the 1880 campaign. Eking out a precarious existence as a sensation-monger on the edge of New York city journalism, *Truth* suddenly found a chance for real notoriety midway through October. A big envelope came to the office with a letter, apparently in General Garfield's handwriting. It was a reply to one Henry L. Morey, of the Employers' Union in Lynn, Massachusetts, expressing the candidate's friendliness to unrestricted Chinese cheap labor. Garfield's willingness to permit free immigration was well known, but this was something much worse: support for businessmen's recruitment and importation of Chinese paupers to do their work for them. Recently deceased, Morey had left this letter among his effects, and now those handling his estate passed it on where it could do the most good.[20] If genuine, the letter was political dynamite, especially in working-class neighborhoods, where foreign contract labor seemed likely to drive low wages even lower.

But was it authentic? The *Truth* staff compared the paper with a facsimile of other writing by Garfield, and after a quick examination, decided that it was genuine enough to boost circulation. The following morning, the paper hit the street corners. That afternoon, staff members carried it down to the Democratic National Committee headquarters, where some of Garfield's colleagues and friends from the House could pass judgment on the handwriting. Their assurance that the letter was the real thing was all the national committee needed, and they were not about to look hard for more. The committee ordered electrotype plates with the Morey letter on them and spread them nationwide.

Democratic readers gobbled the story like starving men. A few days before, their party had suffered crushing defeats in key state elections, and workers frightened that Democratic tariff policies would drive down their wages were the cause. If anything could put the party right with the working class, this letter would do it. Republican doctrine, as the *Wheeling Register* defined it, said, "Levy a tax on pig iron, but let pig tails come free." Democratic parades carried Chinese lanterns, as usual, but this time they were decorated with copies of the Morey letter.[21] It all seemed too good to be true.

As indeed it was. The Morey letter was a clumsy fake. It spelled words wrong, including, quite possibly, Garfield's last name. The covering envelope was postmarked and stamped, to be sure, but with a stamp that did not begin circulating until well after the date on the letter itself. No one in town could remember having met any such person. The Employers' Union did not exist. By the 22nd, the Republican committee knew that they were dealing with a forgery. The next day, Garfield followed up a denial with a genuine letter that Republicans could reprint in facsimile and use for comparisons.[22]

That should have been the end of it. But it wasn't. Leading Democrats shut their eyes to the mounting evidence and kept on yelling. Carefully adding that if it was a forgery, it was certainly a very clever one, Congressman Abram Hewitt of New York assured audiences that the Morey letter was beyond doubt and that he trusted Garfield's signature far more than the candidate's word, which had long since been proven worthless. A few partisan papers handled the whole affair with discretion. Others bolstered the forgery with fresh whoppers. The *Louisville Courier-Journal* divulged a plan by the Chinese-American Six Companies to bring 100,000 Chinese workers over within the coming year, a blow at workers "indorsed by James A. Garfield, Republican candidate for President." It was well known that the Republican chairman had received $50,000 from the Six Companies in San Francisco to help Garfield. What more proof of his intentions did people need?[23]

As the evidence accumulated that the Democratic committee had been diddled, the papers grew more heedless in their assertions. Comparison of the two letters, they had insisted, actually proved Garfield the author of both, because they were exactly alike; now the proof lay in how unalike they were—nobody wrote the same way twice. The very fact that the letter misspelled "companies" with a "ys" only proved authenticity, they argued. Knowing the candidate for an accomplished scholar and aware that such a lapse on his part would be unthinkable, would any forger let such a blunder slip in? Garfield must have made the mistake himself. By the end of the month, Democratic newspapers were printing confirmation of the letter's authenticity, much of it gleaned from testimony in the trial for criminal libel that the Republican National Committee had instituted. A hotel register at Lynn's Kirtland House showed Morey's name among those signing in on February 25, 1879. Just in time for the election, one Samuel S. Morey took the stand to identify Henry L. Morey as his uncle. "Garfield is in favor of the rat-eaters—Chinese cheap labor," the *Clarksville Semi-Weekly Tobacco Leaf* declared. "Chinamen can live on rats and rice and work for twenty-five cents per day. What will become of the colored people in the South if Garfield is elected and brings in cheap John?"[24]

Even as the official count was being made, the libel trial's witnesses proved what Republicans had known all along. Samuel Morey and the character witnesses were exposed as impostors, paid to show up under phony names. The Democratic National Committee footed the bill. A chemist who manufactured ink testified that the hotel registry signature was in an entirely different ink than all the entries before and after it; apparently it had been added later by persons unknown for corroboration. Having "proven" the letter's authenticity every day, the *Louisville Courier-Journal* now declared that it had never been taken in at all and used the exposure to prove that Democrats were much less villainous than Republicans: only amateur scoundrels got caught![25] More than a readiness to do their enemies justice made the rumor-mongers drop the story so fast. Less than a zeal for truth made Republicans keep in on page one well into the next presidential campaign.

The partisan press did more than define the issues. It created a cant of politics, trying to make it the center of people's lives and, perhaps, deceiving later chroniclers into thinking that it actually was. Press distortion and sensation could set the tone for a campaign. Newspapers could rouse enthusiasm or at least testify to its existence where there was none, or give certain issues privilege over others simply by how they covered them. But whether Republican, Democrat, or genuine independent, the mainstream papers reinforced the strength of the two-party system and worked to shut out alternatives to it. This point needs emphasis. The press's growing independence of the two major parties did not change the monopoly that they had on news management. Events worthy of political reportage might change over time. Even so, it was major parties that got the coverage. Their candidates had reporters in tow; their actions won most of the attention; their speeches were more likely to be reported in full, if at all. Other parties hovered on the margins, and how thin that margin was, the mainstream presses decided. To Republicans and Democrats, outlanders, no matter how deeply their concerns touched the voters, no matter what their prospects of electoral success, ranked as sideshows. Coverage treated them accordingly: an occasional reference, without any constant or in-depth reporting, and certainly without any serious discussion of their program.[26]

In the Deep South, the Republicans were the sideshow in a one-party system, and major newspapers scarcely noted a GOP state convention. References to its nominees were few, kindly references almost nonexistent. Editorial page remarks were far more common than news reports. As for local nominations—when they took place, and who, precisely, was running—these might be left entirely unstated. This lack of exposure often worked as a deliberate blackout, to hide a wider choice from voters. Silence was death, especially to a party newly established and one without a cadre of voters trained by habit and tradition to vote for candidates with that particular party label.

All mainstream papers treated third-party paladins as curiosities, much as they would the features in a real circus sideshow. Belittling nicknames abounded: "prohis," "dismalists," the "free lunch party." Familiarities certainly were applied to mainstream politicians, too, though more often as a mark of endearment or an affirmation of the statesman's connection to the common people: "the Old Roman," "the Plumed Knight," "Tall Sycamore of the Wabash," James "Blue Jeans" Williams, "Old Saddlebags" McDonald. Outsiders' names were strictly for laughs: Luman "Calamity" Weller, Benjamin "Spoons" Butler, Solon "Them Steers" Chase, and "Mary Yellin'" Lease. Prohibitionists were always either "political dyspeptics," "cranks," or "frauds." As for working-class candidates, the mainstream press declared them socialists and anarchists—apparently wanting to destroy all government and make it all-powerful at the same time. Where fanaticism seemed less credible, outsiders' motives usually were narrowed down to disappointment, vengeance, and an "insatiable greed of office." Instead of engaging with radicals' arguments, editors found abuse more useful. Trying to extract logic from articles like those, one insurgent complained, was as futile as pressing "the juice out of a common XX soda cracker." News reports regularly understated the numbers at opposition rallies and printed lavish reports about the hopeless feeling that unnamed members of the sideshow parties felt.[27]

This language highlighted a related bias among all the larger, well-established newspapers. Beyond the editorial page, news coverage itself sent a message about legitimate protest movements in America. It did so by defining newsworthy events in ways that were friendly to business and to the secular order, where a country of bigger industries and booming cities was progress, however unevenly the benefits were shared and however much misery the search for profit created.

Independence in a paper did not mean independence of all parties — merely between the two parties. But the independents shared the philosophy common to both parties, the broad mainstream consensus on matters of morals, property, and the proper role of the state. News cost money, money that the parties could no longer provide all of. Advertisements, and increasingly business advertisements, must supply the wherewithal. In 1880, half of newspaper revenue came from advertising, and by 1910, 64 percent. (As a consequence, publishers had all the more incentive to build up circulation among women by adding features unrelated to politics.) Cultivating a readership of consumers paid off handsomely, and not just for business. Dependent on advertising revenue, editors could hardly afford a war on their clients, even if they had wanted one. Nor did they want one. There was a built-in limitation in most papers, a loyalty to and a sense of responsibility to the community in which they published.[28]

This booster's role had always been present. If anything, the extension of the wire services enhanced it. With the mammoth printing presses able to produce cheap newspapers in bulk and the improved facilities for quick delivery, metropolitan papers were spreading farther afield than ever, and making inroads into the markets of their country rivals. Small-town editors able to get along on crude partisanship had to protect their local market. The best way was to do what no big-city paper could, make itself the champion of local interests and boost the county's advantages.[29]

Such a focus, again, made the press an active agent of economic upbuilding, and concentration on a brick-and-mortar notion of a community's progress was peculiarly unfriendly to anything that unsettled promoters' confidence. Capitalism might be robust, but it was notoriously timid. So editors frowned on anything that unsettled the customs, institutions, or business prospects on which prosperity must rest. Except for the carefully channeled disorder of the campaign parade, they had no patience for "agitation" or "fanaticism" and had an outright horror at the presumably disruptive influences of class-based politics. Newspapers shared the notion of most prosperous Americans, that the country was a land of opportunity, where just about anyone could rise, and where every day brought progress beyond the day before. Progress itself might be defined in moral terms on the editorial page, but on the front page, and often in the leading articles, it had a material side. Hard times were not just downplayed. They could be denied completely. "It is lost breath for a ranting demagogue to tell such a people that they are suffering," an Iowa editor insisted in 1890, not very truthfully. "Life . . . in Iowa, to the average citizen, is a life of success."[30]

As news coverage spread beyond politics and as the appeal to consumers increased the need to make the newspaper appealing to women, the press directed itself to reports on society, which usually meant high society. Social affairs of the bon ton were news events. Prominent socialites' deaths warranted an obituary, always laudatory. Union meetings got far less coverage, and sometimes none at all. The poor died unnoted in most cases. For the most part, news about them came in the listing of crimes, arrests, and disorders. As for strikes, editors were likeliest to pay attention to them when violence broke out, and since so much of that came from striking workers, press coverage emphasized the disturbances of the public peace on labor's side far more than the grievances that had caused the strike in the first place. Even without editorial comment, a middle-class subscriber to the metropolitan press could hardly come away from the news reports without viewing the poorer sort as inherently more unstable, turbulent, emotional, and vicious. Such a vision made those who would stir the resentments of the "dangerous classes" all the more frightening, and those who challenged the economic order of the Gilded Age were always doing just that.[31]

Coverage could mislead and slander without uttering a single barefaced lie, but, labor reformers complained, where working-class events came up, the metropolitan dailies had made lying as professional as typesetting. They forged interviews with labor leaders and put rabid speeches in their mouths, reported strikes at an end that were still under way, and turned violence against strikers into assaults on the workers replacing them. One editor surmised that every journalist on the *Chicago Tribune* had to turn his notes over to "the chief liar" for a more thorough distortion. Victims could only rage at lies "adorned with circumstantial precision," put out by "a lot of boys, usually with a dawning mustache," who understood the issues as much "as an ocean herring does . . . the rings of Saturn." Indirectly, the unfair coverage of labor dealt a blow to those parties giving priority to labor's grievances; if workers were in the wrong and got

"Iron and blood. They don't scare worth a cent" (Thomas Nast, *Harper's Weekly*, July 31, 1875). Congressman William D. Kelley of Pennsylvania tries to terrify business with fears of revolution, if the money supply is not expanded. Shocked by such demagoguery, Nast himself readily linked all expansionists with Communism, anarchism, and the breakdown of civilization.

what they deserved, why did they need a party all their own to defend their interests?[32]

One could see the bias of mainstream journals not just in what they covered but in the very phrases they used, ones suggesting that character and wealth were connected: "the best men," "the solid businessmen," "the respectable classes." Accusations of "demagoguery" always had a class bias. In theory, the term could cover any stirring up of base passions in the populace. In practice, though, the offender always was someone rousing the poor against the privileged. Accusations of class warfare never covered appeals stirring up the public against tramps, anarchists, or foreigners, or demands for the use of troops to put down strikers. "Businesslike government" appeared as a term of unalloyed praise, carrying with it the implication that businessmen could do the same tasks better at lower cost. That in itself implied that politicians, by their nature, were lowly, corrupt beings, incompetent, inefficient, and of narrow vision, and that industrialists and merchants were just the opposite. Most of all it was a standing indictment of the threadbare politicians, whose public careers furnished their only source of income.

So it became a compelling indictment to define the political outsiders as failures: failures in politics, forced to make a new party because they could not sell themselves to members of the old, and failures in the "real" world of business, where talent received its reward. In the South, Democratic newspapers commonly depicted Republicans as ne'er-do-wells, vagabonds, and defaulters; whites who dared to join were "scalawags," unlettered, unprincipled, and unpropertied. Republicans tried the same tactic against Democrats in the North, tying them to ignorance, vice, and slum life, but the tactic worked much less well against a party composed of between 40 and 60 percent of the population, especially one with a vigorous press establishment of its own, able to turn such an allegation inside out and use it to prove Republicanism the voice of a purse-proud aristocracy. Against minor parties, both parties used the method zealously.

Clearly, the first need of a robust third-party movement was a means of getting its message out to readers on a regular basis. Only then could Greenbackers or Prohibitionists define the terms of the debate. Only if farmers knew what Greenbackers stood for could they see whether they were indeed, as mainstream newspapers alleged, radicals, Jacobins, and Communists. As the returns were announced in Ohio in 1885, Greenbackers waited in vain to learn how they had done. No newspaper reported the figures, and the state government's official tally listed many Greenback votes in the category "scattering." But to set up an opposition organ took strength in the first place, and the backers of agrarian movements were usually poorer. They could less afford to stay with a paper as steady sub-

scribers, and the countryside afforded slimmer pickings than the city for advertising revenue. Newspapers catering to a black or poor white audience also had
fewer subscribers because their potential customers were less likely to be able to
read. City journalists found that to distribute a daily took the creation of their own
special carrier system; the mainstream metropolitan papers fired news agents
stocking a labor paper among their wares. Unable to afford the expense, labor-
party publishers were cut off by law from mailing out their papers, unless they
limited publication to one issue a week.[33]

Without the patronage of county courthouses, sideshow parties found themselves helpless to compete on fair terms. What were Mississippi's eight Greenback newspapers in 1880 against hundreds of Democratic ones? Far more often
than not, the third-party organ was a weekly, which, at best, would be a partial
antidote to the daily paper that readers counted on for their regular news. A *Bates-
ville Blade*, already well established on a Democratic basis before joining Mississippi Greenbackers, might be able to offer a smattering of news about crops and
local events, but it could not match the news-gathering resources of mainstream
presses able to afford a staff of reporters and extensive Associated Press dispatches. In the cities, all the features that attracted potential readers — wire services, sports, and human-interest stories — the big-city dailies were able to provide far more readily and for much less money. As a consequence, third-party
papers died, usually in their infancy, bought out by mainstream parties or closed
down by hard times.[34]

The dearth of a competitive press skewed political choice worst in the former
Confederate states. During Reconstruction, Republicans managed to set up hundreds of newspapers, and not all of them were short-lived. Some made it through
their first year. A few dozen lingered for half a decade or more. But when Republican governments fell, their journals tumbled with them. In the Border South,
the larger cities — Wheeling, Louisville, St. Louis, and Baltimore — permitted an
enduring Republican organ that, when required, could spread the word statewide. Beyond city limits and in the cotton kingdom, poverty, illiteracy, and commercial boycotts killed the alternative press of the early 1870s. "Most of the Republicans have no use for newspapers, except to put them in the windows when
the glass breaks, under the carpets in the winter, and for other humble domestic purposes," a reporter sneered on a visit to Alabama. It would have been fairer
to say that they had no better use for Democratic papers, and no way of getting
any other.[35]

Between the tradition of partisan journalism and the transforming power of
Gilded Age capitalism, the chances of a political realignment that would break

the two parties' monopoly lessened every year. It was certainly true that the old partisanship had begun to decay. In San Francisco and New York, the Pulitzers and William Randolph Hearsts had built powerful newspapers with a working-class appeal and a dollop of radicalism. They could outperform a *Times*, *Tribune*, *Sun*, or even a *Herald*. But they could not outsell them all, and their radicalism had pretty clear limits. Take out the few spectacular exceptions, and the picture of where the press was headed could have given third-partyites no hope that a breakdown in the Gilded Age political system would give them an opening. Far more visible was a trend among the "independents" and nonpartisans toward a nonpartisanship of a more conservative flavor; editors spoke loudly of the need for a "businesslike" administration for the cities and the banishing of party labels in municipal campaigns.[36] Nonpartisanship of that kind looked askance at organizations committed to notions that could not be expressed on a ledger. It had no place for Socialists, Populists, Prohibitionists, or cranks in general. From a hundred years hence, the end of the "party period" marked a great change on Newspaper Row as anywhere else. But as far as America's economic outcasts were concerned, the change might as well never have happened. Outside city limits, the Democratic "dishrags"—and Republican ones—still lay on insurgents' faces. Always they would find voices of their own, sometimes by the dozens, sometimes by the hundreds. But amid the clamor of the major parties and "independents," theirs was a muted cry. In the end, the secret of third-party failure may not lie merely in what its editors said but in the stillness where no one had the medium to print the words at all. That silence may have been the most damning eloquence of all.

The Best Majority Money Can Buy

On that day the market for votes opened at five dollars, with a brisk demand and strong upward tendency. Many holders declined to enter the market, even to the extent of naming figures, preferring to stimulate inquiry by an affectation of confidence in the value of their franchises. Prices quickly mounted, and many transactions took place at $6, $7 and $8, prompt delivery and strict spot cash. The upward movement continued during the afternoon, and the highest point was reached at 3 P.M., when $10 was freely offered and accepted. The published quotations, however, by no means represent the real strength of the market. A very large number of private transactions took place, and it is said that in many cases as much as $50 was realized for a single vote. [Much complaint was made about goods being sold twice to different purchasers.] It is needless to point out that conduct of this kind is detrimental to the interests of sellers, and if continued at subsequent sales will have a tendency to diminish the value of their wares.—a "business report" from Rhode Island's spring election, *New York Standard*, April 14, 1888.

In November 1888, Delaware gave the country a stunning example of how deep pockets could do away with a pocket-borough. Second smallest of states, it had never let the Democrats down. Those in command could give plenty of good reasons: a tradition of conservatism, a heritage of slavery, and contempt for newfangled notions like equal rights. But Delaware conservatism also rested on relentlessly unfair election laws and a constitution rigged for rural domination. As long as Democratic county officers applied the poll tax requirements selectively, Republicans could never win state offices. As long as New Castle, with half the state's population, had the same number of legislators as Kent or Sussex, the folks at the crossroads would dominate the city-dwellers of Wilmington.[1]

Republicans needed a break, and in 1888 they got one: right in the middle of the opposition's ranks. When Eli Saulsbury, that tall, gaunt, "bird-of-prey-looking figure," sought reelection to the senate, his enemies combined to deny him the all-important support of the legislative delegation from his home county,

Kent. Votes in some of the primary elections were said to have gone as high as thirty-one dollars, and both sides talked carelessly about the fortune spent carrying crossroads precincts like Duck Creek and North Murderkill. Saulsbury may not have added to the senate's intellectual atmosphere except by his absence ("There goes a man who thinks he thinks," one waspish colleague once sneered), but he had no intention of a graceful farewell. If his Democrats could not represent Kent, no Democrats supporting another favorite son would. As the general election approached, Saulsbury's coterie sprang into inaction.[2]

Former district attorney Anthony Higgins, mastermind of the Republican campaign, grasped the possibilities at once. The GOP was sure to carry most of the seats in New Castle and now, it seemed, a decent share of Kent's. That left Sussex, so proverbially Democratic that managers in either party fixed their attention elsewhere. But Delaware's rural electorate also was famous for doing business on a cash basis. Money could buy 1,600 Sussex residents, the Republican committee's secretary calculated, and two out of three were nominal Democrats.

All Higgins needed was the wherewithal. He turned to the Republican National Committee and turned back, unsatisfied. Philadelphia businessmen had more faith and released more funds. Election day came, and Kent County behaved just as Democrats had feared. "Plotting treason" and "insane ambition" had beaten the party, the *Smyrna Record* shrieked. "Eli Saulsbury, whose career began by undermining a brother and whose career has ended by selling a State, thou art the man."[3]

In fact, Republican managers had bought Delaware from quite a few people other than the Saulsburys. Sometimes what they bought was simply their supporters' right to vote their principles. A full turnout depended on the faithful payment of poll taxes. Where they had access to the county books, Republicans went out of their way to hunt down delinquent taxpayers. They ascertained their loyalties and paid the taxes in arrears for those whose vote could be relied on. Sometimes they even paid property taxes. Other times, the voter's choice itself was bought. There was nothing criminal in a voter being handed a little piece of pink, blue, or yellow pasteboard. The figures two, five, and ten by themselves could have any meaning. But, of course, they had only one real meaning, when they were turned in to the local party bagman and exchanged for two-dollar, five-dollar, or ten-dollar bills, respectively.

Democratic leaders swore loud and long, but not at the wickedness of their enemies' actually paying for voters. In East Dover, Democrats themselves had handed out pay vouchers. Together, local pols admitted, the two parties there had accommodated at least 250 voters that way, and 1,500 across the county.

Both sides had done their homework before election day, drawing up lists of potential purchases. In the Georgetown Hundred, Democrats admitted to a list eighty names long, and Republicans to one 125 names long. Together, the two parties bought one voter in four on election day, 1888. Vote-buying was standard. Democrats admitted having done so for years. The outrage came in the fact that this time Republicans had been able to draw on so much more money.[4]

Perhaps the most striking thing was how little onlookers cared. A Wilmington reporter traveled in Sussex County in the wake of the 1888 election, looking for indignation at the vote-buying, and found plenty, but most of it over the whopping price votes had gone for. Everyone in the community knew which of their neighbors had marketed his suffrage. The malefactors did not rank among the social elite, "but most of them hold as high a head as any of their neighbors." Landowners without shame proposed to organizers that they "do a little business together next week," perhaps in the form of covering their property taxes, and in many cases an extra five-dollar bill to seal the bargain. Nobody ever flung the fact into the vote-seller's face. Both parties had acted all along as though buying an election was business as usual. Well aware that the prices, even within a single township, varied, depending on the way an unofficial canvass of the turnout showed that the election was going, the treasurers handling the money had written down the precise amount of money due to each voter before he came to collect it, but they admitted to a second, more significant reason. The parties expected their negotiating teams to keep an itemized list of their converts' value, for future reference. There would always be another election.[5]

Vote-buying was not one of the dirty secrets of Gilded Age politics. It was done out in the open, and, like most other vices, came in different moral shadings. "Votes can be bought if you will just shake the cash at them," an activist assured his congressman. So they could, but how many? And did it make a difference how the cash was shaken? Contemporaries then could have argued, as a few political scientists and historians have since, that the problem, while real, was nowhere near as serious as reformers made out.[6]

For one thing, so many election-day services were paid for legitimately that marking the clear line between an honest and a dishonest vote was impossible. Even purists saw nothing wrong with using money to bring voters to the polls. Any party furnished with carriages enough would bring the housebound and the bedridden or, for that matter, the inmates of public institutions. But what about voters whose inability to get to the polls was pecuniary, rather than physical? In an age when many workers toiled from sunrise to sunset and ten- and eleven-hour days were common, and where laws closed the polls at six or seven in the evening, employees had to depend on being given time off. This did not always happen.[7] Companies might give time off and dock workers' pay for the minutes lost. The potential voter was forced to make a choice between his pocket and his party. Compensation to make those losses good seemed more than justifiable; for partisans able to afford it, it came close to a debt of honor. Parties therefore often provided money for wages lost, or other expenses.

Election-day payments in a way were analogous to the payments to poll watchers, who received several dollars a day for standing around the precinct, keeping an eye out for the tricks that the opposition might play, or for the money for party ticket-peddlers, and providing copies of the ballot to whomever would take them and some last-minute advice about nominees and, perhaps, those whose names the local organization would like to see "scratched." Election-day service was freely given, but it did not always come free. Why, then, should those who cast a ballot for the good cause be compelled to sacrifice their earnings?[8]

One might make the same comparison to another common election-day custom, "treating" the electorate. Candidates might "set 'em up" in the bars, if the law permitted liquor establishments to stay open (not all states did), or at banquet tables. Party organizers might pass out tickets, good for a drink when the saloons did reopen. There might be barbecues or refreshments of other kinds. Except in the direct outlay of cash—which might very well go for drinks anyhow—how different was this practice from spending money to keep a good man loyal? If any voter was permitted to share in the candidate's generosity, with no obligations stated, was it any of the courts' business? (State courts ruling on the matter decided that it was not.)[9]

Indeed, as regulars pointed out, paying for votes was not the same as buying them. The money need not affect a regular's judgment at all; he would never have voted for the opposition. He was simply claiming a reward for services rendered and compensation for attendant inconveniences.[10] In an age when the spoils system covered every office from postmaster to police captain, the distinctions between requiting the labors of a ward heeler and requiting those of a ward constituent were even harder to draw than they would be later on. It was only right that those who did the work should get the benefits; everything from nursery tales to Poor Richard's adages taught that. Politicians who worked to organize the party would get their reward hereafter, in jobs and contracts; those they induced to show up on election day had no such hopes, yet their service made victory possible. How, morally, did a dollar in the hand now differ from a clerk's desk in the hereafter?

Every party shouted that the other side was stealing an election, and often belief outran the facts. Many alleged vote-buying schemes had nothing behind them, or very little. In 1880, Republicans knew for sure that the Democrats had embarked on a massive campaign to buy the Indiana state election in October and give their party a morale boost big enough to inspire them to an all-out effort everywhere in November. The figures varied, but Republicans never had a doubt of the Napoleon of the pending political crime: onetime Indiana congressman and current vice presidential nominee William English, notoriously rich. In fact, as operatives on the ground discovered, Democrats had no such scheme and no such war chest as had been supposed. Far from planning a coup against Republicans, they were troubling themselves trying to find what vast scheme of vote-buying the Republicans were up to. When the election ended, it was they, not their foes, who made the greatest outcry about vote-buying, and not just in Indiana, where the "two-dollar bill" became a synonym for bribery and a vice president elect brought the term "soap" into the national vocabulary. Many of the Democrats' charges about Ohio's results that same day were remarkable ones. One might assume that with James A. Garfield, an Ohioan, heading the Republican presidential ticket, the GOP would not have found carrying his own state difficult. But that was not how the *Cincinnati Enquirer* played the results. The workhouse, the city jail, and the station houses all "were emptied of all who would promise to vote the Republican ticket; money was handled as though it was nothing but brown paper; false swearing was done with a recklessness and abandon almost sublime."[11]

The *Enquirer* reporters may have believed their charges, but then it would have been only natural to have publicized them, whether they were believed or not. Each party had a stake in exaggerating the vote-buying that went on. Doing so gave its own cause legitimacy. They were not defeated by the people; the people were with them—always had been with them. On the contrary, it had been a deliberate effort on the opposition's side to thwart the public will that had denied them the majority that had been their due.

Understandably, then, historians have been skeptical that vote-buying could have made all that much difference. Indeed, looking at the consistency in patterns of voting from one year to the next, they can make a pretty sound case. With a few glaring exceptions, the returns showed no suspicious, large swings in the vote, of the kind that vote-buying might involve.

That confidence, though, may be based on a few misunderstandings. Vote patterns could remain pretty consistent and still tell nothing about the comparative honesty of the returns, if both sides bought voters and if both continued to buy in roughly the same numbers. Paying voters to stay at home would not show up in the same way, and this, too, the parties did as a means of depressing the other side's turnout. Voters who took pay for voting as their beliefs dictated might still vote that way, if convinced that the party needed them and that there really was no money this year.

For, take all the rationalizations and quibbles, the exaggerations and perjured testimony, no sensible observer of the Gilded Age denied that vote-buying happened. Even the naysayers only argued that it was not quite as widespread as suggested, or that the really nefarious cases were elsewhere. Parties worked hard to overcome the dangers that they knew were sure to occur, and to thwart schemes that they saw in the offing. At every polling place there were a few floaters, eligible voters ready to sell their loyalties for cash and ready to withhold them if cash was not given, and often there were many more.[12] Under euphemisms, party correspondence itself admitted vote-buying. Partisan activists asking for "documents" sometimes meant paper products of a very specific kind, and when an organizer boasted that he used money "in the most judicious way I could," the candidate needed no translation. At times, the language was not veiled at all. A close relative of future senator William E. Chandler wrote him in 1875 to mention that he could not vote that year but had induced others to do so. With fifty to a hundred dollars more, others hawking their suffrages could be fixed. "My men cost me $10 apiece, and that is about the quotation, I should say," he added.[13]

As each party pointed out, it could not help itself. To forego election-day payments would be to let the opposition carry the polls by default. There would be just that much more marketable material available, enough to change the results. That the other side *was* up to something all the time, partisans never doubted. In New Hampshire, the *Concord Monitor* admitted that Republicans could not do without the lower-ranking politicians whose ability to sell and deliver votes was their livelihood. And why should they? "Satan must be fought with his own weapon at times." For those who opposed vote-buying, recognition that the opposition had started it and was doing it worse only dissolved all scruples. Acknowledging that "money is a power with our voters," the Republican state chairman in Nevada reminded national leaders that Democrats had bought a victory in 1880. "Put the Republican party on an even footing . . . & we can elect every man on our ticket. On the other hand, give them all the coin & force us to depend on principle alone & they will devide the honors and elect Gov & Congressman." Quizzed about vote-buying, Governor Morgan G. Bulkeley of Connecticut insisted that it was "in the interests of the party." That alone did not justify it, but the wickedness of the voter did; "it is right for a candidate to secure that man's vote, if he is without principle or ignorant, by any means you can use."[14]

Finding buyable voters was, in fact, easy. By the time an election ended, poll watchers had a pretty good idea of the value of each voter, and they often prepared an official list, with prices attached. To prevent any kind of swindling by agents for the purchased voters—who on occasion lacked a full sense of personal honor and collected payment for votes neither negotiated for nor delivered—the vote-buyers' names were kept, too. For days after the election, that list was left open to party members' inspection, "and sometimes of the general public."[15]

Discretion required that the vote-buying be separated as far from the candidate as possible. Proofs of fraud could vitiate an election, even if the courts could not prove that the fraudulent votes had made the difference between victory and defeat. In urban districts, the best method was to open a vote-buying shop, complete with clerks and a manager. It was important that they work without pay and that the clerks—who would be busier as the day went on—voted before they sat down to work. One would serve as cashier, another as paying teller. Runners were hired to do the work outside and to make the bargaining. After the arrangements with a floater were complete, he would be marched to the polls and a ballot put into his hands. If possible, the voter would be kept in ignorance of who he was voting for; it helped prevent him from giving dangerous testimony later on, but often, the floater took an active and unhealthy interest in which side he had taken. When the ballot had been deposited, the runner handed over a poker check or paper slip or some other token. Handing over cash, pols sneered, was the unmistakable mark of "countrymen" and "greenhorns."[16] No professional would hand over an IOU that on the face of it would attest to the purchase-price and could be placed in evidence in some future court case. But the slip or check would have a meaning of its own; the color of the paper might represent the denomination, for instance.

The voter would then go to the payments office and hand the token over to a cashier, who would check off the customer's name and the amount of payment due. The cashier would write out a money order that the voter would take to the teller; the teller would furnish the money. The system was complicated, and deliberately so, to thwart indictments for bribery. The cashier could protest that he had never been told outright just what the voter was being paid for, or, indeed, whether the payee was a voter at all. The teller could claim that he had no grounds to suspect the payee of being a purchased vote; his only duty was to pay off orders presented to him from the cashier.[17]

Necessarily, the methods for vote-buying differed in the rural areas. Purchases had to be done one at a time, by personal visits with the voters. Each party might keep a book of potential hirelings, noting prices and political preferences, but often it was catch-as-catch-can, with voters approached on the spot, taken into a nearby grove of trees or a saloon, and brought back in a friendly condition; of course, this had the attendant risk that some of those approached might spurn the offer and spill the beans. But the risk was not all that great, as long as courts ruled that a contesting candidate had to prove that the number of purchased votes amounted to more than the margin of victory, and as long as recipients of the "silent dollar" could not be compelled by law to say how they had voted.[18]

Vote-buying was a delicate art, because ethics varied from one floater to the next, and so did their prices, though one or two dollars was a common rate for whites most places, and twenty-five cents about as low a rate as black southern-ers would accept. If the *New York Sun* was right, country prices were usually higher, because the purchasers were unable to buy in bulk. Two dollars was New York City's going rate in the 1880s, and five dollars practically unheard of. In country towns, floaters demanded far more, and, when the contest was close, as much as ten to twenty dollars (and—very rarely—got it). Upcountry Tennessee villagers, apparently, could be bought for as little as a glass of whiskey, a plug of tobacco, or a pound of coffee, though a dollar or two was the going rate.[19] A rus-tic who put himself up for sale in the morning could be bought relatively cheaper; the smart ones waited until later to take bids, knowing that the tensions of an election day would press party workers to raise their prices, usually. (Not always; if the poll watchers, in counting the turnout late in the day, thought that their side had outpolled the other, they would not be eager to part with cash, and the going rate for floaters would go down. It also was in the interest of the party with the biggest war chest to offer tremendous rewards for votes early in the day, just to force the opposition to match them and go broke early. Then, with a monopoly on the vote-buying money, the solvent party could set its own terms for voters.)

Some voters were for sale to all; others retailed only for one side and were bought to stay at home by the other. Indeed, the *New York Sun* suggested, most floaters had political preferences. Smart political managers, in determining the price of voters, always marked down which party they leaned to. It could make a difference in expense; selling out one's principles generally went at a higher rate than selling one's vote to the side upholding those principles. Some floaters came to the polls determined to vote but not sure which side to favor. Others would not vote at all, unless motivated with money. Others insisted on voting only for their own side and would accept no payment from the opposition. It would be worthless even offering them money. These were the ones likeliest to insist that they were not being bribed; they were simply being paid for their "time."[20]

Legitimate payments for time and inconvenience were, in fact, one of the most natural covers for outright vote-buying, as everyone knew, and made indictment nearly impossible. People hired to do work for the party were occasionally hired to stay loyal. "We always have had hard work in this county, where the floating vote is so large," journalist A. J. Ricks wrote Senator John Sherman from Massillon, Ohio, in 1885, "and it has been unusually hard this fall, because so many expected to be hired to work. This wholesale use of money is a terrible curse." Those whose loyalty most needed refreshing were men able to deliver some friends. In that case, voters were sold in clumps. Sometimes buying goodwill worked, sometimes not. Charles W. Woolley, one of the most dedicated wireworkers on the Democratic side in Cincinnati, had the misfortune to need help from a personal enemy in the first ward. He overcame the problem, or so he thought, by handing over $375 for "missionary work among the voters." The money went into the recipient's bank account and stayed there. Furious at this failure to deliver goods honestly paid for, Woolley sued; an out-of-court settlement recovered something under half the amount; Woolley took the rest out of his enemy's hide the next time they met.[21]

Money went for other methods that, if not quite vote-buying, would not stand ethical scrutiny. In 1888, Philadelphia's major parties bought up some 100,000 poll tax receipts to enable their poorer supporters to vote and to induce other delinquents to vote right. Party organizers might pay the expenses to procure naturalization papers for the foreign-born who had not been able to afford them on their own, and, to make sure of turning a political profit on the investment, march them to the polls and there hand "them their papers with the understanding that they vote the Democratic Ticket." Such a scheme was certainly proposed, and the county organizer making the suggestion was not so much concerned by the ethics as he was about whether this would be the wisest use of scarce campaign funds.[22]

How many votes could be bought? Figures are extremely imprecise. But the guess of the *Worcester Press* in 1876 was that 8,000 of New Hampshire's 80,000 electors were willing to be bought. Seventeen years later, *Century* magazine echoed the same figure of 10 percent, though it suggested that this estimate was faulty only for being on the low side. (The *Concord Monitor* thought it a little too high, but much closer than the other figure bandied about, of one voter in three.) In New York City, one observer's guess was that, counting together those put on the machine payroll to work for the party and those bought at election time, the number of voters paid for election-day services approached 20 percent, and that was the same guess that a Republican ballot-peddler gave. A city ward manager in Michigan told an investigator that he paid about 5 percent of the voters, and, naturally, the opposition could not have been idle in accommodating still others.[23]

Where did most of the dealing take place? Conventional wisdom credited it to the cities, with their political machines. There, rootless immigrants, unversed in American traditions and with no commitment to American institutions, had no reason to vote their beliefs and, ill-paid as they were, every reason to make the suffrage pay. No one had to ask about the naturalization frauds in New York City in 1868 or the hired voters in Philadelphia four years later.[24]

In fact, vote-selling happened in the countryside and in smaller cities, too. "Practical politicians" insisted that Brooklyn's buyables were nowhere near as many as in the Long Island towns. In Hudson, Newburgh, Poughkeepsie, and Troy, there were election districts where half the eligible vote was believed to be in the market. Some small communities were infamous for their barter and sale. "Pot cannot call kettle black," the *Watertown Daily Times* commented after one election-day retailing. "Both parties were into it apparently by mutual consent and feeling secure from this cause there has been no secrecy in it. Men openly boast of buying and voters boast of the price they were able to get." What made it worse was that Watertown, compared to other towns in the area, had been comparatively clean—unlike Dutchess County, down the Hudson River, where old-timers talked wistfully of the debauch in which party operatives bid as high as forty dollars a vote and Republicans, as a cost-cutting measure, bought off the Democratic convention.[25]

Perhaps even more than the parties themselves, the floaters were the real corrupters of innocent voters, by setting an example for how party patriotism could pay. Those who were bought one year only encouraged others to put themselves into the market the next. The more common vote-buying grew, the more it changed the reward given to a partisan into a quid pro quo, demanded if anything would be done. Too "many voters are coming to look upon suffrage as a thing of sale and purchase," a Cincinnati editor lamented. Some people certainly thought that the problem was worsening, although even with the same proportion of the electorate up for sale, the expense and the absolute numbers of purchased voters would have risen. Until just a few years before, the *Concord Independent Democrat* declared in 1869, vote-buying was unheard of in New Hampshire. The poorest man would have sold his birthright as soon as his ballot.[26] It was a heartfelt complaint, though New Hampshire's reputation for venality and the losers' protests that the winners had bought victory were as old as the Jacksonian party system itself.[27]

Bullying, not just bribery, had its own effect on the popular will. Like vote-buying, personal influence came in different degrees, with different moral shadings. One of the benefits of running a banker or factory owner as the candidate was how well his presence might draw to the ticket those whose livelihood depended on him. Party managers often discussed the usefulness of bringing corporate executives onto their side. Certainly some of what they were thinking about was the moral influence that went with a business leader. Those who admired him — as many employees might well do — or identified with his fortunes might follow him in whatever direction he chose to go. Especially when an executive had enjoyed good labor relations, his endorsement of a ticket carried all the force of a certificate of good character.

That, at least, was how it was rationalized. Sometimes it may have been true. But there was always present the knowledge that a man who controlled so many people's livelihoods could control their votes, and in an age before the secret ballot, this was hard to prevent. Factory owners sent their foremen to the polls to keep an eye on the results. They warned their workers of the consequences of voting wrong; some businessmen threatened to close down the firm if one party triumphed, usually justifying the threat by declaring that the party's economic program would mean industrial ruin. "The fact is, the farmer's 'help' of to-day is a very different sort of personage from the farmer's 'hired man' of ante-bellum days," a Michigander wrote. "At the present time the average farmer takes it for granted his 'help' will go with him to the polls and vote as he directs, especially if he gives him a holiday on that occasion." The party expected it, too; that was what it paid the landowner for when it gave him "due remuneration for the 'time'" he had given his help.[28]

The worst intimidation may have been partisanship itself. Because of the system of passing out ballots and voting, most people who went to the polls would incur the wrath of their political friends if they voted wrong. It may have been for this reason — and not because of solicitude for their own party or a reluctance to commit themselves to the other — that, instead of switching parties, they stayed at home. It was the public nature of that commitment that brought much of the restraint.[29]

That intimidation the parties encouraged, coaxed, and inspired. They castigated traitors in their midst; they blackened the reputations of those who did not go along with them. They insulted, vilified, and, in all, made an escape from party loyalty extremely uncomfortable at the polls. Women wearing Grover Cleveland buttons were reminded that no lady would do any such thing; that it was grounds for suspecting harlotry.[30]

In the South, the pressure and possibly the bribery was more severe and far more effective as a means of depressing the total vote, particularly the Republican portion of it. Threatening language could be veiled or guarded, but it was unmistakable. Editors warned white Republicans that they would be shunned; partisans put up placards ordering them not to attend Republican rallies. Their motives were impugned, their past careers open for public inspection in the newspapers. Blacks were told not to vote or assured that their votes would not be counted. There would be "incidents," usually involving injury or death, as a warning to those blacks still thinking of showing up at the polls. Democratic newspapers insisted that, by embarking on a stumping tour, Republican candidates would only inflame the public mind and that any violence resulting would be their fault exclusively. Regularly, memories of the forcible overthrow of Republican rule during Reconstruction were evoked, not only to remind Democrats of the glory days, when they "redeemed" the South, but to make clear that if the opposition turned out on election day, the same methods would be used again. "It is a crime against the common welfare to run for Congress in opposition to the regular Democratic nominee," one Mississippi congressional committee announced. Any black resident of the shoestring district knew what that meant.[31]

No campaign relied on "bulldozing" alone, as the browbeating and selective murder of Republicans came to be called. As long as there were federal election inspectors, weak as they were, Democrats found it to their interest to make some token gestures toward blacks and to offer some public proofs that the Negro consented to and even appreciated white men's government. As long as any blacks voted, Democrats courted them and publicized every success. They founded all-black campaign clubs and enlisted the members as torchbearers for parades and, when blacks showed up for political rallies, reported their conversion to white orators' irresistible logic. But they also treated them as a commodity to purchase and put to use. The use might be as veiled as Democrats' reimbursement of black spokesmen for "costs" involved in rallying support to the party. It could also be as cynical as that reported of General John B. Gordon's campaign for governor in Georgia, when black voters were enticed into town, feasted, liquored, and then locked in a large hall to keep the opposition from buying them before election day. Guards were stationed at the door, and a military detachment marched them to the voting booths when the polls opened.[32]

Some few blacks actually did vote Democratic from principle. Seeing that there would be no safety for their rights as long as one party took their votes for granted and the others gave their votes up as lost, local black leaders occasionally solicited propositions from either side. Others held out for money. Racial stereotypes strengthened an impression widely shared that black voters were the very kind likeliest to serve as tools and to accept bribes. One never had to ask who was a dishonest voter, said the Nashville *American*; "the color of his face proclaims the presence of one who has a vote to sell for a few cents or barter for a few drinks of whisky."[33] Those assumptions only encouraged Democrats to put black virtue to the test. As for blacks, their poverty and dependence on the good favor of powerful white patrons made it that much harder for them to resist a bribe when offered. Many may have rationalized that taking a bribe was the only way to give their vote value at all. In some places, the one vote that Democratic election inspectors would count would be one that their own side had bought.

Because money so often changed hands and because black interests seemed so clearly on the Republican side, most blacks saw any Democratic support in their race as proof of betrayal at the least and corruption at the likeliest. Republicans could intimidate renegades, too. Black Democrats lost their friends and were estranged from their wives. They were exposed to ridicule and abuse, threatened with physical harm, and sometimes killed. Democratic newspapers reported black supporters burned out of their houses for making a campaign speech and shot off the platform at mass meetings.[34]

In the South, the consequence of vote-buying and intimidation went further than it did in the North. Not many liberal reformers blamed the people themselves for the methods party operatives used to suborn their votes. Some did see a literacy or property test as a way to improve politics in the cities. After all, a demagogue could buy votes among the poor as easily by promising an open-door policy at the treasury for parochial schools and public works construction as by offering them cash in hand. Restricting the suffrage to taxpayers in city elections might create a more responsible government, where those who paid for public services had the sole right of deciding which ones the city should provide. But it was perfectly plain to most Mugwumps that restrictions on voting were a political lost cause. Moreover, they attacked bribery at the polls from the wrong end. The real villains were those handing out the money or threatening people's livelihoods. But then, liberal reformers had different views of the North's "dangerous classes" and the South's. They did not see in any class of society, nor, for the most part, in any ethnic group, a natural criminal element, or one that could not be tamed, corrected, and redeemed. Anyone could learn, and "campaigns of education" were the natural cure for partisanship. It might be improb-

"The greatest of American intimidators north and south. Practical politician: 'Vote as I dictate'" (Thomas Nast, *Harper's Weekly*, November 7, 1885). The cartoon may show how far, by the 1880s, even a former champion of equal rights like Nast had left behind his concern with the very real intimidation of black voters across the South—if not his faith that they were fit to vote.

able that the degraded slum-dweller from Hell's Kitchen would learn to cast his ballot for society's greater good, but it was not impossible.[35] But to southern whites, the Negro was an entirely different matter. Even at their most optimistic, they set limits on how far education could improve him, and some asserted that education only increased his cunning and capacity for mischief.

It followed then that the very methods that Democrats used to hold on to power confirmed their cynicism about universal suffrage. From their own experience, party managers knew that blacks could be bought or bullied into voting right. Every such incident only proved that the ballot box had been polluted by enfranchising a race neither able to protect itself nor willing to resist temptation. By the 1880s, to the charge that blacks voted as unthinking partisans for any scoundrel on a Republican ticket, conservative whites had added a new one: that Negro suffrage was at the root of election fraud and corruption. At every election, there were allegations that the opposition meant to buy up black votes "like fish, mutton, beef, pork, or any other commodity in the city market."[36]

Conservatives saw the shambles where it existed, and even where it did not. Wherever supporters of Prohibition put their proposal before the voters, the election campaign afforded them proof that the worst obstacle they had to face was purchased black voters. It was a convenient explanation for their defeats; the last thing any group wants is to know that the people are against it, and the "people," as far as white southerners used that term in books, polemics, and speeches, had an unspoken color qualification attached. In every statewide referendum, most of the votes for the saloon were white ones. White wards in Memphis and Nashville cast majorities against Tennessee's amendment, and the counties in the western end of the state with the smallest black population voted Prohibition down heavily. Black church leaders and community figures worked for Prohibition, and black women's groups helped white chapters of the Women's Christian Temperance Union to gather signatures and pass on the word in North Carolina communities. Still, the moment the votes were in, Prohibition's sponsors laid the blame for defeat on corrupt or dissolute blacks. A Nashville editor knew why: they had been "hired with whiskey and money to vote against the proposed amendment."[37]

By the 1880s, the paths toward political reform and white supremacy were converging. That same distrust in blacks as voters would not lead to disfranchisement in the North, but it afforded grounds for northern reformers to accept the southern solution.

More general was the feeling that money ruled politics. If voters could be bought, so could officeholders, and the sums needed to carry the floaters had to be paid off somehow—either in favors to the contributors or in graft for oneself. "Plain Bill Tutt," the *Augusta Chronicle*'s occasional columnist, found his efforts for a gubernatorial favorite in 1886 all in vain, and he knew why. The trouble, he summed up, "has been that a great many of the Bills which preceded me were not plain, and unfortunately remained in these counties after this plain Bill had left. . . . A man is a fool in Georgia now, to run for office without having a barrel." When a Dartmouth law professor reported his findings about the expenses that the two parties had incurred in New Hampshire's 1888 state campaign, he dismayed one listener by setting the legitimate expenses at somewhere between $25,000 and $35,000 for each party and the vote-corrupting budget at $100,000 and $175,000, respectively. Protesting the professor's error, former congressman Luther F. McKinney declared on his own knowledge that the sums were far greater. "We all know there is corruption," he told legislators; "that there is no longer a free and honest ballot. The question asked concerning candidates is not, Who is the best man? But, Who has the means to buy the most votes?"[38]

That, reformers warned, was a fatal, a devastating, step. Buying votes, *Harper's Weekly* declared, was "the beginning of the end. To teach men that their votes are merchandise is to dig away the foundations." The moment the voters entered a competition as to who could corrupt fastest and make the corruption stick the firmest, they made politics a race to subvert the republic.[39]

An Eye on the Maine Chance

Thou shalt not steal; an empty feat,
When it's so lucrative to cheat.
—Arthur Hugh Clough, "The Latest Decalogue"

Greenbackism had more of a hold on Maine voters than either party liked to admit, and even as hard times softened across much of the rest of the nation, the passions continued, strong as ever, in Maine. In 1878, Republicans had lost absolute control of the legislature. Greenbackers held the balance of power. Together, Democrats and Greenbackers elected Alonzo H. Garcelon governor. A year later, the Republicans gained the majority in the legislature but not the governorship. With a plurality on his party's side, Garcelon and the state administration used the political machinery to give themselves a legislature more to their liking.

Garcelon was not acting out of hand. As his evidence showed, town officers had flouted myriad technical provisions of the election laws. Irregularities like theirs happened all the time. The question was, would they be considered and held against the officers and would the returns be thrown out? A rigid insistence on the law would disfranchise enough Republican voters to bring in 78 fusion and 61 Republican representatives, and in the senate, 20 fusionists to 11 Republicans.[1] Using the same returning-board methods that had so muddled elections down south, the Democrat-Greenbacker leaders counted out 37 Republican candidates for the Assembly and 9 for the senate who, on the face of the returns, had been elected. That gave the incoming legislature a fusion majority, and, as both sides knew, the majority would certainly declare Garcelon the victor.

Garcelon did not go quite so far; nor did he need to. He simply called into session all those legislators whose seats were out of dispute—which, since the returning board had disqualified so many Republicans, meant one in fusionist hands. That fraction of the legislature would rule on the qualifications of members and decide whom to seat. Technically, at least, the coup looked perfectly legal.[2]

Republicans were furious. Protest rallies met in every city, the greatest uprising of the public, one newspaper asserted, since the firing on Fort Sumter. Already preparing for his presidential bid the following spring, Maine's senator James G. Blaine rushed home from Boston to take command of his party's forces. Unkind critics pointed out that the main argument in favor of General Ulysses S. Grant's nomination over Blaine's was the need for an iron will in the White House. No doubt the violent language that Blaine now voiced was to prove to the Republican Party "that he too can be a 'Strong Man' in a pinch." Alarmists pointed to Garcelon's coup as one more proof of the "Mexicanizing" of the American republic. "The complications there threaten the vital principles of the Republic more seriously than the nullification of South Carolina, in the days of Jackson and Calhoun, or than the electoral contest of 1876," Republican operative and Associated Press manager William Henry Smith wrote in alarm.[3]

As autumn moved into winter, Augusta turned into an armed camp. In the statehouse, the fusionists bolstered their cause with a private militia, to prevent an attack, a takeover, or even the serving of a writ of mandamus on behalf of Republican contestants. Midway through the Christmas season, mob violence erupted in Bangor against the governor's emissaries. Republicans made some clumsy and unsuccessful attempts to bribe several lawmakers to come over to their side, all the clumsier because Democrats, who knew of the whole plot in advance, worked to entrap high party officials, hoping to get evidence enough to send a U.S. senator to jail for bribery. Ministers from their pulpits called for an appeal to arms. Through it all, the press stirred the public with the language of pending revolution. "Bullets and Bayonets!" one set of headlines ran:

> Arming to Overawe the People!
> Gov. Garcelon Collecting Arms at Augusta!
> Attempted Removal of Guns and Ammunition from the Bangor Arsenal!
> A Desecration of Christmas Day!
> A Two-Horse Load of Guns!
> And Thirty-Four Thousand Rounds of Ball Cartridge Hauled Through
> our Streets![4]

A solution came when former senator Lot M. Morrill proposed a face-saving deal: let the governor seek an "advisory opinion" from the state supreme court. Garcelon seized the opportunity. The judges' decision supported Republicans' side of the case. Taking advantage of the temporary absence of the fusionists,

Blaine's allies marched into the statehouse, made up a quorum by giving seats to those claiming seats but who had received no certificates, and organized both branches. That same morning, fusionists held a legislature all their own in the same place, counted the votes cast for governor, and swore in the president of the senate as governor. But General Joshua Chamberlain, who commanded the state militia and had been given a warrant by Garcelon for "protection of public property and the institutions of the State" in the interim, declined to accept the new governor as legal. The Democratic state treasurer refused to recognize warrants drawn on him. In effect, Maine was under temporary military government, for lack of any other.[5]

The supreme court recognized the Republican legislature, and Chamberlain recognized its man for governor as the true governor. Fusionists still held custody of the seal of the state and the election returns. Their sessions were expelled from the statehouse, but they took to meeting on the sidewalks, dating their orders, "State of Maine, House of Representatives, as near as possible." One by one the members drifted away. The Republican legislature seated members all of its own party and strengthened its military force, calling out the militia, garrisoning the statehouse, and putting a Gatling gun by the front gate. Eventually, the crisis passed. "Republicans here in the west are cursing Blaine and [Congressman Eugene] Hale for not taking possession *vie et armis*, but I look at the matter differently," a journalist wrote. "It is better to suffer temporary defeat than to disregard the sacredness of law; for upon this rock, the will of party or the necessity of the *party*, . . . will the Republic split *if it must perish*." That assumed, of course, that the court decided on the merits of the case. Democrats and independent observers knew otherwise. All the disputed points rested on what the actual facts of the election returns were, a matter about which there was no agreement. The Republican-dominated court simply accepted as true the arguments of its own party and based its decision on those assumptions.[6]

Having been cheated of their rights, as they saw it, Democrats and Greenbackers found just enough common ground to arrange fusion. Democrats were so hungry for help in carrying Maine that they even abandoned their own choice for the Greenbacker nominee for governor. Best of all, they had an issue that would let them ignore the much more divisive (and substantial) issue of an expanded money supply. One more time the whole issue played out at the polls. "Three a majority of seven — Maine Supreme Court," one transparency read at a fusionist rally. "We vote for no monarchy. Remember July 4, 1776," "What was the consideration? $1000 a year to each judge," "Supreme Court don't rule this year," "Republican arguments — barrels of flour and ten dollar notes." A vote for

Harrison Plaisted for governor was "a vote for constitutional government, . . . for free and fair elections; for the punishment of bribers, bulldozers and intimidators." A vote for the Republicans endorsed "the revolutionary methods" of party leaders who overthrew "the legal legislature" last winter and sanctioned "the usurpation" by the supreme court that so outraged justice. Explain the results how one pleased; argue, as Republicans did, that tubs of Democratic money had bought the votes. The anger and frustration of the Greenbackers showed itself at the polls in 1880 and gave fusionists the governorship.[7]

Garcelon's "revolution" and Republicans' Gatling-gun restoration took matters to an extreme, to be sure, but the spirit was characteristic of an age. Repeatedly, the party in power tried to find ways of counting itself in again. Election day may have been an expression of the people's will, but through law, administrative decision, and just plain dirty politics, Democrats and Republicans were able to redefine the people's will to suit their own advantage.

In mischievous exaggeration, Boss William Tweed once explained that "the voters did not make the result; the counters made the result." If that really had been true, the Tammany sachem never would have been saying it—or, anyhow, not as a convicted felon, his gang booted out of office, his hand-picked mayor harried from the country. At least in the North, counters could do no more than tweak the numbers. They could not make them up. What fraud at the polls could do was augment a legitimate majority or change a skin-of-one's-teeth defeat into a hair's breadth victory. Election laws really did set bounds on cheating. Both sides employed poll watchers as a safeguard, and neither was slow to challenge illegal voters or to make accusations of fraud, often when none took place. As northern states updated their election laws in the 1880s and 1890s, they increasingly adopted New York's requirement that the election officers come from the two major parties.

Still, to judge from the outcry from all political parties, fraud happened constantly and in a great enough amount to throw some elections into as much doubt as Maine's. There were many ways of swelling a majority, especially in an era when states held their elections on different days. "Colonizations" would import voters from across state lines, lodge them in spare bedrooms over the saloons or in the flophouse district of major cities, hand them a list of the names under which they would claim to be registered, march them to the polls, pay them off, and send them home. (Sometimes there were embarrassing moments when the voter forgot "his" name, or badly mangled a name that, say, might be Polish or Italian and a linguistic mystery to its temporary owner. Fortunately, the inspector, working for the political machine, often was ready to help, or might even greet the voter by name before he could open his mouth.) Other voters gave home addresses that turned out to be lumberyards, vacant lots, and bonded warehouses.[8] Democrats charged that Atlantic City Republicans employed blacks as waiters in the hotels and boardinghouses in the summer just to vote them in November, and they supplemented them with more brigades from Philadelphia, where the GOP had all the votes it needed. Some places allowed any resident to vote and opened the polls to any new arrival willing to swear that he meant to live there henceforth. In West Virginia, Indiana, and Ohio, Democrats assumed that Republicans imported blacks from Kentucky and Virginia, presumably because, all blacks allegedly looking alike, it would be hard to expose a "colonist" voting under some absent black voter's name.[9] Wherever the government had a navy yard, Democrats noticed a swell in the job rolls just before the state election and a lot of layoffs of out-of-state residents right after the polls closed, which was one reason why New Hampshire Democrats moved municipal elections to the same day as Maine's: colonists at the Portsmouth yard might swing one state, but not both. Indeed, the hardest task in lodging-house precincts was not turning out a full vote but rather keeping it down — to 100 percent.[10]

"Resurrectionists" complemented the colonizationist's skills. In every city, registered voters died or moved away between elections. But there was nothing like a close election for raising the dead. Well armed with appropriate names, impostors crowded the polls and voted as they had been paid to. A resourceful "resurrectionist" might vote again under a second name in the precinct next door. In some New York City precincts, the machine voted impostors under any name on the list early in the day; then when the real possessor of the name showed up later on, he would promptly be challenged for trying to "repeat." The looser the registration procedure was, the easier it was to be a "repeater." When, as in New Jersey, would-be voters were spared the trouble of registering in person, the doors were thrown wide open for fraud. But, of course, it took something worse than inattentiveness among election officers when voters in New York City walked out of the polls, having done their civic duty, and took their places in line again, or when, as legend had it, in one St. Louis slum, residents put their goats in the registration rolls.[11]

Anyone could engage in such practices, but it was easier when the election machinery gave protection or the concealing veil of law to those committing fraud. Officers could ignore every challenge to a repeater's vote or accept every spurious challenge to bring voting to a dead stop. Whoever had charge of the polls had far more opportunity to incline things their party's way. Only with the conniving of election supervisors in Philadelphia could 36 registrants claim residence in one house (only 3 of them were legally entitled to the vote), or 150 more in a single block, only 4 of whom existed long enough to answer a subpoena. Efforts to permit authorities to open up ballot boxes where tampering was suspected died a swift death when at the Pennsylvania legislature's hands in 1897. As one legislator explained, "A closed ballot box tells no stories!"[12]

Vote fraud with the aid of election officers was common practice. At least in the city, federal officials could monitor goings-on at the polls.[13] In crossroads towns, no such scrutiny existed. There were any number of cases. One such happened in the quiet country towns of Oskaloosa and Grasshopper Falls, Kansas, in 1868. Many who voted one way later testified that they had really voted the other. The judges orchestrated everything by simply calling off the names of voters from a book and then depositing ballots in the box, as the clerk set down the names. Eighty of the names were fictitious. Two more were not on the rolls. Twenty-two more were people not present on the day of the election. Twenty others were minors. In all, at least a quarter of the total vote cast was illegal. In Mississippi's shoestring district along the Mississippi River, Democratic election officials failed to return ballot boxes from the biggest Republican precincts and adjourned the count while confederates with duplicate keys improved on the vote actually cast, or snipped the edge off bunches of ballots, which could then be declared as mutilated and therefore illegal.[14]

Where a competitive two-party system turned partisans into unofficial deputies, ready to expose any infraction, egregious vote fraud could be prohibitively risky. Down south, where Democrats predominated, many frauds went unreported. Most went unpunished. With Republicans unrepresented on election boards, or selected for their illiteracy, incompetence, or susceptibility to corruption, with state courts packed with Democrats and a heavy Democratic majority ready to dismiss any Republican contestant in an election case, majorities were made to be stolen. Long after the fact, Mississippi Democrats boasted of their tricks. In one precinct, blacks (usually Republican) outnumbered whites twenty to one. Democratic judges did nothing to hinder the voting, but when the time came to send the ballot box to the county seat for the official count, they made sure that handlers down at the wharf shipped it to St. Louis by mistake and sent a bale of cotton in its place, "or the ballot box might, accidentally, be dropped out of the window of a train; in fact, any trick might be employed that seemed to promise a chance of success." When a federal judge intervened at another polling place to appoint a bipartisan panel of inspectors, the Democrats waited until the Republicans had gone to supper and then switched the ballots. On the alert for such tricks, the black officers at a third site vowed to skip dinner. Their white colleagues proposed instead that all the inspectors take their meals together, and one of them went out to fetch sardines and crackers. The Republican inspectors' food had been laced with croton oil, a virulent purgative, and they quickly became so sick that they fled the scene, a participant remarked gleefully, "and the box showed at the count a big majority for the Democrats."[15]

Given the choice, however, both parties would have preferred to fashion their majorities by above-board cheating; that is, by taking every advantage that the law let them get away with. To that end, Democrat and Republican alike shaped the election laws to enhance their own turnout and limit that of the opposition. In some states, they devised systems of separate ballot boxes, assigned for different offices. Northern courts usually ruled that a voter mixing up ballots and putting them in the wrong boxes could still be counted, and for the office intended. In the South, honest mistakes were grounds for invalidating the vote, which, since most of those caught making mistakes were blacks unable to read the labels on the boxes, worked just as white Democrats had intended all along.[16] Where it was politically inconvenient, election officers might fail to open the polls in an area heavily filled with opposition voters, or might see to it that they opened late. Polls might close early, and partisans would be on hand to slow the balloting by challenging every voter on the other side against whom any pretext could be found. If this kept many voters from casting a ballot before closing hour, so much the better. All this the law allowed, and the courts left the details up to the officers' discretion.[17]

Most northern states let vote any adult male who could prove residence for a certain amount of time, usually a year or more, and that he either was a native or had taken out his second set of naturalization papers. The most glaring exception was Rhode Island. The people got all the elections they wanted: governors and legislatures were picked every spring, and constitutional referenda appeared on the ballot all through the year. But quantity counted for little when quality was lacking. Between legislative malapportionment and voting requirements, Rhode Island had the least democratic system in the country—worse than that of Delaware, Mississippi, or even South Carolina. Registration closed four months before the election, when roads were at their most impassable, but that hardly mattered. Until 1888, immigrants could not register at all without owning $134 in real estate (personal property, no matter how large, did not count). "They came here without invitation," one Republican explained brusquely, "and no restrictions are placed on their leaving." When Republicans finally gave ground in 1888, widening the franchise to all adult males who paid a poll tax and could prove two years' residency in Rhode Island, they kept the property-holding qualification for city councilmen and referenda relating to taxation or spending. The taxpaying qualification threw thousands of American-born voters who *had* held the vote at the local level off the rolls.[18]

The concern with suffrage requirements even affected national policy in one particular. There was a definable connection between the admission of western territories and the breaking of the power of the Mormon Church, definable in large part because Republicans knew that Mormons inclined to the Democratic side. In the late 1880s, a majority in either house, predominantly Republican, put through severe oaths and restrictions to disfranchise the Mormons of western territories and make the area safe for Republican officials. For the same reason, members of the party most friendly to woman suffrage—which, in most cases, was not saying much—deprived the women of Utah of the vote that Mormon law had given them, lest they exercise it at their husband's decree to perpetuate the slavery that Mormonism was alleged to have forced them into. To vote, Idaho Mormons had to swear that they belonged to no order that encouraged polygamy. When Mormons changed their doctrines, some Republican registrars refused to give them the oath. Others let them take it and then made arrests for perjury.[19]

Parties in control of state and city governments added to their influence over the election process by the interpretation and selective enforcement of statutes related to making the count. As long as the parties printed up their ballots locally, it was entirely possible for one candidate to lose, even if more voters supported him, simply because of typographical errors from local printers. The discretion given by judges to accept or reject misspelled votes allowed considerable authority to those wishing to juggle the numbers. Michigan and Maine's courts threw out votes that put down a candidate's first two initials instead of his full name. Minnesota's permitted identical ballots, while some 500 votes in Los Angeles were thrown out for one misspelling in 1888.[20]

Other methods of counting in one's own side were more subtle. In New Hampshire, the constitution required that all senators be elected by a majority. Where the two parties were evenly matched, even a measly challenge by some third party would prevent "election by the people." Then the legislature got to fill the vacancy among the three top candidates. In practice, this meant that whichever party carried more seats by majority vote would fill all the rest to suit itself. It did a Republican no good to outrun his nearest opponent by 500 votes, as Edwin Wallace did, if he failed to get a majority and the legislature went Democratic.[21]

That partisanship affected not just seats genuinely in doubt but those where the law had been openly violated to serve one party's interests. Contested elections may underestimate the number of cases in which fraud played a role in defeating one candidate. As long as one side won handily, the other was discouraged from bringing formal charges that might sully but could not change the overall result. Winners never brought challenges, even when sufficient evidence existed to prove fraud by the defeated party. Intimidation, fear, or the knowledge that one's own side had committed acts best not brought into public scrutiny all worked to discourage injured parties. As important as anything else was the knowledge that legislative bodies were less likely to do justice than to judge in the majority party's favor. They might admit that the contestant had a majority—and unseat him by going behind the returns to find fault with some of the ballots counted for his side; they might admit that corruption had been proven and then insist that the challenger prove that enough votes had been fraudulent to change the election result. They might stickle at the technicality of a candidate being ineligible under the law or (if he was one of their own) dismiss it as a trivial consideration, compared to the sacred right of the people to elect whom they pleased. Grand juries would fail to indict for bare-faced scoundrelry—as long as the accused were their scoundrels; after all, the officers picking grand jurors were good partisans themselves. Even on Capitol Hill, it was generally understood that with an occasional exception, no Democratic house would expel one of its own members for cheating blacks out of their rights, and a Republican house would find any excuse to protect its own members and throw out Democratic ones. Only compelling evidence would deflect partisans from the party line. When House investigations were headed by Charles Crisp, a Georgia congressman whose district cast one-thirtieth the vote of that of any of his northern colleagues, it was pure fantasy to expect a fight on the bulldozers *elsewhere* who intimidated, killed, and disfranchised black voters.[22]

Against minor parties, the shutout was extremely effective: Prohibitionists were never likely to get a majority of legislators and to pay injuries back in kind, and as long as the major party was convinced that the sideshow movement was a fraud anyhow, bought and paid for by the opposition, a ruthless insistence on the precise letter of the law or obedience to its extremely elastic spirit entailed no risks.[23] Where the two parties were more evenly matched, however, the anything-goes spirit only invited election disputes and challenges like Governor Garcelon's. New Hampshire had had its own coup in 1875, just after the spring election. Democrats were within a few seats of a senate majority, and outgoing governor James A. Weston decided to give it to them. Instead of letting lawmakers decide who had a right to several disputed seats, he certified Democratic winners in just enough to put the upper house in party hands. Once again, the technicalities of the election laws gave him the excuse to eliminate inconvenient Republican votes. Thousands had marked their ballots for "Natt. Head" in one district. They knew who they were voting for, but the difficulty was that Head's legal first name was Nathaniel. Legally, the failure to set down a nominee's "Christian name" made the ballot count as if it were a blank, and the governor was not one to flout the formalities of the law. He invalidated every ballot with a "Natt." on it. The Democratic contenders were sworn in along with those whose election was not in dispute. Republicans stormed out of the senate in protest and tried to set up a senate all their own. The state supreme court refused to enmesh itself. In vain the *Concord Monitor* raged against the "sapient sneaks" and their "pot-house judgment." The usurpation, if such it was, stood.[24]

Having uncovered forged poll books in Cincinnati, Ohio, Republicans felt themselves every bit as much in the right in 1886 as New Hampshire Democrats had eleven years before, and they, too, felt themselves as justified in playing political hardball. "We intend to bounce the Hamilton county Democrats out of the senate," one lawmaker told a reporter. "We've got a way to do it and we will do it. There will be a howl, but the Democrats have got to go." When Democrats left town, Republicans simply acted as if they *did* have a quorum, and expelled all four Democratic contenders. To make sure that Cincinnati tried no such shenanigans in the future, the legislature set up a registration law for that city and for Cleveland. Nonpartisan election boards were created in Cleveland, Columbus, and Toledo to choose polling-place officials. The real aim was not reform; it was a Republican majority that fraud could not break. The same legislature regerrymandered congressional districts to swell party advantage and created a new board of public works for Cincinnati, one appointed by a Republican governor. From then on, except in unusually bad years, Republicans never had trouble carrying the city.[25]

Altogether, political observers should have been worried that the quality of the popular will was being strained and distorted to suit the parties, and, more particularly, distorted to turn the majority party's temporary majority into a permanent one. Sometime in the late 1870s, a new word entered the political lexicon to cover an alarming phenomenon: "Mexicanization." Reflecting a general impression of government in Mexico, where bayonets and stuffed ballot boxes had turned the outward forms of democratic process into false fronts, the term implied that what had become custom among people of an inferior race was turning into standard practice north of the border, too. The *Nation* summed it up best as the idea "that it is of more importance to elect your own man than to satisfy your opponents that he has been elected fairly."[26]

Those fears gave the 1880 election much of its edginess. Nightmares about General Grant as would-be Caesar or of Republicans cheating Democrats out of the Electoral College resonated because the American political system had been under exceptional stress for so long. Before 1860, it would have been unthinkable that a state or states would make revolution to thwart the result of a presidential election; or that Congress would dictate new terms for state constitutions and impose military force until those terms were met; or that state governments recognized as legal enough to ratify a constitutional amendment would not be recognized as legal enough to send members to Congress; or that rival governments would set up legislatures on either side of the street, inaugurate governors, and create local militias to war against each other. Extraordinary circumstances made all of these measures seem necessary, even right, to the parties that used them, but the cumulative effect was an unhealthy one. With the end of Reconstruction, Democrats and many disaffected Republicans assumed that the stress on the system would end; politics would return to its usual state. But it didn't. After Garcelon's attempted revolution, the tissue ballots of South Carolina in 1878, the parade of witnesses called by a House committee to prove that Republicans had stolen the 1876 election, and the exposure in the press of telegrams proving that the Democratic candidate's friends had tried to raise money to steal it back, anything seemed possible.

No alarm can last forever without fresh outrages to keep it going, and with the comparative peace of James A. Garfield's administration, "Mexicanization" faded from the political vocabulary. The president's assassination by a crazed office seeker drove past perils from the public mind. Suddenly the selfishness of the political scramble seemed the main threat to representative government. Perhaps the problem also became too common to notice. Liberal reformers concentrated their attention on the way that northern city bosses bought their majorities. Looking southward, they would have seen a more disturbing trend. All of the defects of undemocratic government were entrenching themselves. Between the bulldozing and the outright use of fraud at the polls, national politics was moving further from an expression of the public will every year.[27] The problems may have been growing worse everywhere, but in the former Confederate states, the downward steps were bigger ones.

What could happen when all of these methods, legal and lawless, were applied simultaneously to an election? Southern Democrats gave innumerable examples in their efforts to make a solid South. Among the best documented was the failed effort of an agrarian alliance to topple the ruling party in Arkansas. For years, the Wheel, a fraternal association appealing to small farmers, had made its influence felt in politics locally. In 1888, it mounted a statewide challenge. A farmer-labor convention met to choose a Union Labor Party ticket. The platform offered an open appeal to the Knights of Labor and the Farmers' Alliance. It called for the regulation of railroads, the ban of alien landownership, countywide school districts, ballot reform, and a state tax forfeiting excess railroad earnings. For governor, they nominated Dr. Charles M. Norwood, a former Confederate and state senator. Republicans were quick to embrace the movement. At the very least, as former chief justice John McClure explained it, the Wheelers had "less intelligence to do harm than these fellows . . . in now." They did not share the Republican political platform, except in one crucial particular, the commitment to free, fair elections.[28]

Insurgents swore that the usual methods would not be tried on them this time. White men, some still bearing their muskets from Confederate service, could not be browbeaten like Negroes, they warned. "There are half a dozen counties where Winchester will meet Winchester if occasion demands," a reporter assured Republican readers. "Monkeying with the ballot-box will be an amusement attended by greater danger than it has been heretofore in Arkansas."[29]

Democrats met the danger willingly. Suddenly, communities found a need to create regiments of the state militia a fortnight before the election. In Conway County, hitherto a Republican stronghold, Democrats had laid in a supply of rifles for the 1886 election, though not enough to carry the county. There had been shootings then; there were more now. The Union Labor candidate for one county office was killed. By election's eve, both sides were carrying rifles on the streets. Republicans at the capital were not worried. "I have observed that when both sides get ready, it is seldom that anything happens," the former chief justice assured one reporter.[30]

Assurances counted for nothing. On election day, the opposition editor was beaten up. A Republican judge of election was put in jail, and Democrats chose ones of their own. Wild reports spread that if Democrats won, blacks would burn the town of Morrillton, and a citizens' militia was out in force patrolling the streets. At El Dorado, the Union Labor Party had the help of a dissident Democratic newspaper, the *Eagle*. Or at least it did until a week before the election. Then the usual persons unknown broke into the office, smashed the presses, and scattered the type. Other Democratic supporters scattered the electorate. On election morning, armed men guarded every road into town. Whites approaching the "deadline" were required to give the Democratic password, "Cleveland." Those known to be all right but with faulty memories were given a reminder, with the warning that they "would need it before [they] got to the polls." White

Republicans were ordered home. Blacks coming to town were driven away. Some were shot at, and several were whipped. By nightfall, there were reports of sixteen killings in two days in a single county. In Union County, a party of rough-necks, supposedly from across the river in Louisiana, invaded the polling place, grabbed the ballot box, and fled with it. The officers at the polls produced a new box and began the election all over again; but, of course, the only voters now were the Democrats waiting to cast their ballots. These forty-odd votes, and no others, were the ones counted on the final return. Many citizens fled their homes before the polls opened and sought refuge in other counties. Other Republicans left for good.[31]

On the face of the official returns, it was a bitter defeat for the Wheelers and the Union Labor Party. Norwood carried some two dozen counties. In ten others, he took more than 45 percent of the vote. All the same, he had lost. The coalition had taken one-fifth of the legislature and a number of county officials. Yet the bulk of the prizes had gone to the Democrats.[32]

The Wheelers knew that they had been cheated. In fifteen counties (one in five), ruckus, force, and fraud had marred the result. "Seven hundred and ninety-one votes were cast here," a Democratic source reported from Jackson County. "County's total vote, 800. Eagle's majority will be at least two thousand." For a joke, it was singularly ill-timed. Both sides admitted that the Democrats had tried every trick in the polling book to suppress the opposition. By Norwood's own count, he had won by some 5,670 votes.[33]

Pulaski County perhaps furnished the most blatant case. There, at least, peace reigned on election day. The Democratic county judge scrupulously followed state election laws. Every precinct had election judges representing both parties. As soon as the polls closed, the ballot boxes themselves were sent to the county clerk's office, with tally sheets and unofficial statements of returns. Wheelers and Republicans stationed a secret guard around the building to forestall theft. That night, persons unknown pried open the safe with a crowbar and stole the ballot boxes and poll books for ten precincts. Just three of them had Democratic ma-jorities (slight ones), and all, not too surprisingly, were "found" by the county clerk a few days later, when canvassers learned that without them, the Democ-ratic nominee for county sheriff would be the only one on his ticket with a plu-rality. The charred remnants of the six Republican boxes were ultimately discov-ered. In each case, there was other evidence of the boxes' contents: poll books and registered lists of electors gave an accurate count of who voted and how. The county canvassing board, strongly Democratic, had to follow its own judgment. Granting that there were ambiguities about the returns, the board counted the votes as received. Ashley township failed to send in a certified return, but its tally sheet gave a Democratic majority, and the board counted that. Big Rock township had a tremendous Republican majority, according to its tally sheet, duplicate poll book, and uncertified returns, but the board refused them all, insisting that only a certified form would do. A Democratic county ticket was counted in without further difficulty.[34]

Norwood appealed the state returns to the legislature. Both houses agreed to an investigation, but on terms that made justice impossible. The senate demanded that Norwood post bond to pay for the costs of any investigation, if it ruled against him. With a Democratic legislative majority, that seemed dead certain. As everybody knew, Norwood could not afford the $20,000 to $60,000 demanded and was forced to withdraw his appeal—which the governor-elect refused to permit without a formal retraction of the charges. (He didn't get it.) The legislature had no intention of any inquest. Nor would it void the elections and call new ones, even in Pulaski County.[35]

There were plenty of explanations for the box-stealing there: that the losers stole their own boxes to make Democrats look bad and that "whiskey men" had done it to keep Prohibitionists from winning a local referendum. (If the latter were the case, they must have been sampling their own wares, since Prohibition was a sure loser, and, in fact, failed by two to one, with or without stolen precincts added in.) Even Democratic editors knew better. Some of them called for new elections. Four Democratic assemblymen from Pulaski resigned; four Republicans replaced them. But even there, the Union Labor Party got stinted justice. The same majorities should have handed them control of the county offices. A Democratic circuit court decided that on the face of the returns, if the stolen poll books had been counted, the Democrats had lost. But with a touching and rare sense of the injustice of bulldozing, it accused the Republican Party of having discouraged blacks from voting their consciences. If blacks had only been allowed a free ballot, the bench declared, Democrats would have had a perfectly fair margin. By rights, then, the offices belonged to them.[36]

Republicans challenged the returns in several congressional districts. Eventually, their nominees were seated in every case but one. That was the second congressional district, where former governor Powell Clayton's brother John Clayton had lost to the influential Congressman Clifton R. Breckinridge. When the case came before the House, Breckinridge's defenders admitted that frauds had been proven in one place but insisted that these alone were not enough to change the final result, and that proofs elsewhere were incomplete enough to leave the outcome open to a reasonable doubt. The incompleteness was hardly Clayton's fault. Within weeks of the election, he had announced an official challenge of the results and set out across the district to collect the evidence for his case. On January 29, 1889, persons unknown fired through the open window of a hotel parlor and killed him. Witnesses to election frauds were far more shy about coming forward after that, shyer still after the federal supervisor of elections for Breckinridge's district was shot in the head while playing a game of poker. Declaring themselves as shocked as anyone by the assassination, Democrats launched an investigation, turning up nothing, and on that basis denied that the incident had any relevance to the election contest, a conclusion with which the investigating committee chairman, Breckinridge himself, agreed entirely.[37]

Republicans were not about to forget or forgive. "We count Democrats' votes and they steal ours," one banner read in a postpresidential election rally. But indignation made a poor solace. Nothing could be done to redeem the state government, and reforms must begin there, if anywhere.[38] Fraud had taken the heart out of many of the coalition builders. What use was there in mounting a challenge to Democrats on any terms, when it would be overturned so flagrantly?

Nor were Democrats about to make the predictions come true. Many of them may well have agreed with the banner that declared Arkansas "Republican with a free ballot and a fair count." They brought the race issue to the fore, more viciously than before, and started tinkering with the laws to cut Republicans off the poll lists entirely. Two years later, the Democratic machinery was working perfectly, and peaceably—or nearly so. When Republicans printed up 7,000 Union Labor tickets for the election, they had to do so in St. Louis, to prevent them from being seen in advance and counterfeited. When the shipment arrived, several hundred Democrats in Conway County were waiting to mob the delivery agent, grab the tickets, and destroy them. But aside from beating the agent senseless, there was nothing disorderly about it; the crowd was all on horseback under military discipline: the men wore red sashes and carried miniature flags. Heading the crowd was one of the witnesses for Breckinridge's defense in the congressional hearing and several Democrats indicted for ballot-box stealing.[39]

In fact, people were hurt and killed, and far more were cut out of their rights. Advance though blacks might in their own enclaves in that election—and eleven assemblymen and the first black state senator since the 1870s went to Little Rock—the state was further from their control than ever; and disfranchising laws would follow within the next few months to turn back even those local gains.[40] What had happened was that, as with the 1888 outrage, most northerners had stopped caring and most northern papers no longer considered a stolen election newsworthy.

" 'Freedom of suffrage to the blacks means freedom of suffrage to the whites.'—Evarts. Solid South: 'Hurry up, dough-face, and shut up your side. Mine is *solid*' " (Thomas Nast, *Harper's Weekly*, October 23, 1880).

Had the South been a separate country, the consequences would have been grave enough. Because it was part of the United States, the effects touched national policy. Force and fraud made presidents and put Democrats within reach of an electoral majority without their needing to spend on a national campaign. An unfree, unfair count kept the House in their hands and permitted their hold on a substantial minority of the senate. It corrupted the Republican Party itself by turning its southern delegations at national conventions into the representatives of so many rotten boroughs, representing nothing more than the federal offices from which they made their living and delegates ready to sell out to the highest bidder. It created a generation of white southerners unaccustomed to a serious competitive party system—a party system not of "independents," roused this year and vanished the next, or of a series of one-shot party challenges with little common ground, but rather of lasting organizations, with a tradition of having held power in the past and the prospect of regaining it in the future; and it fostered a sense that any such political process was somehow alien, unnatural, and threatening. The mind-set of a solid South was already forming, even before the South had made its solidity permanent. More than all, the "Mexicanization" of the South helped give the mainstream parties a reason for continued existence by giving every Republican good reason to see the issues of Grover Cleveland's day as akin to those of Abraham Lincoln's. There could be no government of the people, by the people, or for the people as long as free government and a fair political process permitted a minority section of the United States to direct its counsels and shift the balance of power to the minority party of the North.

Anything, Lord, but Milwaukee!

Malapportionment and Gerrymandering

Thou shalt not kill; but need'st not strive
Officiously to keep alive.
—Arthur Hugh Clough, "The Latest Decalogue"

Nobody could teach Pennsylvania politicians a thing about rigging the system to suit themselves. In any fair vote, Republicans could carry the state by 50,000. The Keystone State elected one Democratic governor in thirty years, and two in seventy. Still, where the legislature was concerned, the majority left nothing to chance —and next to nothing to the minority.

Even with the fairest apportionment in the world, a districting based on population would have meant some inequalities. The state constitution insisted that any drawing of districts create compact, contiguous forms and that they follow county lines; except where a county deserved more than one congressman, assemblyman, or senator, the boundaries must take in all or nothing. As long as the only combinations possible were of counties bordering on each other, District A would have fewer people than District B. But partisanship aggravated the problem, because, as everywhere, the majority drew borders to permit itself the greatest number of "safe" districts. By 1880, an imaginative eye could pick out configurations on the map like hairpins and spindles.

Nothing would change until the injured party had the power to act, and as long as the gerrymander gave Republicans one branch of the legislature, that time was never. The closest Democrats came to a fair deal occurred after the miracle of 1882: the first Democratic governor in twenty-two years and a majority in the Assembly. Shrewd negotiation might draw a fairer map, especially with Republicans in disarray. But nothing of the kind happened. The senate offered Democrats a better deal than they had, only to be pressed for more. Neither side would budge, and when members' per diem ran out, they went home. An extra session just frayed tempers worse, and by the time the districting question came up again, two years had passed and Republicans had overwhelming margins at both ends of the capitol. There was no pretense of fairness this time. Out of twenty-eight congressional seats, Democrats had a fighting chance in only eleven and a good prospect in only seven. Angrily, Governor Robert Pattison sent in a veto of the districting bill. That was his party's second mistake. Another two years and Republicans controlled the executive mansion, too. As the election-night celebrations wound down, out came the new districting maps. "You'll hardly know Allegheny County," a Pittsburgh Republican boasted, "and there'll not be a Democratic congressional district in the state." There certainly was none west of the Susquehanna.[1]

Pennsylvania's adventures in mapmaking were nothing extraordinary. They highlight the way in which politics set the boundaries of fair play in Gilded Age politics. In principle, the representative system assured consent of the governed and defined districts so that local concerns would have the fullest possible voice. In practice, a system based on representation posed several crucial conditions, ones that hindered the second-largest party and virtually wiped out the influence of any others.

With rare exceptions, American representative bodies were chosen on a district-by-district basis — which, given the old custom of electing at-large all the legislators or aldermen for a city like Boston, was certainly an improvement, since it permitted some say to minorities with a local majority. Generally, state law demanded that the districts have specific borders, and it usually set up conditions like those in Pennsylvania: the shape must be as compact as was practical and the district's various parts must connect with each other. Some state constitutions insisted that districts respect county lines, though, of course, for a populous county where more than one representative was permitted, lawmakers could draw lines within the county, and in some states they could attach part of a city in one county to an adjoining county, providing that they took all of the latter.[2]

All of these regulations assured that any districting based on population would produce only an approximate equality, but states' fundamental laws often made the situation worse by decreeing that any county, no matter how sparsely settled, must have one representative, or by limiting the number of members from another county, no matter how large its population. State senates were the worst in that respect. There, states usually set up a standard other than population for apportioning members.

Connecticut was a case in point. In "the Land of Steady Habits," a dose of real township democracy would have made the habit of electing Republicans to the senate far less steady. When the state wrote its constitution in 1818, that flinty independence, where each town took care of itself, forced an equal voice in the General Assembly for each one. Since Hartford had only 9,000 inhabitants then, the arrangement seemed fairer. But as immigrants flowed into the cities and farmers' children fled the countryside, the balance shifted drastically, until a minority of Yankee Republicans ran a state where Irish and Yorker voices could be heard pretty plainly. Democrats were pulling nearly half the vote in Connecticut by 1864. After 1874, they were outpolling Republicans as often as not. But if more people were voting Democratic, more *towns* voted Republican. It would have taken a landslide, gathered not just in New Haven but from all over, for Democrats to have scraped together the bare majority of legislators needed to elect a U.S. senator.[3]

The same could be said, and then some, for Rhode Island. When the state constitution had been written in 1846, the conservatives saw to it that one person in every four who lived in Providence would have only one seat in every six in the House. With 459 people, Jamestown had just the same voice in the senate as Providence, a city 228 times its size. A full vote in Providence could have elected Democratic governors in Rhode Island. Little short of revolution could have elected a Democratic senator. As for Vermont, any place with twenty voters could declare itself a town, and each town had a right to a legislator. Time changed the size of the electorate but not the representation, which was a lucky thing for the three surviving voters in one "town" who drew lots for the legislative seat rather than schedule an election.[4]

What constitutional mandates could not do, partisanship did. A rough equality of representation might be all very well, but courts usually declined to interfere unless it was very rough, indeed, and until the 1890s, they went out of their way to defer to legislators' inclinations. Given so much discretion, legislatures drew maps without fear and with very little justice. They might get around the requirement that towns not be divided up by declaring each ward in a city a town for apportionment purposes; or they might create a district surrounded by another like the hole in a doughnut, or devise sixteen Assembly districts for places with less than half the required population to qualify for representatives—every single one of them Republican.[5]

Gerrymandering happened everywhere in the wake of party success, and if partisan advantage hung on its results, it did not wait for a new census. In New Hampshire, there were two mapmakings, one in 1891 and the next in 1893. Ohio had half a dozen in ten years, and Indiana barely went through a session in the 1880s without one side or the other fiddling with boundaries. Sometimes the changes were wholesale, sometimes a fine-tuning of two congressional districts where voters had shown more independence of mind than lawmakers appreciated.[6]

Gerrymandering may have served other purposes than the comparative representation of the major parties, although, to judge from the debates and editorial comments, these were more like an afterthought. How a city voted, and not its influence on behalf of city interests, mattered most when district lines were drawn. Commentators often noted how awkward a marriage of discordant constituencies the authorities had worked out, but if, say, the Holyoke district had "a mongrel nature," it sported a Republican pedigree.[7] When legislators anywhere voted on a districting bill, the dividing lines were not rural against urban but rather Democrat against Republican.

Cheating the enemy of its due could be done in different ways. In some places, the dominant party gave itself the largest possible number of potential seats by devising districts with just enough of a margin for its side to make victory feasible. In others, the dominant party fixed boundaries to banish as many of the opposition as was practical into one district, the better to make all the other districts safe. If the foe was sure to win by a thousand votes, it made sense to give him several thousand more, effectively throwing votes away that under other circumstances might have swung an election against the party in power elsewhere.[8] A city the size of Milwaukee in 1860 could be harnessed to enough Republican counties to give the Republicans a fighting chance in most elections. But the city's population grew much faster than the countryside; by 1870, Democrats were able to roll up large enough majorities to have their way, and when the next redistricting took place, a Republican legislature knew that the best it could do was surrender the district entirely and confine Democrats' power elsewhere by attaching Democratic counties to Milwaukee.[9]

Partisanship certainly made for odd shapes on a map; compactness was one of the first requirements to be sacrificed, for party's sake. Iowa's gerrymander was typical. Having had a close call in the 1885 elections, Republicans for the first time began to fear for their majorities. The next session of the legislature took swift action. It redrew the congressional district boundaries, especially to overslaugh the Democrats of Dubuque. Think of a district 175 miles long and, at one point, 5 miles wide, the *Dubuque Herald* protested. Or another, a narrow strip running from the Mississippi River halfway across the state, "simply and purely to place 6,000 Democratic majority in an already strong Democratic district, and place county after county in another to make it Republican." The new Tenth "cavorts over a good part of the state from Winnebago clear around by an indirect journey to Crawford, inclusive." Based on the 1885 state returns, four House seats would have gone Democratic. Under the new dispensation, the odds favored only one.[10]

Naturally, any gerrymander worked against the interests of some of the dominant party. It had to. Manipulate the boundaries though they would, a Republican legislature could never shape them to put every one of their supporters into a Republican district. In every district conceded to the enemy, there would be friends, doomed to lead a forlorn hope. "Anything, Lord, but Milwaukee," the *Racine Journal*'s Republican editor prayed, as mapmakers got to work. (Milwaukee by itself made a district incontestably Democratic by that time.) Still, apportionment, done cunningly, crimped as few in the majority's electorate as possible and interfered with as few sitting members as it could.[11]

But Wisconsin's Republican boss, postmaster Elisha W. Keyes, showed another not uncommon courtesy: he worked out district lines to help out the state's one Democratic congressman, Charles Eldredge. There were some good reasons for it. A river improvement subsidy was pending in Congress, and the boss wanted Wisconsin to give it a unanimous support. That could hardly be done by offending the one member likeliest to balk. Properly played, though, a districting bill at home could give the Democrat that Keyes called "my erring brother" one more incentive for cooperating. "Come, Charley, go in, now," he wrote as the apportionment bill hung fire, "and the Central Committee will stand by you. . . . I notice that all efforts to put you in a Republican district under the new apportionment *some how or other* fail to come to pass—'and you know how it is yourself.' With the injunction 'be virtuous and you will be happy.'" Majority parties in most northern states appreciated that unfairness had practical limits. Redistricting a Republican state to eliminate every single Democratic seat would take the trickiest sort of work and would be so manifestly unfair that it might just shipwreck in court. Leave scraps to the minority party, and its grumblers would subside eventually. Democratic counties, outside a Democratic district, only meant trouble; even most "safe" seats could swing round in an unsafe year. The fewer Democratic counties in Eldredge's district, the more there would be in others.[12]

What happened there happened elsewhere. The most celebrated case was Samuel J. Randall, Democratic Speaker of the House in the late 1870s and Appropriations Committee chairman for most of the next decade. If anyone should have been a high-profile target for Republican attacks, it should have been he. Districting him out of his safe Philadelphia seat should have been easy work. The Third District had a peculiar shape, running along the Delaware River and at right angles with the lines marking the other districts. Straighten those lines, and Philadelphia just might have five Republicans representing it, instead of four, and this without the kind of contorted mapmaking that proved a gerrymander on its face. Yet Randall never found himself in peril at election time.

Randall's talent and seniority, for one thing, made him too valuable for Philadelphia's business community to spare, but two other motives may explain Republicans' forbearance in redistricting. Committed to high tariffs themselves, they were not likely to find a Democrat more to their liking, or a Speaker more useful at crushing out tariff reform bills in his own party. What open enemy could give Republicans so much value? "You are one of the few Democrats I like," the GOP state chairman wrote him in 1885. "An effort will be made to deprive you of your district. . . . I will resist it." When the new apportionment was drawn up in 1887, Senator Don Cameron, boss of the Republican machine, intervened personally to see that Randall got the district lines he wanted.[13]

Taken together, malapportionment and gerrymandering ensured that legislative bodies not only exaggerated the majority will of the state but also thwarted it. In Vermont, 8 percent of the people controlled a majority of senate seats, in Rhode Island, less than 12 percent, in New Jersey, less than 20 percent. In effect, the voter in Michigan's smallest senate district had 2.7 times the clout of one in its largest; the comparable figures in Connecticut's House in 1890 was 199.8. All through the Gilded Age, New York elected Democratic governors more often than not, and from the 1870s into the 1890s, New Jersey elected them without exception. But Republicans controlled the capitol. Barely five thousand votes out of half a million separated the two parties in Indiana, but Republicans guessed that they would need a fifteen thousand majority to carry the legislature.[14]

As a consequence, malapportionment assured that a party with an unfair advantage could translate its power into unfair advantages at other levels. In some New England states, the requirement that it would take an outright majority to elect any state officer carried politics still further from fairness. In New Hampshire, Connecticut, and Rhode Island, the badly skewed legislature got to choose the governor from the top contenders, if none received more than a plurality. With Republicans in unshakeable control in both houses, there was never a doubt as to what their judgment would be. Connecticut Democrats might come out first in the race for governor (and in the 1880s, often did), but they found that the legislature treated a plurality as the people's will only when a Republican had it. Until after the Civil War, the safety catch on Rhode Island's elections hardly ever came into use: not once under the 1846 constitution, and only three times before it. But with the rise of third-party challenges, lawmakers found themselves second-guessing the popular will more and more often: in 1875, in 1880, in 1889,

1890, and 1891, and, in a situation that nearly tumbled the state into civil war, in 1893—and always in a Republican direction.

Malapportioned legislatures helped assure congressional district lines that distorted the larger partisan will of the nation, North and South. Across the North, as of 1880, 1.8 million Republican votes elected ninety congressman, and 1.6 million Democratic votes elected just twenty.[15] The distortion of the popular will was even greater in the Senate. Even with direct election of senators, the 40 percent of Vermonters who voted Democratic, the 45 percent of Michiganders and Wisconsinites who voted Democratic, could not have translated their numbers into a proportionate share of seats; in thirty years, they did not carry one. But malapportioned Republican legislatures made matters worse. Between 1851 and 1891, Democrats held a Senate seat in New York just once, and then for a single term—and only a tremendous landslide gave them the legislative majorities to do so. Democratic pluralities in Connecticut gave them just one Senate term in sixty years. With fair apportionment of the legislatures and one-man, one-vote, Democratic senators would have sat from New York, New Hampshire, and Connecticut throughout the 1880s. Instead, these states all sent unbroken Republican delegations.[16]

The unfair advantage that Republicans had in House and Senate was offset in part by Democrats' gerrymanders down south and by the deliberate suppression of the Republican vote, but not enough to right the balance entirely. What made the situation even worse was the way Republicans rigged the western territories to create prospective states that would make their Senate majority election-proof.

Even as southern states struggled to find their way out of the Union, inhabitants of the territories were mounting campaigns to thrust themselves in. The more experience they had with the instability and incompetence of governors picked for them half a continent away, the more insistent their appeals. Congress readily obliged. Minnesota became a state in 1857, Oregon in 1859, and between 1861 and 1867, the Republicans redrew the map of the entire territorial West, devising boundaries and assigning names. They made Kansas, Nevada, and Nebraska into states; only a presidential veto kept them from admitting more. Over the next twenty-two years, state-making slowed, with just one new admission: Colorado, in 1876. Then in 1889, an omnibus bill brought in North and South Dakota, Washington, and Montana. Wyoming and Idaho followed in 1890, by which time, as the president grumbled, even he was wearying of the free coinage of states.[17]

New states would have been admitted, no matter who controlled Congress. But neither the timing of admission nor the boundaries set was inevitable. Until the late 1850s, it had been customary to admit no territory until it had as many people as the average congressional district and had real prospects of getting many thousands more thereafter. Nevada was different. Scarcely more than a set of mining camps tumbled along the eastern range of the Sierras, its 40,000 inhabitants lived and died as the price of silver dictated. It came in as a rotten borough, a commonwealth uncluttered with people, and time only made it rottener, as the Comstock Lode gave out and the population dwindled.[18]

The Silver State was a notorious example, but it set the pattern for the Gilded Age. Between 1861 and 1896, of the eleven western states admitted, only six had as many people as the average congressional district, and two only half that many. If the old rules had applied, one scholar calculated, Kansas and North Dakota would have entered a year later than they did, Colorado two years later, Montana and Nebraska five years, Nevada and Idaho not until the twentieth century, and, conceivably, Wyoming would be a territory still.[19]

It might be argued that no better system could have been devised, without requiring settlers to wait a generation for full self-government. This might have been true — as long as territorial boundaries were taken as immutable fixtures of the political landscape. But they were no such thing. Nature did not define them; politicians did: Republican politicians and partisanship tempered the state-shapers' designs.

Nevada's borders were purely arbitrary. Conceivably, a very different state could have been devised in 1864, one with the resources to create a more diverse economy and with the population of an average congressional district. Indeed, Congress could have adjusted the state's boundaries at any time in the next twenty years, as long as the lands north, south, and east remained in a territorial condition. Time only made the logic more compelling. By 1880, the silver bonanza had begun to give out. A decade more, and the cattle boom ended as well.[20] With a dwindling tax base and some stray talk about remanding Nevada to a territorial condition, Senator William M. Stewart offered a proposal to have his state absorb some of Utah and Idaho territories. In the end, Nevada was left unaltered, though Stewart's idea received serious consideration.[21] Very likely the partisan advantage of two more Republican senators from Idaho helped make its dismemberment less appealing.

The fluidity of territorial lines was a reality of the Gilded Age. There was no reason, for example, why Dakota Territory should come in as two states, aside from the benefits of having four Republican senators rather than two. Nor was a boundary stretching east to west inevitable. Indeed, from settlement patterns, it might have been just as reasonable to admit everything beyond the Missouri

River as East Dakota, and leave West Dakota in a territorial condition or attach it to Montana and Wyoming. (A Nebraska senator tried to annex much of Dakota to his own state and did get it through the Senate.) With no road connecting the mountainous panhandle of Idaho with the Snake River valley in the south, and with the easiest route one west to the Pacific coast, north to Puget Sound, and then eastward, Congress could reasonably have dispensed with Idaho entirely, annexing its southwestern counties to Oregon and its northern ones to Washington, as inhabitants wanted.[22]

Just as the mapmakers could have created a West of fewer, larger territories that would have been fitter for statehood at the time of admission, so Republican lawmakers could have admitted certain states earlier than they did. Based on population criteria, Oklahoma could have achieved statehood in 1886, twenty-one years before it did so, and Utah, in 1882, rather than in 1896. By the standards of Idaho and Montana, New Mexico would have been fit for admission in 1890, and perhaps Arizona as well. But all of those states would have been chancy for Republicans at best.[23] As it was, the GOP managed to control the Senate by their dominance in a vast, sparsely peopled domain, where, thanks to the constitutional provision assuring each state equal representation, several thousand voters in Nevada held exactly the same influence as one hundred times their number in New York. Eastern malapportionment helped ensure a Congress where a rotten-borough West could swell Republican totals, and these, in turn, added to the Republican advantage in the Electoral College.

Misrepresentation went beyond partisan advantage and crazy-quilt district maps. Even if every state and every district had contained precisely the same number of voters, there was another built-in problem with the one-district-one-representative system. Necessarily, the winner took all, and a minority, though it be 499 out of every thousand votes, counted for nothing. Spread across an entire state, inequities might cancel out, but only if the minority in some places constituted a majority elsewhere, and as long as the statewide majority, in assembling districts, played fair. As long as carrying a state entitled a presidential candidate to all of its electoral votes, the Electoral College would aggravate the problems of unfairness that partisanship had built into the whole system. Winning New York by a thousand votes in 1884, Grover Cleveland won every single electoral vote; carrying well over two-fifths of the electorate in the prairie states, he did not carry a single elector. As a consequence, narrow popular majorities sometimes translated into great electoral margins, and, in 1876 and 1888, the presidential candidate with the most popular votes lost the Electoral College.[24]

The skewing of majority will, then, was compounded by the suppression of the minority's voice. A system of single-member districts and winner-take-all almost invited vote-buying and fraud. In an election where the two major parties were evenly balanced, so much power could ride on so few. The equities of politics between the two major parties, however, pale beside those of the minor ones. Malapportionment, gerrymandering, and winner-take-all discouraged any small party from launching a national campaign and made the odds of success beyond the local level infinitesimal. Unlike the Democrats or Republicans, a third party usually did not even have the consolation of holding a local majority; it was sure to be the minority party everywhere, and that handicap guaranteed far less influence on legislation than either of the major parties had. Twenty-five percent of the vote could, usually did, translate into no legislative seats at all. It made congressional seats a virtual monopoly of the two major parties; up to 1890, nearly all the exceptions were men who, though a sideshow party put forward their names, got most of their backing from either Democrats or Republicans. Experience taught that the best a sideshow party could expect most years was to act as a spoiler, taking enough votes away from one major party ticket to elect the other; its surest way of influencing the process was to subsume some of its own particular principles and make common cause with Democrats or Republicans on a fusion ticket. Necessarily, the third party, whatever small concessions it won, surrendered the purity of its program.

Malapportionment and misrepresentation affected policy, and not just because they affected party fortunes. In states where rural interests held an unfair advantage, it meant a legislative agenda framed for the special benefit of farmers. Not by chance, small Connecticut towns paid less in state property tax than the salaries their assemblymen collected. As in other states, the great burning issue of the mid-1880s was the prohibitive taxation of oleomargarine, and when the governor vetoed the law, it was only to be expected that he came from Hartford.[25]

Conjecturing about an American polity that never was is a risky business. Still, it seems clear that, had there been a full, fair apportionment in northern legislatures, there would have been more Democratic senators; a full, fair count in the South would have increased the number of Republican congressmen there, though perhaps not enough to offset the Democratic gains up north. Even leaving gerrymanders and malapportionment aside, a delay in the admission of western states until population qualifications had been met would have meant a Democratic Senate not just for the four years between 1879 and 1881 and between 1893 and 1895 but for sixteen, from 1877 to 1883 and from 1887 through 1897. Without Colorado's admission, there would have been no crisis over a "stolen election": Samuel Jones Tilden would have won the presidency, with or without the three southern states' returning boards counting him out. For that very reason, Republicans might not have tried counting him out at all: what would have been the point? For the next four years, the Democrats would have controlled both the president and Congress. Without a Republican Senate, there would have been no Republican-dominated Supreme Court. With control of both houses in Congress, Democrats might have proceeded sooner with tariff reform and gone further; the pressure to expand the currency with greenbacks or silver coinage would have been stronger through the whole period. Federal enforcement of fair elections in northern cities might have been wiped out long before the first veto-proof Democratic Congress in over thirty years wiped it out in 1894.[26]

The winner-take-all system was no more a necessary consequence of the American constitutional framework than malapportioned legislatures and gerrymanders were. State law could have declared that the presidential electors be awarded proportionately, based as closely as was practicable on each party's share of the popular vote; or it could have directed that each state have two at-large electors, awarded to the party winning the state, and that each of the others go as his congressional district went. The proposition was less radical than it sounds. Alexander Hamilton had offered some such scheme in 1800, and until the 1820s, many states split their electors between the leading candidates. As long as gerrymandering skewed the overall will of the state to suit party purposes, a district-by-district basis for awarding electors might have distorted the popular will itself, but it would have made a fairer expression of each state's will than the winner-take-all system.[27]

In electing state legislatures, the principle of reflecting the parties' comparative strength could have been carried out by a scheme of proportional representation. Illinois actually put into practice a system of cumulative voting in 1870. Each legislative district balloted for three members, not just one, and every voter could cast three ballots, just as he pleased. In practice, this assured a member from the minority party in each district, as long as the minority amounted to one-fourth of the electorate. Third parties could concentrate their full strength on one nominee and elect him, which is one reason that the Illinois legislature usually contained not just Republicans and Democrats but Greenbackers, Grangers, and Labor Party members. A strongly Republican northern Illinois elected thirty-six Democrats in 1872, while the overwhelmingly Democratic southern counties found room for twenty-three Republicans. A more representative body drew up fairer congressional districts and spent less effort gerrymandering them.[28]

What if, in addition to fair districting and a nonpartisan admission of states, there had been some system of proportional allotment, of the kind that Illinois devised? Given such a system in the apportionment of presidential electors, there might have been a less corrupt political process and one with less emphasis on cheating. Returning boards, such as those in Louisiana or Maine, could hardly have "counted out" a presidential candidate successfully. At most, they would have gained one or two electors, not the lot. Instead of swinging pivotal states, prime targets for colonization and cash payments to floaters, New York, New Jersey, and Indiana politicians could have raised less money, or applied it to making a campaign of education. Much of the incentive for local organizations to carry an election by hook or crook would have vanished with the proportional representation system, and for the same reasons. A solid South would have been impossible, and with it a northern Republican reliance on the bloody shirt to carry votes. Even though the reform would allow blacks just one congressman out of seven in South Carolina, when they deserved four, the Fifty-first Congress would have had forty-seven Republicans on its southern delegations to make the party's case, not the paltry dozen, nearly all of them from the Border South. With proportional representation, any group of voters strong enough in numbers to deserve a representative could put up "the very man they wanted" and "snap their fingers at the 'machine.'" In 1890, there would have been three Union Labor congressmen, five Prohibitionists—and, given the new advantage of going it alone instead of fusing with the Democrats, perhaps a half dozen Greenbackers to stir up the House. Instead of a Republican majority that year, Democrats would have the lead, with one vote less than an outright majority.[29]

What Illinois could do, other states could have attempted. Still, just about none of them did. With the exception of a few experiments—like Michigan's selection of presidential electors by congressional district in 1891—the mainstream parties chose to stick to the old rules and time-dishonored customs of taking whatever they could by the winner-take-all system and the gerrymanderers' prerogative.[30] When it came to power, even a long-victimized party found reform hard to enact.

Reform was stopped cold by the two qualities that gave late-nineteenth-century politics its character: the partisan impulse and the federal system of setting up the rules under which politics flourished. Complain about it though they might when they were in a minority, parties saw gerrymandering as among the perquisites of office. Majorities had a right to rule and, within the bounds of fundamental law, rule absolutely. Any arrangement permitting the opposition a crumb the majority declared an act of purest generosity. Warning that Republicans might just win the legislature, a North Carolina newspaper urged Democrats to keep in mind that the 1891 session would redistrict the state. That Republicans should dare to claim more than one seat out of nine in a state where easily 40 percent of the vote went for Republicans every year was, to the editor, a breathtaking effrontery.[31]

In any case, each side knew that the other would have done the same, if it could, and, thanks to the existence of some forty different state governments, was doing it somewhere already. Defenders of a Republican gerrymander in Iowa justified themselves by pointing to a Democratic one in Alabama; to those denouncing the rigged borders in South Carolina, partisans answered by bringing up the mapmaking atrocities of New England. They were not just shifting blame but pointing out the obvious fact: for one party to reform its practices would only leave it at the mercy of the other. Even if lawmakers did strict justice in one state, they could not control the wiles of politicians in another. Change by national law had one set of consequences — change, state by state, another. The first might indeed move the country closer to a new way of arranging for fuller democracy; the second would allow cheaters to prosper. Between the partisan impulse and the federal outlook, the likeliest motive for any state embarking on such a reform alone was to cheat the opposition of anticipated victory. There was no whiff of fair-mindedness in two legislatures' discussion of a bill allotting presidential electors on a congressional district-by-district basis in 1880. Republicans there never dreamed of legalizing the system everywhere. What they wanted was to put New York and New Jersey out of Democrats' reach, denying them votes needed to elect a president.[32]

Very likely the bill's sponsors felt no twinge of conscience. Nor did they need to. Behind their calculations was an awareness that, left to itself, the political system was already badly broken. As in so much else, the Solid South had carried the discrepancy furthest between voting and political power. In no other section of the country was gerrymandering so complete or so entirely in one party's hands. In no other section did so many lawmakers and presidential electors represent so few eligible voters. From the shoestring district that ran the Mississippi River counties into one black congressional district and permitted a white minority to run the other six as they pleased, to the "black Second" in North Carolina, to the atrocious "Dibble-mander" in South Carolina, shaped to give Samuel Dibble the House seat that fraud and force had failed to win him in 1880, to the laws depriving Republican counties of the power to elect their own officers, Democrats had turned the South into a force to express partisan ends. It had welded a minority's control of a minority section into the controlling force in making presidents and organizing the House.

It was the absence of a fair political system in the South, more than anything else, that made reform so unlikely. Proportional allotment of presidential electors became politically impossible in the North. Conceivably, a constitutional amendment could have made it work. No Solid South would have been possible then. But what if Republican Pennsylvania embarked on the experiment alone? The unfair advantage that southern Democrats had would only turn a probable victory in the presidential race into a sure one.

Policy—The Golden Rule?

Purse'n'All Influence

No graven images may be
Worshiped, except the currency.
—Arthur Hugh Clough, "The Latest Decalogue"

In one sense at least, the Gilded Age seemed to later generations truly an age of gold. Long-discredited by historians, the popular impression persists of a political system where money ruled: either the corporate interests sponsoring their protégés or the millionaires making the Senate their private club.[1]

The truth makes a more unsatisfactory mix. Money mattered. The need and scramble for funds and the constraints that these put on politics make an essential complement to the street display and popular participation. One was impossible without the other. But how far money could buy political happiness and how precisely the money affected the course of politics takes an answer much more carefully weighted and nuanced than the old-fashioned indictments.

At first glance, the sums to carry on a political campaign in the Gilded Age seem surprisingly modest. Partisan newspapers told a different story, to be sure. When it came to actual numbers, reporters swallowed any estimate, and never with more gusto than in the heat of a campaign. What could be more sensational than the "confession" of Ohio gubernatorial candidate George Hoadly that he had spent $50,000 dollars winning the Cincinnati primary elections? (Hoadly's "confession," it turned out, was his failure to scotch a free-floating rumor.) Sometimes they underestimated the other side's war chest; bankruptcy was a perfect way of showing that the enemy's morale was shattered beyond recovery. News like that might hearten one's own supporters. It could even convince potential donors to the opposition not to throw their money away. More often, editors tried to alarm their own party's contributors by making fabulous estimates of the money on the other side: $258,000 to carry Maine in 1884, say, or $2 million to

"The bosses of the Senate" (Joseph Keppler, *Puck*, January 23, 1889).

swing Ohio a month later, and $400,000 to wean Alabama from the Democracy in 1892.[2]

Parties had any number of good reasons for overstating what the enemy spent. Voters could only be stirred up by a sense of imminent peril, and the money-bag bogeyman joined that whole line of other terrors: "British gold," "Rebel claims," Knights of the Golden Circle, and the like. Putting one's opponents in the wrong by suggesting that their cause was too unjust to win on its own merits certainly eased the process of arguing, especially if, on the issues, one's own party had the weaker case. Figuring out the comparative advantages of specific and ad valorem duties baffled some voters and bored others. But anybody could understand the danger of cheap imports (bribe and ballot in hand) from Kentucky into Indiana just before the polls opened. The scaremongers were not just being cynical. If politicians' private letters are any guide, they gulped down unbelievable reports avidly. A month before Indiana's 1868 election, a Republican operative in the south of the state was sure that the foe had put in $135,000 already. His "proof" came "not only in the appearance here and there of strange faces but in unaccountable change of Republicans of note and influence in almost every part of the state." Level-headed congressmen warned that the other side had "unlimited means at its finger ends" or was about to raise millions on millions.[3]

This was fairy-tale finance. More precise, more official, and, at first glance, more plausible calculations came from those in the know. According to Senator

William E. Chandler of New Hampshire, a privileged insider in several Republican campaigns, the national committee never had more than half a million dollars to use in any presidential year before 1896. Nor had its Democratic counterpart. In a presidential year, a party's central committee, even in an important state, considered itself lucky to have as much as Hoadly allegedly put into a one-day city primary.[4]

Arthur L. Conger knew that fact all too well. It was his thankless task to raise funds for Ohio Republicans in 1883. Most years, the party's central committee got by on some $22,000. This year, they found themselves helpless to raise even half as much. Assessments came slowly, and with "some kicking," but "then, there can't be $2,000 raised by that means in the State. It is slow and lots of trouble." Hopeless about raising money in the state, Conger turned east, west, and toward Washington, with mixed results. The president offered promises, the Chicago customhouse apologies, the Illinois business community excuses. One insurance executive proposed to give, instead of money, something unspecified that he declared just as good. Just before the election, Conger came up with just a thousand dollars from the steel kings of Pittsburgh. Checks from New York City's money lords and party solons totaled $525. That the state committee went into ecstasies of gratitude over so little only showed how close it verged on beggary.[5] It ended the campaign far in debt. Five years later, members were still haggling over whose responsibility the IOUs were.

Republicans found their requests a harder sell in 1883 than usual. But the same complaints came two years later, when their prospects had brightened. In "Fire Alarm" Joe Foraker they had a winning gubernatorial nominee in 1885, and the party rank and file was too hungry for victory to haggle over principles. In private, though, Republicans' words of confidence were drowned out by the hollow sound that the campaign war chest emitted.[6]

Those numbers themselves may deceive. Historians cannot begin to guess the actual sums spent, precisely because, as in so many other respects, politics was a federal, not a national, system. No comprehensive official tally covered what individuals, ward leaders, county committees, and candidates put into a contest. If there had been, Ohio's figures surely would have been much higher than the sums that Conger raised. As for the *costs* of a campaign, taking in services tendered for free but compensated for in other ways, those were quite incalculable.

If anything, a state committee's budget should be seen as suggestive, the minimum outlay. The Congers and Bushnells could afford to get by with less because so much of the expense was borne by county and township committees, volunteers, true believers, and political employees. They paid in time or in contributions that sustained the campaign clubs and enhanced the hoopla. Many campaign expenses were invisible: the price to the post office of sending franked documents or of work undone because a government employee had visited home to put the party into fighting trim. No reasonable accounting practice could estimate the value of partisan newsmongering for getting out the vote.

With or without all of these unpurchased, decentralized donations to the cause, the plain fact was that party machinery could not get along without cash in hand. Pageantry carried a big pricetag. As long as Republicans hoped for results from the South, struggling presses clamored for money, and most of the southern state committees could scarcely raise a dime from their black constituencies, most of whom had nothing to give but their votes. They had to look north to the national organization, though even then they had to make do with a paltry few thousand — scarcely enough to throw a decent torchlight procession in Boston. Many of the functions that a growing state would shoulder in the future were still a party's responsibility in 1880. Parties, not governments, paid for poll watchers, ballot boxes, and the ballots themselves. They arranged for their own primaries, financed their own voter registration, and, where they could, assumed the burden of paying poll taxes, legal fees, and charges for furnishing naturalization papers.[7] None of these costs came cheaply.

New York City offered an extreme example. There, three major political organizations vied for power in the 1880s: the Republican Party and the rival Democratic machines, Tammany Hall and County Democracy. Lesser machines and impromptu parties, such as Irving Hall and the United Labor Party, might issue manifestos and run candidates as well. Success depended on a fair count and a good turnout at the polls, both requiring close partisan involvement. Every election district had its polling place, and each needed four inspectors and two clerks, according to law. Since New York had 812 districts in the 1880s, that came to 4,872 election officers, divided equally between the two major parties. Experts guessed that 45,000 more workers than those required by law did party duty at every New York election. As many as four out of five may have taken some compensation. In a normal year, Tammany would spend $75 to $100 for each precinct, County Democracy the same, with Irving Hall getting by on $50, and independent organizations making do on as little as $15.[8]

Voting was only the culminating ceremony. By that time, the parties had taken on other expenses, just producing and distributing the tickets that their loyalists would vote. County Democracy spent $12,000 to $19,000 just printing the ballots. When they were ready, the organization hired workers to fold and bunch them and to address envelopes, stuff them, and send them to prospective voters.

That cost some $6,000 to $8,000 more. Add to this the printing costs for other needs in the campaign, and no strictly political organization in New York City could get by on less than $25,000.[9]

Many expenses were inescapable, even for small, spur-of-the-moment political organizations. When reformers tried to mount an independent municipal campaign against Tammany Hall's candidates in 1882, they kept costs as low as possible; they had far less money to spend than the political machines did. Still, the Citizens' movement paid $25,000 for poll watchers and voting booths, $10,000 for printing ballots, $8,000 for mailing them, and $15,000 for advertising. Hiring halls for mass meetings, renting brass bands, and incidental expenses cost $4,500 more. For a ten-day campaign, all this might seem like an outrageous amount, but it proved to be much less than the Citizens' movement needed. They had overlooked the expense of buying off trouble. Confident that Republicans would back their ticket as the only alternative to Tammany rule, supporters of Allan Campbell's mayoral bid refused to spend $15,000 lining the pocket of Republican poll workers. Indignant district leaders swore vengeance. One of them later allowed that he had been inclined to double-cross Campbell anyhow but that when he found what chiselers the reformers were, "he determined to put the knife in up to the hilt." Another assembled his "boys" and, having told them how the "Independents" had acted, asked their advice. With one voice, they decided to run Tammany's mayoral ticket from the Republican booths "as a proper punishment for . . . niggardliness." Between the rival organizations, all told, politics-as-usual in New York City in the mid-1880s cost some $400,000 a year, and some calculations put it nearer $700,000.[10]

For individual candidates, of course, the figures came to far less than the citywide averages—as long as one left out of the accounting all the expenditure by the party for the general success of its own ticket. Just what those figures were varied, as conditions did. Congressmen themselves could tell how much it cost them personally, itself a fraction of the total amount spent. Members from the South and West ran the least expensive campaigns. There, where politics had not taken on the traits of commercial advertising, oratorical talent went every bit as far as a bankroll in bringing out a good vote. Personal popularity or a war record went further still. In the eastern panhandle of West Virginia in the 1880s, the same old networks of family connection and courthouse influence, barbecues and handshaking that had served for sixty years kept their appeal. Incumbents from agricultural districts could buy reelection comparatively cheaply by mailing out garden seeds and documents at public expense. Congressmen of national prominence often found themselves spared the costs of fund-raising. They were much more valuable to their districts than their districts were to them. Donors rushed to give greatness its due — and prospective challengers rushed away from a proffered nomination.

Northern congressional campaigns cost more, and those in the cities most of all. *New York Sun* correspondent Amos Cummings had an easier time than most. Popular, sure of good write-ups from his chums in the press galleries, he did not seek, much less campaign for, the nomination to Congress in New York City's Sixth District. The Democratic machines offered it to him on a silver platter. Nomination there was as good as election. Even so, Cummings had to give $6,000 to the party treasury for the privilege of running. Others with a bank account behind them were sure to pay far more — their full two years' salary at the least, every time they ran. On average, it was a fair guess that a candidate in the late 1880s paid the equivalent of half his congressional salary, and senators averaged much more than that.[11]

But even in the South, campaigns became more like those of the Northeast. By 1892, reporters in the West Virginia panhandle found all kinds of new innovations: a regular district headquarters in constant touch with county leaders. A full corps of clerks and typists bustled about answering letters and evaluating reports from distant precincts. At the chairman's fingertips were tallies of the names, ages, occupations, politics, and color of every adult male in the Second District. One Georgia member who first won office with $200 and had some change left over soon had to spend $2,000. A Louisiana member spent nothing for his first election and $5,000 in a subsequent campaign.[12]

So money must needs come, but where it came from was far from certain. Could it be gleaned from the robber barons? Democrats loved to leave that impression (at least for Republican funds). Corporations did give, when their own financial interest seemed at stake. National bankers, like Jay Cooke, who provided generously for the Republican Party that gave his house a special relationship as money changer and bond salesman for the government, were no laggards about producing an itemized list after the election as a reminder of favors desired. (They had little choice. From one cabinet member came the bare-faced reminder, "To whom much is given much will be required.") In every campaign, party leaders plotted to pry open wallets up and down Wall Street. The Republican National Committee issued a circular to national banks in 1884, reminding their directors that Democratic victory might doom their charters, now up for renewal. One committeeman tried to have a similar circular sent to the transcontinental railroads, written "to strike them in a tender spot."[13]

The reality, as Conger always found, was that few companies, *as* companies, were willing to give even so much as a well-heeled individual. By and large, business firms did not produce great sums; individual officers might, and they might do so with the company's advantage in view, though more often because of their own partisan loyalties and the way in which partisanship made them see what the company's advantage would be. Soliciting corporate funding on behalf of either party carried risks. Unless one side offered an advantage too plain to gainsay, directors' partisan loyalty would come into play. Let a company fund Republicans' campaign, and Democrats would protest. They might even storm into court with charges of misfeasance. Offending either side had additional risks. Incensed at the stinginess of John Murray Forbes in 1884, the Republican National Committee sent its Nebraska and Iowa managers to pay the railroad executive a special visit and remind him that "if the C B & Q is going to be Democratic in the East it is not going to have Republican shelter in the West & it is mainly in the West & mostly in our two States."[14]

That corporate reluctance helps explain why the GOP had to play up the difference between the parties on the tariff issue. Without unusual exertions, most businesses would be listless about modest reductions or would conveniently forget their promises as the campaign drew to a close; even some contractors with federal contracts failed to advance "a red cent" at times. Less obligated firms were not about to fry their own fat as a public service, unless a free-trade scare sent frissons into the boardrooms. "With all the immense interests of the Tariff at stake, I don't think a single manufacturer gave $20,000," presidential candidate James G. Blaine complained after the 1884 campaign. "I doubt if one gave $10,000."[15]

State races, like Ohio's, needed smaller donations, but they also were less likely to get them. For Conger, with especially good connections to the business community in Akron, investment bankers on Wall Street, and ironmongers nationwide, fund-raising was the same exasperating story every year. In New York, a Republican ally, attorney C. W. Moulton, reported "a growing feeling of alarm" among the party's friends about the Ohio canvass. "The apprehension is so great that I think there is a genuine desire to aid in almost any way," he assured Conger. Any way, as it turned out, except by opening their checkbooks. A week before the election, he had not been able to scrape together one cent. In Pittsburgh, a maker of cast steel declared that Republican victory was vital to his interests and to those of anyone with a stake in tariff legislation — and gave $300. The head of the American Iron and Steel Association, James M. Swank, was no less effusive and no more promising. "If I had not already made such urgent appeals to our people in behalf of Virginia it would have been possible to render our Ohio friends some assistance of consequence," he explained. *If . . .* but he had, and as a result, Swank could only forward on a single check, drawn on the Cambria Iron Company, for $200. The association would give Ohio nothing, "but," Swank wrote, "you will be pleased to learn that we have sent a very liberal supply of tariff tracts into your State."[16]

Contributions came from business *men*, more than from businesses, and not necessarily for business reasons. The distinction is an important one. Individuals hoped to advance their financial interests, but often they gave money primarily out of partisan loyalty and from political aspirations. Gilded Age opinion usually treated businessmen as a separate class from politicians. In fact, the two classes overlapped, in a variety of combinations. There were politicians and businessmen, pure and simple, businessmen in politics, and politicians with heavy business investments. One might look at the roster, certainly incomplete, of great givers to the Democratic campaign fund in 1884: ironmonger William H. Barnum, $27,500; Cooper & Hewitt ironworks, $25,300; German newspaper publisher Oswald Ottendorfer, $18,000; banker Daniel Manning, $13,675; city railroad speculator William C. Whitney, $15,250; railroad king James J. Hill, $10,000; coal and railroad executive Arthur Pue Gorman, $14,908.25; and banker Roswell P. Flower, $16,000. Listed that way, it would seem natural to assume that capital had the Democracy well in hand, but such a description may be misleading. Barnum was a former senator and Gorman a rising figure among Senate insiders. Flower was a congressman and presidential aspirant, already eyeing the governorship that New York would give him seven years hence. Whitney, whose future lay in the transition from a political to a business career, had been a leading figure in the Democratic machinery of New York City. As a leader in the House, wracked with partisan spleen and insomnia, Congressman Abram S. Hewitt looked to Democratic victory for higher political rewards, perhaps a cabinet seat or a future presidential nomination. All these donors were businessmen, but, except in Hill's case, their primary reason for contribution was no business decision, unless one could describe it as a way of protecting their investment in a political vocation. They did not calculate their donations as money spent to make money, nor, in most cases, did they expect a specific payoff. (If they did, some, Hewitt among them, were to be bitterly disappointed.) They were simply the kind of people who gave, who always gave, unless the party adopted policies threatening their financial well-being, and even then that threat must be of the most direct and clearest sort.[17]

The Barnums' investment highlights how indispensable funding from professional politicians was. The same list of contributors that set down Hewitt and Whitney's names included Grover Cleveland himself. The presidential candidate was set down for $10,000—the sum that, before the nomination, he was told would be expected of him, if he wanted to run. Any such list on the Republican side would have credited $65,000 to the GOP nominee, James G. Blaine. And the donation was not unusual. The spoils system not only fostered the *need* for large amounts of money; it also helped solve the problem. Indeed, it remained among the most important solutions all the way into the early 1890s.

At the heart of party finance was the principle of assessment on officeholders in particular and partisans in general. In return for being rewarded an office, the loyal partisan was expected to pay some of his or her salary to campaign funds. There might be more than one levy in a year. In a federal system, each level of government had its own elections and its own campaign finance committees. National, state, county, ward, and district organizations sent out requests. Sometimes an emergency would require the national committee to demand supplementary assessments to match needs. In presidential election years before 1884, the appearance of official party representatives stalking the halls in search of prey was a common sight. No salary was too modest to be overlooked, from municipal scrubwomen to disabled inmates of soldiers' homes and jailhouse wardens.[18]

Reformers put the practice in its bluntest terms, as a highwayman's demand for "your money or your desk." It was true that an appointee might turn away the assessor and get away with it. Of some 100,000 federal employees called on for a contribution in 1878, only some 11,500 responded. But that very much depended on the backing of superiors, and in 1878, with a law recently on the books forbidding assessments and the Hayes administration on record against the practice, desk holders may have felt especially safe from dismissal. On the whole, those who refused one assessment were well advised to submit to others, and those who had given in the past were best protected for exercising their discretion thereafter.[19]

Assessment of small-fry officeholders dwindled considerably after the Pendleton Civil Service Act of 1883. Over time, press attacks strengthened the resolve of those who resisted demands on themselves, and the efforts of the newly created Civil Service Commission made the collection of unlawful assessments an increasingly risky business. Under Theodore Roosevelt's management, the commission became the terror of Republican officeholders and a constant embarrassment, with its high-profile investigation of political practices. James "Ret" Clarkson, former assistant postmaster general and ruthless partisan, agreed with Roosevelt on this issue at least. Those most vulnerable to assessment had always been the party's poor, who were given postmasterships and clerk's positions to keep them from want. Ill-paid as they were, they were the partisans least able to afford the demands made. "I would rather go into any city in America to-day and try to raise $10,000 from the liberal [figures] among businessmen than $1,000 among office-holders," Clarkson wrote.[20]

The Pendleton Act could not shut off the flow of federal assessments entirely, and it did nothing about the dunning that went on at every other level, but the biggest single contributions came not from appointees but from those holding or seeking elective office. From the way politics worked, public office was a party trust fund. When Grover Cleveland ran for reelection, his check to the national committee for $10,000 excited public notice; Republicans even suggested that the president had proven his true feelings about civil service reform by being the most prominent violator of the Pendleton Act. A voluntary contribution did no such thing, though naturally the president's donation added to the moral pressure on officeholders under him to give way to Democratic shakedown artists. But Republicans had a point. Donations like Cleveland's were not optional. They were expected, even demanded, of any nominee.

No one from the White House to the statehouse was immune from dunning. New York City aldermen were taxed $15 to $25 per election precinct. Assemblymen, whose offices had less potential gain, paid $5 to $15. State senators, who had a two-year term and more time to recoup expenses, contributed $20 to $25. That was $5 per precinct less than congressmen paid. If more than one political organization nominated him, he had to give the same assessment to each one. The more lucrative or prestigious the office was, the bigger the mulct a party levied on the nominee. A would-be mayor of New York would need to fork over $25,000 to $30,000, a state supreme court justice, $20,000, a sheriff or county clerk, $10,000, and a district attorney, half as much. The more competitive the race, the higher the assessment was likely to be. As campaign expenses rose, so did the contribution expected of nominees. New Yorkers could remember a time when Tammany's nominee for sheriff paid a mere $2,000 assessment, just after the Civil War—and that was the same John Kelly who, as boss, is said to have set the price at $25,000.[21]

In many cases, an assessment had all the effect of an entry fee. If it was expected from candidates, they must either be businessmen of some means or have rich friends to back them. Otherwise, consideration would be out of the question. Talent, brains, a gift for oratory, social and institutional connections, and influential allies all could overcome the parties' need for funding, and fatheads could not sustain their careers long on a fat bank account. Still, money gave the edge, especially in years when the party was most desperate for funds.

To raise money, managers sought out candidates with a "barrel," or, more pre-

"The prospect in New York. 'What are you going to do about it?'" (Thomas Nast, *Harper's Weekly*, November 11, 1876). Samuel Tilden is poised to buy New York; in fact, the difficulty in prying open the candidate's barrel for any purpose was the despair of Democratic managers.

cisely, a checkbook, that could tide them over till election day. In some cases the money was no more than an incidental advantage. Democrats wanting a presidential candidate in 1876 would have looked closely at any governor of New York, and certainly one with Samuel J. Tilden's savvy. In his well-timed fight on the Tweed Ring and the well-chosen battle against the grafting contractors in New York's upstate Canal Ring—both thick with prominent members of his own party—he made himself, in one senator's words, a representative for "the aggressive honesty which is the dominant idea of the time." But his legendary wealth certainly helped. Democrats were confident that he would tap his barrel liberally to win election. "Any man, of negative character, about whom nothing specially bad could be said, with $20,000 per annum to spend in postage & lithographic fac similes and a thorough knowledge of the local celebrities of each school district . . . could be developed into a statesman & patriot, of equal consequence . . . in three years, more or less," an associate wrote.[22]

If wealth had been a consideration in the 1876 campaign, it became even more so after Tilden's defeat. The closer they looked at him, the less leading Democrats liked the "cold, clammy, selfish wire-puller." In moments of crisis, he proved irresolute, perhaps even cowardly. "He was an unlovely creation and if Dante had known him he would have invented an eighth hell in which to depict his unloveliness," businessman-politician Samuel L. M. Barlow snorted. A series of strokes broke the governor's frail health. A virtual prisoner in his home, nearly blind, unable to speak above a whisper, Tilden yet remained the front-runner for the nomination for eight years, almost to the very day the 1880 and 1884 conventions opened. Nostalgia for the one presidential race that Democrats had come closest to winning and resentment at the way Tilden had been deprived of his reputed right to the presidency gave Tilden part of his appeal. The barrel did the rest, even among those who saw him as a nuisance to the party. In one editor's words, the party seemed prepared to carry Jonah for the sake of Jonah's "passage-money."[23]

Democrats' selection of a vice presidential nominee in 1880 was even more blatant. To be sure, they needed an Indiana man on the ticket; having served in Congress before the Civil War, William English could boast long experience in his state's politics. But the state could boast many men more eloquent, prominent, or popular—just about anybody else, in fact. Since he was a banker, "Ten Per Cent Bill's" very profession stirred resentment among hard-pressed farmers. That fall, the party would have to explain away the many foreclosures and ruined lives that were an inevitable part of a lender doing business. "I will bet you that Bill English is the meanest man in the State, and I will leave it to Democratic witnesses and a Democratic jury," a lawyer allegedly challenged the editor of the state's party organ. "Well, I won't take your bet," the editor replied, "but I will be one of your witnesses." What English did have was money, all of which, it was suspected, would be poured into making Indiana Democratic in the October state election.[24]

English proved a bad investment, just as Tilden had. Neither was as forthcoming with funds as had been hoped. Still, the selection of a vice presidential nominee whose prime quality was his wealth happened often enough. In 1884, Democrats tried to induce West Virginia's former senator, Henry Gassaway Davis, to accept the vice presidency. That his state would be sharply contested in October put him into the running; but there was no doubt that his great wealth came into the consideration. (Twenty years later, Davis *did* accept; by that time he was much richer and, well into his eighties, no doubt much more experienced.) Other New Yorkers would have drawn as well as Levi P. Morton in 1888, but the Republican vice presidential candidate's barrel made him particularly appealing, as did publisher Whitelaw Reid's fortune in 1892.[25]

Vice presidential nominees only reflected a common practice also used in assigning House seats and settling senate races. In most states, business leaders could not buy themselves immediate preferment. Their rise came after long apprenticeship in different capacities of service to the party. Still, one of those capacities was almost always that of being the good provider to the campaign war chest in a time of need, or their potential to give generously for other candidates in the coming campaign.

Many New York congressmen upstate were made in such statesmanlike mold. As long as 1,800 of the 7,000 voters in Schenectady County were deemed buyable, the Republican State Committee needed a moneybags to do the buying. So wealthy contributors became the natural choices of the party in the so-called boodle congressional district. Not far off, in Saratoga, one might find Congressman George West, a Devonshire lad come to America in steerage who now owned eight paper mills. His wealth allowed him to buy a big share in one leading upstate Republican newspaper and complete ownership in another. The seat was his as long as he wanted it and could pay for keeping it—longer, in fact: having declared himself out of the running for another term in 1886, he was renominated by acclamation and reelected. His successor, John Sanford, was a congressman of slightly coarser fiber: carpet fiber, in fact, from the family's Amsterdam factories, and if he missed most roll calls, his attention perked up wonderfully when it came to the woolen duties in which his firm was interested. From the nearby Otsego district came Congressman David Wilber, president of a national bank and victor in a Democratic district after "a campaign noted for its thoroughness and aggressiveness"—and its cash, mostly Wilber's. "King David" was famed for a virtually bottomless purse. "He is a rough rider in politics," one observer wrote, "and when he is a candidate his trail over the district is a golden blaze." That blaze did not illumine the House. Wilber had no talent for public speaking and no gift for making friends, and he was often absent.[26]

Anyone wanting to see a double-barreled campaign need only look at those directing the two major parties' executive committees in a presidential election year. The custom was almost without exception: a merchant, like Edwin D. Morgan of New York or Marshall Jewell of Connecticut, would grace the chairmanship, with the intense political work left to experienced politicians at a lower rank. On the Democratic side, the chairman of choice for years was August Belmont. A prominent New York City banker and representative of the Rothschilds' American interests, he had become chairman before the war and remained for the next twenty years the bankroller of a party desperately in need of funds. His successors would be the able congressman Abram S. Hewitt and wealthy ironmonger William Barnum, a Connecticut ironmaster whose talent in buying votes at home was notorious and whose election to the senate was reputed to have been among his major financial investments. Wealth provided the credentials for many a working member of national and state committees as well, Arthur Conger providing a perfect example. One of Akron's most prominent Republicans, he had begun as a traveling salesman for a manufacturer of mower and reaper blades. Eventually, he became general manager or president of plate-glass and window-glass companies, realty firms, manufactories of tinplate, and a steam-forge concern. A better resume for political influence could not have been devised.[27]

The Congers had political skills and thought themselves at least as much politicians as businessmen. Those skills received ready reward, but it was all the more willingly given because the party expected campaign contributions from them. It was not their own wealth alone that was being tapped. Captains of industry were on intimate terms with others of their kind, the surest men for the task at hand.

What effect did all this money have on the political process? Enormous though the impact was, it did not allow businessmen to dominate the politicians entirely. For the success of their party, many of them were willing to temper their own views, though not so far as to put their business interests into direct peril. To Roswell Flower, election as governor was enough gratification in itself, and Nevada's moneybag senators generally behaved as if the office were an honorific, which took no upkeep thereafter by their attending the sessions of Congress or proposing legislation.

Of course the source of campaign funding did shape political life in several damaging ways. The assessment process, both on candidates and on officeholders, was in effect an informal tax system to sustain the parties. The donors compensated for it out of salaries and fees, paid for by the voters at large. Money for public advertising, contracts handed out to anyone but the lowest bidder, added to the costs of governance, and taxpayers picked up the tab.

The usefulness of assessments was one reason why the spoils system, with all its inefficiencies, survived so long. Cities might choose commissions or nonpartisan boards to handle certain city functions, but the tasks most likely to be put on a merit basis were those with few lucrative rewards attached. Fees from a city clerk's office were tremendous, compared to the rake-off from public libraries or parks. The big money-makers, the police and fire departments and the post offices, a political organization would try to control as long as possible.

The need to repay assessments bred a tacit understanding among hard-eyed party managers that officeholders should be allowed to make what they could from their positions. When in 1881, the Star Route scandals broke, no one should have been surprised to find that contractors carrying mail across the desolate West had been selected for partisan reasons and had milked the government, padded expense accounts, and kicked back a share to their political patrons. That was how the spoils system worked, at its most flagrant. In the cities, it assured a police department full of party workers, who heaped into the campaign war chest a fraction of the take from payoffs and protection money on their beats. Unlicensed concert saloons and green-goods men, pushcart peddlers, peanut vendors, bootblacks, and whorehouses all paid to evade city ordinances, and the police worked as an effective licensing agency, deciding which entrepreneurs should be permitted to run contrary to law and on what terms. A saloon could stay open on Sunday, for a fee. In New Orleans, the assessment on disorderly houses was so well regulated that madams were said to have left the weekly installment for police on the doorstep; no one in the underworld dared lay a finger on it.

Assessing candidates was not all trickle-down corruption. It left a well-founded impression that offices could be bought, sold, or rented, and it discouraged honest men from entering the race. In Rhode Island, the connection between a high office and a fat bankroll became so strong that governorships looked to outsiders like nothing more than a barter. Taken all in all, the Republican organization was "thoroughly rotten to the core," a Prohibitionist told one reporter.[28]

With well-documented cases of "barrel" politics, newspapers readily ascribed corruption to any convention where a rich man was involved. The 1880 race in Ohio's Fourth District was typical. As each county vied for the Republican nomination with a favorite son of its own, the well-heeled Captain Emmanuel Schultz of Miamisburg emerged as a front-runner. Schultz had served an unnoticed term in the statehouse and warmed a chair at the Ohio constitutional convention, but his real assets were ones managers could take to the bank—and had, in the past. Now, if reports were true, Schultz extended that liberality to convention delegates. Seventeen members from Greene County double-crossed their own candidate, and, allegedly, were well paid for doing so. Soon the Democratic incumbent was writing friends back east of a district awash in Schultz's cash. "The money is pouring out in 100$ and 200$ chunks. . . . There are regular agents from the East located at the Hotel in the [Disabled Soldiers'] 'Home' whose sole mission is to buy up the inmates." The only complaint among Republicans rose from those who could "hear the heavy thud, accompanied with silvery strains, of the cooperage as it bounds from rock to rock down the hillsides and along the valleys" but could not get their hands on a penny of it.[29]

Could money deflect a party from its mission or divest it of its natural leaders, the professional politicians? Here the answer is not so clear. Winning election did not necessarily mean a lasting influence. Barrel candidates often made a paltry show in Congress, when it came to legislation. Standard Oil money may have elected Henry B. Payne of Ohio to the Senate, but the seat might as well have been empty for all the influence he wielded, in large part because so many members believed that he had bought his way into their midst; he narrowly escaped expulsion and did not seek a second term. In the House, too, the greatest leaders were those least involved in business: the Holmans, the Randalls, and the Carlisles. But certainly wealth gave those who had it an advantage over those who did not in reaching the point where their talents could be tested by experience.

"Bar'l" politics shifted politics itself in a conservative direction. The concerns of those with wealth were not those of the less propertied, and the wealthy were not likely to support an agenda of change that went against their financial interests. Sometimes the inclinations were overt. A case in point might be the Washburns and Pillsburys of Minneapolis. While they did not dominate Republican politics, the heads of the two great flour-making firms certainly had a very good chance of winning any nomination they wanted. A Pillsbury won the mayoralty in 1884; his son handled the campaign and went to the state senate. William D. Washburn did even better. First elected to the congressional seat in 1878, he served long enough to push through funding for federal improvements on St. Anthony's Falls, above the city. Belatedly, colleagues noticed that the improvements, supposedly for navigation, were really meant to ease the floating of sawlogs and skiffs from timberlands that Washburn owned to his mills downriver. Indeed, the waterpower sites to be enhanced were privately owned by two firms in which the congressmen held stock. The last in a series of appropriations was struck out.[30]

The influence of William L. Scott was broader but again suggestive of how far the interests of a businessman could dovetail with those of a politician. Representing the Erie, Pennsylvania, district in the 1880s, Scott had entered politics as a congressional page forty years earlier. He had been elected mayor twice but, ever since the Civil War, had expanded his political influence by building a fortune, first in railroads, then in coal-land ownership. By 1889, Scott was rated one of the biggest colliers of western Pennsylvania. He boasted himself stockholder in 22,000 miles of railroads and master of a stable of thoroughbreds. There was no chance of his accepting a nomination for governor, the *Philadelphia Record* joked. "How could he live for four years so far from a good race track?"

"Scott is a good fellow and means well, never a doubt of that," Daniel Manning, Grover Cleveland's secretary of the Treasury remarked. That summer, there were even reports that Manning would resign in Scott's favor. He had doubly good reason for gratitude: Scott was staunchly hard-money and spoke eloquently against silver coinage. But Secretary Manning also knew Scott's worth from their dealings when Manning was raising funds for the 1884 presidential campaign. Newspaper estimates (notoriously fishy) put Scott's contribution at $50,000.[31]

But if Scott meant well, he meant especially well for himself. When Democrats were leaning toward a campaign focused on railroad extortions in 1885, Scott was one of the loudest voices against taking on the corporations. He offered cogent reasons, though his own vast holdings could hardly have been far from his mind, any more than former senator William Wallace's investments, themselves at the mercy of the railroads, were far from his when he took the leadership on the other side. Unlike most Pennsylvania politicians, Scott was an outspoken free-trader, which took courage. But Scott was one of the few Pennsylvania businessmen who could afford tariff reform. Coal mines nearer the ocean feared competition from Nova Scotia's mines. Across the Appalachians, Scott had no such fear. Transport costs were prohibitive in themselves, and free trade would open up markets for his product across the Great Lakes in Canada, where consumers thought western Pennsylvania coal a bargain.

Economic and partisan interests merged in Scott, but his wealth allowed him greater influence than other low-tariff Democrats had. By the middle of Cleveland's term, he had become the focus for all the opposition to Samuel J. Randall within the Keystone State. As the administration looked for a challenger to the former Speaker and present chairman of the Appropriations Committee, someone who could break his power at home, its eyes fixed on Scott, whose money and power to grant favors already gave him an influential position. With government patronage directed his way, he could do what no other leader had been able to accomplish. Randall's friends were purged from the state committee, and the delegation sent to the 1888 national convention spoke with Scott's voice.

Once again, it needs to be stressed that there were limits to how far money could silence all the other voices in the party. Only at great cost to the Democratic Party could the Randalls be driven into the wilderness. The further Scott ranged from where rank-and-file Democrats stood, the more tenuous his hold upon them became. Deprived of administration patronage when Cleveland lost his bid for a second term, Scott found his money less than sufficient to hold the party in line. The more he concentrated on making a big profit, the more it cost him politically. There was no paternalism to his mine-owning, no sympathy for laborers' grievances, and no willingness to discuss wage rates with employees. When Scott moved to crush out the mine workers' union during coalfield disturbances in 1889, it was more than his Democratic followers could bear. He became such a liability that his announced retirement from politics came as a relief. Randall lived just long enough to see Scott's influence eclipsed.[32]

The Scotts could never sound the only voice in Democratic counsels, any more than the Stanfords or the Wilbers could dominate Republican ones. What they could do was to make their viewpoint heard and raise the potential cost for the party in offending them. Ohio Republicans might be willing to risk brewers' contributions to their campaign to satisfy temperance advocates in their party; for winning office, votes counted more than dollars. But financial considerations may have helped tame lawmakers' zeal and made them search for liquor laws likely to affect the distilleries more severely than the breweries, and the two-bit grog shops so popular in Democratic neighborhoods more than the more respectable bier-gartens in Republican ones. And, certainly, the ability to contribute to party causes was not the only means that businessmen had of influencing policy and defining lawmakers' agenda. Treated separately from other practices, the counsels of contributors and barrel candidates seem an inadequate explanation for the business-friendly agendas of the two major parties. Taken in combination with corporations' ability to mount lobbying campaigns, the press's dependence on business advertising, and the range of favors and expertise on special matters that businesses could muster, the preeminence of barrel politics helps create a more disturbing picture.

If filling their financial needs was a distraction to the mainstream parties, it was death to the minor ones. Spending money may not have been everything. Campaigns could be waged on a shoestring, and with help from nonpolitical institutions—the evangelical churches from which the Prohibitionists drew so many of their leaders and so much of their money, or the trades unions and farmers' associations with their own networks of communication to members—a third party sometimes could compensate for its empty pockets. But the very causes for which so many outsiders struggled were never well funded. The business sources that major parties could tap were not just closed to them; the very existence of a Labor Party made a powerful incentive for corporations to open their purses to whatever alternative was available. Always the temptation beckoned of running a candidate who could pay his own way, even if his selection was not quite the perfect fit; always, the major parties could tempt the outsiders into an unofficial alliance, exchanging cash for just the slightest tempering of political conscience. If that rotten old Democratic machine Irving Hall could afford to print the tickets for the Labor Party in 1886—if it could provide labor leaders with the official poll watchers that radical candidate for mayor Henry George could not get any other way—were a few thousand labor votes for the Hall's nominations in downtown New York City an unreasonable price in return? What did it matter, really, if labor cast the decisive margin for a notoriously antilabor judge on the state court of appeals if they won city hall in return? That rough-tongued old political bruiser Benjamin Butler might not have been a Greenbacker himself in 1884, when the party nominated him for president; it was almost impudence on his part when, instead of accepting right away, he went to the Democratic National Convention as a delegate, hoping to parlay a smaller nomination into a bigger one. But the newly christened People's Party had not just adopted a kindred spirit to lead it. It had adopted a bunting manufacturer and highly paid attorney, who, when he ran, paid his own way and found himself greeting crowds of admirers and fending off mobs of political spongers simultaneously.[33]

Reformers on the fringe like Henry George knew that money's power kept them from reaching the audience their ideas deserved, and they knew, too, that inside mainstream party ranks, they could never do much more than swell the procession. They had all kinds of remedies to propose. Above all, cheaper campaigns would open the way to candidates of more modest means. There must be laws forbidding the parades and display that campaigns afforded. Reformers must abolish the practice of "treating." Instead of the parties shelling out funds, the government could prepare and distribute an official ballot. Towns and cities could rent out public halls at nominal expense for meetings, just as schoolhouses were used in the countryside. Indeed, George predicted, the parties would be relieved if the law forbade them to take up most of these financial burdens: the torchlights and display were done not just to rouse their own voters but to keep up with the opposition. A law that set the ban on Republican and Democrat alike would be almost welcome.[34]

It did not happen. On the contrary, with the mass production of campaign materials, the 1880s saw politics' own industrial revolution. The passing of the handshake and the barbecue style of campaigning would not make the process any cheaper. Parties' administrative machinery was expanding and so, too, were the lobbies, and one-cause interest groups with exchequers of their own and the power to augment the tracts that parties put out. Swank's association, the WCTU, state federations of labor, all had created the networks to engage in politics. Their spending meant that the day of shoestring campaigns was passing, even as the mainstream parties' monopoly on politics and policy began to dim. It would be the third house, not the third parties, that defined the making of policy in the century to come.

The (Round) House of Legislation

If money dominated politics in the Gilded Age, as critics claimed, the worst offender seemed to be railroad money. Travelers between New York and Philadelphia joked about "the state of Camden & Amboy" and a legislature that ran on a railroad company schedule. At the railroads' behest, New Jersey surrendered prime shore front to them for a song, remitted local taxation, and chose "tools of monopoly" to administer state and city law in ways that would protect the corporations from prosecution. Working within the Republican Party, the Pennsylvania Railroad engineered General William Sewell's election to the Senate in 1881. Antimonopolists rejoiced at his failure to win a second term in 1887 but, to their dismay, found the railroad interests in both parties leagued to elect Rufus Blodgett, a trusty servitor of the Democratic Party's special corporate friend, the Jersey Central.[1]

Blodgett was not likely to feel lonely in Washington; to a jaundiced eye, the Senate looked like the roundhouse of legislation. Directors and railroad presidents worked alongside company attorneys. To judge by how often Judiciary Committee chairman George F. Edmunds missed sessions to attend court, it seemed as if the Vermont Central's distinguished counsel considered the Senate part-time work. Small wonder, then, that nearly all insurgent parties cast the railroads among the leading villains and subverters of representative government.

Railroad influence showed the strains under which the party system operated, and how far money could have its way. The actual story, even in the state of Camden & Amboy, proves more complicated than critics made out, and one reason lay in that most obvious of points about the parties. Where their elected officials may have been out to gain, Republican and Democratic organizations were out to win. Their first loyalty went not to the corporate boardrooms but to maintaining power. In the new industrial order that was coming into being, business had more tools than ever before with which to shape public opinion and affect legislation, but it could not silence its enemies, and, thanks to the machinery of grassroots input on which the parties were based, it could not take business affairs out of the public debate. As economies developed and as the railroads became less essential to the prosperity of a commonwealth, the political calculations changed, and with them the willingness of the mainstream parties to make trouble for everybody's least favorite "monopoly." The more railroad support became a liability at election time, the harder railroad managers found the challenge of taming or subduing those who made and administered the laws—even in railroad-ridden New Jersey.

Money certainly gave the railroads a louder voice in policy making than they otherwise would have had. From company headquarters came a variety of favors for those with influence to spare. The free pass was like money in hand. For impecunious publishers like those of the *Wisconsin Pinery* or the *Sturgeon Bay Advocate*, the only trip they cared to make was one to the bank, to pay off overdue notes. Smart editors could sell their passes and pocket the proceeds. Railroad money built the *Omaha Republican*, and when it spoke, it gave party gospel in just the form the company wanted. Himself on the Union Pacific payroll, the editor protested that his newspaper never would defend any corporate demand that went against "the interests of the party and the people," and, curiously, he never found one that did.[2]

Corporate presidents made loans to politicians and let them know about special openings for investment. Company lobbies grew more subtle, more professional, in their ministrations to the legislature. The Union Pacific maintained the "oil-room" in Lincoln, where members were lubricated with drinks and favors, and the Central Pacific kept up a "bureau" whenever the General Assembly met in Sacramento.[3] Lawyers on retainer were always available to challenge regulatory laws in the courts or to find ways of delaying action. Potentially troublesome politicians were invited (in a private capacity, of course) to make the railroad's cause their own. With sixteen top Mississippi officeholders serving as railroad attorneys even as they wrote legislation covering their companies, with construction contracts handed out to firms that assemblymen owned, the companies had little to fear in Jackson. No bill setting up a regulatory commission was likely to pass Florida's state senate, as long as railroads kept "a dozen glib men" in Tallahassee. "Our senators have chosen their master," one editor grumbled.[4]

He might better have said that the parties had chosen their master. Smart lobbying began in the convention hall, not the legislative cloakroom. Railroads vetted the candidates, packed local caucuses where they could, and, when all else failed, sent employees to the polls with "scratched" tickets in hand, to defeat the most dangerous nominees. Not by chance, the Nebraska Republican Central

Committee called its 1880 convention for September 1; that way, primaries to select delegates would come at the height of harvest season. No matter how much they resented railroad attorneys making the laws, farmers could not take off time to go to the polls. With the Union Pacific's "blacklegs, cappers, and retainers" in full control, the convention wrote a platform deploring railroad extortion and discrimination, and showed their sincerity by nominating railroad servitors for Congress and lieutenant governor. Under the latter's guidance, the next state senate would stack committees with "monopoly cappers," who, an angry editor protested, wore "brass collars under their cravats."[5]

In states where one party held the overwhelming advantage and one railroad dominated economic life, a corporation's sway came near being absolute. With their virtually indestructible Republican majorities and with their dependence on a set of trunk lines, Kansas and Nebraska were almost notoriously railroad-ridden in the early 1880s. Commerce in Nebraska depended on the Union Pacific, coming out of Omaha, and the Burlington, feeding into Lincoln. The two cities and their roads vied for traffic and prominence, and the companies dominated trade statewide on their respective sides of the Platte River. Within Republican ranks, John M. Thurston spoke for the Union Pacific and Charles H. Gere of the *Lincoln State Journal*, for the Burlington.[6]

The Thurstons and Geres were not just gratifying the railroads' will, of course. They were using corporate support to build up their own power within the party. The same web of favors, obligations, and influence gave staying power to Democrats with company connections, as well; indeed, one of the reasons why regulation faltered in Nebraska was that the Union Pacific found places on its payroll for Democratic leaders and gave them one more reason to turn their wrath on moral reformers rather than monopolists. It was also one reason why, no matter how often West Virginia Democrats turned against Henry Gassaway Davis and Johnson N. Camden, they never could get rid of them. Railroad investments led the two men to fortunes in coal mining and industry. In every campaign, their desires and bank accounts were consulted, and when the time came to award senate seats, Davis and Camden were sure to be among the most prominently mentioned choices. Their ability to give jobs and legal work made them sources of patronage, even when the state government went into unfriendly hands, and, in 1885, Camden as senator had a very loud say in how the federal government would allot post offices and revenue collectorships. Sometimes they chose the national committeeman; at other times, they did the work themselves. As the state developed industrially, their power grew to define both the issues on which the parties debated and the stand that Democrats would take in favor of "progress." In league with his Republican son-in-law, Stephen Benton Elkins, Davis would become master of his party in the 1890s and tame it into the bulwark of the very corporate interests that it had once threatened to control.[7]

In every state, the bigger the company was in proportion to other economic interests, the further its influence extended. There was no doubt of James J. Hill's involvement in Minnesota policy making. He had to keep an eye fixed on doings at the capitol. His roads up the Red River valley had developed the state and the Dakotas into the great wheat-producing empire of the Northwest. The railroad magnate financed charities, newspapers, and politicians locally. He arranged loans for South Dakota senator R. F. Pettigrew; he joined real-estate investment ventures with Pettigrew's colleague, Gilbert Pierce. For legislative candidates needing a few hundred dollars in contributions, or newspapers requiring a donation to refresh their zeal, Hill proved a godsend. But Hill's plans spread further: completion of the Great Northern, stretching to the Pacific Ocean, and, eventually, ownership of its rival, the Northern Pacific. National designs needed national access. When Daniel Lamont, the president's private secretary needed a place to invest his wife's money, Hill advised him, and Lamont went on the company payroll after his departure from the White House and cabinet. Serviceable congressmen were given stock certificates in promising townsite speculations and help from Hill's editorial friends.[8]

Well-placed friends certainly made things easier for the Great Northern. President Grover Cleveland invited Hill to dinner. Washington departments gave him early notice of pending decisions. Power brokers in St. Paul consulted him about federal appointments, and those on the Democratic National Committee kept him informed about the way presidential campaigns were going. He was regularly dunned for contributions to carry on Senate campaigns and understandably earned the reverence of fund managers. Access, in turn, brought him further power. When presidents' and governors' doors were always open, Hill could act as the go-between for political favors that his officeholding friends wanted and then put them under further obligation.[9]

The Hills may have been buying access; the Thurstons were buying exclusion. The purpose of company money was not so much to catch politicians' ears as to shut their ears to arguments from the other side. Though rivals in business, Nebraska's competing trunk lines worked together to forestall regulatory legislation. Farmers complained of being mulcted, but nothing got done. One reason was that in Nebraska, as elsewhere, companies were perfectly content to let antimonopoly men propose any bills they pleased—as long as the gatekeeping committees were filled with men guaranteed to keep those bills from coming to a vote. For years, the legislature pleaded that no railroad commission was possible, as long as the state constitution forbade the creation of new salaried positions. Bowing to pressure in 1885, it did set up a commission, with its duties devolved on people already in office and the real work left to secretaries. The secretaries knew nothing about railroad finance and wanted to do even less.[10]

The story could be repeated endlessly, of railroad tycoons directing policy and dominating party counsels with their money and lackeys. Who believed Democratic threats to rein in Jay Gould's railroad monopoly in Missouri, when the party chairman was John O'Day, a high-ranking railroad executive? Certainly not Jay Gould himself, who named one of his railroad cars after the governor, himself one of the most outspoken antimonopolist windbags. In thirteen years, railroad mileage rose 80 percent, but the total assessed value fell by $12 million. Governors unable to prevent a regulatory commission could stack it with noddies and do-nothings. Often, the regulators themselves became apologists for high and discriminatory rates. "We got a Railroad Commission, but the Railroads got the Commissioners," was a common saying in North Carolina, and editor Josephus Daniels declared the panel to be a board in the strictest sense of the term: "long, wooden, and narrow."[11]

Those outside the mainstream parties saw in the railroads more than a menace to government dedicated to the people's will. Rightly, they spotted the most obvious symptom of something out of kilter in the way politics responded to public needs. Since the 1850s, economic groups outside of the party system had usurped the people's prerogative to make policy through their elected representatives. Their ability to muster voters and money gave them control over the caucuses, primaries, and conventions. More visibly than before, lawmakers seemed to hold a divided loyalty between the party and the businesses that had elected them. In the end, the Thurstons, Davises, Blodgetts, and Sewells only seemed living proof that the old party labels were meaningless—that the same set of hands tended the political machinery on both sides of the fence.

The evidence of influence seems heavy enough. It may even make a convincing case that money not only distorted but actually ruled politics and that the capitalists were not just the holders of preferred shares in the political system but its owners outright. Certainly from the plain evidence of railroad tycoons' letters, Greenbackers and Grangers could show politicians bought, bribed, and on bended knee before the tycoons.

Undoubtedly, by the 1880s, the parties faced new conditions and intense new pressures that no partisanship could tame. Instead of appealing to citizens to save a republic in danger of overthrow, they appealed to specific economic groups to save factory doors in danger of closing, or farms in danger of foreclosure. Still, the story of what politicians did about the railroads affords a somewhat more mixed picture of how far company influence actually went.

To start with, any party system responsive to public demand would have gone a long way toward meeting railroads' desires. Support for railroad construction came not just from lawyers, lobbyists, leaflets, and the lagniappes that corporations could pass out to officeholders. Every state, every territory, went through the "railroad mania," and in the first flush of optimism, when every local project in Georgia seemed to open the gates to the China trade, voters subscribed public funds for construction.

The larger political ideology shared by both parties backed them up. All parties agreed that more material goods, produced for less, constituted one of the plainest tokens of progress. Even moral reformers argued that changes in what Americans drank or how they behaved would have side effects as good for their bank accounts as for their souls. Every party promised to foster prosperity or preserve it. To stand against prosperity was to invite defeat. Run competently, railroads were sure to bring prosperity; on that, just about everybody agreed, as well. Inveigh against the Union Pacific though it might, the *Omaha Bee* saw every new railroad project as the making of prosperity and deplored agitators whose programs would endanger development, from agrarians to temperance advocates. In any legislative debate over regulation, the most dangerous argument was that capital would be driven elsewhere and that investment would stop.[12]

Always, too, the railroads' apologists offered a reasonable alternative to regulation: competition. Wider transportation networks not only would add to consumers' convenience. They would bring down rates and give shippers the chance of striking a fairer deal with carriers. New lines always forced the old ones to fight for traffic that they had hitherto taken for granted. That was one reason why railroad rates fell all through the 1880s, though never as far as critics thought an honestly run company could have gone. The ideal, then, would be a state policy so friendly to capital that promoters could set up rival railroads.[13]

Quarrels over regulation therefore did not pit simple right against wrong, nor the People against the Money Power. More often it set areas that had enough railroad facilities against those still waiting for investment. Every change in rates gave one city an advantage, at the expense of others. Politicians with a local outlook therefore were chary about any regulatory reform that left the legislature in charge of setting rates. It invited irrational decision making and a political free-for-all, especially since so many legislatures had sixty- and ninety-day limits on how long they were permitted to sit, far too brief a period to draft a really complex, well-balanced measure. Worse, it induced outright defeat. A regulatory commission was safer, but there, too, any decision on one locality's behalf would work against another's — especially when the city losing out was in another state, with no constituency for the commissioners to satisfy.[14]

Corporation victories, then, came easiest when they had grassroots support. They were also far from complete. Lobbying did not just give the railroads a new means of putting pressure on men who parties elected to office; it also built up a countervailing pressure. By the 1880s, ironmongers, merchants, textile barons, and even glove makers had their own professional lobbies and were able to awaken a politician's constituents to activism on behalf of their own particular special interest. Often as not, they resented railroad exactions as much as any farmer.

That was one reason why the railroads' political dominance was greatest in the fresh-minted states beyond the Mississippi. Areas least developed or just developing needed railroad connections the most; on their thoroughfare to eastern markets all other economic progress depended. But where railroads were the first business organization to set up offices and services in a territory, politicians had no other powerful economic interests to propitiate. The railroads were life and death to the economy of the Dakotas in early days, just as they and the coal mines were to West Virginia up through the end of the century. Whoever dominated the economy there was going to have a disproportionate voice.

This was why western politics in particular and much of southern politics, too, was likeliest to have one or two specific moneyed interests commanding the show — though those interests did not necessarily happen to be railroads. Where one industry predominated, the state's policy would bend to serve it. The economic importance of the timber barons in the northern half of Michigan allowed them to pack local conventions and to speak loudly in the nominating of state tickets. Silver kings were sure to reign in Nevada, where there was practically no other way of making a living. But in New York or Ohio, where industrialist and merchant, railroad and shipper, all had money, influence, and a role to play in dictating the state's prosperity, no John M. Thurston could command public affairs without being countered. Then politicians could play one interest off another and, serving as broker between competing forces, work out an arrangement that, if not entirely in the public interest, came rather closer to the common good of all interests concerned.

Look again at the sway that James J. Hill exerted. Unquestionably, the nation's capital had plenty of administrators and lawmakers eager to oblige the Great Northern. Well-placed senators could stifle a bill or hustle a survey through the Interior Department, and when it came to the small change of politics, the petty favors that cost little in terms of policy but would be fondly remembered, Hill found benefactors in both parties. Revealingly, his most devoted allies came from the territories or those newly fashioned into states. No other economic interest could advance their careers so well as railroads could, and those interests opposing Hill had no weight to throw around. Even then, they could not commit a national administration automatically or rush laws through unamended.[15]

In a more developed state like Minnesota, where wheat and its transport lost their role as the make-all and break-all of economic life, Hill found his plans increasingly stymied. He had friends all over the state; they were men whose support he had earned — quite literally, in hard coin and in favors done. Cushman Davis, governor and later senator, showed him nothing but goodwill. But Hill could not still the opposition. His cash outlay in politics never let him do much more than break even; it helped him block measures more readily than it helped him pass them. When Cushman Davis made a presidential bid in 1896, he counted on support from both Hill's Great Northern and its then-rival, the Northern Pacific. In the Dakotas, it might have been an unbeatable combination, but not in Minnesota. There, a reputation as the railroads' fair-haired boy was enough to rouse a host of enemies. Davis's candidacy foundered in the state and collapsed entirely outside of it.[16]

In the more-developed states, railroad money could influence but never wholly master policy. As Henry Gassaway Davis's career showed, it also had limits in imposing dominion over politics. Had Davis not been a railroad tycoon and a captain of industry, certainly, he could never have become a captain of politics in West Virginia. All the same, the captain found himself constantly having to put down mutinies, and it took more than a handout from the till to give him a hand on the tiller. His wealth helped elect him senator in 1871, but Democrats were not just rewarding his fund-raising skills. Davis had indispensable political qualifications. While other party leaders had a Confederate war record to explain away or had made enemies in the Democratic ranks by their views on how far to concede equal rights to blacks, Davis had been too busy making money to take political positions. With neither disloyalty nor bigotry to explain away, he could draw enough Republican votes to win election.[17]

Davis's money could do a lot (including carry him to a second term), but it had distinct limits in a politics where parades, pamphlets, and panoply counted for so much less than in the North. Beyond Wheeling, the old-fashioned southern style of campaigning, with its barbecues and emphasis on stump-speaking, prevailed. That put tongue-tied magnates like Davis and Camden at a real disadvantage, and the less visible they were, the more they built up their reputation as backstairs manipulators, able to win with a whisper over a public shouting more popular champions' praises. It was not an enviable reputation.[18] From the first, the millionaires found themselves at dagger's point with the Democratic factions they had displaced. Camden's career therefore had as many political defeats as victories. Twice beaten for governor, he won the senatorship in 1881, only after a bruising fight and after having lost his first bid. He could not make that one term deserve another. Davis retired after two terms, well aware that he stood no chance of a third.[19]

In or out of office, the tycoons had prodigious strength, but always tempered by the give-and-take of politics. They could stifle regulatory legislation at the state level and weaken tariff reform in Washington. But back home, they could not keep Democrats from picking gubernatorial candidate E. Willis "Windy" Wilson, an unembarrassed enemy of the railroad interests, or electing university professor and onetime Confederate William L. Wilson to Congress, where he not only bespoke a tariff revision that would cut rates for the sheep- and coal-producers of his own district but rose to chair the Ways and Means Committee.[20]

Nowhere could money buy the railroads political peace, and the reason became increasingly plain. Having promised so much more than they could deliver, the company promoters left every community feeling cheated. By giving a town preferential treatment, any company made nine enemies and, most likely, one ingrate. Disgruntled shippers and consumers complained at how rival towns stole more than their fair share of trade, but the railroads were blamed for making the theft possible in the way they set up their rates to discriminate between patrons. Whenever anything went wrong, all the distrust of Wall Street and Chicago "monopolists" and out-of-state railroad directors turned into fury. The farther away the board of directors was located, the more it suited local politicians as a scapegoat. If the major parties did not support railroad regulation, sideshow parties would, and, what was more, might well win.

James J. Hill's Minnesota was a case in point. Like its Swedes and Germans, the state seemed conservatively progressive. Radical movements rose, only to sputter out. Up to the mid-1870s, railroad companies found it easy to do business in a state that boasted the terminus of a transcontinental line, the Northern Pacific. Hired lobbyists for Jay Cooke's great project became congressmen, and railroad presidents became senators and candidates for governor.[21]

All the same, politics developed an intense agrarian streak, which was only natural, with an intense agrarian streaking through it, Ignatius Donnelly. Once congressman and later a railroad lobbyist, Donnelly fell off the company payrolls straight into the antimonopoly ranks in the early 1870s. In between his crusades to prove that Sir Francis Bacon had written Shakespeare's works and time out to write dystopian novels, the indefatigable "Ig" became a master organizer of resistance movements and farmers' organizations. Beset by the agitation Donnelly roused, the major parties set up a railroad regulatory commission, though they rid themselves of it as soon as the pressure was off. But they could not rid themselves of the "Sage of Nininger." Railroads never hated any Minnesotan so much. "[If there] is a spirit of agrarianism, he is its embodiment," their newspaper voice scolded. "The 'tramps' of course follow his banner; and the communists of society, by instinct, will give him all their support. . . . If there are those who desire a revolution in government and society, Donnelly is their representative and hope."[22]

Donnelly not only survived; he throve. Defeated for Congress again and again, he practically commanded the Farmers' Alliance movement in Minnesota by 1885. Farmers clamored to have him attend Alliance conventions; Democratic candidates begged for his services on the stump. When a mediator and negotiator between the Knights of Labor and the Alliance was needed to form a coalition in 1886, Donnelly was the natural choice.

And Donnelly was finding allies who would never have admitted themselves as such. In a Minnesota boasting myriad economic interests, businesses as well as farm-grown radicals joined the challenge on railroad power.[23] By 1886, the same Democratic Party that had taken "the irrepressible Ig's" support grudgingly two years before and then frozen him out of the patronage after victory was won was almost begging for his goodwill. A coalition put him into the legislature. "Get the mops ready," an Alliance newspaper warned railroads. "You can almost hear the water drip as he squeezes it out of railroad stock." Retired to private life in 1888, the agitator was back two years later. "It would take a universal cataclysm to keep Donnelly under," the *St. Paul Pioneer Press* grumbled.[24]

The same passion against the railroad exactions stirred outside movements elsewhere. California had a far more well-founded reputation of being railroad-run than Minnesota did—and it kept that infamy for a generation longer. Built up as it had been by the Central Pacific's road to the east and by the Southern Pacific system north and south, it knew firsthand the ways in which the "Octopus" could strangle legislation to railroad interests and how the so-called Big Four, who ran the railroad, could make friends on a cash basis. By the 1890s, even the Big Four's master spirit, Collis Huntington, wearied occasionally of his overlordship. "Things have got to such a state, that if a man wants to be constable he thinks he has first to come down to Fourth and Townsend Streets [in San Francisco] to get permission," he grumbled.[25] One Los Angeleno charged that

"Social science solved. The modern Archimedes: '*Eureka! Eureka!*'" (Thomas Nast, *Harper's Weekly*, April 10, 1880).

the Central Pacific fitted every senator with a collar "so that if he is lost or strays he may be recaptured and returned to his lawful owners."[26]

   And yet, if the legislative votes and the campaign speeches were any guide, Huntington would need more than collars; he would have needed a regular posse of retrievers, because senators and representatives kept straying all the time — almost as if most of them had *not* been paid for. Railroad influence had clear limits, as the Big Four's senator, Leland Stanford, found in 1891, when he failed of reelection. Grape growers and wheat farmers, orchard-owners, and raisin producers had their resentments of railroad exactions, and they let their representatives know it. Major cities had a vested interest in breaking the Southern Pacific's exclusive hold.

It was no longer simply a matter of third-party agitation. California's mainstream parties had tapped into resentments of railroad exactions ever since the Civil War. Then, in the mid-1870s, the threat from the sideshow organizations put new steel into the Democratic attack, or at any rate gave Democrats fresh incentives to propose cures to "the great financial cancer." Rousing working-class crowds to fever pitch in the vacant lots of San Francisco, Denis Kearney turned fury against the railroads, the Chinese workers they had imported, and the two mainstream parties that so obediently did their will. For a while, the gentry on Nob Hill trembled at "sand-lot" orators' threats to settle their grievances against the companies with nooses and revolvers. (Residents in California's many Chinatowns had far more reason to tremble, and for years, both parties paid their down payment on antimonopoly sentiments by promising more brutal laws to cut the "Celestials" out of jobs, close them off from America, and send them packing. The remedy was cheap and effective: the Chinese had no votes.) By 1879, the Sandlotter and Workingmen's Party of California had bent both parties in a radical direction. Out of a five-month constitutional convention came a document giving the government explicit power to control the railroads. As the Workingmen's Party vanished, agitation for a forceful regulatory commission became Democrats' fighting cause—literally. In 1884, the state convention put through such intense antimonopoly resolutions that railroad apologists walked out and helped elect Republicans that fall.[27]

Elsewhere, even where railroads controlled party machinery, they could not quell dissent in party ranks. Let the *Omaha Republican* preach Union Pacific gospel; more Nebraskans read the *Bee*, with its stinging attacks on monopoly, and corporation money could not keep the *Republican* from eventually going broke. Nor could it keep an open enemy of the railroads out of the senate in 1881. True, James Van Wyck, mocked as "Crazy Horse" by conservative reporters, looked like a fluke. He got one term and no more. But what may have been most revealing was how embarrassing a job the railroad executives found it to make the legislature retire the senator at the end of six years. Taking advantage of a provision in the state constitution, Van Wyck had invited the voters to cast a preferential ballot for senator. He had won it easily, forcing the legislature to flout the expressed popular will.[28]

That heroic efforts were needed to stifle popular politics even in so Republican a state as Nebraska showed how dangerous it would be for mainstream parties to ignore the clamor against railroad "monopolists." Two years later, Republicans felt hard enough pressed to stick promises of reform into their platform. Within the year, the legislature had broken the promises. But the price was the

Republicans' near loss of the state in 1890, and then the party's survival came only by its surrender to the friends of regulation.

That price mainstream politicians generally were not prepared to pay. As has already been noted, mainstream Minnesota politics always involved a certain amount of containment of forces that endangered not just the railroad interests but the political leadership. By the 1880s, the state had little trouble putting through a welter of regulatory laws, including ones strengthening the railroad commission. To railroad apologists, the commission was effective enough to rank as a positive nuisance. By its power to expose and publicize, it extracted an 8 percent rate reduction from the railroads; how very unlike the Dakota Territory Commission, the *St. Paul Dispatch* thought—those "nice, agreeable, Christian people" who knew "how to approach a railroad company" with a request! In 1887, the state went still further, giving the railroad commission the power to decide what a reasonable rate was and to impose it on the companies—which the United States Supreme Court overturned in 1890 as a denial of due process.[29]

Railroads had won this round and many to follow, but it took the highest tribunal to temper powers given to the state.[30] As gatekeeper for the railroads' interests, the legislature had become an utter failure. Indeed, the Minnesota law showed how far regulation was meant not for show but for effective action. Elsewhere, the same pattern held true. Try as they might, railroads could not stifle regulatory passions. They could hold off radical reform of their freight rates, but they in return had to give way on passenger fares. The price for a sympathetic commission usually was cooperation in producing statistics when called for and in obliging the regulators with recommended changes. But commissions could not be counted on to stay sympathetic, and weak ones only encouraged demagogues to ride into power on the promise of stronger panaceas.[31]

No one would pretend that the laws in Minnesota or elsewhere had put railroads under complete control. Effective regulation was a thing of shreds and patches in some places and an iridescent dream in others. Precisely because elected politicians could never be wholly trusted, the corporations threw their reliance on the courts, and quite possibly some of their legislative friends may have cloaked themselves as railroad regulators, knowing that friendly judges would undo any statute they placed on the books.[32] But regulation did happen, even in California, where many a politician by 1890 found the Southern Pacific collar more like a halter the moment voters saw it for what it was. Even in New Jersey, the railroad interests found their victories costly. Elect Blodgett to the senate though they might, they did so only as a desperate throw to keep out one of their more outspoken and most effective enemies, Governor Leon Abbett. In his first term, he had pushed through a ban on convict labor, regulations for the sale of oleomargarine, and, most alarmingly of all, a tax law shifting more of the burden to the corporations. That the railroads had not been able to keep him from winning the governorship in 1883 showed how limited their power was; their second lesson came when Abbett picked his own successor and kept Blodgett from getting the nomination. Corporations got their third lesson three years later, when Abbett won reelection, and in 1893, he came within a hair of succeeding Blodgett in the senate — and Blodgett himself was so sure of defeat that he had taken himself out of the running months before.[33]

From the railroad issue, a larger lesson about the making of economic policy in the Gilded Age stands out clearly. Republican and Democratic leaders may have been inclined to oblige business where "progress" or "prosperity" seemed at stake, but they were readiest to do favors in the dark, in committee rooms where no responsibility could fall on the great mass of legislators for deeds done, or on the floor where newspaper publicity and constituent pressure had not drawn attention to a measure. Out in the open, where voters were paying attention, the mainstream parties were too dependent on their constituents to be relied on by any one set of corporate interests. They kept their near monopoly on power by responding to the demands they heard. Sometimes they made a sham fight; often, no doubt, they embraced the lesser reform in hopes of weakening demand for the greater: regulation rather than public ownership, a rate-revising commission rather than a rate-setting one. Still, the fights they made within their own ranks showed that a large minority of Democrats in California, Mississippi, and Florida would carry their party to defeat rather than surrender it outright to the monopolists; in Iowa and Minnesota, Republican leaders made real advances to the railroads' opponents, at the cost of political harmony; and in New Hampshire, Colorado, and Nebraska, they fought losing battles, but fought them hard.[34] Van Wyck would be back, as a Farmer's Alliance candidate and then as a Populist. Lawmakers scored small but real victories.

For all these reasons, a serious third-party challenge based on antimonopoly leanings always had an uphill fight. Wherever a competitive two-party system allowed one side to appeal to the railroads' victims, disgruntled voters could take their resentments to the mainstream politicians and expect results. But the politicians expected results, too, and got them: the perpetuation of two-party control in a world of challengers.

Class Warfare, Mainstream-Party Style

"While I have a kind feeling for the laborer, I do not respect him," Ohio's retired radical gadfly Donn Piatt growled. "He is as stupid, ignorant and vicious as the rest of us. The confounded fools, holding the power of reform in their hands, not only consent to oppression, but actually put and fasten the yoke upon their own necks." To those convinced that the new economic order had gone radically wrong, that certainly seemed the case. Amid the mines, mills, and sweatshops, somewhere, Gilded Age voters should have created a serious challenge to the propertied and powerful. And, indeed, the late nineteenth century was littered with two-bit tempests against monopoly and the Money Power. Minor parties elected a cluster of congressmen and occasionally a governor or two and threw regular scares into the two major parties. But if they were always rising, they also were always dying.[1] Surely a powerful, lasting third party with an ideal based on social justice should have developed. What went wrong?

As this book suggests, the whole shape of the American political universe made organizing and keeping up a third-party challenge unusually difficult. Laws and institutions rewarded majorities, not pluralities, and shaped representation to suit the major parties' agenda. The expense of hoopla politics and of paying election-day costs made a minor party movement easiest to build at the local level, and it put statewide, much less national, victories very nearly out its reach. Counting the cost of printing and distributing ballots alone, any worker's movement would get a better return out of organizing a shop floor than mobilizing a neighborhood. Indeed, the very places where mobilizing working-class action could be done the easiest, downtown, was where electioneering cost the most.

Other historians have pointed out that as the industrial system grew more sophisticated in the late nineteenth century, policy making drifted further from campaign politics. Reformers tried to reserve sensitive matters for boards of professionals. These, not lawmakers, would set railroad rates or decide what a fair tariff duty would be; experts would run parks, libraries, and police departments, safe from scrambles for election or demands to share their perquisites with the ward heelers who put them into positions of authority. Needing a constant, well-informed, and consistent presence at the center of power, businesses started putting lobbying agencies on permanent salary and laid by money for influencing public opinion. Political debate could still point in a general direction — toward railroad regulation, say, or tougher liquor laws — but pressure groups and figures with expert knowledge would work out the details in the agencies and legislate in consultation with those who had the power to write the laws.[2]

Yet this explanation explains too little. Certainly the essentials of economic legislation remained with those who drafted the laws and with the pressure groups of those most particularly interested, but that was true of every kind of legislation. Politics could and often did offer general directions and define basic remedies needed. In terms of its realization into concrete action, the political system was just as vague in answering the demands of cultural and ethnic groups precisely as it was the economic ones. Yet mainstream- and third-party politics throve on cultural issues, and a Prohibition Party outlasted all the economic outsider movements, ever controversial but incessantly troublesome to the two major parties. What, then, explained the apparent failure to develop a class-based political alternative?

Those who spoke for Democrats and Republicans would have answered by turning the question on its head: a large class-based party failed to develop not because something in the system went wrong but because it went right. Formed as they were, the two major parties made a permanent alternative party unnecessary by making at least the down payment on reforms demanded, enough to allay discontent or at any rate to confine it to an unprivileged few. Class-based politics, like culturally informed politics, had been there all along. It was not the crazy aunt in the attic of whom the family tries to deny the existence. Quite the reverse: it was a regular and often pampered guest. Bosses, boodle, ballyhoo, blackguarding, and bribery made it hard for a third party to compete on equal terms; the accommodation of its mainstream contenders to class resentments was what made it impossible.

That answer certainly was self-interested, and it overlooked the obvious point: that without those outsider movements, the mainstream parties would have had far less motivation to address issues disquieting to the well-heeled and well-satisfied membership in their ranks. Even so, the answer may not have been wrong. Mainstream politics did not simply ignore class politics. It absorbed it and channeled the resentments. The two great parties adapted their programs to draw the malcontents, and they succeeded not just because of their own cunning but because the leading principles of the parties were broad enough to carry them some distance down the road that their minor-party challengers wanted to go. Far from simply blinding a working-class electorate with phony issues, Republicans and Democrats made themselves the voices, if less commonly, the agents, of social change.

From both parties, of course, came a constant stream of argument that either belittled or denied that America had any basis for class-oriented parties. Editors and scholars argued that in a wholly free political system, there were no classes, or, at least, none that mattered. Where everyone had the vote, everyone had equal power to shape the society through his ballot or protect himself from injury.[3] Anyone with skills could rise, and everyone who deserved to did. The moguls of today might be the mendicants of tomorrow, while bobbin-boys at a Scottish textile loom might live to own castles in the Highlands and steel furnaces at Homestead. Workers doubting it should read Andrew Carnegie's *Triumphant Democracy*, one of Chicago's Republican magnates insisted. Even the poorest of them could afford it: let him "stop beer for two weeks or less, and invest the savings."[4] Where class lines could never harden, class conflict itself had no meaning. Anyone could escape the injuries of class by working up and out of that class. The cure lay not at the polling-booth window but at the schoolhouse door and on the pages of the regularly updated savings bankbook.

Most Americans' rise came in far more modest steps than in a Horatio Alger rags-to-riches saga. For many, the rise came so unobtrusively that they missed it completely. But politics offered its own constant examples until what might seem the exceptional case looked like the natural progress of any good boy deserving favor in an aspiring civilization. Biographical cyclopedias of various counties were crammed with stories of farmers' sons who achieved high position through hard labor and honest dealings, apprentices who came to town with only two shillings in their pockets or fought the battle of life friendless, "single-handed and alone." Politicians prided themselves on their humble beginnings. Very likely some tried to portray them as humbler than they were. When the Democratic Party of Connecticut nominated Judge Luzon B. Morris for governor in 1890, supporters glided over his eminence on the bench. They descanted instead on the "farmer's boy, blacksmith, tool-maker, Yale student, and lawyer, self-supporting ever since he left the farm, as a lad." "He was not born with a silver spoon in his mouth," the *Nashua Telegraph* assured voters of Hiram Tuttle, New Hampshire's gubernatorial nominee that same year, "and he carries himself not as above every man." These were not simply publicists' conceits. Training voters' eyes backward to a candidate's origins, the politicians might keep them from reflecting that Tuttle was a bank president and railroad director nominated for his money.[5] There was another point. Party scribes were selling Morris and Tuttle as common clay (and, incidentally, as the antithesis of a professional politician). But they were also implying that a person's origin defined him thereafter. To have sympathies with the working class, a public figure did not need to be one of them; he only needed to have served time in their ranks, and his mind would be impressed with the ideals, the fears, the aspirations, the interests that they held dear.

Probably those who looked back on the hard grind were likelier to assume that such a rise *could* be done, that it was within the reach of all. Few were about to credit luck, chance, or accident with their advance. Success was due to character, possibly even to pedigree. It would be only natural for society's successes to feel that the system as it stood was a good one, needing only modest tinkering. For readers, the real message about Morris may not have been that he began humbly but that the very qualities permitting his rise made him fit for high office. Indeed, the very concept of the spoils system drove home the idea that rewards went to the deserving. Anyone reading the countless letters asking for patronage could see how deeply the applicants rooted their case in work accomplished and their worthiness for advancement. (And, by contrast, they would note how the tiny fraction of the whole from woman applicants based their request on need, pity, and the role of men as protectors to the helpless. In their own way, they reinforced the connection between business, politics, striving, and manhood — and the separate functions and sphere of womankind.)

That faith in self-help, an exhortation to aspire and achieve, and the promise that rewards would come, was one familiar to all of the American working class, and to many it seemed to ring true. Labor magazines promised the same: with a full, fair system, diligence, sobriety, and good habits would leave the competent with more than a competence. Still, it did not take a labor journalist like John Swinton to tell factory hands that however hard people worked, as the system had developed by the 1880s, it took exceptional abilities or unusual luck to make a millhand into a Morris. Beyond the bromides on the editorial page and the puffery of patricians on page one, any big-city newspaper gave regular evidence of class injustice and what looked very much like class warfare, of shootings in the coalfields and the stoning of strikebreakers, of lockouts, of starving seamstresses, and of pale-faced eight-year-old girls working barefoot at the cotton spindles of Baltic, Connecticut, for ten to fifteen cents for twelve hours' work. Even as preachers in splendid churches told their listeners that everyone lived in comfort in

1888, New York City's dailies reported that 20,000 spent Thanksgiving dinner eating "the bread of charity at public tables."[6]

Neither party could get by entirely on a denial that class conflicts existed. When discontent grew loud enough, they had to admit that there was something wrong somewhere. Every so often, both parties would break into war chants against wealthy malefactors, and each was likelier to do so against wrongdoers in the opposite party, if the other side had raised the subject first.[7] Still, class consciousness within the mainstream parties did not just spring up at expedient moments. It was embedded in the guiding principles of both parties, ready to be taken forth when occasion called for it.

How it was used, generally, and what it said about capitalism itself, differed. Republicans were inclined to feel that all classes could be made to work in harmony, that with the right legislation, employer and employee would benefit alike. Ideally, a business shared its prosperity with pleasanter work conditions and higher wages. Class warfare, Republicans emphasized, only brought on the injury of both; paternal treatment by those in charge and a respect for the talents and judgment of their superiors by those in the workforce could only ensure a less disruptive economy.[8]

Republicans were most inclined to believe that class resentments were a token of a good economic system somehow gone a little out of kilter and that government action fostering development would set all to rights. Still, they were willing to admit that the system did get imbalanced; it needed constant recalibration — one reason why the tariff never could be let alone. A belief that all classes could and should work for the common good, that everyone could gain and nobody lose, did not keep Republicans from admitting that there were such things as monopolies, or that something should be done about their power. But it did treat talk of class injustice as essentially aberrant, a sign that the economic system was not working under its normal conditions.

Some Democrats thought that way, too. Especially in moments of economic disorder, editors who gave theoretical support to workers would come down against strikes, insist on the breadth of opportunity and the sacredness of free contract and the need for managers and laborers to discover the common interest that they both had — usually on the ground that managers had set, where a regard for the public peace and employees' duties mattered most.[9]

But other Democrats did not think that way at all. They saw permanently divergent, irreconcilable interests. One group's gain came at another's loss. No positive working of the system could bridge the chasm between workers and man-

PROMISE AND PERFORMANCE.

BEFORE ELECTION.—Of some consequence. Well taken care of.　　AFTER ELECTION.—"Hey, look out for yourself!"

"Promise and performance. Before election.— Of some consequence. Well taken care of. After election.—'Hey, look out for yourself!'" (F. Graetz, *Puck*, October 15, 1884). Republican candidates James G. Blaine and John Logan are suckering the worker, but the Democratic candidates might have been transposed in the driver's seat with equal justice.

agers. To these Democrats, the problem was not in a system gone wrong but in the system itself. Conflict and competing interests were its natural state. For this reason, no government action could be taken that would not work an injury; and because those with economic influence were likeliest to define any policy made to suit their own ends, laissez-faire voices in the party were especially chary about government acting at all, and convinced from the first that those injured would outnumber those benefited.[10] Workers needed remedies that business would have to pay for, and sacrifices that would make employers poorer were the only way of making employees richer.

Even the most populist Democratic politicians were capitalists in the largest sense: that when they had the money to afford it, they looked for gain. They saw nothing wrong in that. People should earn, save, and invest. But in many Democrats' vision of capitalism, there was also a sense that without constant oversight, the system's biggest winners would have vices that were the exaggeration of their virtues. Business would be selfish, predatory, and shortsighted, in ways that Republicans could not understand. "Whenever I walk through the streets of that Democratic importing city of New York and look at the brownstone fronts, my gorge always rises," Maine congressman Thomas Brackett Reed drawled. "I can never understand why the virtue which I know is on the sidewalk, is not thus rewarded. I do not feel kindly to the people inside. But when I feel that way I know what the feeling is. It is good, honest, high-minded envy. When some other gentlemen [meaning Democrats] have the same feeling they think it's political economy."[11]

Political economy, for many Democrats, was the story of how the owners of those brownstones—not to mention the Park Avenue palaces—had got there, by taxing it out of the wage earners in the cold-water flats and unpainted farmhouses. Government had skewed opportunity to increase the power of the privileged, with land grants for railroads, bounties for shipbuilders, tax breaks, tariffs, and special charters and privileges for national banks. By the 1880s, these constituted the basis for the new economic order. As radicals in and outside the party warned, the concentration of money in the hands of the "Pig Iron Princes and Coal Kings" had brought a new political order into being, one where the people had less say in what government did. The magic word, the one that tied Democratic language tightest to the class-based parties of the Gilded Age, was "monopoly," which in its broad political meaning was any amount of undue private power. A railroad that dominated local markets was a monopoly, even if in theory wagons could haul goods in and out on the country roads. A firm that employed more people than any other in the town was a monopoly; a company with the muscle to set an extortionate price in the marketplace was a monopoly. Most often, the term came to rest on railroad corporations or banks, and on one man in particular, Jay Gould, the infamous Wall Street speculator and builder of railroad empires, who, by the mid-1880s had taken the lead in union-busting.[12]

Gould made a suspiciously easy target. His early career had been infamous. Even respectable business figures had denounced him. He stood apart from other employers with his reputation as a wrecker, not a builder, a manipulator of shares' value rather than the creator of value. Polemicists never forgot his statement that his railroad was Democratic in Democratic states and Republican in Republican ones and his reputed boast that he could hire half the working class to shoot down the other half. No election year would be complete without allegations that Gould's money was buying soap for New York, or that he was "working the railroads" in the Midwest. Still, having exposed him again and again, Democrats offered no proposals for crimping his plans, except to put his Republican friends out of power and themselves in. Workers didn't want the Goulds gibbeted, a labor paper pointed out; they wanted laws "that will make Jay Goulds impossible."[13] Could the whole Democratic antimonopoly cry be equally hollow?

Obviously, the real test of class rhetoric should not be what the parties said but what they did or promised to do. Results were far more mixed and, to true believers in the Labor Party alternative, a mess of makeshift devices, cheats, and gilded lures. "The Democratic party has been remarkably true to its trust," one insurgent joked, "— the Sugar Trust, the Coal Trust, the Iron Trust, and all other 'Trusts.'"[14]

Accommodation to the insurgents varied. The easiest was to hand them a token as proof of good faith and a possible substitute for concrete action to come. In that respect, the ideal was to embody the protesting group in a mainstream party's choice of nominees. If the farmers seemed angry, Democrats could prove their own good intentions simply by nominating a farmer, even one as far removed from the well-turned furrow as Luzon Morris was from the blacksmith's forge. So in 1888, with a farmers' revolt stirring the Arkansas electorate, Democrats put up a man who, according to his apologists, when it "came to actual labor performed" had "higher claims on the laboring classes . . . than a whole cowpen" of agrarian nominees. Touted as "thoroughly [representing] . . . the farmer interests of the state," James P. Eagle was a part-time planter who let his tenants walk behind the plow and whose understanding of farmers' grievances was summed up by his assertion that Arkansas "was never in a more prosperous condition" than at present — something any farmer could have disputed. He saw no need for ballot reform or national aid to education, nor for restrictions on foreign corporations hoarding the land. In the end, Eagle promised farmers nothing, and, after being counted in, delivered it.[15]

Parties' willingness to fob off discontented groups with something symbolic, rather than palpable change, came from more complex forces than the hand of monopoly. It was perfectly true that the parties needed money to keep going, but they needed votes still more. When farmers or trade unions could prove their ability to deliver more than just their officers, the parties responded, welcoming organizations' support and working to earn it. But delivery was a chancy thing in an age when party fealty had so many sources beyond pocketbook interest and all it took was a few loud dissidents (well paid for, perhaps, by the other party) to turn an official endorsement into a hollow honor. Still, the greatest restraining force on radical action was the politician's ingrained fear of risk. The Hippocratic rule applied in altered form to any party aspiring for power: "First, do no harm — to yourself." Any policy that was likely to breed disaffection stood a real chance of costing more than it gained.

Radical changes might well have a constituency inside the party. That was what made third-party challenges all the more worrisome: their potential for drawing away votes that mainstream party managers had always been able to bank on. But addressing this problem had its own element of danger. Redress the Prohibitionists' grievances, and temperance's true believers in GOP ranks would be more than gratified; they would be reinforced with former members of the Prohibition Party. The balance of power between factions would shift, and with it the chances of factional fighting would intensify. Any change in emphasis on the issues would provoke battles, disaffection, walkouts, bad tempers, and worse morale. For all these reasons, every new policy initiative needed to be tied into party tradition, and every new step needed to be tried in a gingerly way. Putting an Irish Catholic on the ticket was a much safer concession, say, than promising to share public funds with parochial schools.[16]

From pragmatists' point of view, a major party's remedies ranged from the ideal to the barely tolerable, depending on the element of risk involved. In the best of all political worlds, the party could satisfy class demands without changing a thing but rhetoric. It would simply offer its policies as a true panacea. It did not take much repackaging.

This was not as fraudulent as it might sound. Both parties really did believe that tariff rates and immigration restrictions would affect workers' fortunes every bit as much as legislation regulating wages and hours. Shut out cheap foreign imports, Republicans insisted, and America shut out cheap foreign labor's competition. Wages would rise, or at least be prevented from falling to the starvation levels of Malays and Manchester textile-spinners. Even radical labor movements like the Knights of Labor agreed that a high tariff, if not the ultimate solution, made an indispensable beginning, just as the restrictions on the sale of goods made by convict labor and the importation of pauper workers on contract from abroad made a good start to any effort to lay a wage-floor below which domestic employers could not descend.[17] A case could even be made that sound-money policies, keeping the currency from inflating and tightening credit, was, in the end, to workers' best interest. They were hurt if bondholders were hurt; when banks went broke, savings accounts went with them; if the financial system could not trust to the value of a dollar, if Congress printed fiat money, unbacked by gold or silver, the economic depression would hit hardest those whose financial security rested most completely in the hands of others, the employees of corporations and the day laborers on construction projects that financial insecurity had made impossible.[18]

That mixture of party tradition and attentiveness to labor's unrest helps explain Democrats' use of the Chinese issue. Having discovered the benefits of race-baiting against the "Black Republican" Party before the war, they found negrophobia an indispensable weapon after the war. Picking on the Chinese seemed like a natural extension, or, perhaps, a potential replacement. By 1870, it was clear that blacks would have the vote and not so clear that white southern Democrats could take it away from them. As the Fifteenth Amendment neared ratification, party leaders realized that the price of their own favorite kind of race-baiting were about to soar. Invective against the "black vomit" could lose votes. On the West Coast, Democrats' constituency cared far less about the blacks they never saw than about the Chinese track-layers and fishermen that they did, and, as party managers must have noticed, Chinese could not vote. A cost-free appeal to prejudice that fit in with party tradition became even more tempting when Republicans lost their political edge in 1874. All at once, Oregon, Nevada, Colorado, and California could swing a national election, if they voted right, and hatred there for the "Celestials" ran strong. Before 1880, campaign parades marched under the glow of Chinese lanterns. After the publication of Garfield's "Morey" letter, they became "Japanese."[19]

The invective against the Chinese was not race prejudice pure and simple; race prejudice is never pure and rarely simple. Its hold in California was strongest among workers who saw Chinese labor as a more immediate threat to their livelihoods than "monopoly" in general. Chinese labor took less pay for work that whites had done. Since most immigrants from across the Pacific came without wife or child, they could afford to. Employers brought in job-lots of "coolies," submissive and ready to work on terms of near slavery. What, then, would happen to the Irish drayman and common laborer? Starving times and company lockouts in the 1870s told them that well enough. Not surprisingly, the Workingmen's Party of Dennis Kearney, the loudest voice in California against the railroad kings and privileged orders, directed its resentments at the Chinese. Kearney might talk of storming the mansions of the mighty and teaching the tycoons at a halter's end, but his Sand-Lotters took out their fury on the powerless but equally threatening Chinese. There was more than race prejudice in the stereopticon motto thrown across a building's wall in Jersey City, "Rice and Rats will not Support American Labor if it does Chinese Laundry-Keepers."[20]

Less ideal, but still within the bounds of reason, a party could incorporate into its message policies for which some, but not all, of the rank and file had been agitating. A protectionist Republican Party might listen most clearly to its tariff reformers and make its greatest concessions to them in a year when the public was making much of "monopoly" and high taxes. Leaders might discover the prime importance, after long neglect, of a contract-labor law, or restrictions on Chinese immigration, or a law against alien landownership. But, here again, the risks of actual division in one's own party from adopting new policies would increase, and the costs on the local level in some states might well rise to prohibitive levels. Even a modest swipe at tariff reform enraged Ohio's wool growers in 1883. What was saloon legislation to them if they were ruined by the lower price that a reduction on the wool schedule allowed? It was in the sheep-producing counties and not just among the German city-dwellers defending their liberty to lift a stein on Sundays that Republicans lost their votes.[21]

Taking up ideas that originated in a third party was riskier still. Then polemicists would need to find some way of rationalizing it to their followers, by tying it into the sacred party texts, with Lincoln, Jefferson, Andrew Jackson, and Adam Smith. The harder this was to do, the more danger that members of the mainstream party would revolt, declaring that, far from their seceding from the party of their fathers, the party was seceding from them.

Least acceptable of all would be the adoption of policies that flew in the face of essential party tradition and violated the most cardinal premises of the party program. One could do it; one could argue that necessity or changed social and economic conditions compelled a shift in outlook. Party leaders could swallow the most outlandish notions, pleading the need to win. But such a conversion experience came rarely, if at all.

In producing a program and in making concessions, then, mainstream parties gave as little as they could afford and conceded as little ground as possible. When picking out planks from the third-party platforms, they plucked those with the greatest popular appeal and promised the least social and economic upheaval. Given a choice between government ownership of the banks and a subtreasury that issued government low-interest loans to farmers, Democrats would choose the subtreasury. Given the choice between setting up such a lending agency and returning to the time-worn policy of basing the money supply on silver as well as gold, they would adopt "free silver" readily.

Accommodation, therefore, always leaned in a conservative direction and toward party tradition. Mainstream parties were likeliest to embrace those reforms with some support among the propertied. That was not only because the parties were beholden to the well-heeled. Support for reform among propertied men gave an excellent cover for radical action. Money defined a man as "safe," "respectable," and even conservative, where his views might not. But it also followed that any successful party had to rely on support from all classes and divergent interests, not just one. A party of farmers alone could not even win in Iowa, unless all farmers thought in terms of their occupational interests only, and farmers just did not think like that, any more than industrial workers did. Some framed their political outlook in a church doorway and voted as Catholic, Lutheran, or Methodist, putting the kingdom of God ahead of the republic of plowhands. Others voted with their eyes on the swinging door of the saloon. Not a few of them limped to the polls, keenly aware that Democratic Rebels had given them the scars that they would bear lifelong.[22] A party based on one class was sure to perish, unless voters in that class identified themselves in no other way when they came up to the voting booth. So any party had to create an appeal that might draw those who saw their interests in terms of class, occupation, or economic condition but would not turn away those who saw matters differently. It added to the Australian ballot's attractiveness that labor parties made it an article of their faith, but no major party was going to adopt it until they could find respectable men, those of education and property, to swell their ranks.[23]

Against all the countervailing forces, the best spur to class-based two-party politics was a robust third party and a crowd of voters ready to break ranks to crowd into it. The greater the threat, the more the major parties were willing to adapt, to win votes never theirs and to keep those that they were in danger of losing. Adapt they did, and they hated it. They resented pressure politics, and editors railed against special interest organizations that threatened to take their votes elsewhere or put their support for the two major parties up for bidding. Newspapers had nothing but contempt for "political" farmers, "the farmers who farm with their mouths."[24]

Still, given the choice, mainstream parties preferred the strategy of "nonpartisanship," where a group chose between the two parties' nominees to a separate party. So, in 1870, Massachusetts Republicans were entirely relieved when the supporters of woman suffrage chose not to endorse the Labor Reform ticket or to launch a ticket of their own. But, they insisted, it was also best for the suffrage movement itself. As the *Springfield Republican* explained, "The unobjectionable course for the Tremont Temple convention to take would seem to be, to appoint a committee to memorialize the state conventions of the two great parties, and to catechize the candidates after their nomination, leaving every voter free to support whoever he preferred, after learning the views of all on the woman suffrage question." Unobjectionable it certainly would have been — to Republicans. With only two choices available and Democrats refusing to concede a thing, no Republican candidate needed to commit himself to anything more than expressing his goodwill.

Quite a different reaction greeted the Labor Reform Party in Massachusetts that same fall. Disaffection had grown there as the labor movement burgeoned in the late 1860s. Now Labor Reformers chose a formidable figure to lead them, one who could appeal to other disgruntled constituencies, including former abolitionists and temperance advocates. For a generation, Wendell Phillips had been the great human trumpet of antislavery and Irish home rule. Phillips made an aggressive, name-calling campaign, and Republicans called names right back. Old friends who knew better called him a front-man for railroad monopolies, a lifelong coward and fake, the leader of "repudiatiors, proscriptionists," strikers, bigots, and communists, the candidate of "idle & noisy men & women, whose maxims are of the most selfish and monopolizing sort & undeserving of respect." That November, Phillips barely budged his party's totals at all.[25]

What Republicans noticed, though, was the narrowness of their own margins. Democrats had tried to outbid Phillips with a labor platform of their own: attacks on a currency and tax system that burdened wage workers, and stage-thunder against "great monopolies" and the "swarms of Mongolians" imported to compete with white employees. With troublesome Labor Reform challenges in New Hampshire and Connecticut and flickering disaffection elsewhere, the majority party would have to supplement its harsh words for class-war demagogues with concessions. In Massachusetts, for the first time, lawmakers took seriously the idea of child-labor legislation and restrictions on the hours that women could be forced to work. Already they had created evening schools for children over the age of twelve and set up the tuition-free Worcester County Free Institute for Industrial Science. In Congress, George Frisbie Hoar of Massachusetts proposed a bill setting up a national commission to look into labor conditions. He found the Congress of 1872 an unusually sympathetic audience. The House passed such a bill by four to one, and the Senate made a token show of interest, at least until the Labor Reform convention proved to amount to little or nothing; then it roused the courage to kill the measure. But Congress did revise the tariff to make a duty-free breakfast table, by removing the tariff on coffee, tea, and sugar. It also put through a broad measure protecting merchant seamen from mulcting and abuse. Congressman Henry L. Dawes of Massachusetts pushed through a bill reimbursing federal workers for pay lost by the failure of the administration to interpret the 1868 eight-hour law properly. No change of heart made the members so solicitous. They looked to the potential threat of a national Labor Reform Party, which, however little it amounted to in the end, was of indeterminate strength. When the Republican National Convention met, it left it to Wendell Phillips and S. P. Cummings of the Knights of St. Crispin to write the labor plank; not by chance the "father of the eight-hour law," Henry Wilson, became the new vice presidential nominee. And just to be on the safe side, the Republicans held a special workingmen's convention that nominated their ticket.[26]

Third-party pressure worked, then. Given the fear of organized labor throwing its strength elsewhere, mainstream politicians were willing to put "class legislation" on the books. Pressure-group politics that had a large constituency could make "nonpartisanship" work far better than it had in Massachusetts with woman suffrage advocates. Still, there was nothing like a sideshow party in a closely contested state to make the two mainstream parties put in bids for its potential supporters. Not by chance, Democrats and Republicans alike discovered a pressing need for laws protecting workers' safety and ensuring the payment of wages in cash at the very moment that the Knights of Labor and the United Labor Party seemed to be making a breakthrough into national politics in 1886.[27]

All this might suggest that the parties gave way to insurgents' demands only when they had to, and when the fear of defeat for doing otherwise loomed before them: the cynical co-opting of radical movements' least radical program, to be dropped when the political pressure let up. That certainly happened sometimes. Let the Granger movement abandon politics, and midwestern states were more inclined to gut their railroad regulation and politicians were likelier to make "progress," not fairness, their goal — a goal which untrammeled enterprise seemed surest to attain. Many bills were offered purely for bunkum.[28] Yet not simply fear but hope drove the mainstream parties to push for legislation. Within their own ranks were leaders who supported "class legislation," not for the votes it would gain, but for the votes it would hold, and because it fit with party doctrine, as their constituents defined it. Always there were party leaders looking for some common interest with outside parties, not only to add votes to their own side, but to reinforce those of a like mind with themselves within their own organization. Calculation drove Iowa Democrats into alliance with Greenbackers. By denouncing banks and railroad robbers, they could draw the votes to raise the Democracy beyond its status as a hopeless minority in the early 1880s.[29] But there had always been Democrats who heard that message, and in that alliance they saw the inevitable joining of natural friends.

What did the mixture of mainstream insurgency and expediency amount to on the statute books? Not as much as it might have if every good bill had gone through — or had been meant to pass in the first place. Proposing measures that sounded good and were sure to smother in committee was a cheap way to make a party's reputation and give it better credentials in the next election campaign. The limits and inadequacies of labor legislation in the Gilded Age cannot be explained away, nor could the mixture of calculation and bad faith with which some of the bills were offered, in the confidence that committees, governors, or judges would do the dirty work that representatives did not dare to do. A much more revealing measure of mainstream parties' commitment could be found in the bills they smothered, often producing something much less controversial as a substitute. New York's 1884 legislature showed its love for labor with laws limiting the hours for street railway drivers and conductors, forbidding cigar making in any tenement's family rooms, and outlawing convict contract labor. With much less fanfare, it defeated a state income tax, child-labor legislation, and a mechanic's lien law. A measure making eight hours a legal day's work was dismissed as "the nonsense of idlers and loafers," and another bill forbidding employers' blacklisting died summarily. Disgusted as one commentator was with such a "toad-eating body," he only knew half of it: Governor Grover Cleveland vetoed the drivers' bill and the courts killed the cigar-making law. Petitioning legislatures for "this or that beggarly measure of justice" seemed pointless, labor editor John Swinton complained. Most of the bills that went through would leave workers "little better off."[30]

But little was better than nothing, and some bills went beyond tokenism. For all the shibboleths of laissez-faire, lawmakers simply could not leave the economy to theorists, Yale professors, and the iron law of wages. In New Jersey, New York, and Maryland, Democrats in the 1880s repealed the laws that had allowed the prosecution of trade unions as conspiracies; in Illinois, a conspiracy law thrown onto the books with little opposition in the wake of the Haymarket bomb-throwing was repealed four years later with virtually no dissent. New Jersey even outlawed the yellow-dog contract in 1894. Democrats there enacted a comprehensive system of state arbitration, as well, though Republicans celebrated their return to power in 1895 by emasculating it. Factory inspectors were appointed in most industrial states, convict labor was forbidden to compete with free labor, and child-labor laws limited what jobs children could do, how many hours they could work, and under what conditions of safety.[31]

Admittedly, all too many labor laws, like piecrusts, seemed made to be broken and were no better than their enforcement—and there policy makers balked. With only one factory inspector for all New Jersey and penalties only for "willful" violators, there was not much chance of bringing malefactors to book. Children could not be "required" to clean moving machinery, but what child who wanted to keep his job would testify that he had acted under compulsion? Yet it was also true that token steps were taken over business resistance and had to face constant pressure in the future for their repeal. Even little steps could lead to bigger ones, as the regulated industries knew. With one factory inspector to publicize abuses, public demand could be built up to insist on the government hiring more. Even something as frail as a bureau of labor statistics, without the power to compel evidence from corporations or to summon witnesses, could lead to more concrete reforms. Pressed for by the Knights of Labor, the agency did not seem radical. A well-informed government afforded the best chance of wise legislation. But even with starveling powers, the members of Massachusetts' board managed to expose abuses and stir the legislature to act, regulating lodging houses and tenements, requiring fire escapes and improvements in ventilation. Bureau publicity helped pass stronger child-labor legislation and provide cheap commuter trains for the working class during morning and evening hours. By 1884, fourteen states had opened similar bureaus; seven years more, and the numbers had doubled.[32]

Workers, like anyone else, could be bought off for less than radical reform. As long as they had a number of demands, not all of them connected to their life on the shop floor, the parties were able to negotiate and maneuver, well aware that they could give some things and not others, and bring about satisfaction.

Why did workers settle for so little? A number of reasons stand out. One reason was that the labor movement, as in so many other things, was of two minds about the possibilities of activist government. The further outside the two-party system an insurgent was, the more he saw politicians at their worst. It was enough, at election time, to choose a worker for the city council or as mayor. A program that went no further than the promise to fire an unfriendly police chief was enough to mobilize workers in ways that a broader agenda never would; for working-class voters, like partisans in all classes, embraced the idea of vindicationist politics, where turning rascals out and sending the enemy a message was achievement enough.

Beyond that, the pathway faded or split into a dozen smaller and obscurer trails, like a paved road turning into a deer track in the woods. Socialists might embrace statist remedies, but other workers felt less certain, and those who hailed from Democratic ranks, where power was especially suspect, doubted most. As they saw it, the men who cheated and lied their way into office were the last ones who should be trusted with broader authority. Just possibly, one editor mused, the happiest country would be one where legislatures were only allowed to meet every thousand years — or never met at all. Any state able to do things for workers could do things to them, and, as countless interventions by troops to keep order on strikebreakers' behalf showed, often would. Amidst the cries for action on toilers' behalf, radicals described a republic in danger from usurpers and tyrants. Freedom was growing less, not more, and power lay in their enemies' hands. Labor editors like Andrew Cameron and radical gadflies like Ohio's Donn Piatt agreed: government could act to protect the producers, certainly, but its main duty was to remove the privileges it had given: abolish the national banking system and put the issuing of paper money into federal hands alone, perhaps, or protect the public domain from speculators and corporations and declare eight hours a legal day's work. Reminded that his plan for government-run railroads and telegraph lines would add to the bureaucracy, Henry George had the perfect answer. Enact his single tax, and it would shrink the officeholding class just as much! The whole mob of customs collectors and tax gatherers could be sent packing.[33]

For many workers, too, the cultural agendas of the mainstream parties were not simply a deterrent from real issues; they were the real issues. They saw themselves first and foremost as Irish, German, English, or Polish. Above all, they saw themselves as white, as threatened by black strikebreakers as by Chinese ones. Cultural issues did not just replace economic ones; they blended in with them. One could be a good Knight of Labor and feel that control of the saloons was vital. Intemperance broke the bank accounts and the families of employees, and, for those who put the need for creating one united movement of the producing classes ahead of moral reform, it meant trouble. If the Republican Party stood for controlling the saloon, a vote for the Republican ticket just might be the best way of raising the working class to the preeminence and respectability it deserved. On the other side, as the Prohibitionist labor leaders in Denver found, for many workers the effort to decree what they did with their leisure time was as unwelcome a control over a free people as any shop-floor ukase. Sooner than vote for Labor Party Dries, they would cast their votes with the Democrats.[34]

Reasons might be plentiful as blackberries. The plain fact, and one that insurgent movements always had to face, was that much of their electoral strength was on loan. Nonpartisan organizations that wanted a change in law or morals found the same. Never was the Women's Christian Temperance Union in such peril as when it endorsed the Prohibition Party. For five years, the organization faced a buffeting from the Republicans in its ranks, convinced that in embracing the impossible best party, the WCTU would only bring in the too-likely worst, throwing governorships and presidencies into the lap of the whiskey-soaked and rum-supported Democracy. Indeed, aligning the movement with any party, dissidents insisted, would make it political, its women trotting wherever the men who ran election campaigns chose to lead them. Commitment to the Republicans smashed Irish fraternal organizations; and commitment to the Democrats in 1884 tore wounds in the civil service reform movement that time never quite healed. The organizations did not exactly commit suicide, but they did themselves damage by underestimating the depth of their members' partisan commitment, and how far many issues, not just one, made them choose their political friends.

Whether from the sudden importance of other issues or the pressures of old party friends, movements promising much amounted to nothing. Granted the mainstream newspapers had more features and more sensations; there still should have been enough of a market to keep labor papers going from one year to the next. With a million working people, surely New York City had room for at least twenty journals "on this side of the fence," editor John Swinton pleaded in 1884. It hardly had room for one. Some readers would not even take labor papers for free, others would take it on no other terms, and still others would subscribe as long as they never had to pay. Swinton's own paper, nationally read, excellently written, and widely acclaimed, never made money. After four years and $40,000 of his own money, Swinton had to shut down.[35]

That same indifference showed even more palpably at the polls. Only the strongest assurances of labor support made Thomas Armstrong agree to run an independent race for governor in 1885. Sure enough, the editor of the *Pittsburgh Labor Tribune* found Pennsylvanians "boiling with enthusiasm" wherever he went. "It seemed as though the very grasshoppers jumped at the sound of his name." Then came election day. Having barely placed ahead of "scattering," Armstrong learned his lesson. When Labor Party organizers tendered him the nomination to Congress eight months later, Armstrong brushed them aside. "The experience of 'labor candidates' in New York would make good stuffing for a comic paper," Swinton wrote sourly in 1886. What good was a People's Party without people? Bitterly, its 1884 standard-bearer Benjamin Butler washed his hands of labor politics henceforth. "I thought the laborers of the new republic were more intelligent," he told a reporter. "They are not intelligent. . . . Nine out of ten of them would sell their votes for $2 apiece. I was a fool to think that this age was any different from any other."[36] He was right, of course, but not in the way he meant. Then and later, workers had sold their votes for much more: the recognition and occasional support of the mainstream parties. In its flexibility when confronted with demands for change, the late party age was indeed no different from any other.

Rounding off the Two and a Half Party System

The Treason of the Ineffectuals

The golden age of the two-party system was a silver age for third and fourth parties. They were never wholly absent, and their potential strength affected how Democrat and Republican made their own appeals. But the one thing a historian may notice first about the outsiders is not the exultation at fighting a righteous cause. Rather, it is the bitterness and resentment spent on each other. In their suspicions lay a clue to the continued dominance of the two major parties and an illustration of how that dominance warped every political organization outside its bounds.

Does anything really need explaining? Every movement breeds its opportunists. The more inexperienced the insurgents, the easier a mark for men on the make they were likely to be. At the sound of the first chink of a coin in the presidential candidate's purse in 1884, the People's Party suddenly found more would-be friends than it knew what to do with, all ready to lend a hand—or, at any rate, with a hand out. "Here were howling orators, bursting with eloquence," one true believer recalled,

> organizers impatient for the harness—"managers" of all degrees of sharpness,—leaders of the gangs that "work the growler,"—high cockalorums of countless clubs,—candidates anxious about their districts,—editors leaner than Job's turkey,—confidence men always on the wink—insiders who knew

a thing or two—martyrs beyond number—influential intriguers whose strength lay in their tongues, wire-pullers deep as a ditch, and twice as thick,—old "war-horses" of the aged People's party [then a few months old],—cranks of the double-twisted variety,—fellows who were "in with the boss,"—strategists, statesmen, old sojers, committeemen, friends of the family, and so on to the end of the chapter. In short, a crew turned up such as never manned any Chinese junk that ever sailed over the Yellow Sea.

Still, who better than pirates to serve the reputed pirate-king of American politics? Never slow to help his friends pry open the Treasury, almost perversely eager to defend bribe givers and congressional back-pay grabs, former general Ben Butler had never been happier than when making public office pay or offending the respectable Brahmins of Beacon Hill and Harvard Yard.[1] This time, rightly, Democrats charged that Butler made Republicans do the paying; without a regular subsidy to his presidential candidacy, the People's Party would call off its campaign, letting an uncounted number of erstwhile Democrats drift back to their old allegiances, delivering crucial northeastern states to Grover Cleveland, the Democratic nominee.[2]

Outcry against "rings" and "conspiracies," assertions of base motives by erstwhile allies also were the common coin of party rhetoric. Democrats and Republicans complained about traitors in their midst all the time. It enforced party discipline; those who moved out of step must be "knocked down with the ragged edge of the bludgeon" as a warning to all the rest. The mind-set that fixed so much of politics into a conspiratorial framework almost naturally spotted the "true inwardness" in every deviance from the party line. Editors explained every rebellion in personal terms. "Soreheads" or "disappointed office-seekers" had raised a ruckus because they had been denied their ambitions. Neglected spoilsmen were only masking their grievances in principle. Partisans loosing their moorings had equally strong reasons for accusing the party from which they came of having changed its moral character.[3]

Even so, major parties seemed to do a better job of controlling their internal quarrels than minor parties did. A passion for divisiveness seemed to be built into most of the agrarian and labor challenges of the Gilded Age and, as their chances of winning elections became more hopeless, the same condition ravaged Republican parties down south. "Adulterous drunkards and gamblers," "the lowest element in southern politics, the Carpet-baggers and the Rum element": no Democrat could have described South Carolina Republicans more forcibly than former Republican congressman Robert Smalls did. It was a standing joke that Alabama Republican leaders, driven from power, devised a party just big enough to hold all the offices. In fact, they devised one just big enough in which to quarrel incessantly over the offices.[4]

The infighting did not affect the Prohibition Party as badly as others, perhaps because it was a different kind of movement, church-oriented and Protestant. Many of its active members were women, shut out of elective office as long as men alone did the voting. And its main goals were comparatively achievable. Yet even among the Prohibitionists, allegations of treachery peppered every campaign. Every time a presidential candidate ran, the cry rose that one major party supplied the means and mapped the campaign appearances simply to beat the other.[5]

What are we to make of it? How could treason and betrayal seem so much stronger in minor parties than major ones? Two simple answers apparently contradict each other: the conspiracy theorists were right, and the pressure of standing outside of the political mainstream fostered a delusional paranoia.

The family quarrels inside any party were an opportunity that the rival organization could not resist taking advantage of. If Republicans spotted disaffection on the Democratic side, they went out of their way to make it fester. Dissident newspapers got clandestine subsidies. Bolters received publicity, praise, and sometimes campaign contributions. New factional organization seemed to spring from nowhere, and, often enough, the architects included members of the opposition. Devising partisan fronts, Potemkin villages with bright pasteboard to hide the hastily erected scaffolding was a necessary political art in Gilded Age America.

One of the most peculiar of the "kept" movements took place in 1872. Only political necessity forced the Democratic Party to endorse the presidential candidacy of editor Horace Greeley. Liberal though his views on amnesty for former Confederates and lavish though his criticisms of black and carpetbag Republican officials may have been, the *New York Tribune* editor was a long way from the Democratic ideal. A lifetime of sympathy for all the "-isms," from feminism to abolitionism and Prohibitionism, and years of invective against Irish voters in particular and Democrats in general made him particularly offensive. For some, reconciliation was impossible, especially among those horrified at the party's abandonment of its opposition to the Reconstruction amendments.[6]

Out of the cluster of unhappy Democrats, one particularly shrill voice was raised. Blanton Duncan had long been the stormy petrel of Kentucky politics. Nativist and Know-Nothing rioter, passionate Unionist and still more fervent secessionist, sometime warrior, cartoonist, polemicist, and brawler, Duncan always veered on the outskirts of politics, looking for a new movement to join and lead. In time, he would publish a Greenback paper and run for Congress, lugging a cannon and a searchlight to his rallies, the first to fire and draw a crowd, the second to turn on himself as he spoke.[7] Now Duncan resolved that true Democrats must call a new national convention at Louisville and choose a candidate all their own.[8]

The convention was as outlandish as its founder. Not a single Democrat of national stature showed. Instead, it had small-fry "*Bourbonidae*" and oddities, like the mad-dog Democratic editor from New York City Mark M. "Brick" Pomeroy. At least five of New York's chosen had won a lasting fame with the police department: their pictures appeared in the rogue's gallery. The leader of the Arkansas delegation failed to attend not from choice; authorities refused to let him out of jail. Delegates wanted to nominate New York lawyer Charles O'Conor for president, and they rightly worried that he might refuse them, especially because his personal messenger read an endless letter saying exactly that. Delegates dozed through it, woke up, and chose him anyhow. Over screams and protests, a majority declared the convention unanimous. With that, a Republican jeered, the "Witenagemot . . . adjourns, decomposes, disintegrates, vanishes, and fades away into the dismal realms of chaos and of night. Faint gibberings and wailings are heard from Mr. Blanton Duncan, Brick Pomeroy, and others, but these die away in the distance. The Ku-Klux rifles and revolvers are heard snapping behind the scenes."[9] The very terms chosen suggested something ephemeral and imaginary, which, of course, the whole movement was. Neither nominee accepted. But it did not matter. Duncan and his friends insisted on running them all the same.

Democrats knew perfectly well what was going on. As the convention gathered to deliberate, two local eminences ran into Duncan, all strut, swell, and swagger, buttonholing "various purple-nosed satellites." The convention was a fraud, they shouted, and he knew it. "You may be sure there is money in the business, or Duncan would not be interested," one exclaimed. When Duncan protested that he had been offered half a million to break up the convention, his antagonists roared that this only proved that the Republican managers had offered him a still higher sum. A few exchanges more brought the quarrelers to blows, Duncan pressing his views home with a chair.[10]

Democrats could not prove the affair the Republican dodge it certainly was. Seeing an opportunity to divide their enemies, Republican leaders across the South induced the national committee to defray would-be delegates' traveling costs to Louisville. Twenty-five thousand circulars on behalf of Duncan's cause blanketed the country, courtesy of James M. Edmunds of the Republican National Committee, who lugged them to the Senate folding room with the franked signatures of leading Republican senators to carry them duty-free through the mails. The national committee even provided money for a brass band. For the next two months, Republicans did all that publicity and payments could to keep the "Independent Democracy" alive. Most partisans voted as their leaders expected, if they voted at all. Still, the third party had served a very plain nuisance value. If the danger of Greeley winning had loomed larger, thousands of Democrats who voted for him or stayed home might have been tempted to cast a vote for O'Conor. In any case, the O'Conor movement acted as a constant witness to the fact that many Democrats went into the campaign unhappy, and that, in itself, dampened political morale and helped lower Democratic turnout.[11]

It would not be the last time national parties cosseted disaffection. The list of party recusants, having discovered the error in their fellows' ways and insisting on the consistency in following their own principles into the opposite camp, was almost a standard in national contests, long before the so-called Mugwump campaign of 1884 brought an army of Republicans, noisy and just numerous enough, over to the Democrats. To judge each side by its professions, one must assume that each ended up restocked heavily—which, since its own former members had abandoned it (usually in "disgust"), never put it at the risk of overcrowding. In one editor's words, politics had many a "political puppet, a Tom-tabard manufactured by [one side's] knaves for the misguidance of [the other's] fools."[12]

Why should minor parties get off any easier? There was no question that as the Prohibition Party's totals rose, Republican margins declined across the North. It would have been a sin against nature for Democrats to have left the Dries alone (or, for that matter, for dram-sellers to have left them alone; temperance supporters charged that the "rum interests" paid Prohibition candidates' way in close legislative districts to rid the capitol of mainstream politicians with more influence). In 1884, Republicans were sure that John P. St. John, the Prohibition nominee for president, worked on a Democratic payroll (it was, in fact, a bankroll: Democrats footed the minor party's expenses in key upstate New York counties). Of course, if Republicans could have paid St. John to take a dive in 1884, they would have done so. For a few glorious days in October, a con-man persuaded some of their chief insiders that they were about to do it.[13]

Mainstream parties also created backfires inside insurgent movements, swaying members from their duty with promise of profit. There certainly was a Labor Reform Party in New Hampshire in 1870. It was genuine; it contained real reformers. It also worked very well with the Democrats and with former congressman George Fogg's coterie of Republicans, who were trying to make the grabs by overweening railroads a defining issue in the spring election. Republican leaders knew a put-up job when they saw it. It certainly was not one of their own; one party manager had come to town at the start of the movement to "*shape* things a little," only to complain that "the thing is in the hands *now* of the Copperheads and means mischief."[14]

Then a month before the election, another reform movement appeared in Manchester with a suspiciously similar name. The Labor League movement, which soon emerged in other cities, spoke for the workingmen's cause—and argued that this cause could best be served by endorsing Republican candidates. Democrats were wary. They had a right to be. Behind the scenes, Republican operatives were hard at work. Most active of all was Union Pacific Railroad Company secretary and Republican Party chairman E. H. Rollins. "It is a *sham* and a *cheat*, by which only *shammers* and *cheaters* will profit," Fogg's Concord paper screamed, and rightly. The more the Labor Reform movement looked divided, the less likely its prospects and the harder to make converts. By the campaign's windup, Democratic managers were delegating some of their followers to cast Labor Reform tickets, just to make the uprising look serious enough to keep former Republicans in the ranks. On election day, the Labor Reform ticket failed to dislodge the party in power. It carried almost no urban wards, though it did surprisingly well in farming communities. As a party, the Labor Reform organization had been dealt a deathblow. Its purpose fulfilled, the Labor League vanished, never to be heard from again.[15]

Charges of treachery that rang from press and podium therefore had a real basis. Editors who pronounced third parties as mere fronts or sellouts were judging present circumstances by past events. At the same time, that very knowledge that third parties could be bought, bent, and broken gave first and second parties an incentive to try it with every new movement that came along. Where minor parties could not be bought, they could be rented to back one candidate or one set of offices. Their newspapers sold out even more cheaply, but editorial "Tomtabards" served just as well. Nobody in New York City was about to be fooled by the appearance of the campaign paper the *Labor Unionist* in 1887. Nobody there read it; nobody was meant to read it. Democrats published it for their own upstate press to quote, as proof of what city workingmen thought.[16]

No insurgent's fear of dirty work and betrayal, then, seemed implausible. Yet fanciful the imaginings were, in many cases; indeed, the obloquy was nearly universal. Hardly a third-party leader escaped the rhetorical traitor's dock. Read the diatribes by General James Baird Weaver's enemies, and his whole career was one of ambition and treachery, first to the Republicans, then to the Prohibition-

MR. WEAVER IN HIS FAVORITE ROLE.

"Mr. Weaver in his favorite role" (Art Young, *Chicago Inter Ocean*, July 11, 1892).

ists, then to the Greenbackers, and finally to the Populists—shocking work for the presidential candidate of the last two organizations. He sold out parties by leaving them, and by staying in them; he betrayed the Greenback Party by refusing to make an alliance with Democrats in 1880 and agreeing to work alongside them four years later. One might assume that the only honest bone in his body was the jawbone of an ass, and that in constant motion speaking economic heresies—or, anyhow, the wrong economic heresies.[17]

Perhaps the general was every bit as cynical as his enemies thought him and his every choice the worst possible for the party that he led. But it is highly unlikely. From the first, Weaver could have saved himself much grief and spared his reputation a lexicon of insults by staying within Republican ranks, or converting to the Democrats outright. To run for president as a Greenbacker in 1880 was worse than hopeless. It was an expensive way to convince the largest possible audience that the general was both fool and knave. One reporter came calling and found a gentle, kindly man — until public affairs intruded on the conversation. On those subjects, the general turned "implacably militant, essentially a Puritan, rigid as iron in his faith." He was, President Grover Cleveland commented, "one of the few men who come to talk with me about something else than politics — about legislation."[18]

Even if Republicans and Democrats had kept their corruption funds to use on each other and saved their abuse for larger game, the very conditions under which third and fourth parties were permitted to exist would have fitted every insurgent for the role of Iscariot, sooner or later. It could not be helped. When leaders carry an organization to defeat, they take the blame, and there was just about nowhere else but defeat to carry a third party. The political system had been shaped by and for the major parties. Beyond its confines, with a national majority beyond reach, outsiders had no good choices.

Whether a party sold out or not usually came when it faced the critical question: should it go the fight alone or make coalition with one of the two major parties? The go-it-aloners made the case, regularly, that a combination of forces would only mean the ruin of the minor party. At the very least, its program would be diluted. But there was the added consideration that members of the minor party usually came from the mainstream parties. And they generally came in off years, when the stakes were less.

It is important, however, to notice that it *was* the off years when discontent usually peaked and that the discontented did not show their strength as much in the presidential years. For this, there were many reasons. For one thing, many a worker or farmer or evangelical looked to state offices for substantive change. Presidential contests were less suited for fulfilling the goals of most reform movements. With so many causes having sectional, but not national, appeal, and with so little money at hand to form a comprehensive system of party machinery from coast to coast, third parties had to content themselves with enclaves, and enclaves never won an electoral majority. The hopelessness of electing a president only dampened enthusiasm for candidates further down the ticket. But it was also true that off years were safer times to register discontent because many of those registering discontent did not *want* out of the two-party system. They wanted to rebuke the party in power, not to destroy it. They were sending a message about issues, in ways that presidential campaigns could not do. Voting for congressmen was a less dangerous way for party loyalists' to express anger.

They did it, too, because it worked. Nothing was plainer about the Gilded Age political system than the willingness of two evenly balanced national parties to make the concessions required to take the force out of any protest movement. Some Prohibitionists would continue to vote for their own party until every tap to every keg in Ohio was closed forever. But it was not from such true believers alone that any minor party was made, and the message from Ohio, and many other places like it, was impossible to miss: it paid to break with one's own party, not so much to bring it down as to set it right.

The outcasts and exiles remembered their old party homes and in their minds wove fantasies about how a return *might* be possible, if only . . . ; that the party *was* solid at the core, given the right leaders . . . ; that the party had left *them*, not they the party. But all of these were half overtures to be invited back. Never a Democrat in good standing, Chief Justice Salmon P. Chase had become one of the most prominent radical Republicans by the end of the Civil War. But even from his prominence on the bench, he dreamed of returning in triumph to a Democratic Party that he, at heart, felt he belonged to, a party of hard money and hostility to privilege but one purged of its prejudice against people of color. Countless southern Redeemers fell into reveries of Whiggish economic programs and of a revived Whig Party, the party of their youth, now hazed with the gold of idealism.

That passion the major parties knew well and played on eagerly. Treason to the party was the blackest of crimes, but a simple repentance could expunge it all, and renegades coming back might even get the hero's welcome that unshaken faithfulness to the cause would never have earned. Again and again, partisans reached out not just to the old loyalties of their recently departed members but to precisely those issues where their old party loyalties remained most consistent, the ones that still held an appeal: the war, the tariff, the predatory interests.

In this lay the great peril of alliances between great parties and little, new ones and old. If third parties must coalesce with one of the major alternatives, they would provoke the desertions that were always just waiting to happen. If they must ally with one major party's great enemy, they would lose many of their own members, who, deep down, could not entirely shake off their fondness for the party to which they had belonged. They would also accustom their own members to see friends in the mainstream organization, where before there had been only suspicion. The more closely the old and new parties worked, the more opportunities the former found to infiltrate, subvert, and suborn members of the latter. "New parties are not built up by remarriages but by divorce absolute, both from bed and board," an insurgent editor summed up.[19]

Preserving political chastity was all the more vital in a party uniquely dependent on its reputation for virtue. Righteous causes had to hold themselves to special standards. Indeed, those special standards were part of the point when a rising of workers or farmers was also a revolt against the corruption of politics-as-usual. "No one—save political strikers—wants a sixpenny edition of either of the old parties," the *Irish World* protested. The last thing they wanted, the first thing they were likely to suspect, was that "the New Movement" had become "an old dodge." Fresh-minted insurgents objected to anything that compromised the party's principles and, having been spurred into leaving the old parties because of deals and compromises committed for the sake of power, felt a particularly keen distress when their allies started doing the same thing. No matter what the need, the charge that "hack politicians" and "Knights of the Political Bum" had charge of affairs was sure to drive away those who, whether they shared the goals on which a fusion took place, could never stand the defilement of deal making.[20]

All the same, the case for the fusionists was a stronger one than it might seem. They could argue, properly, that any choice they made helped one of the two major parties. Failure to make alliance with one of the parties was itself a boon to the other.[21]

The 1880 campaign showed that plainly. Nobody imagined that the Greenbackers would win, and from the major parties' perspective, that made its continued existence absurd. The only question about "the sick man of American politics," as one editor put it, was whether his remains should be sold to the Democrats or whether they should go to his funeral in lonely respectability. Weaver, the presidential nominee, preferred the second. Setting his face against fusion with the Democracy, Weaver denounced the "traitors" who made joint cause with their hard-money enemies and called on party members to refuse any overtures in Indiana. To other members just as sincere as the general, his stand looked like a sellout. The consequences, they insisted, were perfectly clear. Not helping the Democrats facilitated Republicans' election, and a win for the very men whose disastrous financial policy had brought the Greenbackers into being. When an officer on the party committee, Dyer P. Lum, charged that the Republican campaign had bought Weaver's services for $5,000, he found willing listeners.[22] What could Weaver possibly have done to serve neither party's interests? To choose coalition was to help the Democrats; to spurn it was to help the Republicans.[23] There was no other option.

If third parties, fused or free-floating, served the major parties, and if the suspicion of secret deals followed them either way, what was the case for an alliance? It was, in briefest form, a surrender of the full majesty of the insurgents' program, with the recognition that halfway reforms might well forestall the more thorough change that society needed so badly. Coalitions never advanced as far as the Greenback platform might desire. Sometimes they gained nothing beyond the spoils. They almost invited bad faith on the major parties' part in delivering their part of the deal. But they could work; they were worth trying, if the terms were right.

Those terms might well include offices. Sometimes, as the mid-roaders charged, the parceling out of offices was the sole concession the minor party got, and no other. Yet even here, something could be said for the fusionist position. John C. Calhoun had once spoken of "the cohesive power of public plunder." Contemporaries, hearkening to the phrase, concentrated on the last two words; but perhaps the first adjective mattered more.[24] Define it as Calhoun meant it, with "plunder" including all the contracts, spoils of office, and rewards that legitimately came to an election's winners, and it *did* have a "cohesive" power. Offices were emollients, a cure for potential disaffection. The very prospect of winning them could heal a hundred hurts.

As good a case of the cohesive power of an expectation of spoils as can be found took place in New York City in 1884. "Honest John" Kelly's Tammany Hall machine could find plenty of reasons for knifing the Democratic presidential ticket. Tammany had helped Grover Cleveland win the nomination for governor; and all for nothing—Cleveland, true reformer that he was, doled out the spoils to every other political machine in the state, and picked a fight with Tammany Hall at his first opportunity. Tammany's own supporters were, many of them, Irish Catholic. They didn't like the "hay-loft and cheese-press" Democrats upstate much, and they didn't like Grover Cleveland's Presbyterian conscience at all; behind the scenes, they knew, the governor had worked to stifle legislation supportive of Catholic interests. For the Tammany boss to order Cleveland's political throat cut from ear to ear would have seemed natural.

Natural, that is, for a political amateur. Kelly's machine may not have pulled out all the stops on election day, but it delivered a good majority downstate. It had no real choice. Party machines were based on loyalty. To go against the party to which it had always belonged would have set Tammany against many of its members and encouraged disloyalty to its leadership, and might even have had an embarrassing result. The best chance of getting spoils from New York's state government was to send that stiff-necked governor to Washington and put in his more amenable successor, David Bennett Hill. The best chance of winning the spoils in New York City was to have the Democratic national organization behind Tammany's candidates; and if Cleveland won, he would have to allot Tammany at least some federal offices—as indeed he did.[25]

The most lingering cries of treachery in New York City that November rose not from Democrats but from Ben Butler's People's Party. There, allegations flew that this district leader, that member of the executive committee, had sold out to the Republicans and distributed tickets with People's Party candidates quite deliberately left off.[26] If treachery there was, it should have come as no more surprising than Tammany's loyalty. "Public plunder" necessarily could have no cohesive power among those who never had a chance of getting it. And in that case, the divisions, the quarrels in the ranks, continued to fester. Those without the power to reward their followers found it harder to hold those followers, or to keep them from following some other leader who would give them a better chance at sharing in the rewards of success.

As rewards in a larger society—official position—closed off, the only forms of recognition an activist could aspire to, in a minor party, was one of leadership within the party. The fights for control of the central committee or to act as spokesman became all the more bitter. And the weapons with which those in charge could defend their power became all the more weakened.

There was that other spoils of office: the power to make policy. To describe policy as "spoils" is not the cynical conceit it might seem. The right men in power could make pensions easier to obtain through the Pension Bureau, or speed up the flow of money for rivers and harbors. Even a federally subsidized bank that redistributed the wealth through low-interest loans using farmers' crops as collateral qualified as spoils.

Parties were never spoils machines only. They promised changes, or protection against changes. But all this was impossible without the power to deliver. That power minor parties could not have on their own. But without that power, the force driving voters to the polls would be gone. At first, any new party could ignore this problem. Every movement, at its birth, foresaw a great future, and hope made sustaining enough fare for the moment. It was "the men who are defeated and defeated, and defeated who accomplish the great things," radical activist Henry George cried, "and it is better to be defeated and in the right than to be on the winning side and in the wrong."[27]

Stirring words! And the fifty believers in the single tax cheered them to the echo. But these were a far cry from the thousands needed just to win New York City, and George knew it. He must have known, too, that the thousands would not come unless they knew that there were thousands already there, ready to welcome them. With all parties, the highest hopes began to pall the moment the first returns came in. Those in charge began to see what was needed for winning —and how far from winning the party must fall, unless drastic action was taken. Each electoral defeat made that sense of desperation stronger. If, after ten years in existence, the Greenback Party could only round up 156 voters out of nearly a quarter million in New York City, and only 6,000 in Pennsylvania, New York, and Ohio altogether, how long would it be before they won? Losing hope, true believers quit the struggle, and as they did so, the day of victory moved further and further into the future, and then vanished entirely.[28]

The case for the fusionists, then, rested not just on an appreciation of the gains from holding office but on the costs of *not* having a chance at office. To stand pure and alone might seem very well. But insurgents did not run for the solace of their souls. They ran to accomplish great ends, ends that could be achieved only through the taking of power. Time, money, reputation, all had to be drawn on in any campaign. To put heart and soul into a campaign without the least chance of winning, or of even being noticed, was more than most voters were willing to do. Indeed, it might be sounder strategy not to run a ticket at all, if no respectable showing was possible that year. All a "stand-up-and-be-counted" candidacy would do would be to tell onlookers how unpopular the minor party's program was and to discredit it further. Only those with a penchant for lost causes would stay with them after that. Those who sympathized with the basic principles but kept their old party ties would be counted by an unwary public as among the reform's enemies. Labor had tens of thousands of supporters in New York City, but it became harder to prove that when the United Labor Party's presidential candidate took less than 2,000 votes. A humiliating defeat branded its few advocates with "the onus of crankism." Never again would it be as easy to persuade voters to consider the merit in their principles.[29]

Absolute power may indeed corrupt. But the absolute *lack* of power corrodes. It has a devastating impact over the long run on any organization. Failure bred a search for scapegoats, and it was far easier to blame treason at the top than to presume that the failure was in the *message*. Each electoral setback made that search for alternatives more intense and the disagreement about what means could achieve victory more divisive. Victory at the polls, mottled though the results may have been, was the only real solvent for disaffection. It might bring other kinds of disaffection with it, but these were not necessarily as corrosive as defeat —or, more precisely, an overwhelming defeat—was sure to be.

That corrosion made weak movements weaker. It also stilled the voices on which any insurgency relied. Never well funded, the third-party press could not even depend on the true believers to give it the help required. Readers who threw up their caps when a capitalist paper printed a single friendly item "amid an ocean of falsehood and deception" boycotted labor journals that published a single sentence offensive to their views, Joseph R. Buchanan of the *Chicago Labor Enquirer* complained. Editors swore at their colleagues as "dirty anarchists" and betrayers of the class struggle and did capers to see another false friend go broke. Convinced that labor's destiny lay with the Knights of Labor alone, the order's official organ published a list of those labor papers worthy of members' patronage. Most of them were flyspeck weeklies. The newspapers that ranked among the "manhood of labor journalism" appeared nowhere. Within the year, many of them had been boycotted into bankruptcy.[30]

The spectacle of backbiting and frontal assault may have been disheartening, but the real blame for it lay outside, not inside, third-party ranks. Powerlessness bred much of the disaffection, and that powerlessness owed its origin in large part to insurgents having to operate in the political universe that the major parties had created. Once the dissension began, the weakness of the outsiders and of their collective voice simply made conditions worse. The third-party members grew ever more dependent on hostile newspapers for information about what, exactly, their fellow insurgents were fighting about, or fighting for. Every quarrel got the fullest coverage, and, every renegade got front-page publicity as the one honest man fleeing from a political Gomorrah.

All roads, in the end, either went nowhere or ran back to the major parties. Having held firm against fusion, General Weaver himself found the realities inescapable. By 1883, he had begun to move toward the Democrats. He had lost none of his faith; certainly he did not sell out. Iowa's Democratic Party needed reinforcements, and its eye had fallen on those most susceptible to the Greenbackers' antimonopoly arguments. Taking on the railroads for extortion and discrimination, Democrats made overtures to Greenback leaders to join them. A Democratic victory might advance one of the goals that Weaver cared about, and if no victory came, at least the prospect of Greenback support would lend weight to those in the Democracy least wedded to the corporations and friendliest to other parts of the Greenback program.[31] Instead of surrendering his own principles, the general reasoned, he may have brought one major party closer to adopting a few of them.

Of course it meant offices for Weaver, but power was more than a chance to shake the plum tree. It gave the general a national forum for Greenbacker arguments. One man could not budge policy far, but at least a House seat gave him a greater chance than political exile. Even enemies occasionally admitted that the general earned the House's attention in his second spell in Congress. No matter the subject, he debated it instructively and intelligently. He was aggressive and dignified, in all his actions an effective rebuttal to the slur on Greenbackers as anarchists or impracticables. Congressmen found him tolerant, charitable, and reasonable. Colleagues admitted that his principles were honest ones, and, more than that, they were his own—not those of the Democratic Party that had helped elect him. From Congress, his voice was raised for the free coinage of silver, the forfeiture of all land grants made to railroads, government programs to irrigate the West, the creation of a Department of Labor and a publicly owned postal telegraph, and a constitutional amendment for the direct election of senators. If voting for a Democratic Speaker and favoring cuts in the tariff, that "mother of trusts," was the price for fusion, it must have seemed a bargain.[32]

In an ideal world, Weaver would have been settling for too little. But in a polity dominated by two major parties, what good alternative was there? That was perfectly plain when a Republican took his seat in 1888—to the glee of purist Greenbackers. The Republican congressman had no patience with agrarian complaints about railroads and monopolies. He was a believer in business promotion and high tariffs. Having bought up Greenback papers to oppose Weaver and having destroyed the party's most prominent figure, the GOP had wiped out the party not just in the Sixth District but statewide. There would be no danger of that half loaf for Greenbacker principles now; of their demands they could expect not so much as a crumb.[33]

Weaver's own experiences proved to him the obvious. Even with major party support, reform could not go far in Iowa. At least Democrats advanced further than the railroad toadies in the GOP's Burlington Regency. Separate parties, standing aloof, could not make change. But pressure groups within the parties—or, better still, standing just on the edge, in the doorway, ever ready to depart—could force action. It was no sellout of an insurgent movement to gain something now, as long as one held onto the right to agitate for more later. The only question remained, as it had always been: how far could those without real power induce those who controlled the political machinery to give way?

A Little Knight Music

Curtain Down on Bloody Shirt.

Ring Up Curtain on Red Rag.

Stage Directors—During this Change of Bill the Republican Heelers and Strikers will make all the Racket Possible to Conceal the Fact Money is Playing the Star Part.

—Chicago *Knights of Labor*, March 19, 1887

The wonder about the off-year elections in 1886 was their ordinariness. For a dozen years, every midterm had brought a "tidal wave," sweeping Republicans out. But when the returns were in this time, nothing much had happened.

And something should have, for in the bright summer weather before the polls opened, this moment seemed the "workingman's hour." From small beginnings but a twelvemonth since, the Knights of Labor had come to be great nationwide. At their height that summer, they numbered eight hundred thousand and possibly a million, black and white, women and men, skilled and unskilled. Middle-class reformers interested in cooperative enterprise, workers hoping to better their own lot, Socialists, anarchists, temperance advocates, and trade unionists all found a common purpose. Locals tumbled into politics, either to back major-party candidates who agreed with their views or to build a separate labor party, able to take offices out of the hands of politicians and put them back into the hands of the people. "Let the watchword of every workingman be, workingmen to make the laws for workingmen," one labor paper urged, "and let the working-man do his duty to himself and family by voting the straight independent ticket."[1]

That promised revolution did not happen. Reforms changing a society of grasp and grab into the cooperative commonwealth would take national action, but even at its height, the labor movement never came close to getting such action. Indeed, the 1886 elections showed just how hard it was to focus the political system on the Knights' agenda. Most of the working class stayed firm in its faith to the two major parties. Labor politics, the acerbic radical Donn Piatt complained, always ended the same way, "like a tumble-bug in a dusty road, that, having impregnated its lump, dies of sheer exhaustion."[2]

Understanding the Knights' failure takes more than eulogies for the failure of utopian reform, or quite convincing proofs of the overwhelming power of capital. It takes a clear sense of what a typical congressional election year was like, and why no one set of issues could hold the spotlight for long. How did the 1886 elections work? What happened to labor's issues in "the workingman's hour"?

Start with the obvious. Republicans tried to turn the election into a report card on Grover Cleveland's administration and a Democratic House's frustrated effort to lower the tariff. Northern Democrats tried to steer public attention away from the old issues of wartime disloyalty and soldiers' benefits and toward the newer ones of tariff revision and administrative reform. Yet neither side could stick to the issues with which it was most comfortable, not as long as blocs of votes seemed ready to break free from partisan loyalties. Down south, whites grumbled about the Democratic Redeemers, "court-house rings," and "Bourbons." Some wanted a government friendlier to farmers' needs. Others saw the "Rebel brigadiers" as an impediment to the industrial New South, where outside capital and immigration would be welcomed and where a protective tariff would nurture infant industries. In one case, they might support Independent, Greenbacker, or Wheel tickets; in the other, they might break away into Republican ranks. If the Grand Army of the Republic spoke for all Union veterans, even Democratic soldiers up north were fuming at the first president to veto private pension bills and resented the Confederates administering executive departments. Who knew how German Republicans would vote, in states where stricter temperance laws had shut off their Sunday refreshment? Or how many evangelical Protestants would feel sold out by liquor laws that kept the gin mills open the other six days? The possibilities for discombobulating party lines seemed infinite.[3]

That variety of possibilities was precisely why these off-year elections could not be a grand referendum on anything. No one issue made a natural fit in any state; each issue had to fight against others for attention, and each party chose to focus on whatever topics suited it the most. In that sense, at least, the public debate was as partisan editors and stem-winders defined it, but that did not mean that they devised one set of issues—the cultural ones, say, or those where they waved the bloody shirt of sectional passions—to silence others. They designed their campaigns to catch votes, responding to the concerns of their activists, who reflected not only the desire to take a winning position but deep-felt convictions of their own.[4]

For ten years, the number of Republicans who felt strongly about the "rum" issue had been growing and so had the size and scope of organizations like the Women's Christian Temperance Union and the local Law and Order Leagues that made regulation of the liquor traffic their first concern. They could press the managers close, especially since the Prohibition Party had grown from a cluster of cranks into a political party just large enough to throw close elections the wrong way. To send the GOP a message, they were perfectly willing to hand power over to the party most closely associated with the saloonkeepers instead. For many of them, this cause was the one above all others that made them cleave to Republicanism. On the other hand, pragmatists wanted nothing to do with Prohibition, lest it stir the brewers to tap their money barrels for the opposing side. They had to find alternatives that would satisfy everybody but the extra-Dries on the outskirts of the Republican Party and the red-nosed "saloonatics" in the Democratic camp.[5]

In Ohio, Republicans tried one expedient for limiting the number of saloons and their hours of operation and then another. Their final attempt, the Dow Law, meted a license fee on every place selling liquor and endowed it on the counties and townships doing the collecting. It was a law just strong enough to pass constitutional muster, Governor "Fire-Alarm Joe" Foraker explained, and, more important, would let voters say about the whole issue, "Now we are done with it." Jerseyites bickered over whether to go for high license or a constitutional amendment giving townships and counties the right to ban saloons within their borders. When the local optionists from the southern counties beat the licensers in writing the platform, the GOP had to explain itself to the German rank and file in cities at the north end of the state. In particular, the party had to explain why the Dry views of its gubernatorial candidate should mean everything to Prohibitionists but to nobody else. (Prohibitionists, suspecting that they were being offered sucker-bait, ran their own ticket.)[6]

Local option, high license fees, submission of statewide Prohibition amendments: all these issues touched the politics in every state from Kansas on east. These were not artful concoctions by politicians desperate to while away "the workingman's hour" with something less dangerous than class warfare. They were the outgrowth of six years of pressure from beyond the statehouse walls, and of the parties' responses to it. Forced to find common ground between what one candidate described as "the beer-drinking Germans . . . and Prohibition Quakers," Republican managers saw the issues as more immediately dangerous to their own party's support than labor issues could be; Democrats saw them as greater in their potential for gain, but for each of them, to some degree, at least, the liquor question reminded members again of just what defined the essence of the two main parties, and why they had been Democrats or Republicans in the first place.[7] Far more than the Knights of Labor, Prohibition's legions fielded state and local tickets; every bit as much they drew on the classical republican language that tied privileged interests and menaces to the community to selfish and purchased politicians. If the Knights of Labor could not keep the focus on the injuries done to the producing classes, one reason may have been that the "saloonatics" and the "temperanceites" never let them. Much the same could have been said of other groups: the Grand Army of the Republic, with its special interest in pension legislation for its members, the Mugwumps in eastern cities, with their commitment to reform, and the Irish American nationalists, wanting at the very least a commitment to Ireland's right to govern its own affairs. All these groups the parties could ignore at their peril, the more so because so many Irish nationalists held prominent places in the Knights of Labor, and Terence V. Powderly spoke as strongly for home rule as he did for the classless commonwealth.[8]

Workers, then, were addressed as one group among many, clamoring for recognition, and many in the working class were appealed to as Catholics, Germans, Union veterans, or enlistees in the Cold-Water Army of temperance reform. Still, both parties hoped that the Knights of Labor could be turned into a machine for delivering the working-class vote to their side, and each sought it out; both knew that many of their own members had formed a double allegiance, their interests or their long-held sympathies having carried them into the Knights of Labor. Some party managers saw concessions to labor as politically expedient. Others saw it as a fulfillment of a party commitment to equal rights and protective legislation, long overdue and now within their reach.

As has already been noted, there were four ways, at least, of appealing to labor without venturing far from the party programs: antimonopoly, tariff protection, twisting the British lion's tail, and pulling the Chinese immigrant's pigtail. The last two fitted the first two nicely, just as cultural issues mixed comfortably with economic ones, and congressional debates had kept them plainly before the public eye. Under the guidance of House Ways and Means Committee chairman William Ralls Morrison, a modest revision of the tariff had reached the floor, where protectionist Democrats led by Samuel J. Randall had joined hands with Republicans to kill it. Tariff reformers swore vengeance and called for a party purge. Since 1882, federal law had raised barriers against new Chinese immigration, but workers on the West Coast knew from personal experience how pettifoggers could make it meaningless. Every new amendatory bill let Democrats put Republicans on record as friends of "coolie labor." Congressional candidates bickered over which of them had employed Chinese labor and which party had opened Nevada to "rat-eaters." Sylvester Pennoyer, Oregon's Democratic candidate for governor, promised to drive every Chinese resident from the state if elected. His opponent, the *Portland World* revealed, let Chinese do his washing. The terrified Republican candidate rushed into print to deny everything—and was confronted by affidavits proving not only that the Chinese had washed his shirt but that they also undoubtedly had earned their money. "Not the bloody shirt now, but the dirty shirt is the overwhelming question," a disgusted editor commented.[9]

When it came to the Knights themselves, parties played both sides, sometimes simultaneously, but always they pitched their tune to catch labor's ear. As Democrats in upstate Michigan refreshed their alliances with Greenbackers, Detroit's Greenback and Labor parties ran a separate candidate for Congress, with Republican support. In New Jersey, Democrats disappointed the Knights of Labor by nominating for governor Congressman Robert S. Green, a corporation lawyer whose firm had, among its clients, the notorious Jay Gould. But if Republicans' platform made fairer promises, the Democrats could point to a finer performance, under incumbent governor Leon Abbett, and Green had voted for every bill on the Knights' wish list in Washington.[10]

In some places, the major parties took up Knights as their own candidates. In one northern Ohio district, for example, Democrats nominated Dr. Thomas G. Bristor, a dentist from Mansfield. Bristor played up the class issue, denouncing the monopolists and the rich, assailing Ohio's congressional delegation as nineteen lawyers, a banker, and a doctor. South of Columbus, the Democrats tried an even closer alliance. Springfield, Ohio, had become nationally known for William Whiteley's "Champion" mowing and reaping machinery and locally known for his union-busting and subsidized newspaper that denounced union men as anarchists and criminals. Whitely was Republican, and Whitely's money, or so Democrats charged, bought Assembly Speaker Robert Kennedy's GOP nomination to Congress for favors rendered. Against "King Bob" the Knights nominated a prosperous farmer, Thomas R. McMillin. Thirty years a Republican and a recent convert to the Prohibition Party, he would not have received so much as a passing glance from Democrats in ordinary years. But they endorsed "Old Honesty" and predicted an unbeatable combination of insurgents and disaffected supporters of Kennedy's rivals for the nomination.[11]

Elsewhere, the two parties could build on alliances already made with insurgents. At the southern end of Pennsylvania's anthracite belt, Schuylkill County had always been rough terrain for farmers or politicians. Hard drinking, hard fighting, and a hard life characterized coal country. Drunk and disorderly Welsh-, Irish-, and English-born miners settled some of their grievances in brutal killings, and the coal companies in the late 1870s kept order in the same fashion, railroading the so-called Mollie Maguires to the gallows. Employers crushed labor unions, but they could not crush out political insurgency. Instead, the main-line parties took it over. In 1878, the Greenback Party nominated Charles N. Brumm, a small-time inventor who had gone into politics and reinvented himself. Having been a Republican until two years before, he now was able to win a seat in Congress. Republicans adopted him two years later and started a long, mutually profitable alliance with the Greenbacker Party. What Brumm did, in effect, was provide Republican policies with Greenback justifications. What did it matter if he supported the federal arbitration bill, not a very radical measure in itself, touted the high tariff as in the workingman's best interest, and drew pictures of a "whiskey-and-water syndicate of Kentucky and Wall Street" as "at the bottom of all the evils" America suffered?[12]

Kennedy's, Bristor's, and Brumm's campaigns all showed how far the mainstream parties might align themselves with supposed radical alternatives, but they also showed how little radicalism the campaigns had after all. Beyond the candidate, the parties ran the same old way and summoned the standard mainstream arguments. As a leading figure in the local GAR, Brumm waved the bloody shirt more fervently than the red flag. His great moment of notoriety in the Forty-ninth Congress came when he declared that the only Democrats who wore Union blue had had to be drafted into service—a libel on at least 150,000 Ohio Democrats. In each case, Republicans made their case to labor by talking up the protective tariff; indeed, they did that everywhere, directing their argument not so much to a working class as to individual working groups' interests, as carpenters in the Maine shipyards or as puddlers bringing home a steady paycheck in the Pittsburgh iron foundries or, in Bristor's case, to ethnic loyalties (a "British free trader" was the last thing any "loyal Irishman who believes in good wages" could support).[13] For all their talk about "monopolists" and "trusts," Democrats knew that many workingmen's associations and the Knights of Labor cared more about the tariff than any other piece of national legislation, passed or prospective.

Three House contests involving members of the top Democratic leadership made the point plain. The most stunning Republican upset came in William Ralls Morrison's Illinois stronghold. A plainspoken, plain-dressed congressman from the East St. Louis district, Morrison had made himself the champion of tariff reform. His management had helped shut a protectionist out of the speakership and given it to John G. Carlisle of Kentucky, whose opposition to high duties was beyond dispute. By 1886, Morrison had written two tariff bills and was certain to write more. Defeating him would send the plainest kind of message to Democrats elsewhere; if Morrison could be beaten, any of them could be.

For there was not much doubt that "Horizontal Bill's" hold over his district defied an easy overthrow. Over his fourteen years in the House, Republicans kept trying to defeat Morrison, but gerrymanders and popular vote-getters alike had failed.[14]

Enter, then, the shadowy figure of John Jarrett, political hit man. Welsh-born, Jarrett had found work in the Pennsylvania iron country and a career in the Amalgamated Association of Iron and Steel Workers. At one point, he was its president and a highly visible leader in the Knights of Labor. He still presented himself as a simple working man, though he was, in fact, an employer and heavily involved in steel industry projects for making tinplate. As secretary to the American Tin-Plate Association, he had good economic reasons to object to any bill making foreign tinplate duty-free, and as an ardent Republican, he had every reason to detest Morrison. Now Jarrett arrived in East St. Louis, with plenty of money to organize clubs, rent a hall, and do printing. Ostensibly raised by a "working-man's tariff club" in Pittsburgh, the fund came from Pittsburgh industrialists, and most likely from James Swank's American Iron and Steel Association. Jarrett's arrival was one stop in an extensive campaign. He arrived fresh from roiling the waters in the district of Pennsylvania's top tariff reformer, William L. Scott, and would leave to change the outcome in Speaker Carlisle's district.[15]

Still, Jarrett needed discontent to stir into active hostility to the incumbent. He found it on the shop floor and in Knights of Labor locals. Workers' alarm at tariff reform's potential effect was quite real. Democrats later charged that Master Workman Terence V. Powderly himself sent the directive to defeat Morrison. Certainly leading figures in the Knights showed up to pass on the word among coal miners and nail smelters. They found an ideal candidate in Jehu Baker, the last Republican to defeat Morrison, a score of years back. Allowing that some revision in rates might be needed — by the tariff's friends — Baker promised to hold firm on duties shutting out the products of pauper labor. He also vowed to fight against other privileged interests, end the special rights that national banks enjoyed, and hold corporations strictly accountable. And, of course, he favored home rule for Ireland.[16]

Morrison's troubles could have been predicted, but no political insider dreamed of unhorsing John G. Carlisle, Speaker of the House. Just across the river from Cincinnati, the county courthouses around Covington knew how to bring out a Democratic vote whenever it was needed, and, some alleged, a vote conveniently larger than the number actually cast, when a districtwide winning margin called for something special. As if Carlisle would need it! Nobody knew that there was any opposition to him at all. Aware that they could not win in a public display of power, the Knights had organized secretly. Their candidate, George Henry Thoebe, a journeyman woodcarver in the local furniture factory, had been a longtime Democrat before taking up the fight against saloons and for greenback currency. Now he threw as lavish a campaign as he could manage, outside business hours. It cost him just sixteen dollars, most of it for buggy rides, postage stamps, and train fares. His election-day expenses amounted to forty-five cents, two nickels of it going to buy beer for several voters wearied from a long walk to the polls. How much John Jarrett spent on his quiet trip into the district nobody knew.[17]

Tariff talk also targeted the Democrats' other great revenue reformer of the Midwest, Frank Hurd of Toledo. Republicans again chose a candidate with appeal to the working class. Artfully told, Jacob Romeis's story was that of a friendless boy, unable to afford schooling, set to work scrubbing the decks on Great Lake steamships and washing the dishes in the galley. Toledo Greenbackers had made him mayor, and when he sought reelection, Republicans rallied to his side. Now Romeis seemed a sure draw among Knights, "soft-money" men, and all toilers who had sweated for their earnings while "Frank Hurd was training his voice." With Democrats alarmed statewide and with the Toledo congressman used everywhere as a token of the party's secret adherence to free trade, Hurd dodged his own record, tried to change the subject, and even protested himself no free-trader after all.[18]

Carlisle's, Hurd's, and Morrison's contests showed how far customary issues could be applied to special political circumstances, but they also showed how mixed the message from any congressional district might be. Romeis was an eligible candidate not just because he was a onetime Greenbacker but because he was a German and a champion of "personal liberty." In Morrison's district, Jehu Baker openly wooed the German vote and made no secret of his distaste for Prohibition. He even campaigned in the saloons. When all the votes were in, Jarrett and the Knights claimed Morrison's scalp and the credit for Baker's win, but other groups helped deliver the victim: dairy farmers enraged at "Old Axle-Grease's" vote against a tax on oleomargarine, disgruntled would-be postmasters, vengeful enemies from the party upstate, reformers appalled by Democratic ballot-box stuffers in East St. Louis, and the stuffers themselves, who, from their prison cells, could not put in the usual good work for Morrison.[19]

Morrison had good company in defeat. Elsewhere, the tariff and working-class organizations took credit for some notable results. Hurd's "death-bed repentance" could not save him. In the neighboring Ohio district, Bristor lost, despite the solid support of the Knights, which, in so heavily Republican a district, should have surprised nobody, and in Pennsylvania, the Greenback-Republican alliance paid off for Brumm once last time but "King Bob" Kennedy's narrow escape set off alarm bells. One editor noted that Whiteley had given five dollars to Kennedy's campaign, and he gave thanks: at that rate, thirty cents more would have wiped out the Republican county ticket's slim lead, too.[20]

The biggest shocker came in Kentucky, where Speaker Carlisle owed his election to propertied Republicans. As the first reports of canvassers showed Covington going heavily in Thoebe's favor, merchants and professionals closed their offices and escorted their clerks to the polls. Those with telephones summoned home Republicans with day jobs in Cincinnati for some last-minute help. After a slow, possibly creative count by Democratic officials in outlying counties, the Speaker did pull through, and the next House threw out Thoebe's challenge "with laughter and scorn." Still, Democratic editors shook their heads. It had been too close. Didn't the Knights realize that Carlisle had spent his life fighting the power of robber capitalism by his opposition to the protective tariff? Indeed they did; the tariff was the secret of Thoebe's near success. This was his chief issue, and the fear that reform would drive down employees' wages.[21]

Here and there, labor parties made their own mark. In Chicago, the United Labor Party polled 25,000 votes that fall. Sixty-four votes more, and they would have elected a congressman. As it was, their vote took enough strength from the Democrats to hand the county government to the Republicans. Downstate, the Knights elected their ticket in East St. Louis and lesser offices among the miners in Will County. In Milwaukee, the People's Party won the county, the mayor's office, six assembly seats, and the congressional seat. Knights of Labor went to the Colorado state senate and the New Jersey Assembly and made a spirited race for Congress in Richmond.[22]

Still, given the prospects that summer, the Knights had not done particularly well in the midterm elections. Neither party gave them much credit for the national results. Independent labor candidates ran for Congress in Kansas, Kentucky, Maine, Michigan, New York, New Jersey, Ohio, Pennsylvania, and Washington. All of them lost. Republicans picked up twenty-six seats in the House, seventeen short of winning control, and Democrats kept most of the governorships. Hoping to beat "that sycophant of banks and corporations," "Leatherskin" William McKinley, a radical in Ohio discovered Knights of Labor voting against their own congressional nominee because McKinley's name was synonymous with a protective tariff. Ohio's Knights included "some of the biggest flatheads to be found," the organizer complained. "It would require a club as big as a telegraph pole to knock even horse sense into some of their thick skulls."[23]

From the returns, indeed, the striking fact was not labor's clout but the mischief that the temperanceites had caused. In Indiana, Democrats found to their surprise that the third party had done all too well. Its numbers had grown fourfold since 1884. Having picked up the most eligible Republicans already, it now made inroads on both sides. "The prohibitionists get the sky," a local organizer wired headquarters; "the republicans the earth, and the democrats get h--l all along the Wabash."[24]

The Labor Party's hour had passed. It did not seem so then. State tickets would run in various states the following year. Independent tickets threw a scare into the major parties in more than sixty cities. They elected their judicial ticket in Milwaukee and very nearly elected a mayor in Cincinnati. "Every day brings tidings of the uprising of the people," the secretary of the Industrial Union enthused. "We are of a grand army surely."[25]

On the map of the labor movement, all these victories spangled the country in pinpricks of light, but they shone the brighter for the dark background behind them. To win an alderman, even a mayor, permitted only limited change. Certainly a working-class neighborhood would feel the effect of a change in how the police handled tramps and labor demonstrators. More money for sewer lines on the other side of the tracks and for night schools improved the quality of life. Many Knights thought this enough; just doing as their predecessors had done, and doing it better, offered living proof that the common people knew their own business best.[26]

Still, little could be done to right the wrongs in the workplace without some radical change in the kind of governors, senators, congressmen, and presidents elected, and with them the sort of decrees handed down from the bench. As an independent party, labor never made the breakthrough to that higher level. Nine thousand Pennsylvanians voted for labor, and only six hundred in Massachusetts. A Dubuque organizer warned his more eager colleague that any state labor party convention would be "a pitiable farce." Only six members of the state committee even bothered to reply to his letter, and on a list of names in his own congressional district, he received but one answer. In Milwaukee and Kansas City, Socialists bolted the labor ticket, assuring the return of the mainstream parties to power.[27]

When an independent labor party took on more substantial proportions, Democrats and Republicans joined forces to crush it out. Henry George faced an informal arrangement of that sort when he ran for mayor. Theodore Roosevelt was running on the Republican ticket, but nobody had to ask why his totals were unusually small or Democratic ones suspiciously large. Detroit's silk-stocking Republican wards turned out against the labor candidate their party had endorsed for Congress. From San Francisco to Clinton, Iowa, fusion and "citizens'" tickets turned every box—and every poll watcher—against the independent party.[28] When Republicans and Democrats worked together, with their presses providing a loud chorus of scare-talk and their legions of city employees manning the polls, the labor parties discovered how vulnerable they were, standing alone.

Nothing fails like failure, and the sooner it became clear that the Knights of Labor were on the decline, the sooner potential third-party voters cut themselves loose.[29] But there may be other, more practical reasons why failure had been there all along, why every day that the two parties were given to counter the "workingman's hour" would lessen the chances of a sturdy, lasting labor party. To build on sentiments that already existed was one thing; to break the institutional ties and loyalties of workers and induce them to take up new ones—that was quite another. Yet this was precisely what a new party would have to do: it would have to wrench its workers free of their partisan loyalties, already established, only to commit them to a fresh partisanship. Habit, custom, tradition, and ideology all worked against any such action.

As things stood, the Knights could organize workers without shaking any of those loyalties. Indeed, one could see the roles of union membership and party loyalty as working together, as complementary. The protections that a union member sought on the shop floor were analogous to the protections that only law could provide, and to which one party or the other stood committed. Brotherhoods and fraternal orders protected the dignity of labor by asserting the rights of freeborn men, while the high tariff protected that same dignity by keeping wage levels high enough to keep families self-sustaining.

At the same time, the Great Upheaval, as historians have come to call it, was terribly vulnerable to what the mainstream parties did. If, in fact, the Knights did not articulate a radical program, or, indeed, any program at all, then their strength at the polls may have come precisely from their own imprecision: they could be everything and all things to people who wanted *something* and could not agree on what that something was. Create a set of specific demands—Henry George's single tax, mine safety, an end to the wage system—and the constituency that had put labor candidates in might well reconsider their loyalties, rejecting candi-

dates now that they had a program attached to them. As long as the labor uprising had no set program, it was at a disadvantage against political parties that
could offer programs, and take away at least some of their members by putting reforms onto the statute book.

That is very much what the two-party system did. In early 1886, as the Knights
of Labor began to show their power, legislatures leaped into action, and after the
midterm elections, the action was renewed. Historians have noted the spate of
anti-anarchist laws, and laws against conspiracy, the first "Red scare." They may
have underestimated the offerings on labor's behalf that accompanied them. Over
the next two years, a host of measures, not all of them meaningless gestures, went
onto the statute books. With a powerful labor party on the rise, Massachusetts
enacted its first employers' liability law. In New York, Connecticut, New Hampshire, and Maryland, lawmakers showed a similar concern. Wisconsin passed its
first factory-safety laws, covering "all belting, shafting, gearing, and hoists, fly-
wheels, elevators, and drums" in manufacturing establishments, and set up a factory inspector with powers to order reforms.[30]

Not all the alacrity to serve labor came from the year of the Great Upheaval. In
New Jersey and Ohio, Democrats had formed a working alliance with trade unions
years before. But the pressure helped those politicians already friendly to labor
convince recalcitrant rustic lawmakers that the need for action could wait no
longer. As good an example of that mixture of long-term strategy and short-term
expediency could be found in Governor David Bennett Hill of New York. Cour-
teous and calculating, he despised Mugwump notions of reform. His model for
politics was his home town, Elmira, where election day was said to have ended
with the ground white around the polling place from the torn envelopes that
started the morning with payoffs for prospective floaters.[31] With an eye on key
immigrant groups and his support in the downstate metropoli, the governor
stymied toughened liquor laws and defended the right to get drunk as "personal
liberty."

Hill knew all the Democratic shibboleths about the best government govern-
ing least and the immutable laws of economics defining labor's value. He also
knew how to read election returns, and the speedy rise of a labor party in New
York politics alarmed him. It was true, perhaps, that the labor nominee for mayor
of New York City, Henry George, had more going for him than his advocacy of
the working class. But 68,000 alleged "anarchists, communists, socialists, ni-
hilists, terrorists, man-eaters, property-destroyers, incendiaries and traitors of
the red flag" dared the bullies and defied employers' threats of dismissal to put
George in second place. Without the help of a lot of scared Republicans and

without Tammany Hall ward heelers doing a little constructive counting of ballots, the regular Democratic nominee might well have been beaten.[32]

What followed in the next session of the legislature was no gesture, nor some midnight conversion. Hill had counted on laborers' votes in the past; that was one benefit he could expect from fighting temperance activists, and his first years as governor had seen a fair amount of labor legislation enacted. Now that interest in action friendly to labor took on a new intensity and spirit. Not by chance, a month before the 1886 mayoral election, the governor commuted the sentence of some Knights jailed for leading a boycott. When the new legislature convened, there were ten pages of recommendations in the governor's message, not just three. No Republican "hayseed"-dominated legislature was likely to give him everything, nor did it. But in a moment of apparent economic crisis such as the Knights had created, Hill did get Labor Day and for some businesses, the Saturday half holiday. Funds were found to prolong the life of the state arbitration board. A tenement house bill went through, and the number of factory inspectors was increased. Certain safety mechanisms were required in factories, and the yellow-dog contract was forbidden, in either oral or written form. With pleasure and much publicity, he signed a bill forbidding the employment of workers on New York City's streetcars and elevated railroads for more than ten hours at a time.[33]

What Hill had done, in effect, was to invite labor unions to enter politics as allies, rather than as a separate party, using their influence to put through legislation and win a piece of the patronage. The strategy worked very well. Henry George's followers moved to form a permanent labor party in 1887, but the city-run United Labor Party found itself handicapped by an inability to make an appeal to labor significantly more persuasive than Hill's. The State Trades Assembly endorsed Hill and decried the United Labor Party for its strictures on him. "Hill's labor side-show," Republicans jeered; but they could not produce a phenomenon like it. That November, the Democratic state ticket swept through comfortably, and Henry George's party took 70,000 votes statewide—just 2,000 more than he had won in New York City alone the year before.[34]

Hill continued to keep his ties open to labor. When he vetoed a factory inspectors' bill covering women employees' conditions, he was quick to write Terence V. Powderly with assurances that his only reason for doing so had been because of defects in the bill's writing. Next winter, he promised, he would see to it that a better bill passed. That would have his signature, and the lady that Powderly had recommended for an inspectorship would be given friendly consideration. In the years that followed, he asked for other advances to protect labor's right to organize. It was, the *Nation* fumed of one such request, "the most auda-cious piece of demagogism that even he has ever perpetrated."[35]

By itself, politics cannot explain the story of labor's failed moment. Still, it may give a glimpse of how hard it was for any third party based on class or cul-ture to break the two-party monopoly, as long as an America of many interests defined the issues in any campaign. There would not be one dominating voice but a cacophony. Out of the many calls and appeals for various forms of action, the mainstream parties had it within their power to pick and choose which top-ics to emphasize, at least within certain limits. They did not have the ability to stifle an issue completely, even one that made as uncomfortable dealing as that of what to do with the "saloonatics." Still, they could temper the appeal of out-siders by giving way on some things and holding firm on others; and by their command of the places of power — editorial offices, governor's mansions, and legislative seats — they had it in their power to give what no third party could, deeds that could be read as concrete proofs of their good intentions.

Against the blandishments of ideology and statutory provision, those Labor Party supporters who had left Democratic or Republican ranks on vacation, to cast a protest vote or send their old friends a message to reform, faced irresistible temptations. Those who wanted an excuse to return to their old loyalties had it; watching the struggle within the mainstream parties' ranks for the just cause, a Knight might see more clearly than ever that, among his former associates, he *could* make a difference. The Democrats had the power to change America in ways no Union Labor candidate had, or, it became increasingly clear, ever would have.

Bribed, bullied, and bargained with, labor parties tore apart. Their state legis-lators fell earliest from the ranks, breaking pledges and deserting labor nomi-nees' hopeless candidacies, and electing Republican or Democratic hacks to the U.S. Senate instead. Twenty-five Knights sat in Connecticut's Assembly, and only one stood by the Labor Party candidate.[36] In Chicago's mayoral race in 1887, Democrats and Republicans united on their ticket. With brothels, bosses, and boodle on their side, the fusionists carried two votes in three and every alder-manic seat but one, but they had help doing it. Labor papers and Terence Pow-derly himself smeared the candidates, all good trade unionists, for their supposed loyalty to the red flag. William Gleason, on the third party's executive commit-tee, took his followers over to the fusionists. With Democrats' help, he devel-oped his own organization, which opponents derided as the "Free Lunch" party. But it won the official right to the Labor Party label, and at the next city election, it whittled the newly christened "Radical Labor" Party's numbers to 7,000.[37]

In 1888, the working classes had not just one party all their own but four: the two biggest being the United and Union Labor parties. The United Labor Party insisted on making the presidential campaign on Henry George's land-value tax idea, after having expelled Henry George as a traitor. The Union Labor Party appealed to insurgents in the countryside, those who the Farmers' Alliance and the Agricultural Wheel had been indoctrinating out west. For president it ran A. J. Streeter of Illinois, head of the Northern Farmers' Alliance. Streeter did best in Kansas, where the party had no industrial workers on its ticket at all, and made a good showing in Texas, Missouri, and Arkansas, though in at least two of the three, his followers may well have been Republicans looking for any way of casting an opposition vote that Democratic election officers would count. Even where labor had polled a strong vote, organizers found potential support melting away. "The spirit of American manhood is gone," a Dubuque leader mourned. "We are already the slaves of the money power and are glorying in our shame. Our feeble efforts are only the last muscular twitchings of a corpse."[38]

From the Knights of Labor the Union Labor Party got hardly any support. "There is no Knights of Labor ticket in the field," Terence V. Powderly announced, "and the ticket through which the most practical results can be secured is the ticket which the Knights of Labor should support." By "practical results," Powderly may have meant a protective tariff. That was how leading Knights like Charles Litchman and the now-notorious John Jarrett interpreted him. They went Republican. GOP campaign money was funneled into the window-glass workers' union as well. Convinced that free trade would do more to liberate labor than anything else, Henry George cast his lot with Grover Cleveland. In most cities, independent labor party managers threw their support to Republicans or Democrats, and sometimes got local concessions in return. "Fusion has played hell in the sixth district and all labor parties are blotted out except those that for money are willing to assist the old rotten bourbon democracy," an Iowan raged. "A few letters from Gillette the political trader had more influence in this district than ever did Grasshoppers on a Kansas cornfield."[39]

The two major parties trimmed their own arguments with a distinct ethnic and cultural flavor to bid for working-class support. "The log cabin of 1840 has given place to the Chinese wash-house," the *San Francisco Alta California* joked, and it predicted that Harrison would add "bird's nest soup and 'lat pie'" to the White House bill of fare. Republicans promised to save the industrial masses from English wages and the debilitating cheapness of Canadian coal. Both discovered the evils of the "trusts," and when James G. Blaine blurted out to an audience that monopolies were "largely private affairs, with which neither President Cleveland nor any private citizen has any particular right to interfere," the Republican high command scrambled to shut him up.[40] Not in years had Democrats shaped their arguments so much as an attack on monopoly and overweening business interests.

When the election was over, with a few specks of exception, there was no labor party left worth mentioning. "As a national organization a labor party or any other distinctively class party is played out," the Knights of Labor's official organ concluded. "The Union Labor party, which was supposed to represent the Knights of Labor, the Trade Unions, the Farmers' Alliance, the wheel, the Grangers, Anarchism, socialism, Greenbackism, Free Land, Free Labor, Free Transportation, Free Banks and Free Lunch polled about one hundred and fifty thousand votes, and that too after a campaign of brag and bluster such as was never indulged in by a prize fighter." Its lesser rivals ranged from minuscule to invisible; Henry George's once-mighty United Labor Party, shorn of its leaders, barely took in 2,000 votes in New York City—and "took in" were the right words: true to mainstream custom in dealing with lesser rivals, Republicans paid the bills and printed up tickets giving themselves thirty-two of the state's thirty-four presidential electors on it.[41]

What Knights learned, every group learned. The dominant parties did not just control the political process. They used it to deliver. In Iowa and Minnesota, other groups besides labor had attacked the railroad "monopolists" in 1886 and forced the parties to shift toward stiffer regulatory measures. Companies that gave lip service to a national commission were hardly pleased with the bill that Congress put through that winter, establishing the Interstate Commerce Commission (ICC), though they allowed that southern Democrats could have given them far worse. On the state level, corporate spokesmen found themselves everywhere on the defensive. "The legislative mills are grinding out law for the railways with the utmost liberality," the *Railway Age* growled, "as will be seen from the carefully compiled epitome given in this journal each week." The *Age* knew where to lay the blame for laws against discrimination, pools, and cheaper prices for freight carried long distances: with the Congress and the model that the ICC had given to state legislation. It might have just as easily blamed the election returns.[42]

Yet was there not another, powerful lesson to be learned from the 1886 returns? The old issues, the outmoded ones that liberal reformers and Knights wanted to cast aside, could not be exorcised so easily as that. In the end, Democratic ascendancy in the House rested on one simple fact: the suppression of an open political process down south. However far the agrarian rebels in the Wheel may have trimmed Democratic margins in the Arkansas legislature, neither it nor the Alliance nor the Knights had done a thing to keep a solid South from send-ing an overwhelming Democratic delegation to Congress. From South Carolina to the Rio Grande, not a single Republican won. Nationwide, there were just 40 seats where the winner took over 80 percent of the vote — and 34 were in the South; 17 more gave two-thirds or more of their votes to one party — and 10 were southern. In all, of the 88 congressional seats where a candidate got more than 60 percent of the vote, all but 16 were Democratic ones, and 62 of those Demo-crats came from the South. As long as "usurpers" held southern districts that they were not entitled to and gave Democrats the majority in national councils that no free process would have allowed, Republicans, even working-class ones, would have every right to turn their resentments southward. Like it or not, the incomplete freedom that the Civil War had given to black southerners was to them of greater moment than the narrowing freedom of white Americans, in a world of expanding capital.

The Fix Is In

Little bars of "soap,"
Little bags of "sand,"
Make a great commotion
In this voting land.
—from the *Boston Times*, quoted in *St. Joseph
    Daily Gazette*, November 11, 1884

Politics was too important to leave to the politicians. Reform must come. On that point a growing chorus agreed in the Gilded Age. The only question was, on whose terms should the system be changed? Here, the answer revealed what had been clear all along. Neither businessmen nor idealists controlled the political process. Politicians owned and dominated it, and while they could not quash reform entirely, they used their power to meld it to suit themselves.

One would not imagine that fact, to judge from the first cries of triumph and the claims of original authorship that came from those least political of partisans, the liberal reformers. The Mugwumps had a gentleman's disagreement with those running the political machinery. How could gentlemen have anything else in an age of grab, graft, grist, and grease? Often college educated and born to affluence, they looked down on the party scramblers, and, indeed, on much of the dollar-scrambling that went with it. They never packed a party caucus; indeed, their lament was that so few people with their civic responsibility attended one at all. Mugwumps were not out just to make government work cleaner and better but to change what it did and what kind of people had the loudest voice in making policy. Seeing a political system where business lobbies and appeals to the "dangerous classes" had made politics a dispensary and idealism or long-range precepts of government dispensable, they looked to a change in the rules to rescue the public good.[1]

"Public good" like "citizen" was a very elastic term. For the narrowest interpreter, like Edwin L. Godkin of the *Nation*, "reform" dwindled to little more than honesty and efficiency in public affairs, a mixture of judiciously applied nightsticks and sound double-entry bookkeeping. At all events, policy makers had no business using the city treasury as a cornucopia for politicians, or, for that matter, for their constituents. Cities should rule themselves, but respectable, well-informed citizens should run the cities, not "demagogues" bent on "class legislation." Other reformers took a broader view of government than Godkin did. But even they worried about a partisanship that used its hold on power to buy votes, if not in cash, then in contracts and statutory handouts: a private pension bill for a deserter or a logrolling river and harbor bill that found a little something for Cheesequake Creek.[2]

The Godkins had a case. Partisanship made governance into a statutory higgledy-piggledy, inconsistent as a whole except in its readiness to please powerful groups. When liberals deplored "special interest" and "class" legislation, the terms also covered the grabs to serve the upper classes, the hungry railroad corporations demanding subsidies, and the tariff tinkerers putting local advantage ahead of national good.

Mugwumps were not alone in seeing a need to overhaul the machinery. All the outsiders, the third and fourth parties, the professionals and businessmen troubled by the inefficiency of the national state, echoed the indictment of a system that worked so much for the benefit of the placeholders and spoilsmen. Expanding corporations wanted a government that was predictable, or at least comprehensible. Permanent specialized lobbying machinery and trade organizations that helped individual firms express their views in one voice were among the Gilded Age's growth industries. Bombastic editors to the contrary, businessmen knew they could not control politics, knew, indeed, that the search for votes or douceurs gave politicians regular incentives to promise controls on them. Run by its own laws of supply and demand, politics looked less like an art or a profession and more like a trade, a very coarse one, much in need of policing.[3]

A tradition older than the party system itself underlay the unease. Ever since the founding of the republic, there had been a suspicion of "professional" politicians — one reason for the emphasis on short-term congressmen and annual elections of state officials and officeholders "fresh from the people." One can make too much of a culture of jokes about lawyers and politicians as self-interested, corrupt, greedy, and predatory, but the imagery was a constant backdrop to the more chaste self-descriptions that partisans gave of themselves. Some of it could be traced to the classical republican idea that power corrupted and that anyone with ambition automatically showed his unfitness for the place he sought. The

Puritan ethic, too, had emphasized the moral superiority of those whose work produced something tangible: farmers ranking ahead of bankers, brokers, lawyers, or "jacks in office." Both skeins of thought reinforced an instinctive, traditional distrust of government, with its "tax-eaters." At all events, the political class was something apart from the people, and, it was alleged, even dared to rate itself as the "best society," manifestly worthier than those who entrusted it with power. To till the soil, a reform paper charged, was "to practically shut [oneself] out from all positions of trust and honor. The man who works for a living either as a farmer or mechanic, is not regarded by political managers as a fit man for office—he is too apt to have some impracticable notions about honesty."[4]

The years after the Civil War did not improve the image. Politics may have been no more putrid than in the 1850s, but the metropolitan press had greater resources for nosing out scandals and broadcasting them to a wider audience. For various reasons, including the political aspirations of some great editors, the "press gang" was keener to expose the incompetence and corruption in government. For white southerners, an attack on federal politicians dealt a blow to the central authority that had imposed and then protected a new biracial political order in the former Confederate states. Discrediting those who held power, they could discredit the uses of power to safeguard blacks' right to vote and Republicans' right to compete with Democrats on equal terms. Reform movements offered candidates whose lack of official experience underscored their worthiness. While Iowa Republicans threw the usual parades and played the political game, a reporter noted, Luman "Calamity" Weller ran a people's campaign for Congress. While the pro's laughed at him,

> he was quietly, with his trousers in his boots, cutting across lots, through corn-fields and wheat stubble, and talking with the grangers in the glare of their own back-log fires. . . . The result of these consultations was that Weller seemed to know better than anybody else why the hens did not lay, or the shoats prosper, or money was scarce, and what was the remedy. And so they came to talk of Weller as the man who understood what was the matter with things and how to straighten them out. And so they nominated him, and when the time came they elected him.

As for that longtime office seeker and party insider editor Horace Greeley of the *New York Tribune*, his supporters billed his presidential candidacy as eminently apolitical. He was the author of "What I Know about Farming," the hearty woodsman pictured in rustic surroundings.[5]

By the mid-1870s, what flickering faith in the possibilities of public authority that the Civil War had let loose had faded out. From what those in charge could tell, most people wanted cheaper government and less of it. The image of the politician was reinforced by novelists and satirists: the copperhead hacks like Petroleum V. Nasby of David Ross Locke's creation, the oleaginous Senator Abner Dilworthy of Mark Twain and Charles Dudley Warner's *Gilded Age*, who was protected in the end from punishment by colleagues just as morally blind as himself, and the charming "moral lunatic" Silas Ratcliff in Henry Adams's *Democracy*, modeled on Maine senator James G. Blaine. Seventeen states held constitutional conventions between 1877 and 1887. Usually the outcomes spoke a clear distrust of politicians. Generally, the documents were lengthened with restrictions on what legislators could do and how often they could meet to do it. At the same time, voters were less likely than ever even to trust constitution makers; they rejected six conventions' work in ten years.[6]

The unfriendly image was one that parties had to play against. Not by chance, they touted candidates more for their rise to success, their domestic virtues, or, in postwar years, their war records than for accomplishments of statecraft. In their own way, they were distancing them from the image of politicians. Regularly, newspapers would hail a selection for office by highlighting his "sterling virtue," "manly qualities" or whatever traits might put his personal character ahead of his persona as a partisan. Any trusting reader of a county history would be astonished at how energetically offices sought men (and caught them — doubtless after a severe struggle), and how often worthy citizens were "called upon" to accept a responsibility or "prevailed upon" to keep it. Few epithets were more insulting than "the officeholders' ticket" or "professional politician," and the parties used both liberally (a well-worn candidate on one's own side, by contrast, might be "a ripe parliamentarian" or "an old pioneer of conceded ability and experience").[7] The very energy with which partisan presses feigned their "independence" was a testimonial to the suspicion in which politics was held.

A small group of reformers put the blame on party itself, not on the parties. To them the idea that wicked men had hijacked political organizations begged the question: did the very nature of political organization give wicked men their chance? Perhaps it was the very process of attaching party labels to the competing sides that brought out the worst in ideological fights and tempted voters to let the name on top of the ticket blind them to the character of the men listed beneath it. If that was so, then any steps to reform the parties was doomed to fail. Institutional changes might clean up present abuses, but the spirit of party itself would find ways of making the new laws serve partisan purposes.[8]

They had a point, but most of the vocal critics of "bosses" did not insist that an America without party was practical or even would be a good thing. Nonpartisanship might work in local contests or municipal races, where there was more of a chance of the electorate knowing the candidates personally and where the issues did not lend themselves as easily to partisan formulas. Elsewhere, party labels had their uses as identifiers of distinctive sets of beliefs and policies. Rather, the crying need was for "a more honest and better informed partisanship," with "less jingle and better journalism." Either by limiting who voted or by changing the way campaigns worked, an educated electorate must be created, brave enough to vote its conscience, breaking party bonds when necessary.[9] The greatest source of rewards for winning, the great incentive for putting this year's success ahead of the country's good, was the whole principle of letting the victor award the offices and contracts to followers. From that, one reformer complained, came a system where "hundreds of thousands of parasitical vagabonds fastened in the country's vitals; professional office-seekers and contract-mongers, preying on the country, debauching elections, prostituting public office, robbing the public treasury, destroying the instinct of independent self-support, resorting to violence and bribery to carry elections, to be swapped over the bargain-counter for public trusts that did not belong to their stewards."[10] That spoils system must be trimmed away. Some of the vital functions of administration should pass out of politics entirely and into boards of nonpartisan experts.

Without influential friends, though, reform must fail. Independents lacked the clout to cast political life anew. Nor did they have staying power. Unfairly, New York's ward boss George Washington Plunkitt would sneer that they were "mornin' glories," or dilettantes. The real truth was that activists only lightly connected to the two-party system never had much of a chance to wield authority for long, even when they wanted to. Their entry into public life was the result of indignation, spurred on by immediate events. As the events faded in memory and the indignation cooled, the old party claims renewed their force among the voters. A few concessions from the regulars, a few events that reasserted the old issues, and the revolt could be tempered, even if it was not entirely suppressed.

Cloaked in a little brief authority, a reformer had to act quickly or work with the mainstream politicians, whose support was always conditional on the passage of reforms that were least likely to damage their own interests and disrupt the system as they knew it. The more a change in the rules promised to give them command of the field, the way a good gerrymander would, the brighter their reform sympathies shone. At best, then, every change in the structure of politics only offered the *potential* for making the system work more fairly.

This was certainly true of the spoils system. It was manifestly inefficient, breed-

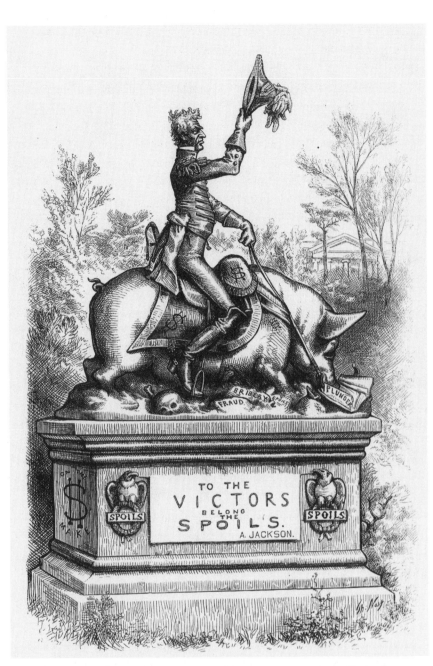

"In memoriam—Our civil service as it was" (Thomas Nast, *Harper's Weekly*, April 28, 1877). Like most reformers, Nast celebrated the death of the old system decades too soon. And, as a good Republican, he blamed its evils on Andrew Jackson, Democrats' patron saint.

ing corruption and the barter of perquisites for votes, providing campaign funds for the major parties and encouraging shakedowns of officeholders. Spoilsmen, as reformers pointed out, made even the poorest city-dweller pay in rotten service, "foul water, dirty and ill-paved streets, poor and high-priced gas, inefficient policemen," and businesslike responsibilities handled "upon a political basis."[11]

An age of increasingly complex public responsibilities needed a professional civil service, one where workers put their administrative duties ahead of partisan ones. But civil service reformers would have argued that more was at stake than making the government machinery run smoothly and cheaply. Spoilsmanship united personal and partisan advantage to create a system where the main purpose was winning office rather than doing anything with it. It impeded a party's commitments to causes where there was no immediate political payoff and resisted any changes that would interfere with "public office as a private snap." Lowering the moral tone of government service, partisanship was virtually unable to distinguish between public and private advantage, and hard put to discipline wrongdoers who had been of service to their party. It invited corruption, collusion, and incoherence.[12] A merit system and an end to assessments would not solve all America's problems. Still, they would be the first essential steps before government could be entrusted with new responsibilities. Appointed commissions could master the intricacies of their field in ways that no party-packed body could. Government *for* the people might indeed be possible only by making it less one *of* and *by* the people.

The decisive force, however, for passage of the first federal civil service act was not moral indignation but partisan calculations. As Republicans lost the House in 1882 by thumping majorities, they looked to the coming presidential election with a fresh dread. That Democrats might win it seemed very possible. Then all the offices would be vacated, not just in the same old way of the last twenty years, but far worse; the change from one Republican administration to another never led to the same kind of scramble and dismissals that a shift from a Republican to a Democratic administration would. Deserving partisans needed protection. Suddenly, Republicans saw the need for civil service reform, and immediately. They created a system with a small number of jobs chosen by civil service rules, but with the built-in guarantee of infinite expansion by presidential directive.[13]

At the same time, Democrats saw the bill as a chance to deprive Republicans of their campaign funds, by shutting off the flow of assessments and of donning the garments of reform to improve their political image. So the Pendleton Act came into being. Instantly, the merit system covered departmental clerks in Washington and in the biggest eleven customhouses and twenty-three post offices in the country. In ten years, the number of offices covered tripled. Wherever its pro-visions went into practice, government service became cheaper, more efficient, with less of the jarring turnover in personnel of the past.[14]

It was an advance, certainly, but not the revolution that reformers had hoped. Covering only about 11 percent of the offices at first, it left 117,284 positions un-trammeled, a banquet of spoils larger than Ulysses S. Grant had inherited when he entered the White House in 1869. It afforded a model to the states, but few of them chose to adopt it. Reformers offered bills in a dozen states. Only two, New York and Massachusetts, passed anything. Philadelphia and New York put en-claves of the municipal service under civil service rules; Milwaukee applied them to the fire and police departments. Few other cities followed their example.[15]

At the national level, presidents did indeed expand the system. Civil service rules covered 13,789 employees in 1884, 30,626 in 1890, and 94,893 by 1900. Es-pecially where the government's needs required expert technical skills or cleri-cal training, and where little profit was involved, the parties had no objection to mandating reform. Still, even those with reform records showed a keen interest in finding excuses for the dismissal of opponents before their time. Presidents re-freshed their reform instincts as they neared retirement and had the chance to keep their successor from meddling with a whole category of officeholders.[16]

The more important an office was for political purposes, the more rewards it had at its disposal, and the more certain it was that it would remain a patronage job. Jobs of special use to the politicians remained outside of civil service cover-age, and these expanded faster than the others. Outside of the cities, where mer-chants insisted on a professional mail and customs service, the parties had their field representatives ensconced in every office where there was money to be made. On average, that gave a congressman 200 favors to dispense, assuming that he be-longed to the president's party, and senators filled the rest, as well as the most im-portant unclassified offices. Legal or not, the extortion of assessments continued.[17]

Most of all, the basic principle of a nonpartisan civil service did not come about. When Republicans were fired, the successor might well have to pass a test, but the indispensable requirement was that he hold to the Democratic faith. Of the 2,359 postal officials at the president's appointment, Grover Cleveland's first administration removed 2,000, one reformer pointed out; of 52,699 lower post office clerks, 40,000 were replaced. And Cleveland was widely acclaimed as the most reform-minded president of his day! He looked even better after Ben-jamin Harrison's appointees picked up the headsman's ax. Committed to econ-omy and efficiency, businessman John Wanamaker was one of the most innova-tive postmasters general in half a century. But changes like a board of promotion that gave weight to merit in raising employees from one rank to the next never kept him from applying it to Republicans exclusively. Within months of his taking office, Assistant Postmaster James "Ret" Clarkson had fired nearly all the Democratic postmasters in the country, a service identical to Adlai Stevenson's during the first months of Cleveland's administration four years before. At all costs, deciding who should be promoted should stay with Wanamaker's own partisan-packed board rather than be left to the nonpartisans on the Civil Service Commission.[18]

A strong, effective Civil Service Commission would have been essential to making the system work, but there, the politicians had all the discretion they needed to hinder reform. Not until the Progressive Era would civil service reform take deep and meaningful form in the federal government. Even then, the use of government patronage to serve partisan purposes continued, often in pretty flagrant form, up to the passage of the Hatch Act of 1939.[19]

An equally large constituency appealed for "purity of elections" laws to end intimidation, vote-buying, and outrages at the polls. Because the problem came in so many varieties, it needed a number of solutions. At the very least, upper-class reformers argued, the vote should be trimmed to those with intelligence enough to read a ballot and character enough to heed their own consciences: immigrants able to read English and able to prove their residency by showing their naturalization papers and taxpayers with a stake in society. Paupers and jailbirds could not be trusted with the suffrage. To do away with colonizers and repeaters, every state needed an efficient registration system and, to forestall the resurrectionists, one that updated its rolls on a regular basis, so that the dead could be kept from deciding the fate of the living with a well-directed vote. Checks on the power of election officers to reject votes as they saw fit and of one party to monopolize the offices of authority were certainly needed, too, and many states strengthened legislation against voters selling their suffrages or politicians buying votes.[20]

Because money lay behind so many of the corrupting agencies on election day, states also considered laws throwing daylight on just who gave money to candidates, and how much. In the wake of the 1888 election, Democrats argued that an immediate exposure of corporations from whom the "fat" had been fried would scare off the big givers and cut down on the vote-buying money. Add to that a set of stipulations about what money could be used for, set spending limits, proportioned to the size of a candidate's constituency, limit the number of hands through which disbursement of funds could be made, the *Nation* argued, and campaign spending would slump.[21]

Given these incentives, New York put through the first such publicity law in

1890, and over the next three years, California, Colorado, Kansas, Michigan, and Missouri all followed suit. Another decade and fourteen states had some such law. With few exceptions, the laws worked poorly. Perhaps that was how they were meant to work. New York outlawed the corrupt use of money but, since it covered only candidates and not political committees, left spending limits untouched. Not that it mattered; the state set up no agency to enforce the law. Disclosure without spending limits gave only the semblance of reform. Five states thought even minimal laws were too strong and repealed them when the pressure for reform faded. Nor could any state law bring national committees to book. They were freer than ever to fry the fat. If anything, the laws only enhanced the fund-raising power of the Matt Quays. More often than ever, the national committees became the first place contributors would put their funds; there, at least, their donations could stay confidential. Money intended for a state could be laundered that way; the state committee could credit the money to the national one, and not to the original donors.[22]

What laws against bribery passed were only sporadically enforced. No reformer believed that they caught more than a fraction of wrongdoers. State legislatures put through an occasional bill forbidding employers to intimidate their workers into voting right, but, again, enforcement was so lax and the means of evasion so palpable that arrests hardly ever occurred.[23]

Registration laws were far more common. Between 1860 and 1880, just about every northern state put one through, and often built on it, widening the scope and closing up unexpected loopholes. In the next twenty years, South and West followed suit. Such laws certainly made privately sponsored vote fraud harder, but, again, partisan ends determined a statute's particulars, and those who passed the laws cared most about cutting down the vote given to their opponents. "I will tell you why we have passed this amendment," an Indiana lawmaker explained of one proposed measure in 1879. "We think you Democrats have carried this State by fraud for the last ten years, and *we* want to put a stop to it." In some states, such as Minnesota, registration went no further than cities with 40,000 people or more. In 1873, New York Republicans applied it to cities, more often than not Democratic, and continued to exempt towns with 10,000 people or fewer until 1913; Democrats, making a like calculation, briefly imposed registration on the countryside. Naturally, a partisan purpose was enough to discredit any law, and Indiana's constitutional amendment failed. No registration law passed court review until 1911. New Jersey Republicans tried to apply registration in cities of over 6,400, and Democratic governor Leon Abbett, who could see just as easily as they who this would burden, vetoed it.[24]

Just how registration worked, of course, determined whether it would work at all. A law like New York's in 1865, permitting voters to add their names to the lists up to the Saturday night before an election, almost invited repeaters to register under phony names on the last day or two; election officers would have just one working day to spot fraud, and that was nowhere near enough time. When the legislature tried to close the registration on the previous Thursday, a Democratic governor vetoed it, arguing that it discriminated against people who were still minors on that last day but would be of age when the polls opened. Maryland chose to require registration every three years; reformers protested that only annual registration assured honest elections. Where one registered mattered, too. Signing up at the ward level, as opposed to the precinct level, assured that registers and poll watchers would find it much harder to know whether the applicant was a genuine resident. The provision "enables the rounders to get in their work," the *Baltimore American* protested.[25]

Registration laws, by their nature, impeded a full turnout in the working class. Because they usually required a term of residency, they cut off those who changed their abodes regularly, and the smaller the precincts were made, the more likely that poorer voters, changing dwellings, would disfranchise themselves. The more poorly paid a worker was the more likely he was to shift lodgings or to leave town looking for a job. Landlords could drive tenants off the rolls by forcing them to vacate thirty days before an election. Any such discriminations, Democrats argued, hurt their own rank and file worse than Republicans', which was why Republicans enacted residency requirements.[26]

Indeed, registration laws, in the wrong hands, might even permit a more thorough subversion of the people's will than had a wide-open system. If the law required that the registrant's color be noted, as Maryland's statute did, it became an invitation to harassment and selective trickery. After reforms, designing politicians could not vote phantoms as easily, but the registration board could. Partisans on it could swell the rolls with phony names or strike hundreds of names of the opposition off, by apparent oversight. The more complicated the law's provisions the more excuses it gave for disqualifying those likely to vote incorrectly. North Carolina registrars rejected voters because they were epileptics, or because their wives lived in different precincts from themselves, or because the official registry failed to list their occupation, or because they "looked" too young. Republicans who had omitted to give their birthplace were turned away, and Democrats, including the registrar himself, were allowed to waive the requirement. Clearly, registrar-fashioned law bore "no more likeness to reform than a circus rider to Shakespeare."[27]

As with so many other manipulations of who could vote and how, the registration laws worked most viciously down south. There, Democrats found them one of the most useful hurdles to black voting, and to dampening Republican turnout generally. Virginia's 1884 law was typical. Enacted by Democrats as soon as they had driven the opposition from control, it let voters choose the three-person panel that named local election officials. There was no provision for a minority representation. "The Anderson-McCormick bill was passed in the interest of the white people of Virginia," the *Richmond Dispatch* explained; it was a law framed "to perpetuate the rule of the white man in Virginia." It certainly worked that way. With one-party policing, Democratic ballot-box stuffing became infinitely easier, and election judges used their authority to challenge black voters' identity, reject their votes, or slow the process in black neighborhoods so that the polls would close with many still waiting to cast a ballot. In the first state test of the law's usefulness, Democrats easily elected a governor, and angry Readjusters noticed that the counties that Democrats won included those with large black majorities. In Norfolk alone, the *Richmond Whig* protested, at least a thousand blacks were turned away from the polls.[28]

Almost all of the election reform laws had one final drawback. Covering the main event, they left primaries alone. It was still possible to call a caucus to choose delegates on short public notice or on none, to flood the primary election with bought-up members of the opposite party, to vote colonizationists to tamper with the returns, and to ignore all the specific safeguards that a general election made mandatory. But, of course, the only choices left to the voters were the ones that a packed caucus or a snap primary decreed.[29]

The last great reform of Gilded Age politics came with the enactment of the Australian ballot. Unable to police vote-buying, reformers argued, there must be some way of making the commodity worthless, and the way to do that was to give every voter a wide choice of candidates in absolute privacy. In the sense that a ticket could be folded or carried in one's vest pocket, citizens already had a secret ballot, but they were party ballots, with just one side's set of nominees, and as long as poll workers distributed them at the polls and had some leeway in the kind of print used and the color of paper, voters would have to work to keep their vote confidential or to split their suffrages between different nominees. It took special effort to "scratch" offensive partisans' names, a burden that party machines counted on when they ran respectable men at the top of the ticket and rascals farther down. To prevent intimidation and bribery, the ballot would need to become still more secret: one officially prepared at government expense, containing every important party's nominees, and available only from authorities at the election precinct. Dubbed the Australian ballot because of its origin, it gained wider attention in 1883, when the British parliament enshrined it in a corrupt-practices act. Louisville added the provision to its city charter in 1888, and Kentucky lawmakers broadened it a year later to include other cities. In 1891, it became part of a new state constitution.[30]

Reformers proclaimed its success even before the results were in. The Australian plan was well worth having, they argued, not just because floaters could be bought, but because anyone degraded enough to sell his suffrage lacked the honesty to stay bought. In fact, the *Troy Daily Press* argued, the "inherent 'cussedness' of the man mean enough to make merchandise of his right of suffrage" actually would prompt him to vote against any ticket he had promised to support.[31] With no means of knowing that he was getting his money's worth, a poll worker would withhold payments; with no need for an election-day shopping spree, parties would fry less fat. Barrel candidates would lose their advantage over purer, if poorer, statesmen. Countryside, not just cities, would feel reform's tonic effects. Community pressure to conform was worst where everyone knew everyone else. Under the new system, nobody would be the wiser. Labor Party supporters predicted that the Australian ballot would banish the employer's spies from the polls and break management's power to vote workers against their own interests. Agrarian reformers knew that small farmers dependent on their richer creditors and even tenant farmers could vote without fear, once the curtains on the polling booth closed around them before they made their choice.[32]

All these groups helped provide the Australian ballot with a wider audience and helped build popular support for its enactment, but what may have really shifted the balance was the recruitment of mainstream politicians to the movement. By no coincidence, the passion for reform broke out suddenly, even convulsively, in the months after the 1888 presidential election. After the cheating in West Virginia, Republicans had particular grounds, as Democrats had in Delaware and Indiana. As chief victim of the "blocks of five," Grover Cleveland naturally came out in the Australian ballot's favor. The Democratic press joined the chorus more heartily, perhaps, from fear that 1888 would set the pattern, with Republicans outdoing them at frying the fat and turning it into soap. In the Northeast, Republicans made the calculation that any official ballot would discourage illiterate voters, and that, they suspected, could only work to their benefit in Democratic cities. Connecticut Democrats counted on reform to weaken the force of the immense sums ($10,000 in Hartford alone, it was alleged) that had made "Bulkeleyism" a synonym for vote-buying in 1888.[33]

Indeed, politicians, regardless of party, could find reasons of their own for wanting election reform. Party-printed ballots were useful in some ways and in others a costly nuisance. A mistake in proofreading could cost one side votes it deserved. Worse still, local leaders found it all the easier to knife the county or state ticket by printing up ballots with particular variations. The right kind of reform would permit individual ticket-splitting, perhaps, but by setting up an official ballot sanctioned by those leading the state party, it would confound the wholesale ticket-splitting of a double-crossing ward heeler.[34]

With such support, states tumbled over themselves to endorse the "Marsupial Plan." One state enacted it in 1888, nine in 1889, seven in 1890, eighteen in 1891 —two of those being revisions of laws passed earlier. Maine Republicans had deplored reform as a "degrading foreign invention, designed originally . . . for use among the convicts," but by 1891, the governor gave in to public pressure and endorsed just such a law, and the Republican legislature put it through. By 1892, the secret ballot had triumphed in some form in every nonsouthern state except Idaho and Kansas. Four of the five states in the Border South and two in the Upper South had enacted it as well.[35]

Did it work? Reformers thought so, at least at first. What the Australian ballot did do was make it harder to carry elections by "individual electioneering," as one editor termed the influences, from intimidation and bribery to heartfelt discussion. A less-bought electorate conceivably would spend more time mulling over the issues, and one able to split its tickets more easily would need to work harder to familiarize itself with the full range of choices. For all these reasons, some newspapers boasted that the change in law had given the press "a power never before possessed" and incidentally encouraged a well-informed citizenry.[36]

Yet two-party politics not only survived; it thrived. Freed from the intimidation of voting as their Republican neighbors expected, New England farmers went to the polls and voted . . . just about the same as usual. The same was true everywhere—at least of those who still could vote. "The ballot law which we have used in this state for four years . . . has served the state well and the Republican party better," a New Hampshire Republican wrote Senator William Chandler.[37]

The reasons were not far to seek. Intimidation may have received a check. "Working men walked proudly into the reserved stalls and voted as Lords of their own suffrage," an observer boasted. But partisans soon found that they could still buy votes reliably, if they needed to, simply by paying potential enemies to refrain from voting, or the opposition's local leaders to spare any exertion to get out the vote. Reformers had also underestimated how far money had been used not to win but to reinforce individuals' loyalties and missed a fact that politicians knew perfectly well. Those who sold their vote often considered it a business transaction.[38] Paid for their votes, they delivered. Vote-buying may have slackened. It came nowhere close to ending.

Far from freeing voters to cast a ballot as conscience dictated, observers discovered that "kangaroo reform" intimidated some of them into absence from the polls. When Vermont Republicans failed to turn out in 1892, the party press blamed the Australian ballot. Farmers' "sensitiveness" and "timidity" kept them away from the polls. Able to read and write decently but bewildered by the complicated instructions for casting the newfangled ballot, they were too proud to reveal their ignorance by asking for help. The argument was self-serving, of course. Apparently the Democratic Party, that organized agglomeration of ignorance, in Republicans' view, had found no difficulty with the Australian ballot; *their* vote was up. Perhaps it was that they simply had no shame and were unembarrassed to ask directions. More likely, they made up their own real losses with Republican converts: 1892 was a bad year for the GOP. But the intimidating factor of a strange balloting system, particularly in the countryside where party machinery was less well suited to assembling the faithful for a crash course in ballot use, certainly must have played a part in a number of places. Elsewhere, parties organized schools to teach their voters how to use the Australian ballot, erected mock voting stalls for dress rehearsals, and distributed copies of a "specimen ballot" sent out by authorities—one reason why Tammany Hall's forebodings that they would lose 40,000 votes in 1890 proved a wild exaggeration, and why the real problems with mishandled ballots in Chicago came in "the kid glove, or gilt-edged polling places." Newspapers printed facsimiles, with explanations of the way to vote a straight party line and warnings about what to avoid. Even reformers used to "scratching" a ballot had some unlearning to do; defacing a ballot in the old way carried a one-year jail term and a $1,000 fine in New Hampshire.[39]

The Australian ballot worked as more than a literacy test for the unlettered. Slow readers found themselves partly disfranchised because they ran out of the time permitted to them before reaching the end of the ballot; very likely impatience cut down on a full vote as well, both because citizens spent longer waiting in line for their chance to enter the polling booth than they had done in the old days when a paper slip, already prepared, could be placed in the box, and because the longer the list of offices to be filled was, the likelier the voter was to quit before reaching the bottom of the page. Just trying to hold Pennsylvania's official ballot, fifty-two inches long and twenty-two inches wide, was an ordeal in itself. Voters with an unclear grasp of the directions marked their ballots for two different candidates for the same office; on these grounds, officials threw out 15,000 Republican votes in 1892 in Massachusetts alone. Some of these problems time and experience could overcome, of course. After instruction, voters found that they could pass through the polls at about 200 an hour. Still, at least in the short term, the *Berlin Independent* commented, the official ballot "was a document which caused some solemn hours of meditation." Its first trial had been a complete success, a Manchester newspaper agreed, "as a means of depriving voters of the right of suffrage."[40]

But there was also a problem with the laws themselves. As with so much else in Gilded Age policy, the federal system assured many variations on ballot reform, and partisan advantage was one of the forces determining how the law operated. Republican and Democratic lawmakers decided on what terms election reform would take place, and the terms they set, invariably, would keep their most crucial advantages in controlling the whole process. Vermont Republicans first confined the law to the larger cities, where Democrats had their biggest turnout and, according to their reputation as foreigners and illiterates, were likeliest to have trouble coping with the new ballot. In Connecticut, parties still wrote the tickets and passed them out; all the secrecy came in the provision of an enclosed booth, where the elector could deposit his ballot without a political heeler breathing down his neck.[41] But, of course, everything depended on the precautions to make sure that the voting booth *was* closed off from view, and on that, the law remained conveniently vague.

Partisans found other ways to keep their own hold over the ballot. "There's voters of ours so dumb that you couldn't drive this way of voting into their heads with a pile-driver or a trip-hammer," a Tammany ward heeler warned. So instead of the "blanket" ballot, New York and several other states arranged to let the state print each party's official ticket separately and permitted election officers to accept ballots printed up by the parties, too. They also allowed the "paster," a stick-on slip, which local candidates could hand out to their friends, to gum next to the appropriate office on an official ballot. In fact, city poll workers passed out pasters as electoral security blankets: a daunted voter could simply walk into the booth with five ready-gummed pasters in his pocket, stick them in the blank places, and not worry about checking off names. To help his unlettered constituents know the right paster from the wrong, New York's ward boss, Tim "Dry Dollar" Sullivan, scented his with peppermint. With twelve different kinds of unofficial ballots being peddled on election day in 1892, politicians were not so much confounded by the new system as they were confused. Even the governor flubbed his first attempt at a paster ballot.[42]

Election reform did not necessarily mean disfranchisement of illiterate voters, especially where the majority party saw it to its advantage to keep them voting.

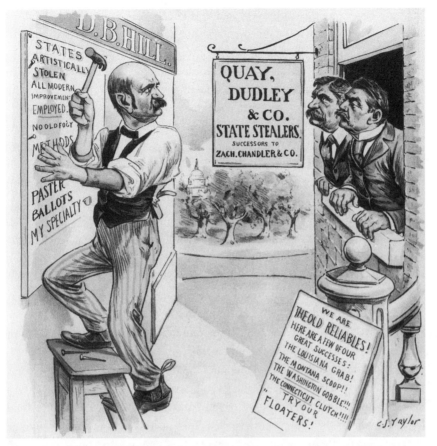

"A hustling competitor. Dave Hill: 'What are you looking at? You fellows can't have the field all to yourselves. I'm here for business, too!'" (C. J. Taylor, *Puck*, December 9, 1891).

Any New York voter who was "physically disabled" could admit a poll worker into the booth with him, and in some neighborhoods the clink of a coin in the hand was all that it took to produce disability in the most robust of voters, each of whom entered the booth. New Hampshire law permitted anyone needing assistance in marking a ballot to ask for aid from the election officer of his own party, and in some towns the moderator asked illiterates to specify which party's services they required. As "an arrangement to facilitate the purchasing of votes and knowing that you get what you pay for, the new secret ballot is just a howling success," a manufacturer complained.[43]

Where the two-party system was most competitive, both parties found it to their interest to organize the ballot by parties rather than list candidates alphabetically, office by office. That way, a simple check mark at the top could allow straight party voting, without the potential mischance of a voter not being able to read names (in Pennsylvania this privilege was restricted to the two major parties; Populists would need to place a check by each name in their columns). In New York, voters could tell one party slate from the other by the symbol at the top. Ticket-splitting was now restricted to the literate only. Some states tried the double-marking system as a compromise with party regularity and illiteracy. At the top of the ballot, a voter could check a single box, thus voting the entire party slate, or he could mark each of the boxes by individual names, the better to split his ticket. Not all states tried this method, and those that did, like Maine, found limitless confusion in voters who would mark the same ballot *both* ways.[44]

Such a situation assured that election officials would gain a power never before possessed. Thanks to the demands of an official ballot, the state became the gatekeeper for political alternatives. Only those parties with a place on the ballot had any chance of being voted for. This was all very well for the mainstream two parties, each of which had a place by habit and by virtue of their numbers. But insurgents found themselves barred by requirements that they reach a certain proportion of the vote or collect a certain number of signatures in order to qualify. Money that could ill be spared would now need to go for the preliminaries to a campaign rather than to persuasion, and in some states, labor parties found themselves ruled out entirely. Even fifteen hundred signatures seemed a daunting number for the People's Party in West Virginia, and when they formed less than a month before election day in a congressional district, the rules made it impossible for them to gain official recognition in more than one county. Few independent parties could collect the 10,000 signatures necessary to field an official state ticket in New York, and regulations discouraged putting forth any incomplete ticket—a nominee for governor, say, without picking names for all the other state officers. Rightly, the *Nation* protested that the real aim of such laws there and in California and Pennsylvania was to kill independent nominations. Elsewhere, the real impact came at the local levels.[45]

Officials now could control the process as they liked. It was up to them to decide which signatures were genuine on petitions for a place on the ballot or to refuse allowance of petitions. The technicalities of the law could be used effectively to deny one group the right to a Democratic Party label, on behalf of another, or to set the disqualification of a party on the basis of technicalities.[46]

The Australian ballot also gave white southerners a new reason for cutting blacks from the vote. The last thing Democrats could afford was a reform that would put black voters beyond their power to buy or intimidate. An Australian ballot could be made harmless only by making sure that its advantages were for whites only. So southern legislatures lagged in taking up the innovation, and those that did ringed it round with other measures assuring a smaller, whiter electorate. Indeed, as some northern reformers pointed out, the Australian ballot itself could give the white South just what it had been unable to arrange since the passage of the Fifteenth Amendment, the legal disfranchisement of an entire race. In effect, it acted as a literacy test. It deprived a certain number of Democrats' white supporters of their vote, but that was an acceptable price for changes disfranchising the great bulk of Republicans' black ones. Reform would also put election day and the interpretation of the intricacies of the law more securely than ever into the hands of Democratic election-judges.

Combined with a poll tax and the requirement that voters show the receipts as proof of payment, the Australian ballot became part of the repertory of a putatively color-blind set of regulations. It also gave the disfranchisers protective coloring; to northern liberals, for whom election reform had become the necessity of the hour, enactment of ballot reform proved the goodness of white leaders' intentions. They were not trying to get rid of black voters — only corrupt and ignorant ones. They had enlisted in a crusade to purify politics, and reformers, like any other group, did not scrutinize too closely the motivations of their own allies. Under cover of the Australian ballot movement, northern perceptions of the workings of southern prejudice became duller than ever. The ballot, Professor N. S. Shaler reminded readers, was as dangerous as a gun; lacking proper education, blacks could never use it properly—and, he let readers infer, would be less worrisome if disarmed of it.[47] In fact, the real effect of the Australian ballot was to further a process well under way by the end of the 1880s, to solidify an already solid Democratic South and to tilt the advantages even further toward the conservative white Democratic leaders who had come to see political power as their exclusive property.

Plainly, reform's potential lay less in the idealists' figuring of its results than in the way the laws were written and the limits set upon them, and in the purposes for which they were enforced. In both cases, the strongest determining factors were those people with the political power to translate public outcry into action and to deflect it in the direction best suiting themselves. The professional politicians who ran the system were not about to make a new system that would dismantle the parties. An American people, accustomed to party, was not about to raise the kind of pressure needed to make the politicos do so. The hour of reform was a fleeting one as long as the two-party system remained strong. Changes in law made no difference without a change in the attitudes that had befouled the political process.

This the Mugwumps had seen plainly. The problem of an apathetic or selfish public would not go away of itself; it was a condition of public life that itself needed correction for the system to be made anew. Gentlemen who had not soiled themselves in politics must involve themselves. Individuals should set their own goals toward some higher interest than a pension or a protective tariff. So the reformers chided, chivied, and encouraged. They reached out for alliances with the pulpit. They called for campaigns of education, convinced that the more information the people got, the more they would see beyond their own personal interests to the higher good of the nation.

In this Mugwumps, like the Progressives that succeeded them, were more clear-eyed than their idealistic language may suggest. They may have believed that the political system could be restored to the people's hands or to the public interest by the enactment of structural changes on politics: in the next generation, these included referendum, initiative, recall, nonpartisan tickets in city elections, a city commission form of government, and direct election of senators. Corruption might be ended, pundits opined, if every convention gave way to a primary, and if attendance in the primaries was made compulsory so that the people who did not expect offices would find a reason to quit their comfortable homes to do their duty.[48] But as the last suggestion indicates, they did not always deceive themselves that changing the machinery would change the character of American politics — not by itself. Machinery was neutral. "Without public spirit anarchy follows," a reformer summed up. "Our youth should be taught at the family and church altars, at school and by example, this obligation — like the precepts of religion and temperance, honor and patriotism — that attendance at the caucuses and primary elections is the first duty of the citizen and cannot be neglected without personal dishonor and danger to the Republic."[49]

The language itself opened a possibility that many reformers outside the Mugwump ranks had suggested all along: if the problem was a lack of virtue, of moral fiber in politics, might not the real answer lie in woman suffrage? For if women were motivated by right and wrong, where men acted out of a search for advantage, the best way to win the war on rascality and rapacity might be to call on the reserves. So the Prohibition Party had argued, and so the Populists of the West would insist. States had accepted the logic of the argument when they dropped the gender qualification in school district elections. "Your regular politician takes to stealing almost as naturally as a duck takes to water," an Ohio delegate told the state constitutional convention. But where women went, "corruption is apt to disappear." In the ladies, another delegate predicted, vote-buyers would find "an incorruptible phalanx, which they could not purchase." Give women the vote, a radical newspaper urged, and "those qualities of the feminine mind and character complementary to the masculine mind and character" would be brought to bear on social questions. Drunken brawls would end at the polls, a suffragist promised, and "the very angelic presence of women" would quell all "the rude outrages and insults" of election day. (And, in fact, some observers in the 1890s saw exactly that: as women appeared at the polls to electioneer, lawmakers hastened to clean up politics with laws closing polls earlier in the evening, forbidding bonfires, celebratory riots, and the "treating" of voters during the campaign.) The Australian ballot itself, by making voting a more genteel business, made the polling place safer for women's attendance, and campaigns of education seemed to be taking the masculine edge off politics. The great hopes of reformers in this, as in everything else, would go unmet. But in their argument, no observer of Gilded Age politics could have disagreed: that what America needed most, a "quicker intelligence and higher conscience for the management of public affairs," could not come through politics-as-usual, guided by the politicians-as-usual.[50]

Dishing the Pops

So hurrah, hurrah for the great P. P.!
1 = 7 and 0 = 3,
A is B, and X is Z;
And the People's Party knows it!
—from the *New York Sun*, copied in the
Philadelphia Press, July 7, 1892

Four years after the "workingman's hour," it seemed as if farmers had seized the day. From the western prairies and the cotton fields of an impoverished South, low prices and overproduction had made mockery of America's success myth: the better their crops, the poorer a return producers earned. Sunk into debt, often to the point of ruin, angry men and women turned to politics, and the Farmers' Alliance, a fraternal society and mutual self-help organization, threw itself into the 1890 campaign to compel candidates to favor the reforms that mainstream politics had not. Exasperated by the failure of western Republicans and southern Democrats to provide for meaningful changes, insurgents elected congressmen and governors. A year later, their most forceful advocates banded together with other activists to create the People's Party. The Populists, as they came to be known, would bring a different kind of color and excitement to politics, and unease to the financial centers of the East. "Everywhere as I went through the aisles of the House, I saw it and heard it," Hamlin Garland wrote. "Place-holders were beginning to tremble; but in the midst of it the men who were advocating right and justice instead of policy sat eager, ready for the struggle."[1]

The story of the Populist revolt makes dramatic reading for those who love their history as a confrontation between good and evil, the oppressors and the oppressed. Instead of the claptrap of the stereotypical Gilded Age campaign, outsiders took on Wall Street, the extortionate railroads, and all the banded corporations of the Money Power. Populism stood as the best and, to some historians' thinking, last hope of confronting an industrial order that treated people like commodities and government as the lapdog of propertied interests. If only it could have succeeded![2]

But it did not succeed. Those who held power were not about to surrender it graciously. Where slander, manipulation, deceit, and trickery could not do the job, there was always the fraud that counted dogs, mules, and the inhabitants of graveyards against Congressman Tom Watson in Georgia, and the force that dynamited Populist presses in Louisiana and filled the streets of Wilmington, North Carolina, with a white mob prepared to kill any black that chanced its way.[3]

These are bitter truths, but not the whole truth. To mourn for an opportunity missed is easier when we slight how little real opportunity there was to mourn for. As should be clear already, the Populists were not simply beaten. They had just about no chance of succeeding nationally. Except in their scale of operations, the owners of the political system did not rouse themselves and use extraordinary measures to make their world safe for Democracy—and Republicanism. They did what they had been doing all along. Their means were the well-refined, clearly designed ones by which they had thrust third parties onto the outskirts of politics. Not for the first time, the reigning parties realized that their command of the law gave them a power against which the Populists were helpless and that their years of building up partisan loyalties were a force that no new movement, no matter how fervid its evangelism, could counter.

Generally, the rise and decay of Populism has been seen in the context of the farmers' complaints and, somewhat less commonly, in the broader fabric of insurgency and organized movements of discontent during the Gilded Age. It can be understood in no better way, but it also needs to be seen from the perspective of two-party politics and politicians. Without that context, much about the sudden rise of the farmers' movement, the awkward translation into a third party, and its crushing destruction cannot be well explained.

At least until 1892, the People's Party really was a sideshow. Given the choice of enemies, Republican and Democrat preferred meting out blows to each other, and over the past four years, they had been unusually ruthless in doing so. There were good reasons for doing so.

Republicans had won a portentous victory in 1888. Taking the Electoral College but coming in second in the popular vote, Benjamin Harrison had carried a smaller share of the total vote than any Republican since 1860. Democrats lost the House, but so narrowly that the speakership became quite literally a matter of life or death, dependent on how many Republican members died before the session opened. Firm control depended on filling disputed seats.[4]

More was at stake than putting a Republican in the chair. With patronage and the right kind of legislation, the party could bring in a loyal West and bring over a New South. Give Republicans a fairer chance down south, and they would provide the two dozen seats the GOP needed to make its House majority firm. Give statehood selectively, and eight fresh Republican senators would place the upper house beyond capture. At the very least, Republicanism would go into the 1892 election nineteen electoral votes richer than before. Even with a solid Democratic South, they were within sight of a lock on the Electoral College.[5]

But as the returns from below the Mason-Dixon Line in 1888 showed, congressional action must happen at once. If the Republicans lagged inactive, there was every chance of a South solid enough to put Democrats within a few votes of a foolproof electoral majority. A year later, the off-year elections up north gave an even more ominous warning. States that the GOP had counted on in the past looked uncertain, and others were trending Democratic. Beyond that, the electorate seemed more unpredictable. How the newly adopted Australian ballot would change the electorate, nobody knew for sure. But a new politics, where a minority party could become a majority one, seemed quite possible.

Indeed, action down south made it look downright probable. Republicans won most of their victories up north, but in every House election, their majority had depended on that saving remnant from the former slave states. But the shock of losing the White House and control of both branches of Congress had given Democrats one more shove toward making the South as solid for themselves in state and congressional races as it was in presidential elections. In Florida, Democrats took advantage of the slimmed-down electorate and the rigged legislature that a registration law and gerrymander had given them to shove through a poll tax requirement for voting and an eight-box law, which effectively disfranchised the large illiterate Republican population of the state. North Carolina lawmakers pushed through a tougher registration law that was sure to make it harder for any opposition party to bring out its full strength. With a frank determination to shut blacks out of the franchise, Tennessee required registration before every election in any town or city that had cast 500 votes or more in 1888 and enacted a poll tax, which in 1890 became the requirement for any prospective voter. That winter, Mississippi Democrats spared themselves future difficulties with Republican city government in Jackson by enacting a new charter changing the ward lines, as a southern newspaper explained, "so as to give perpetual control of the board of aldermen to the white people," and by imposing street and poll taxes on all prospective voters. Compared to what had gone before, perhaps these ranked as reforms; Democrats had carried the last municipal election with Winchester rifles and by stationing armed mobs around the polls to drive off legal voters.[6]

Not in a decade had the nation seen so much outright bulldozing: bullying and intimidation in Virginia's gubernatorial election, a coup d'état in Jackson, Mississippi, mobbing and assassination in Arkansas, open fraud in Louisiana. A legislative election in Baton Rouge began with threats and ended in ballot-box stuffing. Republican election commissioners were assaulted and party activists knocked down while the sheriff and city police watched tranquilly. Just five Republicans had voted in the recent election in a four-county area of Georgia, and one was horsewhipped for it. The House majority needed no southern correspondents to tell them the facts. Seventeen contested election cases, most of them from the South, supplied eloquent testimony enough.[7]

With such apprehensions members assembled at the Capitol late that autumn, and with such expectations both sides prepared for the roughest kind of combat. Though they stood a good dozen seats in the minority in the House, Democrats were fully prepared to stop things completely. To govern, Republicans would need more discipline from the chair than they had had in a generation, and a change in the rules. Thomas Brackett Reed was ready to give them both. He directed the clerk to count members as present, whether they spoke up or not. Having given the House a permanent quorum, he faced down Democratic filibusterers and pushed through changes in the rules expanding his own power to check the flow of debate, refuse dilatory motions, and define House business.[8]

Reed's new rules set off what might seem, in retrospect, a childish explosion. Democrats swore, screamed, and waved their fists, and one member, to escape being counted, kicked down the locked doors confining him in the House chamber. Yet Democrats felt that the system was being rigged — not just that the majority could have its way, but that due process could be thwarted. They accused the "Czar" of counting not just faces on the floor but customers in the Capitol's barbershop to get his quorums. What made it worse was that Reed's "majority" represented a minority of the votes cast. As a political economist noted, Republicans had taken 48.2 percent of the votes for the House, and Democrats 49.6 percent. Instead of having a majority of three, the GOP should have been behind by four. Gerrymandering gave them their edge (just as rough tactics and control of the polls down south gave Democrats their national plurality — though of course Democrats were not about to mention that!).[9] Nor could Democrats ignore the reason why Reed made his rulings when he did, and what was at stake: not a tariff, nor a pension law, but the Republicans' ability to add to their actual majority by counting in their party's candidates in contested elections down south. Case after case came up, and regular as clockwork, the Republicans voted their man in. "What's the use of electing Democrats to Congress, anyhow?" an editor stormed. "Why not let Reed select the men he wants to misrepresent the different districts of the South, and save the trouble and expense of holding elections?"[10]

Party control allowed the "Billion-Dollar Congress" to do prodigious things, and, not by chance, things strengthening the party's hold, like the admission of Wyoming and Idaho to join four other new-made Republican states. Of course, there were other grounds. Yet Republicans never overlooked the partisan advantage. Idaho might have come in Democratic, but Republicans had fixed voting requirements to cut most Mormons out, and Republican judges refused to register even those Mormons who could take the required oath. For the territories of Arizona and New Mexico, much more safely Democratic, there was no thought of bestowing statehood. As for Utah, with far more than the necessary population and far too few of them Republicans, its admission was unthinkable.[11]

The effort to crack the Solid South raised much more passion. Now, if ever, the first steps toward a free ballot and a fair count must be taken. The federal elections bill built on the past enforcement acts permitting national supervision at the polls.[12] Behind it all was an obvious commitment to restore fair play to the national election process, in a South that was drifting further every year from the arrangement that existed at Reconstruction's end, of moderate infringements on blacks' right to vote. Democrats jawed about liberty, a Mississippian wrote. "Well, now, 'liberty' is a grand subject. . . . And yet we hear an appeal in the name of 'Liberty' for the right to stuff a ballot-box and make fraudulent returns."[13]

Democrats had never liked supervision of the polls and could see all the possibilities in a system of Republican election officials, supervisors, and marshals backed by military force. Badges and bayonets could protect black voters coming to cast a vote or a baker's dozen. Under the proposed measure — quickly dubbed the "Force bill" by its foes — authorities could dictate majorities as they liked or turn into "a lot of hell-hounds to hound down our freemen and run them from the polling-places." Did anyone seriously imagine that the new law would apply only in the cotton states? Like its predecessors on the books, it would strengthen Republicans' ability to meddle in the returns at Cincinnati, New York, and San Francisco. The "blocks of five" in Indianapolis now would have an escort, armed with court orders and instructions from the attorney general. "Since the Praetorian guard stood upon the ramparts of the Eternal City and proclaimed that the whole Roman world would be sold at auction there has never been presented to the world so dangerous a proposition," Tennessee congressman Benton McMillin roared.[14]

With some crucial defections from their own ranks and mounting criticism from both parties, Republican senators agreed to delay consideration until after the off-year elections. Some thought, rightly as it turned out, that this would kill the Force bill for good. Still, Democrats could not afford to leave anything to chance. The majority party was almost sure to lose seats in the House come the midterm election. It had few to spare. A little statutory nudging, and even a dead-even result among the voters could give Democrats control again. In Maryland, the legislature determined to see that never again would Republicans take five seats in six, or, if they could help it, a single one. A registration law, administered by Democratic boards, now raised new barriers to blacks, native or imported, voting at all. Republicans admitted that many of their constituents migrated out of the southern counties to Baltimore or Washington to find work as bellboys, carriage drivers, and day laborers and often returned only around election time. Now anyone absent for six months from their place of residence was thrown off the lists. District boundaries were changed to give one of the leading Baltimore Democrats defeated in 1888 a safe return and to relegate Republican areas to a solitary enclave in the mountainous panhandle of the state. Kentucky Democrats fiddled with congressional district lines to spare themselves the embarrassment of as many as three Republican congressmen from the mountain counties. Tennessee had already redistricted the Republican Third for the same purpose. In addition to a wholesale slaughter of Republican officials and state commissions, New Jersey Democrats set their eyes on a Senate seat and overhauled Assembly districts so that they would get forty-two seats to Republicans' eighteen. "Before we go home we are going to redistrict the State so that we can come back next year, and wipe out what we forget to repeal this," a Newark legislator explained. Ohio Democrats gerrymandered so lavishly that they won a national notoriety. By the draftsmen's calculations, the new map would put fifteen of the twenty-one seats out of Republicans' reach. "This was Democratic day in the House," a reporter gloated, "and how the Republicans squirmed and kicked when the medicine they have been administering to the Democrats for the past four years was forced down their throats."[15]

After the midterm elections, every day was Democratic day in the U.S. House, as well. Republicans were swept out for many reasons, and the gerrymanders, while they worked as planned, only swelled an enormous majority—which, like the one before it, was a gross exaggeration of Democrats' modest increase in their overall popular vote. "There is only a grease-spot left of the Republican party," one editor crowed. "And there wouldn't have been that if it had not been for the left-over fat they fried out of the monopolies two years ago." Only the crassest manipulation left two of the "grease-spots" unscrubbed, and those left a very dirty mark indeed—a clear sign of how harsh parties in distress could be. Pettifoggery and a manipulation of the technicalities of the law saved Republicans control of the New Hampshire legislature; but then a year after that, the same talent for manipulating every legal advantage that the election statutes provided allowed Governor David Bennett Hill to "steal" the New York Senate for Democrats and thus ensure, for the first time in a quarter century, a redistricting that would give his party its due.[16] And the southern drift away from a two-party system only gathered speed. In Tennessee, the election laws had what one editor called "magical effects," breaking down Republican strongholds and cutting the opposition in half. Florida's "reforms" produced record-setting Democratic majorities, Mississippi's constitutional convention effectively created a polity open to whites only, Arkansas did much the same, and Alabama lawmakers shifted district lines, as they openly admitted, to leave blacks powerless to affect any candidate's chances of going to Congress.[17]

Let one hard-knuckle struggle stand for all. In Connecticut, Democrats carried the state senate for the first time in fifteen years. Republicans held on to the House. The real problem was the governorship. On the face of the returns, at least, Democrats had won a clear majority for the whole state ticket, governor included. The state canvassing board so certified and sent its report to the capitol, where members had the constitutional duty to declare the official winners. Republican assemblymen declared their right to go behind the returns. They put together a select committee (all Republicans) to investigate. Its five members insisted that some ink-specked votes rejected by local officers should be counted for the Republican side. The letter, if not the spirit of the law, lay with Democrats. But everyone knew what was at stake. Counting those ballots would take away Luzon B. Morris's majority and leave him with just 50 percent—enough to let the legislature name the winner. Thanks to a system of apportionment in the House that permitted towns casting 42,019 votes to elect 133 Republicans while towns casting 92,235 votes elected only 119 Democrats, Republicans would have a five-vote edge on the joint ballot when the legislature met. Democrats in the senate refused to accept the Assembly's action. Each side saw itself as forestalling pettifoggery. The battle, the *Waterbury Daily Republican* scoffed, was a struggle "between the Connecticut constitution and a Bridgeport ink-speck."

In this deadlock, Governor Morgan C. Bulkeley seized the chance to serve himself by serving his party. Since the legislature refused to go into joint session and certify the winners, he announced, that only left one governor: himself. He and all the other incumbent state officers, including the candidates clearly beaten last fall, would hold office after their terms expired. With the House refusing to pass budget bills, there would be no funds for Bulkeley's government. The chief executive simply borrowed $300,000 from his own life insurance firm to pay expenses and earned the name "the Crowbar Governor" when he descended on the capitol to force open meeting rooms that Democrats had locked for their own personal use. Peace came gradually, and justice was never more than piecemeal. Not until mid-1892 did judges on the Supreme Court of Errors decide, and they followed the Republican Party line, denying Morris his outright majority and declaring Bulkeley governor until a successor was "duly qualified."[18]

The message was unmistakable: however manipulative the parties could be in normal times, their readiness to rig the system to their advantage only grew as the political balance grew less stable. Republicans and Democrats did not need to throw out their scruples when it came to legislating and cheating Populists out of their due. By 1892, they had become hardened offenders. Against that array of weapons, already polished and bright with use, a new-made party could scarcely hope to prevail.

Yet its promise at first seemed great—very like the Labor parties in 1886 or the Greenbackers in 1878, many of whose members now found a new home in the Populist ranks. Two-party hegemony, as has been noted, was artificially stimulated and protected by those in charge of the system. That made it harder for minor parties to operate. Yet operate they did. In presidential-election years, the electorate would scurry back to the major parties, but there was scarcely an off year without its uprising, and, often as not, the lesser players in the party system were the ones that set it off.

Those phenomena were strongest in the South and West. One reason—not the only one, perhaps, but certainly among the most substantial—was the break with party tradition down south and the short span of time for founding such a tradition out west. Party structures that east of the Mississippi and north of the Ohio had kept their form since the late 1850s and had strengthened their own hold by drawing on principles and traditions dating back to Andrew Jackson's day were interrupted by disunion and war, and especially so in the Confederate South. There, true Republican and Democratic parties of the Gilded Age came into their own only in the late 1860s. In the High Plains and Rockies, territorial status delayed the formation of parties that operated on the same issues and under the same constraints as eastern parties until late. In Montana or the Dakotas, political strife often looked more like the struggle of Court against Country in colonial times, which was only right: with their dependence on distant authorities for their governors and most of their laws, territories were the closest equivalent to colonies that the Constitution permitted. It made for a vigorous politics —and in New Mexico downright homicidal ones—but ones distinctly unlike those in Illinois or New Hampshire. Add to that the other problem, that from the 1870s on, the number of inhabitants grew substantially on the prairies and that therefore the electorate, from one election to another, included a comparatively large number of strangers, newcomers to the local system, and the growth of party habits faced a considerable challenge. The problems of first-generation organizations translating themselves into second-generation and permanent ones therefore were delayed and more acute than in the East and Midwest.[19]

As Garland's remark suggested, Populism shared something with all of the other revolts, that of the Mugwumps included. Through their protests ran a strong current of anger, not just at the money lords, but at politicians- and politics-as-usual. The real message of the Farmers' Alliance, one Alliancewoman explained, was that "politics should be made a science of government rather than a means of securing offices and patronage." Farmers' enemies were the "time-servers," "place-holders," "office-holding class," the trimmers and shufflers that packed caucuses made possible. They built on the vision of politics as a conspiracy in the broadest sense: the secret backroom deal, the corruption of public servants, the hidden payoff. An old cry was given new voice when Annie L. Diggs, one of the leading editorial voices of Kansas Populism, explained why it was only right that women join the farmers' revolt. It was precisely because men's politics was a "dirty pool." Whatever affected home and family was a woman's business. Now the ladies in the Alliance traced their own hard lives back to the laws that men had made. "They say, 'Our homes are threatened by the dirty pool. The pool must go.'" Compared to the mainstream parties' view, this was radical, certainly. Yet Prohibitionists would have nodded and understood, not just the need to bring women into the process, but the inherent corruption of two-party politics. By contrast, the insurgents' leaders came from the blacksmith forge, as Leonidas Polk, chief of the Alliance, did, or from one of the finest ranches in California, as Marion Cannon of the California Alliance did. Alliance vice president H. L. Loucks "could never be a politician," one woman Populist told readers. "His unquestioning devotion to all that seems to him to be right makes him entirely fearless of consequences. He could never parley for one moment, nor look expediency in the face." Nor was it surprising in Georgia congressman Tom Watson to argue for government ownership of the railroads as a blow at political, not economic, evils. Nationalization, he wrote, would remove "the greatest danger to popular government, to purity in elections, to honesty in the courts, to integrity among our lawmakers."[20]

There was, then, a tradition of third-party protest, broader than the grievances of producers and the exploited. That restlessness was one that major parties had to consider and came to expect from one election to the next. But uprisings in off years were no new, unexpected threat that the major parties were unequipped to deal with. They had been dealing with them all along, and they knew from past experience that many a protest vote was just that, a vacation from the major parties in an off year, not so much to send them packing as to send them a message. Many of those who would desert the Grand Old Party when it could afford a loss were sure to return to it, at the first beckoning or when its services were really needed.

The worst danger the major parties faced, then, may not have been the creation of a separate party, just in time for the presidential election, but the danger that the insurgent groups would take over the Republican or Democratic organizations. If that happened, the Alliances might be able to call to their aid not just a list of demands but the long-indoctrinated principles of party loyalty. The danger was not just theoretical. When the Farmers' Alliances pressed into politics in 1890, they fielded separate nominees for Congress in some places, but in many others, they worked within the existing system, packing conventions and primaries to select their favorites, endorsing major-party candidates, and bidding for their support. That enhanced the movement's power significantly.[21] It allowed many a discontented voter the opportunity to register protest without breaking outside of a two-party system into something new. And, as in the past, they were most willing to do so because it was not a presidential year. Take away those two conditions — create a new party, making the formal break with the political system, and set the protest in a presidential year — and the farmers' uprising was sure to see its advance slowed, or even reversed.

Indeed, from the first, Populism built on party loyalties and not just party disaffections. Historians have noted the Populist fondness for bogeymen: Shylocks, the Money Power, Jay Gould, the Rothschilds. Undoubtedly, the insurgents included a prodigious supply of political cranks; every party did. And some of them had wild visions of a Money Power capable of pulling every string and arranging every program to suit themselves. But, as should be clear by now, the Populists' conspiratorial viewpoint may not have been so much a proof of their oddity as their typicality. Indeed, the very bogies that Populists chose had been road-tested by Republicans and Democrats over twenty years: the Wall Street goldbugs' conspiracy to demonetize silver, for example. The bankers' plot, like Jay Gould and the Money Power, was a standard of Democratic rhetoric. Naturally, Kansas Populists saw their troubles within the context of an English conspiracy against the producers. Kansas Populists included many lapsed Republicans, and Republicans had for a generation been making John Bull the bugaboo to terrify their constituents to the polls.[22] In so heavily a Republican state as Kansas, voters would immediately recognize and appreciate the argument. It made conversion easier. The break from a mainstream organization to a new one was nowhere near so jarring, if there were continuities of language and of demonologies. Indeed, partisans could persuade themselves that they were carrying on the same fight as before, though under a different party label. They had kept the faith.

Keeping faith was easier within the parties rather than without, and so at first the most intense pressures to adapt and change were inside the major party ranks, led not just by committed third-party men but by those whose loyalty to the good old cause had never been in doubt. In response, applying the same lure they had used with the Knights, Democrats picked Alliance members as their candidates; nominating men with the right credentials, as past experience had so often shown, was a cheaper way to buy insurgents' support than adopting Alliance principles, and especially taking up the notion of a government-run subtreasury, exclusively framed to give easy credit to farmers of wheat, corn, and cotton. (When the Alliance insisted on writing its subtreasury idea into party platforms, Democratic managers balked. In Mississippi and Tennessee, they made repudiation of the "utopian scheme of converting the national treasury into a pawnbroker shop" a condition for party membership.) Once more, Democrats appealed to members of the Alliance to save it as an agency of nonpartisan reform by destroying it as a political force. To petition the legislature for change might fall within its rights; to intrude on parties' exclusive domain—to pack caucuses and endorse candidates—was to set foot on forbidden ground, and, if the past was any guide, one that might as well have been posted with signs warning, "Trespassers will be shot." If party loyalty had not been so long inculcated and so strongly held, the warnings and appeals could not have worked, but they did—or at least well enough. Of 175 Alliance-affiliated legislators in Georgia, the Populists won over just 14. An Alliance organizer told the story of Populist leader Ignatius Donnelly's visit to Hell. There he saw a group of men standing obliviously on a white-hot furnace. "Those are farmers who are shingled with mortgages and were not in the Alliance," the devil explained. "They are too green to burn, and so I have set them up to dry. They do not even know that they are in h--l." To judge from the flood of resignations from the Alliance the moment it tried to translate itself into a separate Populist party, h--l suddenly had more recruits than it could handle. Or perhaps to many of them, to be lost to the party around which their political cosmology had always turned was to be shut out of Heaven.[23]

Once the insurgents had been pared down and the irreconcilables shifted into a party all their own, then Democrats and Republicans had their work half-done for them—indeed, more than half-done, when the foe was no more than half-made. The People's Party was just assembling its machinery. No longer just a mass movement, it had not quite become an organization. That would take time, money, and media, and the mainstream parties were not likely to give it a fair access to any of those. Building a new party took more than simply assembling the voters. There must be the constant indoctrination of a party press, the political culture that the two-party system had made so natural.

Instead, the indoctrination was overwhelmingly on the other side, against the Populists, thanks to the entrenched position of the two-party and independent press. The bias appeared even in reporting that was intended to be fair and impartial. It could be found most blatantly in every political article. There, the mainstream press followed its usual tradition of defining Populists in terms of how they would affect the real party system's agenda rather than in terms of their own program: Democratic highlighted how the Alliance stood "shoulder to shoulder" with the Republican "niggers of Arkansas," and Republicans harped on how the Populism would bring in policies that once had been "promised in the event of the success of the Confederacy." One generation after an era when states actually had owned railroad lines, eastern newspapers looked on the Populist call for government ownership of the railroads and discovered revolution, communism, socialism, and anarchism. As they did so often in the past, newspapers belittled the minor party leaders as cranks and outcasts, and, most important, as hicks: "Milkman" Otis (a prosperous dairy owner) and "Red Rooster" Kem, for example. Just scanning the press, Governor Davis "Bloody Bridles" Waite of Colorado could find a host of fresh nicknames if he did not like the one: the Human Windmill, Pop-headed Governor, the Old Buzzard, the Chief Unpopulist, the Devil's Cuckoo, the Whiskered Bloodsucker, the Western Child Governor, the Scratch Executive, Old Blasphemy, Colorado's Cancer, His Royal Paresis, His Gory Ruleness, Old Non Compos Mentis, Old Notoriety. As for the Populist voters themselves, they were failures in a society where no capable person could fail, and, worse, poor sports about it.

Why should the farmer delve and ditch?
Why should the farmer's wife darn and stitch?

The Government can make 'em rich;
   And the People's Party knows it![24]

Abuse was aimed not just to denigrate but to intimidate those who might join the Populists and their supporters. Metropolitan reporters used savage, loaded language: "this Alliance pest . . . not unlike some other plagues of politics that have swept over the world," "the bacillus and its antidote," a "secret organization, bound together by mystic ties." And when editors declared that mob violence was more than "the atheistic, anarchistic, communistic editor of the *People's Party Paper*" deserved, they only made it likelier that the same violence would be visited on those daring to read it.[25]

"The slaveholder's whip still cracks," one insurgent journalist wrote bitterly, "but the courageous pistol and bowie knife are replaced by slander and suppression." Editors found room for bogus reports that Populist congressman "Sockless Jerry" Simpson was dying and that Populist chairman Herman Taubeneck was working out deals in Chicago to elect a Democratic secretary of state to the senate; they published incredible discoveries of anarchist conspiracies to blow up the Capitol and the White House, lacking the least shred of evidence; but they carefully left out reports of Populist state conventions, refused to publish their platforms, and shut their columns to letter-writers arguing the People's Party viewpoint. On election night, 1894, Indiana's Populist leaders paid for a special wire to their headquarters so that they could get the first returns of party victories out west. Western Union never sent them, nor, indeed, reports to the dailies. From the states where Populists had the highest expectations, not a line of news came, and from others, only the Republican and Democratic votes were transmitted. Just denying whoppers from the Associated Press would fill a reform paper's weekly columns completely, one journalist complained. Editors should save work by running a regular warning at the masthead: "If it is sent out by the Associated or United Press never believe it until it is proved to be true."[26]

When it came to a reply, Populism faced the same handicaps that third parties and southern Republicans had known so well. In scattered cases, Democratic or Prohibition newspapers would endorse an Alliance ticket, if the price was right. Some struggling county publishers might sell press, establishment, and goodwill for as little as $2,000. Populists could find an editorial voice (and, indeed, in Texas, fifty-three at one time), but it was slight compared to the mainstream parties', and often it was a struggle to find talented editors willing to work for a pittance in a concern never far from bankruptcy. Fifty years before, the competition would have been more equal. Then most newspapers were weeklies, and news was not their first or guiding function nor what readers seemed to desire. Now things were worrisomely different. Populist four-pagers, issued once a week, faced off against eight-page dailies, twelve-page metropolitan sheets, thick with pictures, sensational articles, family advice, and all the media that so many Americans had come to expect. Very likely many a subscriber to a Populist paper took a regular daily as well. But that meant that on a daily basis, the readers were given a view of the world at odds with what the Populists gave them. When victory seemed within reach, insurgent papers "sprang up like Jonah's gourd—in a night," as one editor put it. And, he might have added, they withered just as quickly.[27]

Along with the inducements to return to party loyalty, both rhetorical and programmatic, the two main parties used the same old methods of legislating to lengthen the odds against the outs carrying an election. Some of their advantages took no legislating at all. Leave the system of electing congressmen by districts and winner-take-all as it was and the Populist presence in the House would be insignificant—as, except in talent, it was. As one political economist pointed out, with any relation to total votes cast for their party, Prohibitionists should have had five congressmen in Reed's "Billion-Dollar Congress"; and in the House of 1893, Populists should have had thirty-one members instead of eight, and forty-two rather than seven in the Congress that followed—and, incidentally, the balance of power in both. But the mainstream parties were not about to leave ill enough alone. In the West, Republicans wrote up Australian ballot laws that made fusion between Populists and Democrats harder. Fresh requirements for putting a party's name on the ballot were too costly or time-consuming for third parties to meet. If no candidate's name could be placed more than once on the official ballot, Democrats and Populists would have to choose slates all their own and expect little help from those unwilling to go beyond a party label, and a ballot law that organized the names by office rather than by party did just that. By giving state officials the power to say in what order names would be printed on such a ballot, Republicans made sure that the GOP came first, and this, in close elections, could make all the difference.[28]

In the Deep South, beatings, killings, and evictions kept the Democratic hosts together. "It is the religious duty of Democrats to rob Populists and Republicans of their votes whenever and wherever the opportunity presents itself and any failure to do so will be a violation of true Louisiana Democratic teaching," the foremost party paper in northern Louisiana asserted. "The Populists and Republicans are our legitimate political prey. Rob them! You bet! What are we here for?"[29] It was universally admitted that Democrats bought black floaters in Alabama and Georgia. "With about $5.00 or $10.00 I could make a considerable change in this vicinity," one party worker wrote Thomas G. Jones, who was running for governor of Alabama against agrarian leader Reuben Kolb. "Send me . . . a little money to be used among the floating (negro) vote," another pleaded. Some Alabama convicts were given pardons on promising to vote Democratic, and many blacks were counted as having cast a Democratic vote without leaving the cemetery where they lay. Only Democrats claimed that Kolb had lost the governorship fair and square, and not even all of them believed it.[30] Paupers in Rome, Georgia's, poorhouse were let loose to vote Democratic in 1894; asking whether they had qualified by paying their poll tax would have been a waste of breath, and election officers were unwilling to embarrass them by finding out. That same delicacy may have explained why, when the mentally retarded were marched to the polls and asked whether they were tax defaulters, the judges did not take their confession into account and let them vote — after seeing to it that they had Democratic ballots in hand.[31]

Having triumphed, southern Democrats saved themselves the trouble of cheating in the future. The movement, already well under way to save themselves from independent challenges, took on new momentum. In the name of "reform," planters and partisans reshaped the election law to make the South solid indeed. Playing up the racial issue worked because so many Farmers' Alliance members parted company with Populists the moment issues of white supremacy came up and because momentary Populists carried their Democratic nightmares with them. "You are kept apart that you may be separately fleeced of your earnings," Tom Watson told Georgians, white and black. "You are made to hate each other because upon that hatred is rested the keystone of the arch of financial despotism which enslaves you both." But even Watson made points by accusing a Democratic president of having opened New York's white schools to black children.[32]

Having survived the Populist challenge, southern leaders now could use racial fears to justify laws cutting blacks out of the vote. This dirty work the poll tax, literacy test, and new registration laws did quite effectively, and in doing so gave Populists no Republican Party worth allying itself with. But, under Democratic guidance, the laws also cut out white voters by the tens of thousands, and Populist ones more than all the others. When Alabama's constitution-makers wrote a requirement of good character into the franchise, one delegate protested the vagueness. Could Christ himself have passed such a test, he asked. That, another delegate answered, depended entirely on how he intended to vote.[33]

Outrageous the events certainly were. They destroyed what frail hopes the People's Party had nationwide by wrecking considerably stronger hopes in the

South. But they were extraordinary and new only in degree. The closing out and co-opting of minor parties had begun before Populism came into being, and the intimidation and use of force was an old, old story. Laws defining how people could vote and what they could vote for had precedents dating back to the first Australian ballot laws of 1888 and 1889, to the registration laws of a generation, and to the gerrymanders of a century.

All the same, laws and tricks did not stand alone. The binding power of party loyalty and changes in the rules for political competition did much to hold the Populist Party's numbers down. But there were other reasons why the Populists failed, and why the Democrats in the South and the Republicans in the West were able to regain their grip on the machinery. As they had done with the Knights of Labor, the Grangers, and the Prohibitionists, the mainstream organizations stooped to conquer. Power allowed them to do what the Populists rarely could, by turning promises of reform into what, at least to a careless eye, might appear to be legal fulfillments.

The lesson could not have been lost on politicians that the initial breakage in party loyalties had been the greatest in state parties that could not change. One-party systems, or ones where the regular opposition was doomed to unavoidable defeat, just invited a challenge from outside. In Nebraska and Kansas, the Republican Party made perfunctory nods to the demands of the Farmers' Alliances. In 1888, its convention promised reforms to put the railroads in check. Promises were easy. When the legislature met, the promises were broken. Furious at betrayal, the Alliance leaders looked for alternatives. Among the Democrats, they could find none. "We have more sunshine and more wind, more republican stinkers and democratic dough-faces than most any other state," a Nebraskan insurgent fumed. Railroad attorneys and spokesmen for laissez-faire dominated Democratic councils. Accustomed to holding its Irish and German loyalists with appeals to "personal liberty," the outs would venture no further than the saloon door, when looking for an issue. Nor had the Democracy built an organization strong enough to knock Republicans of their pins, whatever beliefs it adopted. So the activists of the Alliance embraced third-party alternatives and threw their force into shaping a movement that elected congressmen and senators.[34]

The story in Iowa was very different. There, the Democratic Party had discovered from long practice that an appeal to the Greenbackers and a stand in favor of railroad regulation, combined with the liquor issue, could bring them within sight of victory. Republicans had seen it, too. In the late 1880s, their governor had taken on the railroads and pushed for reforms. Much that he wanted went on the books, often against the open resistance of those in his own party,

who were fearful that regulation would endanger "progress" and drive investment capital from a rapidly developing state. The Farmers' Alliance learned a
very different lesson from that of their confederates in Nebraska or Kansas. Working within the existing parties had succeeded in the past and could in the future.
Two-party politics worked. There was no need to build any other kind.[35]

The lessons for the major parties were obvious, even if experience with other
challenges had not long since taught them. Potential Populists, like potential supporters of the Prohibition or Greenback parties, could be held to their old party
loyalties by concessions, that the traditions still tugging at Populists' sympathies
would bring many of them back, if they could have tokens that their grievances
would be met. They would settle for less, far less than the whole Populist program; it need only be enough to let them justify themselves in returning to the
good old cause.

What followed, then, was not so much an open war of Populists and the main
parties but a struggle different in each state, for control, a mixture of accommodation and intimidation, of emulation and ridicule, of cooperation, co-optation,
and coalition.[36] Parties changed their programs and their personnel, the better
to draw the Populists back.

The conversion was not simply opportunism, though there must have been
plenty of cynical calculation of how much could be given to gratify the discontented. The reforms each party was readiest to adopt were those with the widest
appeal within their own ranks, among those members who would not desert.
Necessarily, this meant the safest reforms: not subtreasury but silver, not railroad
ownership but regulation. It had been the same way with the temperance crusade
—not Prohibition but license and Sunday closings. This was not simply the ob-
tuseness of the propertied, unable to understand the need, the hunger, the misery out there or deafened by the language of ordered progress that major parties
had spoken for so long. It was the simple knowledge that the collection of the
most votes entailed conceding as little as possible, to keep their own ranks united
from the first.

This consideration was strengthened by the knowledge, ripe from past experience, that no concessions would win *all* the disaffected. No minor party could
be wiped out completely. At its core would be those so alienated from the major
party system, so disaffected from politics-as-usual, that any concession by a major
party would be looked on as a snare, or a delusion. For some third-party people,
indeed, there was as much satisfaction in voting *apart* as there was for major
party constituents in voting the regular ticket, regardless of its makeup. And of
course, as major party organizers knew, third parties were full of partisans who

had come from *somewhere* within the mainstream system and would go back there and only there, if they went back at all.

Putting everything in terms of such calculation does the mainstream parties an injustice. Just as with the Knights' uprising and the Greenback movement, the force that bred insurgency did not strike just those who deserted the mainstream organizations but those who remained. They roiled state conventions, imposed their will on the platform, and in many cases dictated the candidates. Appealing to those conservatives who, like themselves, wanted the money supply reflated with the free coinage of silver, they nominated men who wanted more: election reform, employer liability laws, laws against corporate armies and alien landownership, and tax reform.[37]

Parties had to make concessions, not just to win the defectors, but to hold that potentially larger force, the loyalists for the moment, those who might well defect, unless action was taken. More than that, though, the leaven of discontent worked its way up through the party, giving the reformers the votes they needed to capture conventions and nominate candidates, and giving them the hope that they could prevail, because the politicians in the middle, most concerned about office, would heed any cry of protest all the more, for the losses into third-party ranks. It was certainly true that every vote that left the party for good weakened the power of the reformers in the mainstream parties. But every vote that left in an off year was a *potential* loss, a defector that might yet be brought back, if action were taken, and taken now. That strengthened the power of the reformers to sway voters that they could not convince by reason or ideological argument. In addition, the anger that ran through the political system made many loyalists demand change and work for it within the system. And work they did. Looked at from the perspective of the Populists, the 1890s proved a barren decade of disappointments and electoral defeat. But from another perspective, the 1890s had much the look of a proto-Progressive Era. In state after state, where insurgency was at its strongest, reforms did take place.[38]

This is not to say that the reforms went far enough to satisfy the Populists (or, in the case of Kansas, that they long outlived the Populists' own ascendancy). That ingrained distrust of national authority or any policy that might weaken the sway of white males over society kept southern Democrats from embracing a number of reforms that third-party advocates believed essential. That faith in promotion and progress that both parties shared made them more cautious in hard times about anything that would risk bringing a sluggish economy to a dead stop. New Mexico Populists wanted far more than normal schools and a secret ballot: they wanted blows at the land monopolists, the cattle kings, and the railroad extortionists, none of which Democrats there dared to tackle. In South Carolina, it was all very well for Ben Tillman, the "one-eyed plowboy," to run for governor as the farmer's friend, but how did he show his friendship? To his efforts, South Carolina owed the creation of a state primary and a liquor regulatory system. The state's agricultural college was strengthened, and its railroad commission won new powers to set railroad rates. Cheaper government and a lowered state debt meant less onerous taxes. But compared to the great Populist demands, these were a pittance, if not utterly irrelevant, and under Tillman's guidance the state wrote a new constitution closing the door more firmly than ever on black voting and a competitive party system.[39]

Indeed, without the ideology of Populism, the premises of the movement, all such changes were a change in the letter, not the spirit, of American institutions. They permitted those committed to economic development, to progress, and to a special care for the rights of property and the traditions of substantive due process to offer reforms that would be translated in extremely conservative ways. The commonwealth that the Populists envisioned involved more than laws mandating fair railroad rates, even if such laws had had the force of Newton's three laws of physics. It involved a transformation (or, as they saw it, a retrogression) in the society's sense of its priorities and the proper deference due to farmers, producers, workers, and capitalists.[40] That Populist commonwealth was no nearer for a mandated primary or a direct election of senators, certainly not when the Money Power could simply apply its unrighteous profits in a different way to choosing corporation lawyers for high office.

Nor can we say that all of the reforms were sincere. Spanking-new laws, full of high promise, were meaningless without the enforcement mechanisms behind them. Many more were patchworks. But even halfhearted reform might make a beginning. Nor can all the acts by mainstream parties be dismissed so cynically. There was nothing illusory about Texas governor James Hogg's railroad reforms; any corporation executive watching his road slide toward bankruptcy could have testified to that. By 1894, James Nugent, the head of the Texas Populists, had all but conceded the fact. Endorsing the laws as "wise and just," he had to assure audiences that if the People's Party won office, it would leave them on the books.[41] And there is no saying how many Populists had joined the movement for the ideology, and how many for the remedying of concrete abuses. Democrats and Republicans gambled, and gambled successfully, that many of the disaffected wanted a change in specifics and had thought no further than that.

Very likely they did not think as far as to wonder why Populist leaders had been able to deliver so little. But it was a question worth asking, for the mainstream parties had so written the rules of legislative action that sideshow parties faced the steepest of hurdles. Party caucuses and party discipline decided who would be Speaker and, on Capitol Hill, the makeup of committees that vetted legislative proposals. Under the circumstances, Populists who slipped into power found their bills little better than wastepaper and their speeches unheard. As long as the mainstream parties in House and Senate chose the committees, Populist congressmen would be shunted onto two-bit committees; their bills would be reported unfavorably or, as often happened, not even given the publicity of getting reported at all. In vain their members rose, begging for recognition. Given the blackout treatment, they were hard put even to make the case for their side before the chamber — and were then dismissed with that insult based on the injury done them, that they were incompetent to legislate, because they did not know how to get things done. No wonder, by 1897, those Populists still in Congress lost heart and gave up even offering bills and motions of inquiry, and even quit voting on bills. They had been made all but invisible already, a standing argument both for the uselessness of seeking action from Congress as the system had made it at present and for the miniscule value any voter would get from choosing a champion outside the two major parties.[42]

The pattern of concessions on matters of policy, then, did more than drain away potential Populist votes. It also made all the more plausible the invitation of the two major parties to a coalition of interests where, in return for cooperation, the weaker member of the alliance could win influence where it might amount to concrete change in the future. As long as fusion simply meant a divvying of the offices, the straight-outs had a powerful argument. No victory would amount to anything, except in finding seats for the seat-warmers. As long as the conservatives controlled the old parties, the case could be made that Populists, by electing a "Populist democrat," just sent him to be "swallowed up in a lot of goldbug democrats." It was, an editor declared, like "the rat's deposit in a barrel of wheat. The labor is not worth the pains." But the situation would change if the Democratic Party could be moved from its corporate moorings and if western Populism could not hold onto its control of the state government without outside help. Then some kind of negotiations was bound to begin — and, inevitably, did begin. There would have to be concessions, certainly, but Populist leaders like Governor Lewelling of Kansas could tell themselves that they gave up nothing essential. After all, the two issues surest to offend Democrats were Prohibition and woman suffrage, and neither one lay at the heart of the Populist program. What they may not have calculated on was that an alliance once made had a way of becoming permanent. Having worked with Democrats so well, many a Populist might soften his resistance to becoming a Democrat in the end—as General James Baird Weaver and "Sockless Jerry" Simpson would do. Only a deluded reformer could hope that by fusing, a smaller party could take over a larger one. "That is the way Jonah captured the whale. . . . Fight on your own line if it takes all summer—and winter," a mid-roader appealed. But that, of course, was the point. Without fusion, Populists might just fight till doomsday, and come no closer to winning any of their demands.[43]

The strength of the Populists may have owed something to the number of leaders trained outside either of the main parties, and so not as instinctively hostile to one party in particular as any Democrat or Republican had been trained to be. Many of their leaders had honed their skills in earlier campaigns, as Union Labor or Prohibition or Greenbacker activists. That experience may have taught them not just the practicality but the necessity of fusion with one of the mainstream organizations. Even then, they were in a very small minority. Most Populists had come from the mainstream parties, and many of them would return there, as the third party's prospects faded. Coalition with one party was sure to waken all the traditional distrusts of the other. The old issues that had divided recent allies came to the fore. Some who would have agreed to an alliance with one major party balked at any arrangement with the other as a betrayal of Populist purity, and some of the most ardent middle-of-the-roaders, determined to keep the organization from moving toward the Democratic or Republican side of the political highway, had had long experience fashioning alliances in the past. Given the duty of choosing sides, ex-Republicans and ex-Democrats were sure to choose differently. Any coalition out west made that sure. "Nothing has so helped the Republican cause as the now open and avowed fusion between the Democracy and the Farmers' Alliance," gloated the *St. Paul Pioneer-Press*. Farmers dallying with a purportedly independent Alliance renewed their old love. "There is no fact of politics better established than the power of a party name."[44]

When it came to a pooling of resources between Republicans and Populists, the unattractiveness of fusion worked the same way down south, but the race issue made matters far worse, and when, in 1896, the national party chose a presidential candidate that the Populists ended up endorsing, it made a problematic situation positively impossible. Many of the strongest opponents of a national alliance with the Democrats were former Democrats themselves. A combination of two weak parties might do very well, and that was how it was, between Democrats and Populists in Colorado, say. But in Georgia, combination with the Democrats meant the strongest party gobbling up the weakest. It meant joining hands with the party in which most of the vested economic interests in the state had an honored place. At best, the Populists might get a few crumbs of federal patronage if they won—but nothing more. In Georgia or Texas, a Democratic-Populist alliance meant a merger with the one state party that had no need for and no interest in fusion against Republicans. By contrast, the frail GOP states down south could win in no other way but fusion. That party, at least, might be willing to bid for Populists' services. Democrats were not just Populists' rivals in the cotton kingdom but their assassins—literally. As one reform journalist put it, the line between parties was at least one row of graves wide. The last thing a Mississippi agrarian leader like Frank Burkitt was about to do was cozy up to the "putrid, putrescent, putrefying political moribund carcass of bourbon democracy." One editor put the case exactly for at least some Populists everywhere when he protested that they hadn't left their old parties "for the purpose of being 'fused' back again. Their object in leaving is to find something better."[45]

In one sense, the outsider parties were lucky to have the Money Power to inveigh against. Then they could apply some of their boundless talents for vituperation to some other object than each other. "The great reformation movement for the purification of politics has fallen into the control of tricksters," the *Kincaid Kronicle* fulminated after the Populist candidate for Congress was forced to withdraw in one Kansas district, and a Democratic banker put in his place. "Principles have been traded for expedients. The high moral plane has been abandoned." It was "a stupendous and perfectly shameless traffic for office," the *Kansas Agitator* echoed. When Minnesota's Alliance-Democratic coalition produced statutory chicken feed in 1891, much of the blame should have fallen to Democrats. But reformers reserved their loudest thunders for the trimmers in their own midst. Within two years, Alliancemen were inviting their friends to attend the order's state convention, "with *war paint* on with tomahawk and scalping knife."[46]

A collective picture, assembled from harsh language, makes an unedifying portrait. The longer they worked with one another and the further off the day of victory seemed, the more Populist leaders leveled damning judgments at each other's competence, intentions, and morals. "The Democracy raped our convention while our own leaders held the struggling victim," Ignatius Donnelly wrote in 1896. Six years before, he had spotted enemies of the people nesting in the Farmers' Alliance. "These men must be *isolated* and *destroyed*," he advised an editorial ally; two state elections later, the editor took the convention floor to call Donnelly a "fat brute." Donnelly's friends cut him short by shutting off the lights and ending the meeting.[47]

Historians take the vituperation seriously; indeed, there is nothing more interesting about so much of Populist scholarship as the search for betrayers and fools, who succeeded by sharp practice and deceit. On occasion, the middle-of-the-roaders are seen as the emblems of purity, the fusionists as time-servers, and opportunists hungry for gain.[48] Yet perhaps purists miss the larger reality: that with the grip that the two-party system had on the laws and on its ability to translate desires into statutes, there was no road open to anything more than a local victory for third parties, no matter which way they went. Some of them, the mid-roaders or straight-outs, held out the hope that if their party only stood aloof, the Democrats would have to come to terms; once they disbanded, a new party—different from Populist or Democratic, but where all like-minded reformers could meet as equals, would come into being. As long as Democrats knew they could have Populist backing more cheaply, what incentive would there be for them to go out of business?[49] It was a fine hope, untainted by the reality of party loyalty and the means any mainstream organization had at its disposal. Take the middle of the road though Populists might, it led to the same dead end that the fusionist journey would, and must, as long as the winner-take-all system assured that even a sizable minority would gain precisely nothing. Historians have also read the invective out of a larger context. For the story of *all* the minor parties on the left in the 1870s and 1880s was one of fission and disrepute. The quarreling ran deep and raged constantly. Always it worsened as poor showings at the polls occasioned the search for scapegoats.

Unable to make policy or control the debate, unable to promise spoils or the emotional rush of victory, Populism came out of the 1896 election an emotional wreck. Mid-roaders and fusionists spent the next four years struggling to drive each other out of the ranks. As the midterm elections approached in 1898, enemies of fusion, rallied by Philadelphia industrialist-publisher Wharton Barker, worked up a call for a special national convention in Cincinnati. Its main aim was to drive the traitors from control of the national committee and purge those who cared "more for the preservation of the People's Party than of the people's rights." "Let no man mistake. The issue is drawn between fusion and straight Populists, between life and death for the People's party. If the People's Party is to be saved the time to pass on the issue is now."[50]

Even then, that looked like an immense *if*. Straight-outs threw their energies against fusion, state by state. There were walkouts and separate slates fielded by fusionists and mid-roaders. When the Cincinnati convention met, to paltry attendance and pallid enthusiasm in September, it nominated Wharton Barker for president, not so much for his rather fresh conversion to Populism as for his reputed bankroll. About half the delegates walked out, refusing to accept the decision. Many of them went over to the Democrats, which, Barker asserted, was exactly what he had wanted to have happen.[51]

As long as two and three met together, Populists continued to find enemies in their midst. Had there been as many Populist papers read as there were Populist members read out, the cause would have found converts everywhere.[52]

The warring chieftains rescued remnants, permanently ruined. In 1900, Populists held two conventions. Fusionists dominated one, straight-outs the other. By fall, it became clear that the purified party would do worse than the corrupted one, or that, no matter how many traitors were removed, there were always others to distrust. Internal fighting had completely destroyed the party organization, and once-active members informed Luman Weller that they had drifted "'out of politics' except to vote" and discouraged any effort to reorganize. Party organizers in Iowa reported little hope; only a few regulars "have not turned traitor." A full state and presidential electoral ticket would be a good idea, certainly, but nobody could think of anyone to fill it up with, and local organizers hoped that those in charge at the state level could propose some names. Getting the Populist ticket on the ballot would take signatures, but the few old faithful who could be trusted were too disheartened to sign.[53] The elections passed, and, for all practical purposes, so did the Populist parties. Once again, the looking for scapegoats began. Lack of power proved as debilitating as the lack of confidence in Populists' purity; and there were fewer Populists in good standing to do the work that needed doing. What was the point of competing, with no end, no goal, no triumph in sight? Better, perhaps, to find some new party, able to accomplish the ends.

It sounded so familiar. Yet, in a larger perspective, the destruction of the Populists was something special, because the peril had been greater and the steps taken to contain it were more lasting and devastating against a national, class-based party. The laws defining a new political universe crimped the prospect of third-party power for years to come. There would be third and fourth parties, to be sure—a Socialist mayor in Bridgeport and Socialist congressmen from Milwaukee and the lower east side of New York, Non-Partisan League governors in the Dakotas, Farmer-Labor lawmakers in Minnesota, and Progressives from Wisconsin in the Senate. Until the end of World War II, the two-party system would still have to fend off and bend to regular challenges from outside its ranks, some of them locally severe or momentarily perilous. With a wary eye on the rising power of the Socialist Party, presidents might call for less drastic reforms; to cajole Progressives into the Democratic camp, Woodrow Wilson's New Freedom program would spread out to encompass many of the causes that Theodore Roosevelt's third party held dear. But the incessant, ubiquitous pressure from the sidelines, never wholly stilled, which had characterized Gilded Age politics, really came to an end. The Populist Party died. The Prohibition Party became a political joke, too minor to hold the balance of power between major parties or even to merit a footnote in historical texts.

With that control of the outside pressure, the need to bring about change within the parties became all the stronger, but the need of party managers to bend before the pressure lessened. For twenty years, minor parties had forced parties to make concessions. If there was no place for discontented partisans to go, there could be no walkout worth worrying about. The only thing a major party had to fear was stiff competition from the other major party, and that, in the South and much of the North, no longer existed. Taken as a whole, the United States had a two-party system by 1900. Taken state by state, it often looked more like two collections of one-party systems.

None of this froze the political system. Reform was still possible; even as the Populist Party died, a progressive movement swept up both the major parties, with results fattening the statute books of every state. The Prohibitionists, abandoning reform by means of a separate, futile third party in states too lopsidedly aligned with Democrats or Republicans, created a nonpartisan organization, the Anti-Saloon League, tendering favor and punishment to mainstream candidates for any step, however small, in advance of where policy had been until now. It worked so well that we might overlook the moral: change must come within the structure of two indissoluble major parties, if political action was to bring it at all. Increasingly, the forces for change came from those who gave their money to the national parties and to the organized pressure groups untrammeled by party loyalties but with the arguments and inducements to make lawmakers define what most needed to be done in ways that suited the lobbyists' agendas. In such a definition, those with the most effective organization had the advantage, and these increasingly were those with the means of making legislators listen. Over time, the preponderance of pressure groups lay with those who had money, not votes, at their disposal, and among those who had votes to deliver, the strongest force came from those rich enough to mobilize them, by shaping a public opinion tailor-made to order.

Parties to a Conspiracy

Party games did not end with the Populists, though the need for playing them diminished. With the Australian ballot and the shift in campaign methods, the abandonment of parades and the growth of a metropolitan press only fitfully keen on politics, the old partisan world gave way to a new, and one quite a bit less exciting. Reformers would get the blame for putting the vote out of the reach of illiterates and the civil service out of the grasp of politicians chosen by governments fresh from the people, but it was the parties themselves that adopted the changes for reasons of their own; if they no longer had faith in campaigns of hoopla, it was because the campaigns no longer seemed to be working. If voter turnout slumped, the parties helped depress it, too. They had never wanted big turnouts for the sake of the fullest possible participation; what the politicians wanted was to have *their* supporters show up. If that could be arranged with a slimmed-down electorate, if, indeed, a much smaller electorate skewed the odds in their direction, that sacrifice white southern Democrats paid gladly.

For one reason why the old participatory system vanished was because the majority parties had done their work so well. Having won control, they consolidated their power to add to the obstacles in the way of the opposition regaining power. The big political story of the 1890s was the unmaking of the competitive two-party system in America, at least in most states, for a generation — and all of this happened before there was a Populist threat to counter. With the 1892 presidential election, Democrats seemed[1] to be poised on the verge of becoming the majority party.[2] Little could they have imagined that an economic collapse would turn them into a wrangling crowd and turn their local differences over the tariff and currency questions into fatal divisions. A new political order emerged with

AFTER ELECTION.

GRANGER.—" Wall, if that air picter don't scare away the crows, I dunno what will!"

"After election. Granger: 'Wall, if that air picter don't scare away the crows, I dunno what will!'" (Frederick Opper, *Puck*, September 17, 1884).

a solid Democratic South and a North where Republicans had things their own way in all but a few enclaves. States once competitive had been locked up for either side, and there they would stay well into the twentieth century. For this situation the foundation had been laid years earlier. After the mid-1890s, the western states worked precisely as Republicans expected, guaranteeing them a solid command of the Senate and an extra edge in the Electoral College; and the South had been legislated into secure Democratic strongholds.[3] Party tricks would continue. New York's rural Republicans would rewrite the state constitution to keep their advantage over downstate Democrats, and those in Connecticut and Rhode Island would count on rotten boroughs and election laws to handicap any challengers. But the competitiveness that might have inspired voters to turn out in record numbers was gone, and as civil service reform expanded its coverage, the rewards that would make party operatives do their worst no longer beckoned them.

Just before the 1916 election, a reporter from the *Columbus Evening Dispatch* called on a few of the old poll watchers from the glory days of crowd-pleasing politics. A few of them had fond memories of the good old days, when, as one of them put it, "there were as many election laws as there are literary societies in Iceland." Incessant fistfights, "perhaps a murder or two, vote-buying in whole-sale quantities, and corruption around the polls that would have made Boss Tweed think he was an amateur" had livened elections in the Gilded Age they re-called. Mathias Martin was in his early sixties, but he remembered four decades before, when he had served as judge in the Hayes-Tilden election. "Judges were appointed on the morning of the election," he told the journalist. "The party that had the most representatives at the polls got two of the three judges, and then what chance did the minority have?" Martin laughed at the memory:

> So, of course, precinct chiefs rousted all their henchmen out of bed early to get the two judges. That was half the election. The judge asked the voter what party he belonged to: if he disagreed with the judge, that gentleman would toss the voter's ballot into the waste-basket and slip in his own vote. It was easy then, because there was no uniformity of ballots. Now, down in the South End, which was solidly Democratic, the judges would take pity on the Repub-licans and let the minority judge slip in a few votes. Double voting? Wholesale importation of voters? With no registration, what would you expect?[4]

For the poll watchers, nostalgia gave these donnybrooks a feel of romance, even innocence. Nearly a century later, the temptation is even stronger to envy an electorate treated to lusty politicking. With so much governance left to unelected commissions and so much campaigning confined to glossy televised advertising, Americans may rue the system that they have lost. The party machines seem to have had so many vices we admire, and the reformers, with their view of an apo-litical, antiseptic process, so many of the virtues we detest. A careless reading of scholars' works about Gilded Age political culture would only drive home the point.

The victims of Gilded Age politics knew better. Meeting in Omaha in 1892, the Populist Party reckoned the price of politics-as-usual. "We meet in the midst of a nation brought to the verge of moral, political and material ruin," its platform began. "Corruption dominates the ballot-box, the Legislatures, the Congress, and touches even the ermine of the bench." Behind the gaudy show that the two major parties had put on, the system was rigged to give the professional politicians every unfair advantage. Democrats in Alabama and Louisiana stole the state elections—in Louisiana, as usual. Kansas Republicans held a legislative majority with Gatling guns and rifle-toting partisans, a brazenness unheard of . . . at least since the retirement of Connecticut's unelected "crowbar governor" just weeks before.[5] Georgia's dogs, mules, and honored dead cast Democratic votes enough to drive Tom Watson, the Populist's chief southern spokesman, from the House, but then, South Carolina Republicans and Henry George's Labor Party could have raised the quick and the dead as witnesses to how Democrats had made their defeat sure.

The campaign circus performed to record crowds; we will not see its like again. The major parties defined real issues, with consequences as close as the factory shop floor or the saloon door. They promised much, and delivered some. Always those outside the mainstream had a say: the third parties whose programs the major parties raided for votes, the labor organizations and farmers' groups seeking concessions or recognition, the women whose ability to awaken and organize the electorate on moral issues forced backroom bosses to find some accommodation. Self-interest and principle alike kept the politicians from turning into the messenger boys of the great financial interests. In the best sense, the Gilded Age political process did work, better and more fairly than the goo-goos made out. But in essence, the critics were right. The system was as the professional politicians made it. They wanted no level playing field, no full, wide expression of a people's will that the major parties could not control. Their purpose was to win, and to do that, they drew the rules to serve themselves.

That is one reason why when the Populist movement arose it had so little chance and why so many of its members found nowhere else to go but into a fusion that prolonged the party's life even as it made its ultimate demise inevitable. It took no extraordinary effort to rig the system against Populists, and no unusual wrestling with partisan conscience. Poll taxes—registration requirements—hurdles for any minor party to leap before it was permitted a place on the ballot at all: the mechanisms were endless.[6] Bogeyman figures misled the voters or simplified issues into fakery: John Bull, Shylock, the Money Power. But all these methods had been standard practice in the Gilded Age system for twenty years. Parties had cheated each other with gerrymanders, rigged the election process, and disputed returns in every court and with every technicality at their command. Partisan vote-counting boards and requirements selectively enforced stole

"The state of the pine tree; or, a nice Christmas tree" (Thomas Nast, *Harper's Weekly*, January 10, 1880).

enough southern states to give Democrats a fair chance of winning Congress; malapportioned legislatures and franchise requirements up north helped Republicans steal it back again. Even when reforms came, they were drawn to protect the party machines as far as possible, or to give one machine advantage over its rivals.

The limitations of popular politics were greater than could be cured by pointing to bribe takers and calling instead for the election of "honest men" or friends of the people. Not all the collective integrity in the world could make up for a process where the most important criterion for nominating a candidate to Congress or denying him a second term was the need to give some other county the chance to fill the seat. The parochialism, the all-too-obvious skill at rousing and channeling emotion, the magnificence of the two parties' machinery for manipulating the voters for partisan ends, and, most of all, the ethical flexibility that placed winning ahead of just about anything, more than outright scandals, allowed that paradox still with us, of an electorate that despised politics in general as a vulgar trade, even as it turned out to turn the rascals in. It was not reformers alone, with their battle for civil service reform and the unofficial literacy test of a secret ballot and their insistence on campaign of "education" that thwarted a truly representative democracy. That ideal had been compromised long since. Its sworn defenders, the partisans, had shaped, skewed, and at times subverted it to suit their own ends. To those who look back today with fondness on so energetic a system, to the popular politics of E. L. Godkin's day, the reformers' cure may seem far worse than the disease it treated. Perhaps. But the disease was worse than we may imagine.

The rumble of gun carriages in Bangor's streets mingles with the party songs that glee clubs sang. The whiff of gunpowder came not just from fireworks but from gunfire in Arkansas. Put-up jobs, whispering campaigns, forged letters, rotten boroughs, and tissue ballots were facts of life, every bit as much as the statutes on farmers' and laborers' behalf. Politics is a messy business. It cannot help being so. All the same, in seeing the evils of our own time, it is well to hear in Godkin's words the true epitaph on his age, neither romanticized nor simplified: "We shall win, but what a victory!"

Abbreviations

AmN	*American Nonconformist*
BWC	*Bangor Whig and Courier*
ChaN&C	*Charleston News & Courier*
ChanMSS (LC)	William E. Chandler MSS, Library of Congress, Washington
ChanMSS (NHHS)	William E. Chandler MSS, New Hampshire Historical Society, Concord
ChiTi	*Chicago Times*
ChiTr	*Chicago Tribune*
CinCG	*Cincinnati Commercial Gazette*
CinEnq	*Cincinnati Enquirer*
CinGaz	*Cincinnati Gazette*
ClPD	*Cleveland Plain Dealer*
CMMHC	Calvin M. McClung Historical Collection, Knox County Public Library System, Knoxville
ConMon	*Concord Daily Monitor*
CR	*Congressional Record*
DEN	*Detroit Evening News*
DMSR	*Des Moines Iowa State Register*
HML	Rutherford B. Hayes Memorial Library, Fremont, Ohio
HW	*Harper's Weekly*
InJ	*Indianapolis Journal*
InN	*Indianapolis News*
InSen	*Indianapolis Daily Sentinel*
ISHS	Illinois State Historical Society, Springfield
IW&AIL	*Irish World and American Industrial Liberator*
JSP	*John Swinton's Paper*
KoL	*Knights of Labor*
LC	Library of Congress, Washington
LC-J	*Louisville Courier-Journal*
LRArkG	*Little Rock Arkansas Gazette*
ManU	*Manchester Daily Union*

MHS	Minnesota Historical Society, St. Paul
NAR	*North American Review*
NOrT-D	*New Orleans Times-Democrat*
NYEP	*New York Evening Post*
NYH	*New York Herald*
NYS	*New York Sun*
NYSL	New York State Library, Albany
NYStan	*New York Standard*
NYT	*New York Times*
NYTr	*New York Tribune*
NYW	*New York World*
ODB	*Omaha Daily Bee*
PhilRec	*Philadelphia Record*
PiPo	*Pittsburgh Post*
RanMSS	Samuel J. Randall MSS, Rare Book and Manuscript Library, University of Pennsylvania, Philadelphia
RJ	*Racine Journal*
SFAltaC	*San Francisco Alta California*
SHSW	State Historical Society of Wisconsin, Madison
SprRep	*Springfield Republican*
StLG-D	*St. Louis Globe-Democrat*
StLP-D	*St. Louis Post-Dispatch*
StPGW	*St. Paul Great West*
StPP-P	*St. Paul Daily Pioneer-Press*
SU	Stanford University, Palo Alto
WilEvEv	*Wilmington Every Evening*
WVC	West Virginia Collection, West Virginia University Library, Morganton

Preface

1. C. Cushing to William E. Chandler, October 22, 1868, ChanMSS (NHHS).

2. *Washington Post*, May 18, 1897.

3. The best examples of the corruptionist school are Matthew Josephson's *Politicos*, Ginger's *Age of Excess*, and, with greater credibility and more careful research, Ginger's *Altgeld's America* and Myers's *Tammany Hall*. Those whose description of the joys of political culture may entrance the reader far beyond the author's intent include McGerr, *Decline of Popular Politics*; Jean H. Baker, *Affairs of Party*, Silbey, *American Political Nation*, and, with much more detail given to the darker workings of organizational politics and the limited effectiveness of reform, Reynolds, *Testing Democracy*. Keyssar's *Right to Vote*, concerning only the gradual disfranchisement in postwar America, without dwelling on the hoopla, stands in a class by itself. All of them are excellent, and, while I lay far more emphasis on the disconcerting methods of the mainstream partisans and share Reynolds's recognition of the larger role played by politicians in deciding how reform would be implemented (if at all), I have learned

much from McGerr's book and am sold on his conclusion of the deadening impact that "advertised" politics had on voter turnout. For the dismissal of politics itself as a vastly overrated concern, in which popular participation was shallow, misinformed, or meaningless, large voter turnout no proof that the public had engaged with the real issues, and an America in which interested partisans put on a tremendous show for their own personal advantage, Altschuler and Blumin's stimulating *Rude Republic* stands alone. It is remotely possible, though, that study of manuscript sources outside of Cornell's library and of newspapers from some, or any, city larger than Syracuse, New York, for a period of the Gilded Age extending beyond three years may afford a different insight into how nineteenth-century politics worked.

4. This is a point well emphasized in a much narrower context, in Yearley, *Money Machines*.

5. How politicians' responsiveness to organized groups worked is part of the story in Hammack, *Power and Society*, and Kousser, "Restoring Politics to Political History," 592–94, and can be deduced in Campbell, *Representative Democracy*.

6. For example, Stewart and Weingast, "Stacking the Senate," 223–71; McCormick and Reynolds, "Outlawing 'Treachery,'" 835–58; Argersinger, "Value of the Vote," 279–98, Argersinger, "Place on the Ballot," 290–300; and Perman, *Struggle for Mastery*.

7. For the appeal to a larger definition of politics, see Daniel W. Howe, "Evangelical Movement and Political Culture," 235–36, and Paula Baker, "Domestication of Politics," 620–48.

8. As note, again, McGerr, *Decline of Popular Politics*, and Sproat, *Best Men*, the latter a study that may give Godkin and the talkers—as opposed to the doers—far more weight than they deserve. A far more sympathetic portrait appears in Blodgett, *Gentle Reformers*; McFarland, *Mugwumps, Morals, and Politics*; Hoogenboom, *Outlawing the Spoils*; and Klebanow, "E. L. Godkin," 52–75.

Chapter One

1. The best treatments of the 1888 election are the chapters in H. Wayne Morgan's *From Hayes to McKinley*; Marcus's *Grand Old Party*; and Nevins's *Grover Cleveland*; see also McDaniel, "Presidential Election of 1888," and Reitano, *Tariff Question*.

2. For "Grandpa's Hat," see *Puck*, July–November 1888; see also transparency, *Buffalo Courier*, November 4, 1888.

3. *NYS*, September 27, 1888.

4. On the choices of 1872, see James Rood Doolittle to his wife, September 12, 1872, Doolittle MSS, SHSW; *StPP-P*, November 1, 2, 1872; and "Annus Domini, 1873–74–75," 4, 5, 31.

5. *Milwaukee Journal*, November 5, 1888; *NYS*, November 18, 1888; James S. Martin to Joseph Fifer, September 8, 1888, Fifer MSS, ISHS.

6. Edwards, "Gender in American Politics," 28–32, 129; *NYH*, October 28, November 4, 1888; *NYS*, July 15, September 27, 30, October 1, 8, 1888, November 4, 1888; *ChiTr*, August 3, 1888; *SFAltaC*, August 3, 1888; *Baltimore American*, October 23, 1888; H. Wayne Morgan, *From Hayes to McKinley*, 316.

7. *NYStan*, July 21, 1888; *InN*, October 10, 1888.

8. *NYT*, November 25, December 2, 1888; *NYS*, November 26, December 15, 1888; *Evansville Courier*, November 9, 11, 1888; *PiPo*, December 11, 12, 1888.

9. Edwards, "Gender in American Politics," 143–45, 159–65; Reitano, *Tariff Question*, 79, 81.

10. *ManU*, October 31, 1888; *San Francisco Chronicle*, November 5, 1888; Benjamin F. Jones to Stephen B. Elkins, January 24, 1888, Elkins MSS, WVC.

11. *PiPo*, October 30, 1888; *SFAltaC*, July 2, 1888; *NYH*, October 17, 1888.

12. "Campaign Lying," *HW*, September 29, 1888, p. 727; *ManU*, September 20, 21, 1888; *Nation*, August 9, October 4, 11, 18, 1888; *NOrT-D*, September 3, 1888.

13. *SFAltaC*, July 2, 1888.

14. R. Hal Williams, *Democratic Party and California Politics*, 120–24; *SFAltaC*, July 9, 11, November 3, 6, 1888; *CinEnq*, August 18, 23, 1888; *NYH*, September 2, 1888; *StLP-D*, August 8, 1888; "The Chinese Treaty," *Nation*, September 6, 1888, p. 184, September 13, 1888, p. 201.

15. Richard W. Townshend to David A. Wells, May 16, 1888, Wells MSS, LC; *SFAltaC*, July 16, 1888; *CinEnq*, August 22, 1888; *Nation*, August 16, 1888, p. 122; *ManU*, July 31, October 31, 1888; *PiPo*, August 1, 15, 1888.

16. "Campaigning in Congress," *HW*, September 22, 1888, p. 706; *PiPo*, August 25, 1888; Arthur Pue Gorman to Samuel J. Randall, August 22, 27, 1888, RanMSS; John C. Spooner to Henry C. Payne, August 24, 1888, Spooner MSS, LC.

17. *PiPo*, September 12, 1888; Nevins, *Grover Cleveland*, 428; Charles L. Lamberton to Samuel J. Randall, September 10, 1888, RanMSS.

18. Nevins, *Grover Cleveland*, 429–31; *NYH*, November 4, 1888; *StLP-D*, October 29, 31, 1888; *Baltimore American*, October 25, 26, 1888.

19. Frank Willing Leach, "Twenty Years with Quay," *Philadelphia North American*, October 9, 1904; Wharton Barker to Levi P. Morton, August 13, 1888, Quay MSS, LC.

20. Marcus, *Grand Old Party*, 137–39; Kehl, *Boss Rule*, 98–99.

21. "Campaign Contributions" and "Hubbellism," *HW*, September 8, 1888, p. 667; "Black-Mailing," ibid., September 29, 1888, p. 727; *NYTr*, September 9, 1888.

22. Nevins, *Grover Cleveland*, 437; "Mere Mugwumpery," *HW*, December 8, 1888, p. 931; Leach, "Twenty Years with Quay"; *NYStan*, December 15, 1888; Marcus, *Grand Old Party*, 134.

23. Kehl, *Boss Rule*, 99, 103–06; Leach, "Twenty Years with Quay."

24. Jensen, *Winning of the Midwest*, 28–29; *CinEnq*, August 31, 1888; Henry C. Lea to Lucius B. Swift, October 24, 1888, Swift MSS, Indiana State Library, Indianapolis; J. N. Huston to Stephen B. Elkins, October 15, 1888, Elkins MSS, LC.

25. Marcus, *Grand Old Party*, 144–45; Jensen, *Winning of the Midwest*, 29–30; Baumgardner, "1888 Presidential Election?" 421–25; *InN*, November 2, 3, 1888. For the story of Magee's money, see *NYS*, December 17, 1888.

26. *WilEvEv*, November 23, 1888.

27. See Jacobs, "West Virginia Gubernatorial Contest."

28. Hair, *Bourbonism and Agrarian Protest*, 138–40; *NOrT-D*, November 6, 1888; "Tried and true Republicans" to William E. Chandler, April 18, 1888, Henry Clay Warmoth to ——, July 16, 1888, Butler Adams to ——, July 13, 1888, and M. J. C. Lavallaise to the president of the Republican state committee, April 19, 1888, ChanMSS (LC).

29. *StLG-D*, August 31, September 12, 15, 1888.

30. *DEN*, October 26, 27, 1888; *Savannah Tribune*, April 6, 1889; Job Harrol to Leonidas Houk, July 18, 1890, Houk MSS, CMMHC.

31. *ChiTr*, October 10, 1888.

32. E. M. Brayton to William E. Chandler, December 17, 1888, ChanMSS (LC); *DEN*, October 30, November 2, 1888; Kantrowitz, *Ben Tillman*, 202–5.

33. Edward A. Miller, *Gullah Statesman*, 162–63.

34. *ODB*, November 11, 1888.

35. McDaniel, "Presidential Election of 1888," 190–91; H. Wayne Morgan, *From Hayes to McKinley*, 317; *Evansville Courier*, November 9, 1888. On North Carolina, see Daniel L. Russell to William E. Chandler, February 25, 1890, ChanMSS (LC); Frank Willing Leach, "Twenty Years with Quay," *Philadelphia North American*, October 9, 1904; and Anderson, *Race and Politics*, 160–61.

36. Parker, *Recollections of Grover Cleveland*, 342–44; Daniel Lamont to David Bennett Hill, November 7, 1888, Hill MSS (Bixby Collection), NYSL.

37. Nevins, *Grover Cleveland* 437–38; Boomhower, "'To Secure Honest Elections,'" 321–22; *Pittsburgh Post*, December 12, 1888; *NYStan*, November 17, 1888; "Money in Elections," *HW*, November 24, 1888, pp. 886–87.

38. H. Wayne Morgan, *From Hayes to McKinley*, 318; *NYS*, December 29, 1888; H. Smythe to Samuel J. Randall, December 8, 1888, Adoniram J. Warner to Randall, November 17, 1888, John Morris to Randall, November 12, 1888, and George W. Ladd to Randall, November 15, 1888, RanMSS.

39. *PiPo*, December 27, 1888.

40. Polakoff, *Politics of Inertia*, 201–314; Taylor, *Louisiana Reconstructed*, 240–49, 268–73, 291–96, 484–89; Thompson, "Leadership in Arkansas Reconstruction," 175–285; King, "Counting the Votes," 169–91; Current, *Those Terrible Carpetbaggers*, 233–35, 240–42.

41. Peskin, *Garfield*, 507–10; *NYH*, October 26, 1880; James A. Garfield to William E. Chandler, November 8, 1880, ChanMSS (NHHS); W. Davis to Bard, November 22, 1880, Bard MSS, Huntington Library, San Marino, Calif.; *Brooklyn Daily Eagle*, March 21, 1884.

42. R. C. McCormick to William E. Chandler, October 5, 1880, ChanMSS (LC); Peskin, *Garfield*, 505; *Norfolk Virginian*, August 2, 1883; *InN*, June 21, 1884; *InJ*, October 12, 1880; George F. Howe, *Chester A. Arthur*, 129.

43. On the Grange opposition to Matthews as a railroad attorney, see Ainsworth and Maltese, "National Grange Influence," 41–62; McHargue, "Appointments to the Supreme Court," 614; and Magrath, *Morrison R. Waite*, 246.

Chapter Two

1. *Omaha Republican*, September 29, 1888.

2. *Atchison Daily Champion*, October 31, 1886.

3. John E. Owens, "The Welsh in Politics," *NAR* 157 (December 1893): 635–36; *Minneapolis Tribune*, October 26, 1890, and, on the same point, see also *New Haven Daily Morning Journal and Courier*, October 6, 1888. For the ethnocultural component, see Kolbe, "Culture," 243–52; Jensen, "Religious and Occupational Roots," 325–43; and Jensen, *Winning of the Midwest*, 69–85.

4. *ConMon*, October 17, 1890; *ChiTr*, July 31, 1884; *Raleigh News & Observer*, September 25, 1890.

5. Robinson, *Thomas B. Reed*, 108; R. Hal Williams, "'Dry Bones and Dead Language': The Democratic Party," in H. Wayne Morgan, ed., *Gilded Age*, 131–32, 141–44; *Nation*, November 24, 1881.

6. Oliver Johnson, "The Paramount Question," *Independent*, October 28, 1880, pp. 5–6; *RJ*, December 21, 1870, March 1, 1871; Robinson, *Thomas B. Reed*, 271; *ChiTr*, September 15, 1887; *Hartford Daily Courant*, February 1, 1869; see also "D. P.," *CinEnq*, March 9, 1878, and *DMSR*, July 2, 1880.

7. Calhoun, "Civil Religion and Gilded Age Presidency," 656–63; Calhoun, "Political Economy in the Gilded Age," 291–310; Zachariah Chandler to John E. Bryant, August 7, 1876, Bryant MSS, Duke University Library, Durham, N.C.

8. *DMSR*, October 5, 1884; *Atchison Daily Champion*, October 31, 1886; *Elmira Weekly Advertiser*, September 24, 1880; *East Liverpool Potters' Gazette*, October 9, 1879; "Murray," *InN*, June 3, 1885.

9. Jean H. Baker, *Affairs of Party*, 249–58, 344–52; *ChaN&C*, October 4, 1880; *LRArkG*, July 29, 1888.

10. *ChaN&C*, September 13, October 5, 1880; Jean H. Baker, *Affairs of Party*, 342–44.

11. Kousser, "Towards 'Total Political History,'" 546–49; *BWC*, October 16, 1884; John Hay to Whitelaw Reid, October 15, 1879, Reid MSS, LC.

12. *StLG-D*, October 2, 6, 1886; Ostrogorski, *Democracy and Organization*, 2:335; *InJ*, October 19, 1870; *InN*, November 7, 1884; Peck, *Twenty Years of the Republic*, 88.

13. Jensen, *Winning of the Midwest*, 104–05; Jean H. Baker, *Affairs of Party*, 56–63; Palermo, "Rules of the Game," 488–90; Hammarberg, "Analysis of American Electoral Data," 647–52; *NYH*, October 18, 1888; "Ithuriel," *CinEnq*, September 17, 1880.

14. Altschuler and Blumin, *Rude Republic*, 265–67; Jensen, *Winning of the Midwest*, 9–10; Hammarberg, "Analysis of American Electoral Data," 650; *NYS*, September 29, 1888; *Davenport Daily Democrat*, October 10, 1870; *StLG-D*, November 7, 1876; *Minneapolis Tribune*, November 5, 1890; James T. Noble to Alexander Long, September 22, 1876, Long MSS, Cincinnati Historical Society, Cincinnati; *Philadelphia Public Ledger*, November 2, 1880.

15. Hofstadter, *Idea of a Party System*; Altschuler and Blumin, *Rude Republic*; Formisano, "Political Character," 683–709; Carwardine, *Evangelicals and Politics*; Bridges, "Creating Cultures of Reform," 1–23.

16. *ManU*, March 11, 1871; *NYW*, May 16, 1870; *Nation*, March 2, April 20, 1871; Carlos White, *Ecca Femina*, 148–57; Kraditor, *Ideas of Woman Suffrage*, 25–27.

17. Altschuler and Blumin, *Rude Republic*, 193–96, 220–25; Ayers, *Promise of the New South*, 37.

18. *CinCG*, September 26, 1886; *Xenia Republican*, October 5, 1886; *CinEnq*, September 30, 1886; *ClPD*, October 12, 1886.

19. On Mugwumpery, see Dobson, *Politics in the Gilded Age*, 164–68, 188–90; Sproat, *Best Men*, 273–81; Blodgett, "Mugwump Reputation," 867–87; McFarland, *Mugwumps, Morals, and Politics*, 18–54; McGerr, *Decline of Popular Politics*, 42–45.

20. *Woodbury Constitution and Farmers' and Mechanics' Advertiser*, May 1, 1872; *Carson City Morning Appeal*, October 5, 1886; *Davenport Daily Democrat*, October 10, 1870;

Burlington Hawk-Eye, August 16, 1890; *RJ*, September 21, 1870; *ChiTi*, September 29, October 2, 5, 1876.

21. "A Good Word from New Jersey," *HW*, February 8, 1890, p. 98; *Nation*, September 23, October 14, 1880.

22. J. L. Spalding, "The Basis of Popular Government," *NAR* 139 (September 1884): 207; *NYT*, August 28, 1880; *IW&AIL*, June 19, 1880; "Flanagan," *NYS*, July 29, 1880.

23. "Scratching," *HW*, November 22, 1879, p. 918; "Two Pictures," *HW*, March 22, 1890, p. 214; Julius H. Seelye, "The Moral Character in Politics," *NAR* 139 (October 1884): 301–3; Dorman B. Eaton, "Parties and Independents," *NAR* 144 (June 1887): 554–58; *InN*, October 30, 1888; *Chattanooga Daily Times*, July 23, 1882.

24. McMath, *American Populism*, 53–80; Deverell, *Railroad Crossing*, 42–46; Hamm, *Shaping the Eighteenth Amendment*, 22–33; Goldberg, *Army of Women*, 46–48, 90–91.

25. Henry George, "The New Party," *NAR* 145 (July 1887): 1–4; *AmN*, March 29, 1894; *KoL*, October 16, 1886. For a dissenting view, see Voss-Hubbard, "'Third Party Tradition' Reconsidered," 121–50.

26. Michael F. Holt, "Primacy of Party Reasserted," 151–57; Formisano, "'Party Period' Revisited," 93–120.

27. *SprRep*, July 8, 1876; *NYEP*, October 20, 1892.

28. McCall, *Thomas Brackett Reed*, 123.

29. *BWC*, August 25, 1876; *RJ*, September 21, 1870.

30. And not just Mugwumps. See *StPGW*, October 7, 1892.

31. George E. Waring, "Government by Party," *NAR* 163 (November 1896): 589–90; *Kansas State Record*, October 16, 1872; T. B. Whitledge to B. Benson Cahoon, April 21, 1880, Cahoon MSS, Missouri Historical Society, St. Louis; *NYH*, October 18, 1888; David A. Wells to Samuel J. Tilden, March 15, 1876, Tilden MSS, New York Public Library, New York.

32. *Jackson Clarion*, October 15, 1884; *Memphis Commercial Appeal*, October 15, 24, 1886; *ChaN&C*, November 2, 1880; *Atlanta Constitution*, July 18, 1886.

33. *ChaN&C*, October 23, 1880; for "dividing time" in Arkansas, see *LRArkG*, July 13, 15, 1888.

34. See Olsen, *Carpetbagger's Crusade*, 49–182, 312–31, and Current, *Those Terrible Carpetbaggers*, 199–210, 367–82, 401–6.

35. Albion W. Tourgee to Benjamin Harrison, June 29, 1888, Harrison MSS, LC.

Chapter Three

1. *StLG-D*, June 6, 1884.

2. P. L. Jaslin to Edwin D. Morgan, October 10, 1876, Morgan MSS, NYSL; James R. Randall to Alexander Stephens, November 10, 1872, Stephens MSS, LC; *CinGaz*, September 28, 30, 1872; Jean H. Baker, *Affairs of Party*, 287–91; Jensen, *Winning of the Midwest*, 11. On women, see *DMSR*, October 2, 1884, and *Milwaukee Sentinel*, November 3, 1884. On reformers, see *InJ*, July 14, September 14, 1884; *ChiTr*, September 10, 1884; and *Wheeling Intelligencer*, July 21, 1884.

3. Kornbluh, *Why America Stopped Voting*, 23.

4. Ibid., 23–25; Ostrogorski, *Democracy and Organization*, 2:226–28, 245–48.

5. Kornbluh, *Why America Stopped Voting*, 27–28; *Springfield Globe-Republic*, November 1, 1886.

6. Charles L. Flanagan to John Sherman, September 16, 1880, Sherman MSS, LC; Charles W. Johnson to Knute Nelson, September 21, 1878, Nelson MSS, MHS. For a full listing of campaign papers, see Miles, comp., *People's Voice*. For speeches, see Stephen Mallory White to John H. Wise, July 27, 1888, White MSS, SU; J. W. Stevenson to Samuel J. Randall, September 8, 1880, RanMSS; and *ChiTr*, July 28, 1888. For almanacs, see *Tribune Almanac* (New York: Tribune Publishing Co., 1860–93). On campaign biographies, see Ostrogorski, *Democracy and Organization*, 2:329; *Dial* 1 (September 1880): 81–84; and *NYT*, August 28, 1880.

7. Douglas, *Golden Age of the Newspaper*, 83–86; *Philadelphia Public Ledger*, October 27, November 2, 1880.

8. *Cazenovia Republican*, October 16, 1884; *ChiTr*, October 29, 1886, September 4, 1890; *StLG-D*, October 4, 1886; *Watertown Daily Times*, October 6, 1888; *Milwaukee Journal*, October 6, 1888; Joseph W. Fifer to J. M. Gillette, May 19, 1892, Fifer MSS, Illinois State Historical Society, Springfield.

9. *NYS*, July 15, October 8, November 4, 1888.

10. *NYH*, November 1, 1872; *InSen*, September 10, 11, 13, 1872.

11. Ostrogorski, *Democracy and Organization*, 2:332–36; *NYH*, October 22, 1888.

12. *InSen*, August 14, 1872; Henry George, "Money in Elections," *NAR* 136 (February 1883): 209; Reynolds, *Testing Democracy*, 34; Jean H. Baker, "The Ceremonies of Politics: Nineteenth-Century Rituals of National Affirmation," in Cooper, Holt, and McCardell, eds., *Master's Due*, 161–64.

13. Ostrogorski, *Democracy and Organization*, 2:310–11; Robinson, *Thomas B. Reed*, 271.

14. *InN*, September 13, 1890; William Dudley Foulke, "Campaigning in the West," *NAR* 156 (January 1893): 128; *PhilRec*, August 12, 1888; *Brooklyn Daily Eagle*, July 10, 1885; Lucius Q. C. Lamar to William H. Trescot, October 4, 1876, Trescot MSS, South Caroliniana Collection, University of South Carolina, Columbia; *StLG-D*, June 27, 1880, September 21, 1888.

15. *NYH*, August 21, 1892; Henry M. Hoyt to Nathaniel P. Banks, September 5, 1876, Banks MSS, LC; memorandum from the New York Democratic State Committee, October 19, 1880, RanMSS.

16. William Birney to William E. Chandler, August 20, 1880, ChanMSS (LC); F. W. Holls to Will, November 6, 1888, Holls MSS, Columbia University, New York; *Brooklyn Daily Eagle*, November 11, 1888.

17. *DMSR*, August 25, 1880; James S. Clarkson to Jonathan P. Dolliver, May 8, September 18, 1885, T. J. Porter to Dolliver, March 2, 1885, and Charles Beardsley to Dolliver, September 18, November 2, 1885, Dolliver MSS, State Historical Society of Iowa, Iowa City.

18. House, "Democratic State Central Committee of Indiana," 196–99; *InSen*, August 27, 1872; "Pickaway," *CinEnq*, February 1, 1881; Charles Beardsley to Jonathan P. Dolliver, September 8, 1885, Dolliver MSS, State Historical Society of Iowa, Iowa City.

19. Ostrogorski, *Democracy and Organization*, 2:286–92; *PiPo*, February 20, 1886; *NYH*, October 23, 24, 1888; *NYT*, October 6, 1888; R. P. Hammond to Stephen Mallory White, October 19, 1892, White MSS, SU.

20. P. L. Jaslin to Edwin D. Morgan, October 10, 1876, Morgan MSS, NYSL; H. Wayne

Morgan, *From Hayes to McKinley*, 302; *Newark Evening News*, November 3, 1888; Fred B. Phillips to B. B. Cahoon, September 21, 1880, Cahoon MSS, Missouri Historical Society, St. Louis.

21. Daniel J. Ryan, "Clubs in Politics," *NAR* 146 (February 1888): 174–76; Joseph H. Manley, "Permanent Republican Clubs," *NAR* 146 (March 1888): 257–58; *NYT*, July 6, 12, 1888.

22. Edwards, "Gender in American Politics," 69, 129,; *NYS*, November 18, 1888; Kornbluh, *Why America Stopped Voting*, 12–16; Jensen, *Winning of the Midwest*, 2–4; Kleppner, *Who Voted?*, 32–39; Doyle, "Social Theory and New Communities," 160–61.

23. Altschuler and Blumin, *Rude Republic*, 210–15; George to Leonidas C. Houk, June 10, 1880, Houk MSS, CMMHC.

24. Ostrogorski, *Democracy and Organization*, 2:285–86; John R. Brierly to Stephen M. White, April 24, 1884, White MSS, SU.

25. Ostrogorski, *Democracy and Organization*, 207–13, 309–10; House, "Democratic State Central Committee of Indiana," 187–88; *Baltimore Sun*, October 19, 1892; Joseph Knowlton to Charles W. Johnson, October 24, 1878, and Johnson to Knute Nelson, October 11, 1878, Nelson MSS, MHS; John H. Farley to William C. Whitney, October 25, 1892, Whitney MSS, LC.

26. Ostrogorski, *Democracy and Organization*, 2:281–85; William H. Barnum to Samuel J. Randall, August 20, 1880, RanMSS.

27. *StPGW*, September 30, 1892; Charles W. Johnson to Knute Nelson, September 30, 1878, Nelson MSS, MHS; *Lexington Morning Transcript*, July 10, 1887.

28. *ChiTi*, October 2, 1876.

29. Ibid., October 22, 1876; *NYT*, October 6, 1888.

30. *NYS*, October 31, 1886; Jean H. Baker, *Affairs of Party*, 305–9; Samuel J. Tilden to Daniel Lamont, October 26, 1870, Lamont MSS, LC.

31. Reynolds, *Testing Democracy*, 43–46; *Boston Post*, November 7, 1866.

32. *StLG-D*, October 25, 1884; *NYEP*, October 28, 1884; C. Augustus Haviland to Benjamin F. Butler, October 12, 1884, Butler MSS, LC.

33. Ostrogorski, *Democracy and Organization*, 2:213–21; B. G. Caulfield to Francis Kernan, October 12, 1876, Kernan Family MSS, Cornell University, Ithaca, N.Y.; *AmN*, April 5, 1894; George Walton Green, "Facts about the Caucus and the Primary," *NAR* 137 (September 1883): 257–69; *Detroit Labor Leaf*, October 12, 1886.

34. Ostrogorski, *Democracy and Organization*, 2:231–37.

35. *IW&AIL*, October 16, 1880.

36. *ChiTi*, March 18, 1876; *PhilRec*, November 6, 1886; *ChiTr*, October 25, 1886; *StLG-D*, October 31, 1886; *Washington Post*, December 19, 1891.

37. *StLG-D*, June 27, 1880.

38. *SFAltaC*, July 5, 1884.

39. *NYH*, September 18, 1892.

40. "General Hancock and Rebel Claims" and "Dangerous Doctrine," *HW*, October 16, 1880, pp. 658–59; *Springfield Illinois State Register*, July 17, 1880; *Detroit Free Press*, October 5, 1880; *East Liverpool Potters' Gazette*, July 8, 1880; *DMSR*, July 10, 15, 25, 1880; *Albany Evening Journal*, September 29, October 1, 1880.

41. *Philadelphia Public Ledger*, November 5, 1880; *InN*, November 5, 1888.

42. On the logic of negative campaigning in risk-averse societies and its special usefulness in dealing with indifferent voters, see Riker, "Why Negative Campaigning Is Rational," 224–70.

43. F. D. Huntington, "Vituperation in Politics," *NAR* 140 (January 1885): 4–7.

44. *Philadelphia Public Ledger*, November 5, 1880.

45. *NYH*, September 8, 1876, November 2, 1888; *PhilRec*, September 25, 1886; *Newark Evening News*, November 2, 1888.

46. *Huntsville Gazette*, September 17, 1884; *NOrT-D*, October 29, 1884; *Corpus Christi Caller*, April 11, 1886; *St. Louis Republican*, November 3, 1884; Vandal, "Policy of Violence," 175–81; Vandal, "Politics and Violence," 23–42.

47. *Philadelphia Public Ledger*, October 7, 1880; *InN*, October 16, 1888; *Mechanicville (N.Y.) Mercury*, October 31, 1884.

48. Altschuler and Blumin, *Rude Republic*, 225–34; Edward Everett Hale, "The Tree of Political Knowledge," *NAR* 148 (May 1889): 565–66; *ChiTi*, October 14, 1876.

49. William Walter Phelps, "Permanent Republican Clubs," *NAR* 146 (March 1888): 243; Joseph H. Manley, "Permanent Republican Clubs," ibid., 258.

50. Ostrogorski, *Democracy and Organization*, 2:329–30; *Portland Daily Oregonian*, May 29, 1886; William Dudley Foulke, "Campaigning in the West," *NAR* 156 (January 1893): 126; *NYT*, August 28, 1880; *ChiTr*, October 1, 1880; *Boston Herald*, October 25, 1888; see also *Hartford Daily Courant*, October 13, 1888.

Chapter Four

1. *IW&AIL*, December 27, 1879; *St. Paul Anti-Monopolist*, July 25, 1878; *HW*, January 31, 1880, p. 66, April 10, 1880, p. 226; A. Churchell to Samuel J. Randall, March 24, 1879, RanMSS; *Plattsburgh Republican*, June 5, 1880.

2. *IW&AIL*, June 19, 1880; *Frankfort Tri-Weekly Yeoman*, June 10, 1880.

3. *HW*, January 24, 1880, p. 50.

4. *CR*, 46th Cong., 2d sess., appendix, 268–70 (June 15, 1880); *Independent*, November 11, 1880, p. 16; *HW*, October 2, 1880, p. 626; *NYT*, August 30, 1880; *Elmira Weekly Advertiser*, August 13, October 15, 1880; *StPP-P*, November 5, 1880; *Albany Evening Journal*, September 25, 1880; Reeves, *Gentleman Boss*, 195.

5. *Independent*, September 30, 1880, p. 17, October 21, 1880, pp. 1–2; *Albany Evening Journal*, September 17, 1880 (claims); *Elmira Weekly Advertiser*, October 15, 1880; *NYT*, August 26, 1880; *StPP-P*, October 2, 1880.

6. *LC-J*, July 23, July 31, 1880.

7. *Raleigh News & Observer*, November 2, 1880.

8. *LC-J*, September 28, 1880; *ChaN&C*, October 2, 1880.

9. *ChaN&C*, October 9, 1880; *LC-J*, September 28, October 15, 1880.

10. *ChaN&C*, October 4, 9, 1880; *Nation*, October 14, 1880; *LC-J*, October 6, 27, 1880.

11. *Henderson Reporter*, October 28, 1880; "O. O. S.," *LC-J*, October 5, 23; ibid., July 19, 22, 1880: *Albany Evening Journal*, July 1, 1880; *StLG-D*, July 9, 1880.

12. "Outis," *Raleigh News & Observer*, November 8, 1880; *Plattsburgh Republican*, November 6, 1880; *Paducah Daily News*, November 4, 1880.

13. W. E. Johnston to Elihu Washburne, January 7, 1880, Washburne MSS, LC; Victor E. Piollett to Samuel J. Randall, November 4, 1880, RanMSS.

14. *Detroit Free Press*, July 28, 1880; *Nation*, September 30, 1880; *CinGaz*, September 16, 1880; *LC-J*, September 12, 1880; *Albany Evening Journal*, September 23, October 2, 1880; Sam Ward to Thomas F. Bayard, September 16, 1880, Bayard MSS, LC. For Hancock's "treason" in 1868 and 1877, see *CinGaz*, July 21, 1880; *Nation*, August 5, 1880; and *LC-J*, July 22, 1880.

15. Hofstadter, *Paranoid Style in American Politics*, 3–40; Jean H. Baker, *Affairs of Party*, 165–71; Rodgers, "Liberty, Will, and Violence," 150–59; Wertheim, "Indianapolis Treason Trials," 246–60; *Poughkeepsie Daily Eagle*, November 2, 1880.

16. *HW*, August 25, 1888, p. 627, September 15, 1888, p. 687.

17. McFarlane, "Opposition to British Agricultural Investment," 115–30; "Nativism or Not?" 233–39; *IW&AIL*, April 19, May 3, 1884.

18. John Roach to James G. Blaine, June 12, 1884, Blaine MSS, LC; *ConMon*, October 23, 1884; *DMSR*, October 7, 11, 26, 1884, August 8, September 13, 14, 1890; John A. Henderson to Benjamin Harrison, October 28, 1888, Harrison MSS, LC.

19. Reitano, *Tariff Question*, 98–101; *Lewiston Journal*, August 28, 1884. For similar language, see *Zanesville Daily Courier*, November 1, 1884; *IW&AIL*, November 8, 15, 1884.

20. *Milwaukee Sentinel*, October 27, 1884; *Auburn Daily Advertiser*, July 16, 1884; *Milwaukee Sentinel*, October 27, 1884; *BWC*, August 30, 1884; *ChiTr*, October 10, 1884; *NYEP*, October 24, 1884; *Brooklyn Daily Eagle*, July 1, 1884.

21. Tarbell, *Tariff in Our Times*, 158–68; John C. Spooner to Harry H. Smith, July 31, 1888, Spooner MSS, LC; *Baltimore American*, October 13, 27, 1888; *Hartford Daily Courant*, November 6, 1888.

22. *NYH*, October 2, 16, 22, November 4, 1888; McDaniel, "Presidential Election of 1888," 156–57; Charles Lamberton to Samuel J. Randall, November 2, 1888, RanMSS; Blanton Duncan to Daniel Lamont, September 8, 1888, Lamont MSS, LC.

23. *East Liverpool Potters' Gazette*, November 4, 1876, November 4, 1880; *Elmira Weekly Advertiser*, October 22, 1880.

24. Henry Ward to Samuel J. Randall, August 2, 1885, RanMSS.

25. Edwin D. Morgan to Edwards Pierrepont, October 19, 1876, Hayes MSS, HML; W. R. Holloway to Morgan, September 28, 1876, Morgan MSS, NYSL.

26. See, for example, James S. Ashley, "The Impending Political Advance," *Arena* 14 (November 1895): 430; John J. Ingalls, "Fetichism in the Campaign," *NAR* 146 (June 1888): 651; John E. Milholland, "The Danger Point in American Politics," *NAR* 164 (January 1897): 94.

27. Thomas E. Hatch to William E. Chandler, October 1, 1880, ChanMSS (NHHS).

28. Frank Willing Leach, "Twenty Years with Quay," *Philadelphia North American*, October 9, 1904; *StLG-D*, September 8, 1888; *Memphis Daily Appeal*, November 1, 1884; *LRArkG*, July 20, 22, August 22, September 23, 1888.

29. *Crystal Springs Monitor*, August 12, 19, September 9, October 28, 1882; *Jackson Weekly Clarion*, October 4, 11, 1882.

30. House Report 306, 51st Cong., 1st sess., "Featherston vs. Cate," 4–6, 8–10; *StLG-D*, August 30, 1888; *LRArkG*, July 11, 12, 13, 14, 22, September 23, 1888; Rice, *Negro in Texas*, 98–99; Moneyhon, "Black Politics in Arkansas," 228–29.

31. Marvin F. Russell, "Republican Party of Arkansas," 86–87; *LRArkG*, July 22, 1888; *HW*, August 18, 1888, p. 606.

Chapter Five

1. Ritchie, *Press Gallery*, 109–10, 115–21; Emery, *Press and America*, 243–44; McGerr, *Decline of Popular Politics*, 114–19; clipping, *Midway News*, March 5, 1892, Castle MSS, MHS.

2. Davis, Providence Journal, 43–52; Hart, St. Louis Globe-Democrat, 136–60; McGerr, *Decline of Popular Politics*, 119; *Reno Evening Gazette*, November 4, 5, 1890.

3. Mott, *American Journalism*, 443–44, 480–83; George T. Rider, "The Pretensions of Journalism," *NAR* 135 (December 1882): 472; McGerr, *Decline of Popular Politics*, 125–28; on Sunday editions, see *NYS*, December 7, 1884.

4. *Chicago Daily News*, May 5, 1884; Mott, *American Journalism*, 501–3; Schuneman, "Art or Photography," 43; *St. Paul Dispatch*, August 5, 1886.

5. Summers, *Press Gang*, 45–47; Hurd, comp., *History of Fairfield County*, 230; Morton L. Montgomery, comp., *Historical and Biographical Annals*, 61; Ellis and Evans, *History of Lancaster County*, 500–507.

6. Conrad, Wilson, and Wilson, Milwaukee Journal, 24–25, 31–35; *Waterbury Daily Republican*, September 8, 11, 1890; *NYH*, October–November 1888.

7. Brann, *Brann the Iconoclast*, vol. 10; *Chattanooga Daily Times*, September 29, 1882, September 5, 1884; *St. Paul Dispatch*, August 5, 1886.

8. Summers, *Press Gang*, 60–61; *Clarksville Semi-Weekly Tobacco Leaf*, November 9, 1880; *Chicago Daily News*, May 5, 1884; *Brunswick Telegraph*, May 14, 1886; *PhilRec*, June 20, 1886; *Chattanooga Daily Times*, October 7, 1882.

9. House, "Democratic State Central Committee of Indiana," 192–94; McGerr, *Decline of Popular Politics*, 130; bill from *Raleigh Sentinel* for 1872 campaign, Barringer MSS, Southern Historical Collection, University of North Carolina, Chapel Hill; *Springfield Daily Illinois State Register*, July 17, 1880.

10. *Burlington Saturday Evening Post*, October 28, 1882; Summers, *Press Gang*, 47–48; J. E. Brown to Stephen M. White, June 11, 1892, White MSS, SU.

11. Juergens, *Joseph Pulitzer*, 89–91, 353–54; *Brooklyn Daily Eagle*, October 1, 1885; McGerr, *Decline of Popular Politics*, 123–24; Jacob Childs to William V. Byars, October 17, 1887, Byars MSS, Missouri Historical Society, St. Louis; John Bigelow to Whitelaw Reid, February 21, 1892, Reid MSS, LC.

12. West, *Satire on Stone*, 115–23, 195–96; Juergens, *Joseph Pulitzer*, 98–105; Walt McDougall, "Old Days on the World," *American Mercury* 4 (January 1925): 21.

13. *StLG-D*, May 12, 1884; McGerr, *Decline of Popular Politics*, 15–17; *SFAltaC*, October 17, 1888.

14. Clark, *Southern Country Editor*, 22–26; *Journalist*, March 1, 1890; Joseph Barbiere to Samuel J. Randall, January 16, 1883, RanMSS; Mark R. Plaisted to Stephen M. White, December 20, 1892, White to F. V. Dewey, December 10, 1892, and White to Charles W. Humphreys, December 9, 1892, White MSS, SU.

15. Samuel Woods to Isabella Woods, February 25, 1872, Ambler MSS, WVC; Henry G. Davis to Lewis Baker, June 17, August 31, October 11, 1869, August 27, November 4, 1870,

February 10, September 7, 24, 1874, March 6, 1877, September 18, 1880, November 30, 1882, January 8, 1883, April 2, 1885, and Davis to R. G. Barr, October 5, 1885, Davis MSS, WVC.

16. N. N. Hoffman to Waitman T. Willey, March 25, 1868, Willey MSS, WVC; Dick Austin to Leonidas C. Houk, November 20, 1882, Houk MSS, CMMHC; *Salem Daily Statesman*, May 11, 12, 1886.

17. *Reno Evening Gazette*, October 31, 1890; "Memphis," *Journalist*, May 30, 1890; *St. Paul Daily Globe*, September 23, 1890.

18. *Mechanicville Era*, September 28, 1882; McGerr, *Decline of Popular Politics*, 18–19.

19. *Knoxville Journal*, November 6, 1886; *Chicago Daily News*, May 23, 1884.

20. *NYH*, October 22, 23, 1880; Peskin, *Garfield*, 506–7. The best full-dress summations of the whole affair are in Gyory's superb *Closing the Gate*, 203–11, and Hinckley, "Politics of Sinophobia," 381–99.

21. *NYH*, October 21, 22, November 5, 14, 1880; *Wheeling Register*, November 1, 1880; *Dubuque Daily Herald*, November 3, 1880.

22. Peskin, *Garfield*, 507; *NYH*, October 24, 1880.

23. *NYH*, October 25, 26, 1880; *Chattanooga Daily Times*, November 13, 1880; *LC-J*, October 26, 28, 1880.

24. *Frankfort Tri-Weekly Yeoman*, November 2, 1880; *NYH*, October 27, 1880; *LC-J*, October 27, November 2, 1880; *Detroit Free Press*, October 31, 1880; *Clarksville Semi-Weekly Tobacco Leaf*, November 2, 1880.

25. *LC-J*, November 10, 11, 12, 13, 1880.

26. Thomas Harrison Baker, Memphis Commercial Appeal, 142–43; *JSP*, May 11, 1884, February 6, 1887; *NYStan*, January 22, 1887, March 12, 1890.

27. Rodgers, "Liberty, Will, and Violence," 141; *Salem Daily Statesman*, April 30, 1890; *Burlington Hawk-Eye*, August 16, 19, 1890; *StPP-P*, November 5, 1878; W. Scott Morgan, *History of the Wheel*; Cresswell, *Multi-Party Politics*, 149; *AmN*, June 7, 1894.

28. Emery, *Press and America*, 267–70; Harry J. Sherman, "It Pays," *Journalist*, May 24, 1890; Griffith and Talmadge, *Georgia Journalism*, 110–11; Schudson, *Discovering the News*, 93, 99–102; Rider, "Pretensions of Journalism," 473–74.

29. Clark, *Southern Country Editor*, 26–29; "Country Journalism," *Journalist*, May 24, 1890; *Baltimore Sun*, July 15, 1892.

30. Nord, *Communities of Journalism*, 136–38; Catherine H. Spence, "Effective Voting the Only Effective Moralizer in Politics," *Arena* 10 (November 1894): 773–74; *DMSR*, September 12, 1890.

31. Nord, *Communities of Journalism*, 138–45; Summers, *Press Gang*, 73–74; *JSP*, December 23, 1883, November 21, 1886.

32. *JSP*, July 13, December 21, 1884, August 15, 1886; *IW&AIL*, November 13, 1880; *Chicago Labor Enquirer*, March 6, April 23, 1887; *StPGW*, February 13, 1891.

33. *ODB*, September 21, 29, 1890; *StPP-P*, November 5, 1878; *JSP*, October 25, November 15, 1885; *Chicago Labor Enquirer*, April 9, May 3, 1887.

34. Cresswell, *Multi-Party Politics*, 55–57, 149; for births and deaths, see *IW&AIL*, July 3, 1880; *St. Paul Anti-Monopolist*, August 29, September 5, 1878; and *JSP*, July 6, 1884, October 25, 1885.

35. "E. G. D.," *NYT*, October 3, 1892; "The Negro Press in Arkansas," *Journalist*, April 5,

1890; "St. Louis," ibid., November 29, 1890; Marvin F. Russell, "Republican Party of Arkansas," 177–78; Cresswell, *Multi-Party Politics*, 55, 90.

36. Nord, *Communities of Journalism*, 154–57; McGerr, *Decline of Popular Politics*, 124–28.

Chapter Six

1. *NYH*, January 10, 1889; Munroe, *History of Delaware*, 147–48.

2. *NYTr*, April 4, 1886; clipping, April 27, 1885, Carpenter Scrapbooks, Carpenter MSS, LC; *NYS*, November 18, 1888; *WilEvEv*, August 28, 31, 1888.

3. *WilEvEv*, November 10, 23, 1888. Matt Quay's personal secretary later would claim that the money did come from the national committee, but this could not have been to his own personal knowledge: he was helping "fix" North Carolina at the time. See Frank Willing Leach, "Twenty Years with Quay," *Philadelphia North American*, October 30, 1904.

4. *WilEvEv*, November 23, 1888.

5. Ibid. For the same attitude across the state line, see A Pennsylvanian, "The Ills of Pennsylvania," *Atlantic* 88 (October 1901): 561–62.

6. C. L. Robinson to John C. Houk, October 28, 1894, Houk MSS, CMMHC; Jensen, *Winning of the Midwest*, 35–36; Jean H. Baker, *Affairs of Party*, 314–15. The issue of vote fraud—which usually mingles vote-buying and coercion, and the different ways of cheating in making the result—has inspired a vast literature. Among the skeptics are Howard W. Allen and K. Warren Allen, "Vote Fraud and Data Validity," in Clubb, Flanigan, and Zingale, eds., *Analyzing Electoral History*, 157–69; Burnham, "Theory and Voting Research," 1018; Burnham, "Those High Nineteenth-Century Turnouts," 616–18; Mayfield, "Voting Fraud in Early-Twentieth-Century Pittsburgh," 59–84; and Keyssar, *Right to Vote*, 159–61. For a convincing and thorough refutation showing that fraud was seen by more than the Mugwumps and that the proofs rested on far more than anecdotal evidence, readers should see Argersinger, "New Perspectives on Election Fraud," 669–87.

7. D. B. Simpson to John C. Houk, November 23, 1894, and S. Edy Franklin to Houk, September 20, 1894, Houk MSS, CMMHC; *Nation*, January 3, 1889, p. 10; *Howard v. Jacoby*, 14 Lanc. Bar. 31, 3 Pennsylvania Co. Ct. R 436 (1882).

8. *InN*, June 21, 1884.

9. J. W. Bates affidavit, March 19, 1894, Lindsay Rose affidavit, March 19, 1894, and O. P. Runyan affidavit, March 20, 1894, Houk MSS, CMMHC; "A. R.," *Nation*, December 9, 1880; *Thomas Moonlight v. William H. Bond*, 17 Kans. 351 (1876).

10. Pennsylvanian, "Ills of Pennsylvania," 562; U. S. Trammell to John C. Houk, October 29, 1894, Houk MSS, CMMHC.

11. House, "Democratic State Central Committee of Indiana," 201–02; *InN*, June 21, 1884; *NYS*, December 11, 1884; *CinEnq*, October 13, 1880, August 31, 1888.

12. "W. P.," *Nation*, December 16, 1880; "A. R."; *NYS*, December 11, 14, 1884; *NYH*, March 4, 1884; *InN*, June 21, 1884; *LC-J*, October 31, 1884.

13. G. B. Creekmore list of campaign expenses, November 6, 1894, and Joe Foute to Houk, November 17, 1894, Houk MSS, CMMHC; Richardson, *William E. Chandler*, 165.

14. A. J. Johnson to John C. Houk, October 6, 1894, John H. Collins to Houk, October 29,

1894, and U. S. Trammell to Houk, October 29, 1894, Houk MSS, CMMHC; *ConMon*, August 16, 1881; "'The Bar'l,'" *HW*, October 23, 1880, p. 674; *Outlook*, January 14, 1905, p. 99; Baney, "Yankees and the City," 104; John N. B. Clarke to William E. Chandler, February 21, 1868, ChanMSS (NHHS); *Concord Labor Reform Dispatch*, February 11, 1870; William W. Bishop to William E. Chandler, June 17, 1882, ChanMSS (LC).

15. *NYStan*, October 20, 1888; Robert Culton affidavit, March 17, 1894, Houk MSS, CMMHC; *LC-J*, October 31, 1884; *WilEvEv*, November 23, 1888.

16. *Newark Evening News*, November 10, 1888.

17. *NYS*, November 25, 1888. A similar system operated in Newark. See *Newark Evening News*, November 10, 1888.

18. *NYS*, November 25, 1888. For dozens of affidavits about just such a country election, some by voters who were approached and refused, see the Houk MSS for March 12–19, 1894, CMMHC. For court decisions, see *Patton v. Coates*, 41 Arkansas 111; *Tullos v. Lane*, 45 Louisiana Ann. 333; and *People v. Cicott*, 16 Michigan 283.

19. Edgar J. Levey, "An Election in New York," *NAR* 145 (December 1887): 681; *NYStan*, April 21, 1888; Henry George, "Money in Elections," *NAR* 136 (February 1883): 202; *NYS*, December 11, 1884, November 25, 1888; Thomas E. Will, "Political Corruption: How Best Oppose?" *Arena* 10 (November 1894): 848; David A. Biggs to John C. Houk, October 22, 1894, and L. R. Carden to Houk, October 28, 1894, Houk MSS, CMMHC; "M. C.," *Nation*, November 18, 1880; *Concord Labor Reform Dispatch*, February 11, 1870.

20. Levey, "Election in New York," 681; *NYS*, November 25, 1888; Jack Johnson affidavit, March 17, 1894, Houk MSS, CMMHC.

21. Jack to John C. Houk, October 26, 1894, and W. H. McCarroll to Houk, October 19, 1894, Houk MSS, CMMHC; *CinGaz*, April 17, 1871.

22. *NYH*, November 2, 1872; for a similar arrangement that came into court, see *Howard v. Jacoby*, 14 Lanc. Bar. 31, 3 Pa. Co. Ct. R 436, 2 York Leg. Rec. 216 (1882); *NYStan*, November 12, 1887, November 3, 1888; A. J. Ricks to John Sherman, October 12, 1885, Sherman MSS, LC; and F. A. Healy to Wendell Anderson, October 11, 1876, Anderson MSS, SHSW.

23. Richardson, *William E. Chandler*, 165; *ConMon*, August 16, 1881; *LC-J*, October 31, 1884; "M. C.," *Nation*, November 18, 1880; "W. P.," ibid., December 16, 1880; Ivins, *Machine Politics*, 58, 77; Thomas E. Will, "Political Corruption: How Best Oppose?" *Arena* 10 (November 1894): 845.

24. Ostrogorski, *Democracy and Organization*, 2:345; *Newark Evening News*, November 10, 1888.

25. *NYStan*, October 20, 1888; *Watertown Daily Times*, November 10, 1888; Henry George, "Money in Elections," *NAR* 136 (February 1883): 202–3; *NYT*, October 17, 1888.

26. James J. Faran to William Allen, September 17, 1876, Allen MSS, LC; *Hartford Daily Courant*, February 22, 1869.

27. As note Aaron H. Cragin to Mason W. Tappan, March 16, 1856, Gilman Marston to Tappan, February 22, 1859, and Leonard Chase to Tappan, March 13, 1859, Tappan MSS, New Hampshire Historical Society, Concord; Henry Hibbard to John H. George, January 25, 1854, and John S. Wall to George, March 3, 1854, George MSS, New Hampshire Historical Society, Concord.

28. On industrial intimidation, see "A. R.," *Nation*, December 9, 1880; "Michigan," ibid.,

January 3, 1889; W. C. Plummer to Samuel J. Randall, December 4, 1878, RanMSS. For a denial of charges, see *East Liverpool Potters' Gazette*, October 28, 1880; for skepticism, see Jensen, *Winning of the Midwest*, 48–57; for strong confirmation, see Argersinger, "New Perspectives on Election Fraud," 673, and Gould, *Wyoming*, 117–18; on voting farmhands, see Pennsylvanian, "Ills of Pennsylvania," 562, and Thomas E. Will, "Political Corruption: How Best Oppose?" *Arena* 10 (November 1894): 848.

29. *NYStan*, October 20, 1888; Jensen, *Winning of the Midwest*, 45–46.

30. *StLG-D*, September 20, 1884.

31. *Greenville News*, cited in "Sectionalism," *HW*, March 23, 1889, p. 219; Cresswell, *Multi-Party Politics*, 85–86; Anderson, *Race and Politics*, 154–60; Rice, *Negro in Texas*, 114–27; *Jackson Clarion*, October 29, 1884; *NOrT-D*, October 28, 31, 1884; *Memphis Daily Appeal*, November 4, 1884; *Memphis Commercial Appeal*, October 26, 1884; *StLG-D*, October 15, 1886.

32. *NOrT-D*, October 12, 1884; *New Orleans Daily Picayune*, October 4, 1884; Rice, *Negro in Texas*, 96; *Memphis Daily Appeal*, October 26, 1884; *Augusta Chronicle*, July 7, 1886.

33. Cartwright, *Triumph of Jim Crow*, 84–86, 210; *StLG-D*, October 30, 1886; Ostrogorski, *Democracy and Organization*, 2:344–45; "Boodle Politics," *HW*, April 6, 1889, p. 258; *LC-J*, October 31, 1884; John H. Purnell to William E. Chandler, July 23, 1890, ChanMSS (LC).

34. Cartwright, *Triumph of Jim Crow*, 59–60; Giggie, "Spiritual Politics of Disfranchisement," 258–64; *Memphis Daily Appeal*, November 4, 1884; *NOrT-D*, October 27, 28, 29, 1884; *StLG-D*, October 30, 1886; *Jones v. Glidwell*, 53 Arkansas 161 (1890).

35. John A. Kasson, "Municipal Reform," *NAR* 137 (September 1883): 224–29 (city property qualification); Henry Melrose, "Who are the Culprits?" *NAR* 146 (June 1888): 711; Edward Everett Hale, "The Tree of Political Knowledge," *NAR* 148 (May 1889): 567–69; *NYStan*, March 31, 1888.

36. *Austin Statesman*, October 27, 1886.

37. "A Mississippi View," *HW*, March 8, 1890, p. 174; *Memphis Commercial Appeal*, August 4, 1886; Cartwright, *Triumph of Jim Crow*, 205–6.

38. *ConMon*, July 17, 1889; *Augusta Chronicle*, July 1, 1886.

39. "'Bar'l,'" p. 674.

Chapter Seven

1. "Garcelon's Purge," *HW*, January 19, 1880, pp. 10–11; *BWC*, November 12, 13, 14, December 20, 25, 1879; *Nation*, November 20, December 18, 25, 1879.

2. *Lewiston Evening Journal*, January 1, 1880.

3. *BWC*, December 20, 1879, January 2, 1880; Eugene Hale to William E. Chandler, December 16, 1879, ChanMSS (LC); *Nation*, January 1, 1880; *Independent*, January 8, 1880, p. 17; William Henry Smith to Orange Jacobs, January 12, 1880, Smith MSS, Box 10: Letterbooks, Ohio Historical Society, Columbus.

4. *NYH*, January 10, 1880; William E. Chandler to Whitelaw Reid, December 27, 1879, Reid MSS, LC; Eugene Hale to William E. Chandler, December 17, 1879, ChanMSS (LC); *BWC*, December 27, 1879; *Portland Eastern Argus*, September 7, 1880.

5. *Nation*, January 1, 8, 15, 1880; *NYH*, January 5, 8, 9, 13, 1880; *Lewiston Evening Journal*, January 10, 12, 13, 1880.

6. *Lewiston Evening Journal*, January 14, 17, 19, 21, 28, 30, February 2, 1880; *Independent*, January 22, 1880, p. 22; *Nation*, January 22, 29, 1880; Eugene Hale to William Chandler, n.d. [January 1880], ChanMSS (LC); William Henry Smith to Orange Jacobs, January 12, 1880, Smith MSS, Box 10: Letterbooks, Ohio Historical Society, Columbus.

7. *Portland Eastern Argus*, September 4, 8, 9, 13, 1880; *IW&AIL*, August 7, 1880; *Nation*, September 23, 1880; James G. Blaine to William E. Chandler, September 15, 1880, ChanMSS (NHHS).

8. *CinGaz*, November 8, 1870; Henry A. Gumbleton, "The Lodging-House Vote in New York," *NAR* 144 (June 1887): 631–35.

9. *InSen*, October 2, 8, 1872; *Trenton Daily True American*, September 10, 1888; *Wheeling Intelligencer*, October 24, 25, November 2, 8, 1892; *PiPo*, October 15, 1892; *Baltimore Sun*, October 17, 19, 1892; James J. Faran to William Allen, September 17, 1876, Allen MSS, LC.

10. *Springfield Weekly Republican*, September 18, 1874; John W. Goff, "Juggling with the Ballot," *NAR* 158 (February 1894): 203–5; *Nation*, October 14, 1880; *NYH*, November 2, 1882.

11. Ostrogorski, *Democracy and Organization*, 2:303–4; *Mechanicville Mercury*, November 7, 1884; *NYTr*, September 3, 1888; Goff, "Juggling with the Ballot," 205–8; *Trenton Daily True American*, September 10, 1888; *JSP*, November 21, 1886.

12. John E. Milholland, "The Danger Point in American Politics," *NAR* 164 (January 1897): 94; M. L. Mansfield affidavit, March 17, 1894, Houk MSS, CMMHC; *NYH*, November 3, 1882; Clinton Rogers Woodruff, "Philadelphia's Election Frauds," *Arena* 24 (October 1900): 397–404.

13. Though not always. See Henry C. Wright, *Bossism in Cincinnati*, 20–23.

14. *Atchison, Topeka & Santa Fe Railroad Company v. Jefferson County Commissioners*, 17 Kans. 29 (1876); Goff, "Juggling with the Ballot," 205–6; *InSen*, September 26, 1872; J. F. Dayton to Luman H. Weller, November 12, 1884, Weller MSS, SHSW; *StLG-D*, November 1, 1886; *Nation*, June 21, 1884.

15. On partisan and illiterate inspectors, see House Report 1905, 51st Cong., 1st sess., "McDuffie vs. Turpin," majority report, 8–12; on refusal to accept Republican ballots, see "Goodrich v. Bullock," House Report 2899, 51st Cong., 1st sess., 3–12, and *IW&AIL*, November 13, 1880; on Mississippi trickery, see Wirt A. Williams, ed., *Bolivar County, Mississippi*, 162–63.

16. For northern decisions, see *Parvin v. Wimberg*, 130 Indiana 561 (1892): *People v. Bates*, 11 Michigan 362 (1863); *Young v. Deming*, 9 Utah 204 (1893); and *State v. Holran*, 85 Wisconsin 94 (1893).

17. *In re Contested Election of Walker*, 3 Luz. Reg. 130 (Pennsylvania, 1874); *Marks v. Park*, 7 Leg. Gaz. 70 (1875); *Clark v. Leathers*, 5 S.W. 576 (Kentucky, 1887); *InSen*, August 20, 1872. But see also *In re Melvin*, 68 Pennsylvania St. 333 (1871).

18. *NYH*, November 1, 1882; H. B. Anthony, "Limited Suffrage in Rhode Island," *NAR* 137 (November 1883): 413–21; Abraham Payne, "Constitutional Reform in Rhode Island," ibid., 142 (April 1886): 332–36; *StLP-D*, March 10, 1887; *NYStan*, April 21, 1888.

19. Limbaugh, *Rocky Mountain Carpetbaggers*, 43–56; *NYStan*, November 24, 1888, February 12, 1890.

20. *NYT*, October 7, 1880; *Behrensmeyer v. Kreitz*, 135 Illinois 591 (1891); *In re Opinion of Justices*, 64 Maine 596 (1875); *People v. Cicott*, 16 Michigan 283 (1867); *Newton v. Newell*, 26 Minnesota 529 (1880); *Rodenbough v. Wolverton*, 2 Lehigh Val. Law Rep. 285 (1883); *Riefsnyder v. Musser*, 12 Wkly. Notes Cas. 155 (1881); Stephen M. White to J. F. Sullivan, November 8, 1888, White MSS, SU.

21. *ConMon*, June 7, 9, 1875.

22. Argersinger, "New Perspectives on Election Fraud," 682; Cresswell, *Multi-Party Politics*; Anderson, *Race and Politics*, 160–61, 50–51; "Election Investigations by the Courts," *HW*, January 4, 1890, p. 3; *CR*, 46th Cong., 2d sess., appendix, 164 (May 11, 1880); House Report 1905, 51st Cong., 1st sess., "McDuffie vs. Turpin," 2–4; *CR*, 51st Cong., 1st sess., 9627 (September 3, 1890); Thomas B. Reed, "Contested Elections," *NAR* 151 (July 1890): 112–20.

23. Powderly, *Path I Trod*, 68–71; Oestreicher, "Socialism and the Knights of Labor," 1–12; Argersinger, "New Perspectives on Election Fraud," 676.

24. *NYH*, June 9, 1875; *ConMon*, June 3, 7, 8, 9, 14, 1875.

25. *ClPD*, January 7, 1886; Walters, *Joseph Benson Foraker*, 38–39; Henry C. Wright, *Bossism in Cincinnati*, 25–26, 30–31.

26. *Chattanooga Daily Times*, November 3, 1880; "The Republican Party and a Third Term," *HW*, January 31, 1880, p. 66; *Nation*, December 25, 1879, p. 434.

27. "The Colored Vote," *HW*, April 14, 1888, p. 262; Henry Watterson, "The Hysteria of Sectional Agitation," *Forum* (Spring 1888).

28. Henningson, "'Root Hog or Die,'" 197–216; Elkins, "Agricultural Wheel," 152–73; Paisley, "Political Wheelers," 3–13; Segraves, "Arkansas Politics," 178; *LRArkG*, April 11, 1888.

29. Paisley, "Political Wheelers," 13–16; *StLG-D*, September 3, 1888.

30. *CR*, 51st Cong., 1st sess., 9744–46 (September 5, 1890); *StLG-D*, September 3, 1888.

31. Welch, "Violence and the Decline of Black Politics," 368–70; *StLG-D*, September 5, 6, 15, 1888; Barnes, *Who Killed John Clayton?* 374–83.

32. Paisley, "Political Wheelers," 17–18; Segraves, "Arkansas Politics," 182; Marvin F. Russell, "Republican Party of Arkansas," 90. Much more of the story, in rich and grim detail, appears in Barnes, *Who Killed John Clayton?*.

33. *StLG-D*, September 4, 8, 1888; House Report 306, 51st Cong., 1st sess., "Featherston vs. Cate," 26–51; *CR*, 51st Cong., 1st sess., 9625–27 (September 3, 1890).

34. *StLG-D*, September 7, 8, 14, 15, 1888.

35. Segraves, "Arkansas Politics," 184–85.

36. *StLG-D*, September 8, 1888; Segraves, "Arkansas Politics," 185; Marvin F. Russell, "Republican Party of Arkansas," 88–90; *LRArkG*, January 9, 1889.

37. "Clayton vs. Breckinridge," House Report 2912, 51st Cong., 1st sess., majority report, 4–5, minority report, 14–15, 26–66; "The Clayton Murder," *HW*, February 16, 1889, p. 122; Logan S. Roots, "Assassination as a Political Argument," *NAR* 148 (March 1889): 280–81; Marvin F. Russell, "Republican Party of Arkansas," 97–99; Barnes, "Who Killed John M. Clayton?" 383–401.

38. *StLG-D*, November 14, 1888.

39. *CR*, 51st Cong., 1st sess., 9625 (September 3, 1890); Barnes, "Who Killed John M. Clayton?" 401–3; *Trenton Daily True American*, September 3, 1890.

40. Moneyhon, "Black Politics in Arkansas," 240–45.

Chapter Eight

1. McClure, *Old Time Notes of Pennsylvania*, 2:545–47; *Philadelphia Weekly Times*, May 30, June 6, 13, 20, 1885; *Pennsylvania Legislative Record*, pp. 1688 (May 14, 1885); pp. 2169–70 (June 1, 1885); *PiPo*, November 5, 1886; *Philadelphia Inquirer*, August 27, 28, 29, 1888; *NYTr*, September 2, 1888.

2. Argersinger, "Value of the Vote," 61–63. *In re Baird*, 142 NY 523, 37 N.E. 619 (1894); *State v. Cunningham*, 83 Wisconsin 90, 53 N.W. 35, 35 Am. St. Rep. 27; *Parker v. State*, 133 Indiana 178, 32 N.E. 836; *People v. Thompson*, 155 Illinois 451, 40 N.E. 307.

3. Baney, *Yankees and the City*, 49–51, 55–56, 91–92; Argersinger, "Value of the Vote," 67–71, 74–75.

4. *StLP-D*, March 10, 1887; "Corp," *SprRep*, November 7, 1868; Shank and Roeck, *New Jersey's Experience*, 7; Shank, *New Jersey Reapportionment Politics*, 33–34.

5. For the recognition of legislative discretion (though in certain respects overturning state law), see *People v. Thompson*, 155 Illinois 451, 401 N.E. 307 (1895); *In Re Baird*, 66 Hun. 335, 20 N.Y. Supp. 470 (1892); *Denney v. State*, 144 Indiana 503, 42 N.E. 929 (1896); and dissent in *State v. Cunningham*, 83 Wisconsin 90, 53 N.W. 35. For creative districting, see *State v. Cunningham*, 83 Wisconsin 90; *In Re Baird*, 66 Hun. 335; and *Dubuque Herald*, April 17, 1886.

6. *East Liverpool Potters' Gazette*, October 17, 1878; *Sandusky Weekly Register*, November 24, 1886; Argersinger, "Value of the Vote," 72. For screwy results, see Commons, *Proportional Representation*, 53–54, 59–62.

7. *Pennsylvania Legislative Record*, p. 1689 (May 14, 1885); *Birmingham Age*, September 6, 1886; *StLG-D*, November 1, 1886; *Boston Herald*, September 18, 1882.

8. George W. Marston to William E. Chandler, August 3, 1894, ChanMSS (NHHS).

9. *ChiTi*, August 20, October 25, 28, 1876.

10. *ChiTr*, October 16, 1886; *Dubuque Herald*, April 15, 16, 18, 27, October 8, 1886.

11. *Racine Journal*, December 7, 1870; Jeremiah Rusk to Elisha W. Keyes, January 10, 25, 1872, George W. Hazelton to Keyes, January 24, 1872, and Andrew Elmore to Keyes, February 20, 1872, Keyes MSS, SHSW.

12. Andrew E. Elmore to Elisha W. Keyes, February 20, 1872, and Keyes to Eldredge, February 11, 1872 (italics added), Keyes MSS, SHSW.

13. *PhilRec*, July 22, August 29, October 18, 31, 1886; *NYS*, November 28, 1884; *ChaN&C*, November 24, 1883; William H. Kemble to Samuel J. Randall, March 2, 1877, William J. Harrity to Randall, December 4, 1885, W. Fletcher to Randall, February 9, 1885, and George McGowan to Randall, February 25, 1885, RanMSS; Quay, "Philadelphia Democrats," 47, 206; *Philadelphia North American*, October 20, 1886.

14. *Baltimore Sun*, September 22, 1886; *StLG-D*, November 28, 1888; Commons, *Proportional Representation*, 65–68; Argersinger, "Value of the Vote," 68–70.

15. Argersinger, "Value of the Vote," 75–76; *CR*, 47th Cong., 1st sess., appendix, 522 (July 20, 1882).

16. *Baltimore Sun*, September 29, 1892.

17. Lamar, *Dakota Territory*, 244–85; Dunn, *From Harrison to Harding*, 76.

18. *NYW*, April 18, May 2, 1870.

19. On Idaho, see *NYH*, July 2, 1890; on New Mexico, see *NYTr*, May 22, 26, 1874, and "Gideon," *ChiTi*, May 27, 1874; Stewart and Weingast, "Stacking the Senate," 223–71.

20. Lillard, *Desert Challenge*, 27–29, 44–45.

21. Limbaugh, *Rocky Mountain Carpetbaggers*, 78–79; *Carson City Morning Appeal*, June 6, 1886; *Reno Evening Gazette*, July 14, 1890.

22. Leonard, "Southwestern Boundaries," 52–53; *StPP-P*, November 16, 1878; Byron M. Smith to Samuel J. Randall, January 31, 1883, W. R. Brierly to Randall, October 3, 1885, and B. M. Smith to Randall, January 19, 1886, RanMSS; *Omaha Daily Bee*, May 25, 1880; Wells, "Idaho's Season of Political Distress," 60–64.

23. W. R. Brierly to Samuel J. Randall, December 12, 1888, RanMSS; *NYH*, July 1, 1890; Harry Ames to John Sherman, June 15, 1890, Sherman MSS, LC; Limbaugh, *Rocky Mountain Carpetbaggers*, 181–83.

24. On the Electoral College problem, see James S. Ashley, "The Impending Political Advance," *Arena* 14 (November 1895): 433–35, and McKnight, *Electoral System of the United States*, 336–37.

25. Argersinger, "Value of the Vote," 64–65; Baney, "Yankees and the City," 96–110.

26. Stewart and Weingast, "Stacking the Senate," 223–71.

27. *NYStan*, March 26, 1890; *PiPo*, January 8, 1889; "Presidential Election by Districts," *HW*, February 7, 1880, p. 82; *Nation*, December 18, 1879, p. 417; F. A. P. Barnard, "How Shall the President Be Elected?" *NAR* 140 (February 1885): 101–8; S. M. Merrill, "Our Electoral System," *NAR* 163 (October 1896): 410–13; reportedly, such a proportional arrangement was part of the Democratic-Populist program, if they won in 1896. See Walter Clark, "If Silver Wins," *NAR* 163 (October 1896): 467–68.

28. Argersinger, "Value of the Vote," 83–87; Benjamin F. Meyers, "The Single Vote in Congressional Elections," *NAR* 150 (June 1890): 782–85; W. D. McCrackan, "Proportional Representation," *Arena* 7 (February 1893): 290–97; W. D. McCrackan, "Politics as a Career," *Arena* 11 (January 1895): 236–37. For the case for proportional representation, see Hoag and Hallett, *Proportional Representation*, 58–102.

29. Catherine H. Spence, "Effective Voting the Only Effective Moralizer of Politics," *Arena* 10 (November 1894): 770–75; Tyson, "Needed Political Reforms," 612–13.

30. *Nation*, May 7, 1891.

31. *Raleigh News & Observer*, September 21, October 5, 1890.

32. *NYStan*, March 26, 1890; "Choosing Presidential Electors," *HW*, January 3, 1880, p. 3; *Nation*, December 18, 1879, January 22, 1880.

Chapter Nine

1. "Purse'n'all influence" from a letter of Albion W. Tourgee to Benjamin Harrison, June 29, 1888, Harrison MSS, LC; Josephson, *Politicos*, 290, 327–33, 338–40, 444–48; "The Bosses of the Senate," centerfold, *Puck*, January 23, 1889.

2. Henry Ward to Samuel J. Randall, September 12, 1884, RanMSS; *NYT*, October 2, 1892; *Bangor Commercial*, September 4, 1884 (with allegations of two packages of $50,000 sent to Maine by Democrats); *CinEnq*, September 29, 1884; *CinGaz*, November 8, 1870 (which declared that Tammany Hall had spent $100,000 on a torchlight parade); *CinEnq*, September 1, October 13, 15, 1870 (which alleged that Congressman Robert Schenck had demanded a $50,000 exchequer from protected interests before running again); and, as antidote, S. C. Boynton to William E. Chandler, September 25, 1870, and Henry D. Cooke to Chandler, September 26, 1870, ChanMSS (LC).

3. D. W. Voyles to William E. Chandler, September 12, October 20, 1868, ChanMSS (LC); Fuller to Thomas Jenckes, July 11, 1868, Jenckes MSS, LC; George C. Tichenor to John Sherman, September 18, 1880, Sherman MSS, LC.

4. House, "Democratic State Central Committee of Indiana," 189; Polakoff, *Politics of Inertia*, 128–29, 139; Abram S. Hewitt to Samuel J. Tilden, September 2, 1876, Tilden MSS, New York Public Library, New York. For Chandler's figures, see William E. Chandler to Whitelaw Reid, November 1, 1904, Reid MSS, LC.

5. Charles Foster to Arthur L. Conger, July 29, August 25, 1883, Letterbooks, Foster MSS, Ohio Historical Society, Columbus; John F. Oglevee to Arthur L. Conger, September 20, 26, October 4, 17, 1883, James M. Swank to Conger, September 26, 27, 1883, Jesse Spaulding to Conger, September 28, 1883, William H. Robertson to Conger, September 22, 1883, and James W. Alexander to Conger, September 28, 1883, Conger MSS, HML.

6. Asa S. Bushnell to Conger, September 4, 12, 23, 1885, Conger MSS, HML.

7. A. J. Wright to J. M. S. Williams, December 16, 1868, William E. Chandler to Claflin, November 20, 1868, and James A. Briggs to Claflin, September 8, 1868, Claflin MSS, HML; Thomas Coggeshall to Thomas J. Jenckes, October 22, 1868, Jenckes MSS, LC. For money raised specifically "for the defense of the polls," see Charles J. Canda to William C. Whitney, November 11, 1884, Whitney MSS, LC; and Lewis B. Gunckel to Jay Cooke, October 1, 1868, Cooke MSS, Historical Society of Pennsylvania, Philadelphia.

8. Ivins, *Machine Politics*, 39–42; see also figures per precinct in *CinEnq*, September 29, 1884, and Thomas E. Will, "Political Corruption: How Best Oppose?" *Arena* 10 (November 1894): 845.

9. Ivins, *Machine Politics*, 59; *NYStan*, November 26, 1887; *JSP*, June 26, 1887.

10. Ivins, *Machine Politics*, 59–63.

11. *StLG-D*, August 19, 1888; Henry George, "Money in Elections," *NAR* 136 (February 1883): 202.

12. *Baltimore Sun*, October 21, 1892; *Wheeling Intelligencer*, July 27, 1892; *NYT*, October 17, 1892; *StLG-D*, August 19, 1888; Edward Bragg to William F. Vilas, November 15, 1884, Vilas MSS, SHSW.

13. Richardson, *William E. Chandler*, 96–98; William E. Chandler to Henry D. Cooke, June 14, September 19, 1868, March 1, 1872, Jay Cooke to Henry D. Cooke, July 6, 1868, Oc-

tober 25, 1872, and Hugh McCulloch to Jay Cooke, October 2, 1872, Cooke MSS, Historical Society of Pennsylvania, Philadelphia; George F. Dawson to John A. Logan, October 8, 1884, Logan MSS, LC.

14. James S. Clarkson to James G. Blaine, June 26, 1884, Blaine MSS, LC.

15. William E. Chandler to Jay Cooke, October 22, 1872, H. C. Fahnestock to Jay Cooke, October 25, 1872, and Henry H. Bingham to William E. Chandler, November 22, 1872, Cooke MSS, Historical Society of Pennsylvania, Philadelphia; Richardson, *William E. Chandler*, 145; Kehl, *Boss Rule*, 98; James G. Blaine to Whitelaw Reid, January 26, 1888, Reid MSS, LC.

16. Samuel Thomas to Arthur L. Conger, September 24, 1885, W. S. King to Conger, September 21, 1885, Hussey, Howe & Company to Conger, September 23, 1885, William G. Park to Conger, September 23, 1885, C. W. Moulton to Conger, October 3, 1885, and James M. Swank to Conger, September 23, October 6, 1885, Conger MSS, HML.

17. Charles J. Canda to William C. Whitney, October 4, 24, 31, November 11, 1884, Whitney MSS, LC.

18. Dorman B. Eaton, "Political Assessments," *NAR* 135 (September 1882): 197–21; Edwin D. Morgan to Zachariah Chandler, September 1, 1876, Morgan MSS, NYSL; Henry C. Payne to A. C. Botkin, October 30, 1876, Smith MSS, Ohio Historical Society, Columbus; *InN*, November 3, 1884; Edward S. Bragg to William F. Vilas, November 5, 1884, Vilas MSS, SHSW.

19. Howlett to Elihu Washburne, July 13, 1868, Washburne MSS, LC; William W. Flint to Charles Willard, August 28, 1872, Willard MSS, Vermont Historical Society, Montpelier; "'Voluntary' Contributions," *HW*, November 22, 1879, p. 918.

20. Whitelaw Reid to James G. Blaine, October 18, 1884, Reid MSS, LC; Joseph Cannon to Edward McPherson, July 29, 1884, McPherson MSS, LC; *NYEP*, September 15, 1884; James S. Clarkson to E. Halford, April 23, 1892, Harrison MSS, LC.

21. Ivins, *Machine Politics*, 54–58, 65–67; *NYStan*, October 20, 1888, January 5, 1889; "A Millionaire Senate," *HW*, November 30, 1889, p. 951.

22. Polakoff, *Politics of Inertia*, 112–13; A. T. Glaze to William A. Anderson, June 17, 1876, Anderson MSS, SHSW; Eugene Casserly to Manton Marble, November 26, 1874, and S. L. M. Barlow to Marble, August 16, 1886, Marble MSS, LC.

23. Summers, *Rum, Romanism, and Rebellion*, 37–40, 146–48; S. L. M. Barlow to Manton Marble, August 16, 1886, Marble MSS, LC; *Puck*, April 7, 1880, p. 70.

24. *IW&AIL*, August 7, 1880; *Louisville Commercial*, August 4, 1880; *NYH*, September 11, 1880; *Nation*, August 19, September 9, October 14, 1880. *Chattanooga Daily Times*, October 16, 1880.

25. House, "Democratic State Central Committee of Indiana," 191–92, 204–5.

26. *NYT*, October 7, 1888; *NYH*, October 9, 19, 1886, October 18, 1888; *National Cyclopedia of American Biography*, 7:144, 40:16; *Troy Daily Press*, October 30, 1890; *Memorial Addresses on . . . David Wilber*, 3–4, 8; Walter H. Bunn to Daniel Lamont, October 21, 1886, Cleveland MSS, LC.

27. *National Cyclopedia of American Biography*, 2:206–7.

28. "Rhode Island," *HW*, April 21, 1888, p. 278; *StLP-D*, March 10, 1887.

29. John A. McMahon to Samuel J. Randall, September 12, 1880, RanMSS; *CinEnq*, July 22, 30, August 3, 7, September 17, 1880.

30. *Minneapolis Tribune*, April 2, 1884; *CR*, 47th Cong., 2d sess., 3521–22 (March 1, 1883).

31. J. J. Faran to William Allen, October 27, 1876, Allen MSS, LC; Daniel Manning to Manton Marble, March 9, 1886, Marble MSS, LC; *PhilRec*, June 15, July 12, 1886; Rathegeber, "Democratic Party in Pennsylvania," 133.

32. *PhilRec*, August 8, 11, 14, 1886; Rathegeber, "Democratic Party in Pennsylvania," 144.

33. Peterson, "People's Party of Kansas," 240–42; *JSP*, May 25, June 1, July 12, 1884, June 14, 1885.

34. George, "Money in Elections," 206–9.

Chapter Ten

1. *NYH*, January 25, 1883; *Newark Daily Advertiser*, September 14, October 24, 26, 1883; *PhilRec*, November 28, 1887; Sackett, *Modern Battles of Trenton*, 276–83.

2. N. M. Hubbard, "Bribery by Railway Passes," *NAR* 138 (January 1884): 89–99; *Debates and Proceedings*, 1:500 (November 23, 1878); *StPP-P*, February 5, 1884.

3. "Testimony Taken by the U.S. Pacific Railway Commission," 50th Cong., 1st sess., Senate Exec. Doc. 51, pp. 1336–39; W. H. Goucher to Stephen Mallory White, January 12, 1888, White MSS, SU; *StLP-D*, November 1, 3, 1886.

4. Bromberg, "Pure Democracy," 276–93; Ferguson, "Agrarianism in Mississippi," 281–83; *Tallahassee Floridian*, May 13, 1893; Onslow Stearns to William E. Chandler, May 6, 1870, ChanMSS (NHHS); Stephen Mallory White to J. D. Bicknell, January 1, 1887, and White to Creed Haymond, March 18, 1887, White MSS, SU.

5. *Omaha Daily Bee*, August 31, September 4, 7, 27, 1880; "Testimony Taken by the U.S. Pacific Railway Commission," 1335–39; Daniels, *Tar-Heel Editor*, 393–94.

6. Ostler, *Prairie Populism*, 75, 87.

7. John Alexander Williams, *Captains of Industry*, 3–5, 125–40.

8. Francis H. Weeks to James J. Hill, October 2, 1888, Daniel Lamont to Hill, August 15, September 5, October 9, 1888, Ignatius Donnelly to Hill, February 27, 1885, E. T. Nichols to Hill, April 18, 1892, Hill to W. A. Stephens, October 19, 1888, John T. Morgan to Hill, June 1, 1888, and H. B. Strait to Hill, October 10, 1888, Hill MSS, James J. Hill Library, St. Paul, Minn.

9. Merrill, *Bourbon Democracy*, 174–78; W. Thomas White, "Gilded Age Businessman," 439–56; R. F. Pettigrew to James J. Hill, January 13, October 5, 1893, January 9, 1895, W. C. Plummer to Hill, April 19, 1896, Daniel Lamont to Hill, September 5, 1888, September 19, 1896, Hill to Cushman K. Davis, March 11, 1897, Lamont to Hill, September 5, October 9, 1888, and Don M. Dickinson to Hill, August 6, 1892, Hill MSS, James J. Hill Library, St. Paul, Minn.

10. *Omaha Daily Bee*, September 9, 1880, June 29, 1881; Parsons, *Populist Context*, 6; "Testimony Taken by the U.S. Pacific Railway Commission," 1338–39, 1342–43, 1504, 1524–25.

11. George W. Julian, "Railway Influence in the Land Office," *NAR* 136 (March 1883): 237–56; *StLP-D*, October 4, 7, 1882, January 3, 4, February 24, March 9, 1887; *Topeka Daily Capital*, November 27, 1886; Ferguson, "Agrarianism in Mississippi," 279–84; Burton, "Wisconsin's First Railroad Commission," 197–98; Daniels, *Tar-Heel Editor*, 394–97.

12. Gerrit L. Lansing, "The Railway and the State," *NAR* 138 (May 1884): 463–65; *Omaha Republican*, September 17, 1888; Ferguson, "Agrarianism in Mississippi," 283–84; *Jackson Clarion-Ledger*, February 16, 23, 1888; *Chattanooga Daily Times*, September 20, 1884.

13. Lansing, "Railway and the State," 465–68; *StPP-P*, January 28, 1884.

14. Ferguson, "Agrarianism in Mississippi," 290; Going, *Bourbon Democracy in Alabama*, 133–34; *StLP-D*, March 7, 1887; John T. Doyle to Stephen M. White, December 29, 1892, White MSS, SU.

15. Gilbert Pierce to James J. Hill, December 6, 1889, Alexander McKenzie to Hill, January 7, 1887, R. F. Pettigrew to Hill, November 10, 1891, August 6, 1892, December 15, 1894, January 5, April 8, 1895, and J. Tod & Company to Hill, July 14, 1892, Hill MSS, James J. Hill Library, St. Paul, Minn.; W. Thomas White, "War of the Railroad Kings," 37–54; W. Thomas White, "Gilded Age Businessman," 441–42.

16. Frank B. Kellogg to Cushman Davis, February 24, 28, March 1, 1896, Davis MSS, WVC; H. E. Hoard to Henry A. Castle, February 8, 1896, and William P. Dunnington to Castle, March 21, 1896, Castle MSS, MHS.

17. Samuel Woods to Isabella Woods, March 5, 1872, Ambler MSS, WVC.

18. John Alexander Williams, *Captains of Industry*, 11.

19. *Wheeling Daily Intelligencer*, April 8, 1884, April 9, 1886; John Alexander Williams, *Captains of Industry*, 11–14.

20. Festus Summers, *William L. Wilson*, 43–44; *Wheeling Daily Intelligencer*, April 19, August 2, 1884; *ChiTr*, September 29, 1884; John Alexander Williams, *Captains of Industry*, 56–65.

21. *StPP-P*, September 16, 1890; *St. Paul Daily Globe*, October 9, 1890.

22. Ridge, *Ignatius Donnelly*, 186; *StPP-P*, November 5, 14, 1878; *St. Paul Anti-Monopolist*, November 14, 1878.

23. *StPP-P*, February 5, 11, 17, 1884; Christianson, *Minnesota*, 125.

24. Ridge, *Ignatius Donnelly*, 248–52; Merrill, *Bourbon Democracy*, 191–93.

25. Deverell, *Railroad Crossing*, 129–31; Issel and Cherny, *San Francisco*, 122. San Francisco was where the Southern Pacific had its offices.

26. California Constitutional Convention *Debates*, 1:501 (November 23, 1878).

27. M. Thomas to Thomas V. Cator, November 26, 1892, Cator MSS, SU; John T. Doyle to Manton Marble, May 15, 1876, Marble MSS, LC; Shumsky, *Evolution of Political Protest*, 209–12; R. Hal Williams, *Democratic Party and California Politics*, 28–50.

28. Ostler, *Prairie Populism*, 75–76; Parsons, *Populist Context*, 5–6, 14–15; *St. Joseph Daily Gazette*, August 18, 1886; *ChTi*, October 29, 1886; *StLP-D*, November 27, 1886.

29. Christianson, *Minnesota*, 127, 166–67; *St. Paul Dispatch*, July 21, 1886; *Winona Daily Republican*, August 11, 25, 1886; Ely, "Railroad Question Revisited," 124–31. Minnesota quickly passed a new rate law that fit the constitutional requirements.

30. Harry P. Robinson, "State Regulation of Railways," *NAR* 166 (April 1898): 398–407.

31. Going, *Bourbon Democracy in Alabama*, 136–38; Ferguson, "Agrarianism in Mississippi," 294–99; Barr, *Reconstruction to Reform*, 96, 105; Brockman, "Railroads, Radicals, and Democrats," 232–33, 287–300.

32. Roger L. Hart, *Redeemers, Bourbons, and Populists*, 75–77; R. Hal Williams, *Democratic Party and California Politics*, 28–50, 206–32.

33. *Newark Daily Advertiser*, April 1, 2, 3, 4, 18, 1884; Hogarty, *Leon Abbett's New Jersey*, 197–220, 224–27, 257–62.

34. On Kansas, see Press, "Kansas Conflict," 321–22; on Colorado, see *Omaha Daily Bee*, September 1, 1888.

Chapter Eleven

1. *JSP*, January 10, 1886. Immense, excellent work has been done on the third-party challenges of the 1870s and 1880s. Among the most suggestive are Kleppner, *Third Electoral System*, 257–97; Fink, *Workingmen's Democracy*; Goodwyn, *Democratic Promise*; McMath, *Populist Vanguard*; Ridge, *Ignatius Donnelly*; Unger, *Greenback Era*; and Cresswell, *Multi-Party Politics*.

2. Silbey, *American Political Nation*, 225–29; Formisano, "'Party Period' Revisited"; Oestreicher, "Socialism and the Knights of Labor."

3. Richard Grant White, "Class Distinctions in the United States," *NAR* 137 (September 1883): 231–46; Stephen B. Elkins, "The Labor Crisis," *NAR* 142 (June 1886): 601.

4. Fine, *Laissez Faire and the General-Welfare State*, 80–85, 98–102; *KoL*, August 21, 1886; *NYStan*, December 22, 1888.

5. Chadbourne, ed., *State of New York*, 2:126, 229; Hurd, comp., *History of Fairfield County*, 143–44, 150–51; Ruoff, comp., *Schuylkill County*, 250, 294, 302; *ConMon*, September 18, 22, 1890; *NYEP*, October 30, 1890; Willey, ed., *State Builders*, 223–24.

6. *JSP*, June 15, July 6, 1884, April 26, 1885; *NYStan*, December 8, 22, 1888.

7. See, for example, the Iowa Democratic platform in McPherson, *Hand-Book of Politics for 1878*, 162.

8. "Class Politics," *HW*, November 13, 1886, p. 726; Jensen, *Winning of the Midwest*, 17–18; Elkins, "Labor Crisis," 610–16; Reitano, *Tariff Question*, 74, 81, 85, 99.

9. Siracusa, *Mechanical People*, 214; see also McPherson, *Hand-Book of Politics for 1878*, 158, 165, and Sproat, *Best Men*, 218–21, 227–29.

10. See, for example, *St. Paul Pioneer*, October 25, 31, 1873, and Jensen, *Winning of the Midwest*, 19–20.

11. McCall, *Thomas Brackett Reed*, 158–59.

12. McPherson, *Hand-Book of Politics for 1878*, 160, 162, 165; McPherson, *Hand-Book of Politics for 1882*, 165, 166; *ClPD*, October 21, 1884; *Hocking Sentinel*, August 23, 30, September 13, October 4, 1883; *Circleville Democrat & Watchman*, September 14, 1883.

13. Klein, *Jay Gould*, 162–66, 337–39, 302–94; Malin, "Democratic Party and Atchison," 159–64; Edward Morrell to Samuel J. Randall, January 25, 1877, RanMSS; *JSP*, February 6, 1887; *KoL*, October 2, 1886.

14. *AmN*, June 21, 1894.

15. Segraves, "Arkansas Politics," pp. 179–80; *LRArkG*, June 6, July 4, 20, 29, August 8, 1888. The same tactic applied to ethnic groups, too, of course. See Luebke, *Immigrants and Politics*, 134–36.

16. *IW&AIL*, November 24, 1883.

17. Reitano, *Tariff Question*, 75–82.

18. Nugent, *Money and American Society*, 264–65.

19. John L. Swift to Michener, July 17, 1888, Harrison MSS, LC; *NYS*, November 4, 28, 1888; Gyory, *Closing the Gate*, 76–79, 136–68.

20. Shumsky, *Evolution of Political Protest*, 175–78; *NYS*, September 27, 1888; *SFAltaC*, November 2, 3, 4, 1888.

21. McFarlane, "Nativism or Not?" 238–41; Summers, *Rum, Romanism, and Rebellion*, 90.

22. McNall, *Road to Rebellion*, 278; Kleppner, *Third Electoral System*, 144–80; Jensen, *Winning of the Midwest* 24–25; Luebke, *Immigrants and Politics*, 130–31; McFarland and Oshio, "Civil War Military Service," 169–74.

23. Argersinger, "New Perspectives on Election Fraud," 677. On business support for railroad regulation, see George H. Miller, *Railroads and the Granger Laws*, 99–102, 125–29, and Treleven, "Railroads, Elevators, and Grain Dealers," 205–22. On labor and radical support for the Australian ballot, see *NYStan*, November 12, 1887, April 21, December 15, 1888, February 5, March 12, 26, 1890.

24. *LRArkG*, July 4, 1888.

25. Baum, *Civil War Party System*, 151–53; Stewart, *Wendell Phillips*, 300–304; *SprRep*, September 29, 30, October 22, 24, 29, 31, 1870; Montgomery, *Beyond Equality*, 368–69; *Boston Evening Transcript*, November 7, 1870.

26. Montgomery, *Beyond Equality*, 371–73; Taussig, *Tariff History*, 182–89; Jewell, *Among Our Sailors*, 39–69, 155, 267–68.

27. *KoL*, September 18, 1886; *JSP*, May 25, 1884, August 30, 1885; Asher, "Failure and Fulfillment," 201–4; Cosmas, "Democracy in Search of Issues," 107; for the agrarian equivalent, see Ostler, *Prairie Populism*, 55–68.

28. For an example of such hypocrisy on a national scale, see *JSP*, June 15, 1884; on the retreat from the "Granger laws," see George H. Miller, *Railroads and the Granger Laws*, 116, 137–39, 160, and Cosmas, "Democracy in Search of Issues," 108.

29. Cosmas, "Democracy in Search of Issues," 94–96; *NYTr*, April 5, 20, 1883; *JSP*, February 6, 1887; Ostler, *Prairie Populism*, 42–48.

30. *Detroit Labor Leaf*, October 20, 1886; *KoL*, October 16, 1886, April 25, 1887; *JSP*, May 11, 25, June 1, 1884, April 12, 26, June 7, October 11, 1885, January 17, 1886; *New York Standard*, April 16, 1887; "The Menace of Legislation," *NAR* 165 (August 1897): 243–46.

31. Newman, *Labor Legislation of New Jersey*, 26, 52–53, 72–73; Commons, *History of Labor*, 2:508; Staley, *Illinois State Federation of Labor*, 152, 154–55, 158, 160–61, 165.

32. *JSP*, May 11, 1884, August 7, 1887; *KoL*, August 14, 1886; Henry George, "Labor in Pennsylvania," *NAR* 156 (September 1886): 269–71; Newman, *Labor Legislation of New Jersey*, 79–81; MacDonald, "Early History of Labor Statistics," 267–78; Clague, *Bureau of Labor Statistics*, 4–9.

33. Leon Fink, "The Uses of Political Power: Toward a Theory of the Labor Movement in the Era of the Knights of Labor," in Frisch and Walkowitz, eds., *Working-Class America*, 106–7, 116–17; *AmN*, January 19, 1893; *JSP*, November 21, 1886, February 13, 1887; *NYStan*, March 31, July 14, 1888; Scheirov, "Political Cultures," 387–91.

34. Duis, *Saloon*, 143–57; James Edward Wright, *Politics of Populism*, 26–28; Brundage, "Producing Classes," 40–48.

35. *KoL*, April 23, 1887; *Chicago Labor Enquirer*, May 12, 1887, July 7, 1888; *JSP*, January 6, 1884, January 17, 1886, August 7, 21, 1887.

36. *JSP*, October 4, 1885, June 27, 1886.

Chapter Twelve

1. *JSP*, December 14, 1884.

2. James Clarkson to James G. Blaine, September 2, 1884, Blaine MSS, LC; Benjamin F. Butler to William E. Chandler, September 24, 1884, N. A. Plympton to Butler [October 9, 1884], October 10, 1884, and W. A. Fowler to Butler, October 7, 8, 1884, Butler MSS, LC.

3. *NYT*, August 22, 1872; Chauncey F. Black to Samuel J. Randall, July 1875, RanMSS; *InSen*, August 17, 22, 1872; *Kansas State Record*, November 6, 1872.

4. On Union Labor quarrels, see J. R. Sovereign to Luman H. Weller, October 15, 1889, L. H. Griffith to Weller, October 20, 1889, W. T. Wright to Weller, June 24, 1889, and Anna D. Weaver to Weller, January 15, 1888, Weller MSS. Quotations from Edward A. Miller, *Gullah Statesman*, 185–86; see also Uya, *From Slavery to Public Service*, 116–18, 121–23, 127–29. On Republicans, see Holt, *Black over White*, 218–23, and *PiPo*, April 30, 1892.

5. Kleppner, *Third Electoral System*, 243–50; *JSP*, October 14, 1885; Gail Hamilton, "Prohibition in Politics," *NAR* 140 (June 1885): 510–12.

6. Herschel V. Johnson to Alexander Stephens, November 14, 1872, Stephens MSS; *CinGaz*, September 28, 1872; *ChiTi*, October 6, 1872.

7. Boyd, "Neutrality and Peace," 49–52, 175–83; *St. Paul Anti-Monopolist*, June 27, 1878; *Worcester Daily Spy*, October 12, 1878; Blanton Duncan to Rutherford B. Hayes, January 7, August 13, 1877, Hayes MSS, HML; *AmN*, May 24, 1894.

8. *InSen*, August 8, 1872; *LC-J*, August 27, 28, 29, September 1, 2, 3, 4, 1872.

9. Nevins and Thomas, eds., *Diary of George Templeton Strong*, 4:433–35; *NYTr* September 3, 4, 5, 1872.

10. *NYTr*, September 3, 1872.

11. *InSen*, August 9, 12, 17, 20, 22, 24, 27, September 30, October 7, 21, 1872; *LC-J*, August 28, 1872; *NYTr*, September 5, 1872; Thomas B. Carroll to Edwin D. Morgan, October 9, 1872, and Morgan to Carroll, September 21, 1872, Morgan MSS, NYSL; James H. Scott to Horatio Seymour, September 30, 1872, Seymour MSS, NYSL; Bigelow, *Letters and Memorials of Samuel J. Tilden*, vol. 1, August 20, 1872; Herschel V. Johnson to Alexander Stephens, November 14, 1872, Stephens MSS; Isaac McConihe to Francis Kernan, September 6, 1872, and J. H. Prentiss to Kernan, August 16, 1872, Kernan Family MSS, Cornell University, Ithaca.

12. Brann, *Brann the Iconoclast*, 8:82.

13. Hamilton, "Prohibition in Politics," 513–20; James S. Ashley, "The Impending Political Advance," *Arena* 14 (November 1895): 430; Summers, *Rum, Romanism, and Rebellion*, 230–37.

14. Richardson, *William E. Chandler*, 85–89; *ManU*, February 24, 1870; McKinney, "Politics of Protest," 149–70; E. H. Rollins to William E. Chandler, January 19, 20, 30, February 6, 15, 1870, ChanMSS (NHHS).

15. E. H. Rollins to William E. Chandler, January 29, 30, February 15, 1870, ChanMSS

(NHHS); *ConMon*, February 24, 1870; *Concord Labor Reform Dispatch*, February 11, 1870; E. H. Rollins to Henry W. Blair, February 26, 1870, and Charles H. Roberts to Blair, February 26, 1870, Blair MSS, New Hampshire Historical Society, Concord; McKinney, "Politics of Protest," 156.

16. *Chicago Labor Enquirer*, April 9, May 14, June 11, 1887; *NYStan*, November 19, 1887; *JSP*, June 26, 1887.

17. E. O. Davis to Luman H. Weller, June 16, 1888, Weller MSS, SHSW; *DMS*, August 28, 1884, November 7, 1886; Goodwyn, *Democratic Promise*, 440–42, 459–63, 480–87. Long outdated, the general's only biography is Haynes, *James Baird Weaver*.

18. Charles E. Russell, *Bare Hands and Stone Walls*, 71–72; Annie L. Diggs, "The Farmers' Alliance and Some of Its Leaders," *Arena* 5 (April 1892): 601–3; Haynes, *James Baird Weaver*, 289; *StPP-P*, October 5, 1880.

19. *AmN*, June 21, July 5, 1894.

20. *IW&AIL*, June 26, 1880; *JSP*, June 26, August 7, 1887; *KoL*, August 14, 1886.

21. — to Carrington Phelps, September 15, 1890, Tawney MSS, MHS.

22. *ChiTi*, September 26, 27, October 2, 1880; *NYT*, October 6, 1880; *LC-J*, October 5, 1880; *StPP-P*, October 5, 1880; *IW&AIL*, August 7, October 23, 1880.

23. For a similar example in Michigan in 1888, see *NYStan*, September 8, 1888.

24. *JSP*, November 21, 1886.

25. Summers, *Rum, Romanism, and Rebellion*, 119–22, 150–52, 275–78, 288.

26. *JSP*, November 9, 1884, August 30, October 11, 18, 1885; Summers, *Rum, Romanism, and Rebellion*, 237–39.

27. *NYStan*, November 17, 1888.

28. *JSP*, November 29, 1885; Henry S. Wilcox to Luman H. Weller, January 4, 1888, Weller MSS, SHSW; Kousser, "Towards 'Total Political History,'" 533–34, 539.

29. *NYStan*, April 7, 14, 28, November 10, 1888.

30. *JSP*, June 19, 26, August 21, 1887; *Chicago Labor Enquirer*, April 23, May 14, June 11, 1887, August 18, 1888; *KoL*, April 23, May 14, 1887; *NYStan*, September 15, 1888.

31. Ostler, *Prairie Populism*, 43, 61.

32. Haynes, *James Baird Weaver*, 287; *ChiTi*, October 13, 1886; *StLG-D*, September 23, 1888. For a similar cooperation, see Doolen, "Pastor in Politics," 112–22.

33. *DMSR*, October 28, 30, November 8, 1888, September 11, 1890; *Omaha Daily Bee*, November 12, 1888.

Chapter Thirteen

1. Foner, *History of the Labor Movement*, 2:53–70; *KoL*, September 18, 1886.

2. *JSP*, November 21, 1886.

3. Hirshson, *Farewell to the Bloody Shirt*, 143–52; Ayers, *Promise of the New South*, 37–40, 46–48, 216–21.

4. D. H. Goodell to William E. Chandler, August 10, 1886, ChanMSS (NHHS).

5. Kerr, *Organized for Prohibition*, 44–65; Hamm, *Shaping the 18th Amendment*, 19–55; A. P. Davis to William E. Chandler, January 14, April 14, 1886, ChanMSS (NHHS); Benjamin Harrison to J. J. Todd, August 24, 1886, Harrison MSS, LC.

6. Walters, *Joseph Benson Foraker*, 39; Joseph B. Foraker to Thomas McDougall, February 26, 1886, Foraker MSS; *NYH*, October 5, 6, 9, 11, 17, 1886; *Newark Evening News*, October 14, November 3, 1886; *Trenton State Gazette*, October 15, 1886. For Indiana, see *ChiTr*, September 2, 1886, and *InSen*, October 11, 12, 13, 1886.

7. Kolesar, "Limits of Partisanship," 104–5; Campbell, "Prohibition and Democracy," 87–116; Luebke, *Immigrants and Politics*, 138–39.

8. *InSen*, October 12, 1886.

9. *Trenton State Gazette*, October 16, 1886; *Carson City Morning Appeal*, October 23, 29, 30, 1886; *San Francisco Examiner*, October 26, 28, 29, 1886; *Salem Daily Statesman*, May 29, 1886; *Portland Daily Oregonian*, May 14, 15, 28, 29, 1886.

10. *Detroit Labor Leaf*, March 3, October 20, November 3, 1886; *Trenton State Gazette*, September 29, October 1, 15, 1886; *PhilRec*, September 28, October 4, 1886; *NYH*, October 5, 6, 17, 1886.

11. *Cincinnati Commercial Gazette*, September 10, 25, October 1, 3, 1886; *Springfield Globe-Republic*, October 27, 30, November 1, 1886; *Circleville Democratic Herald*, October 27, 1886; 30, 1886; *CinEnq*, September 28, October 29, 1886.

12. Broehl, *Molly Maguires*; Berthoff, "Social Order of Anthracite Region," 261–91; Ruoff, comp., *Schuylkill County*, 248–50; *CR*, 50th Cong., 1st sess., p. 3102 (April 18, 1888).

13. *PiPo*, June 28, 1886; *Norwalk Daily Reflector*, October 26, 27, 29, 30, November 1, 3, 1886; *Sandusky Weekly Register*, September 29, 1886; *Springfield Globe-Republic*, October 25, 1886.

14. *StLP-D*, October 21, 1884.

15. *ChiTi*, October 7, 1886; Merrill, *Bourbon Democracy in the Middle West*, 190; *ChiTr*, November 5, 1886; *LC-J*, November 8, 1886; *Pittsburgh Post*, May 10, 1886.

16. *ChiTr*, November 11, 1886; *ChiTi*, October 7, November 13, 188; *StLG-D*, October 3, November 4, 1886.

17. Barnes, *John G. Carlisle*, 128–30; *Louisville Commercial*, November 4, 1886; *LC-J*, November 5, 1886; *StLP-D*, November 9, 1886.

18. *Toledo Blade*, October 4, 6, 7, 11, 1886; *Biographical Cyclopedia and Portrait Gallery*, 2:349–50; *Sandusky Weekly Register*, October 13, 1886; J. J. Dull to Samuel J. Randall, November 4, 1886, RanMSS.

19. *Chicago Daily News*, October 27, 1886; *ChTr*, November 14, 1886; *StLG-D*, November 5, 1886; *KoL*, December 1, 1886.

20. *Sandusky Weekly Register*, November 3, 10, 1886; *StLP-D*, November 2, 3, 1886; *Springfield Globe-Republic*, November 3, 4, 6, 10, 1886.

21. *StLP-D*, November 4, 9, 1886; *Louisville Commercial*, November 4, 1886; *LC-J*, November 5, 6, 1886; "MacFarland," *PhilRec*, January 21, 29, 1888; Wilson Diary, January 21, 1888, WVC.

22. *JSP*, November 14, 21, 28, 1886; *KoL*, November 13, 1886; "The Labor Vote," *HW*, November 20, 1886, p. 742.

23. *Canton Repository*, September 27, October 1, 12, 1886; *JSP*, November 7, 14, 21, 1886, February 6, 1887.

24. *ChiTr*, November 5, 6, 1886; *InN*, November 4, 1886.

25. Foner, *History of Labor Movement*, 2: 145–46; Fink, *Workingmen's Democracy*, 26–29; S. L. Douglass to Luman H. Weller, December 30, 1886, Weller MSS, SHSW.

26. Fink, *Workingmen's Democracy*, 30–35.

27. E. S. Wicklin to Luman H. Weller, March 29, 1887, Weller MSS, SHSW.

28. *Detroit Labor Leaf*, November 3, 1886; *Chicago Labor Enquirer*, November 5, 1887; *JSP*, November 28, 1886; *Dubuque Herald*, March 16, 17, 25, April 1, 3, 4, 1888.

29. As note Henry S. Wilcox to Luman H. Weller, January 4, 1888 [poss. 1889], Weller MSS, SHSW.

30. *JSP*, January 30, February 6, 13, June 5, 1887; Baney, *Yankees and the City*, 114–18; Lazerow, "'Workingman's Hour,'" 218–19; Haferbecker, *Wisconsin Labor Laws*, 18–19.

31. For a thorough exposure, see *NYStan*, April 21, November 3, 1888.

32. Barker, *Henry George*, 455–81; *JSP*, October 17, 24, 31, November 7, 21, 1886; Hammack, *Power and Society*, 174–81.

33. Bass, "*I Am A Democrat*," 51–71; *JSP*, October 18, 1885, January 17, 1886, February 6, June 12, 19, 1887; *NYStan*, April 2, 1887; Gordon, "Labor Boycott," 288–89; Stimson, "Democracy and the Laboring Man," 605–19.

34. Foner, *History of Labor Movement*, 2:147–53; *NYStan*, November 3, 1888; *Chicago Labor Enquirer*, September 10, 1887.

35. David B. Hill to Terence V. Powderly, June 18, 1889, and Hill to J. T. McKechne, June 18, 1889, Hill MSS, NYSL; Bass, "*I Am a Democrat*," 51–71, 176; *Nation*, July 26, 1888.

36. *JSP*, January 30, February 6, 1887.

37. Staley, *Illinois State Federation of Labor*, 73–75; *KoL*, April 16, 23, 1887; *Chicago Labor Enquirer*, March 16, 23, 30, April 6, 1887, January 14, March 31, 1888; *JSP*, March 27, May 1, 1887; *ChiTi*, October 14, 1888, *ChiTr*, September 2, October 26, 1888.

38. *NYStan*, March 17, April 14, May 15, 28, September 15, 1888; E. S. Wicklin to Luman H. Weller, April 5, 1888, and A. J. Streeter to Weller, May 26, 1888, Weller MSS, SHSW.

39. *NYStan*, April 7, July 7, September 22, 1888; Barker, *Henry George*, 514–16; *StLP-D*, September 30, 1888; S. F. Norton to Luman H. Weller, May 1, 1888, and E. O. Davis to Weller, June 16, 1888, Weller MSS, SHSW.

40. *SFAltaC*, July 3, 16, 1888; *StLG-D*, August 20, 21, 1888; *PiPo*, August 17, 18, 1888; Kehl, *Boss Rule*, 101–2.

41. Staley, *Illinois State Federation of Labor*, 81; *NYStan*, November 10, 17, 1888.

42. Ostler, "Why the Populist Party Was Strong," 461–67; *Railway Age*, February 18, 1887.

Chapter Fourteen

1. McFarland, *Mugwumps, Morals, and Politics*, 13–15, 22–26, 50–54.

2. Sproat, *Best Men*, 145–66, 172–84, 205–18; Preble Tucker, "The Good-Government Clubs," *NAR* 159 (September 1894): 384.

3. Argersinger, "New Perspectives on Election Fraud," 675–77; Silbey, *American Political Nation*, 192–95, 224–32.

4. Mayo, "Republicanism, Antipartyism," 3–20; Paula Baker, *Moral Frameworks of Public Life*; Kruman, "Second Party System," 509–37; Formisano, "'Party Period' Revisited," 97–100; *Concord Labor Reform Dispatch*, February 25, 1870.

5. "F. B. W.," *ChiTi*, October 14, 1884; *Dubuque Herald*, October 31, 1884; *Concord Labor Reform Dispatch*, February 11, 1870; Van Deusen, *Horace Greeley*, 412.

6. Summers, *Era of Good Stealings*, 118–21, 134–36; Altschuler and Blumin, *Rude Republic*, 184–97; Keller, *Affairs of State*, 319–20; Luce, *Legislative Problems*, 561–69.

7. *DMSR*, August 2, September 11, October 28, 1884; *Dubuque Herald*, September 20, 1884; Chadbourne, ed., *State of New York*, 2:210, 216, 222; Ruoff, comp., *Schuylkill County*, 239; *St. Paul Pioneer*, October 11, 29, 1873.

8. McCormick, *Party Period and Public Policy*, 231–58; Cecil Logsdale, "The College Man in Politics," *Arena* 22 (December 1899): 753; George E. Waring, "Government by Party," *NAR* 163 (November 1896): 585–94.

9. Dorman B. Eaton, "Parties and Independents," *NAR* 144 (June 1887): 551–52; Preble Tucker, "The Good-Government Clubs," *NAR* 159 (September 1894): 384; Stephen M. Merrill, "Evolution of Political Parties," *NAR* 159 (November 1894): 574; Rossiter Johnson, "A Perilous Balance," *NAR* 146 (April 1888): 426.

10. Frank Vrooman, "Spoils and the Civil Service," *Arena* 37 (February 1907): 155.

11. Andrew D. White, "Do the Spoils Belong to the Victor?" *NAR* 134 (February 1882): 112–24; Villard, *Fighting Years*, 122; Blodgett, *Gentle Reformers*, 30–40; Wayne MacVeagh to "my dear sir," February 20, 1884, MacVeagh MSS, Historical Society of Pennsylvania, Philadelphia.

12. Hoogenboom, *Outlawing the Spoils*, 1–12; Summers, *Era of Good Stealings*, 89–95; E. L. Godkin, "The Civil Service Reform Controversy," *NAR* 134 (April 1882): 379–94.

13. Leonard White, *Republican Era*, 301–2.

14. Hoogenboom, *Outlawing the Spoils*, 247–52; Skowronek, *Building a New American State*, 71–72; Dorman B. Eaton, "Two Years of Civil Service Reform," *NAR* 141 (July 1885): 19–23; Charles Lyman, "Ten Years of Civil Service Reform," *NAR* 157 (1893): 574.

15. Hoogenboom, *Outlawing the Spoils*, 260; *Civil Service Record* 9 (February 1892): 66.

16. Keller, *Affairs of State*, 313; Leonard White, *Republican Era*, 317–22; Joseph French Johnson, "Is Civil Service Reform in Peril?" *NAR* 169 (November 1899): 678–93; H. T. Newcomb, "The Crisis of Civil Service Reform," *NAR* 166 (February 1898): 196–203.

17. "Black-Mailing Government Clerks," *HW*, October 9, 1891, pp. 742–43; "Blackmailing," *HW*, October 17, 1891, p. 790.

18. Leonard White, *Republican Era*, 311–12; Frank Vrooman, "The Present Status of our Civil Service," *Arena* 37 (March 1907): 277; Charles Lyman, "Ten Years of Civil Service Reform," *NAR* 157 (1893): 574–79; Skowronek, *Building a New American State*, 76–77.

19. Leonard White, *Republican Era*, 313–14; Theodore Roosevelt, "Six Years of Civil Service Reform," *Scribner's Magazine*, 18 (1895): 239; Skowronek, *Building a New American State*, 72–73; Vrooman, "Present Status," 278–81.

20. On the mixed success of propertied reformers to cut immigrants, paupers, nonresidents, and felons out of the vote, see Alexander Keyssar's thorough account in *Right to Vote*, 119–72. On laws against vote-buying, see *Meriden Daily Republican*, January 9, 1884; *NYH*, February 7, 1883; *Nation*, January 24, 1889, February 19, 1891; and *Pennsylvania Laws*, 1881, Act No. 77 (June 8, 1881).

21. "Public Accounting for Election Expenses," *HW*, June 21, 1890, p. 478; Charles Claflin Allen, "Electoral Reform Legislation," *Arena* 3 (December 1890): 92–96; *Nation*, January 24, June 13, 1889.

22. *Nation*, January 24, June 13, 1889; Joseph B. Bishop, "Insufficient Restriction of Cam-

paign Expenditures," *Forum* 15 (April 1893): 148; Ostrogorski, *Democracy and Organization*, 2:347–48; Overacker, *Money in Elections*, 292–94.

23. DeLancey Nicholl, "An Unpunished Constitutional Crime," *NAR* (January 1888): 28–30; *Nation*, January 24, 1889; *CinEnq*, October 14, 1879; Boomhower, "'To Secure Honest Elections,'" 326; Petersen, "Prelude to Progressivism," 132.

24. *LC-J*, February 4, 1879; *InN*, March 28, 1884; *NYT*, October 5, 1868, March 12, 1884; Harris, *Registration of Voters*, 65–79, 85; *Baltimore Sun*, September 29, 1892; for a comparative listing of registration requirements, see J. Chester Lyman, "Our Inequalities of Suffrage," *NAR* 144 (March 1887): 306.

25. Allen Thorndike Rice, "Recent Reforms in Balloting," *NAR* 143 (December 1886): 629; *NYT*, October 5, 1868; *Baltimore American*, February 27, 1890.

26. Keyssar, *Right to Vote*, 153–58; *LC-J*, February 9, 1879; Avey, *Demobilization of American Voters*, 50–51.

27. Bromberg, "Pure Democracy," 179–80; *Baltimore American*, March 11, November 6, 1890.

28. Wynes, *Race Relations in Virginia*, 40–42.

29. John E. Milholland, "The Danger Point in American Politics," *NAR* 164 (January 1897): 97–105.

30. *State v. Adams*, 65 Indiana 393 (1879); *State v. McKinnon*, 8 Oregon 493 (1880); *People v. Kilduff*, 15 Illinois (5 Pec) 492 (1854); *Kellogg v. Hickman*, 12 Colorado 256 (1888); Fredman, *Australian Ballot*, 5–19; *Independent*, January 15, 1880, pp. 2–3.

31. Allen Thorndike Rice, "The Next National Reform," *NAR* 148 (January 1889): 83–84; *Troy Daily Press*, October 25, 1890. For a reformer's shrewd dissent, see Allen, "Electoral Reform Legislation," 92.

32. Fredman, *Australian Ballot*, 33–38; *CR*, 50th Cong., 1st sess., p. 5217 (June 13, 1888); *NYEP*, September 17, 1892; Terence V. Powderly to W. L. Stark, April 7, 1892, Powderly MSS, Catholic University, Washington.

33. McFarland, *Mugwumps, Morals, and Politics*, 65; *Nation*, October 22, 1891; Boomhower, "'To Secure Honest Elections,'" 324–36; Edward M. Shepard to David B. Hill, March 22, 1890, Shepard MSS, Columbia University, New York; David B. Hill to Frank Jones, July 17, 1889, Hill MSS (Bixby Collection), NYSL.

34. Reynolds and McCormick, "Outlawing 'Treachery,'" 835–58; W. D. Hoard to John Coit Spooner, August 25, 1890, Spooner MSS, LC.

35. *St. Paul Daily Globe*, November 4, 1890; *Nation*, January 15, 1891; Joseph B. Bishop, "The Secret Ballot in Thirty-Three States," *Forum*, January 1892, pp. 589–91; *PhilRec*, November 5, 1892.

36. W. A. Holland to Breckinridge, January 9, 1893, Breckinridge Family MSS, LC.

37. George F. Page to William E. Chandler, January 26, 1895, ChanMSS (NHHS).

38. Hiram C. Clarke to Timothy S. Williams, November 7, 1890, Williams MSS, New York Public Library, New York; Reynolds, "'Silent Dollar,'" 203; "Bluenose," in *Nation*, January 10, 1889; *AmN*, June 28, 1894; *StPGW*, November 18, 1892; on taking pay to absent oneself, see "Timely Hints," *HW*, January 25, 1890, p. 62.

39. *NYEP*, October 4, 1890, September 16, 17, 1892; *Chicago Inter Ocean*, October 26, 1892; *Nation*, April 30, 1891; *Washington Critic*, March 4, 1890; *Troy Daily Press*, October 23,

24, 1890; *StLG-D*, October 4, 1892; *Baltimore Sun*, September 29, 1892; *Laconia Democrat*, November 4, 1892.

40. *Exeter News-Letter*, November 11, 1892; *ConMon*, November 8, 1892; *Laconia Democrat*, November 4, 11, 1892; *Berlin Independent*, November 9, 23, 30, 1892.

41. *ManU*, November 26, 1890; *NYEP*, October 30, 1890, September 21, 1892; Morgan G. Bulkeley, "The New Method of Voting," *NAR* 149 (December 1889): 754–55; *SprRep*, November 9, 1890.

42. "The Paster and the Blanket Ballot," *HW*, October 24, 1891, pp. 814–15; "Let Us Have Ballot Reform," *HW*, October 31, 1891, pp. 838–39; *Baltimore American*, November 6, 1890; Charles T. Saxton, "The New Method of Voting," *NAR* 149 (December 1889): 751–52; *Baltimore Sun*, September 29, 1892; Bass, "*I Am a Democrat*," 98–99, 128–34, 148–55; "H. T. P.," *Boston Evening Transcript*, November 11, 1892.

43. *StLG-D*, March 24, 1891; *Troy Daily Press*, October 17, 1890; *Baltimore American*, February 27, 1890; *Laconia Democrat*, November 11, 1892; John W. Goff, "Juggling with the Ballot," *NAR* 158 (February 1894): 207–8.

44. Charles Saxton, "Changes in My Ballot Bill," *NAR* 150 (April 1890): 532; N. Matthews to Timothy S. Williams, March 14, 1890, Williams MSS, New York Public Library, New York; Chrislock, "Politics of Protest," 135–36; George F. Page to William E. Chandler, January 26, 1895, ChanMSS (NHHS).

45. Reynolds, *Testing Democracy*, 64–69; McCormick, *From Realignment to Reform*, 114–18; N. Matthews to Timothy S. Williams, March 14, 1890, Williams MSS, New York Public Library, New York; *Baltimore Sun*, October 19, 1892; *Nation*, April 9, May 14, 28, June 18, 1891; Charles C. Binney, "The Merits and Defects of the Pennsylvania Ballot Law of 1891," *Annals of the American Academy of Political and Social Science* 2 (1892): 751–71; Terence V. Powderly to Thomas E. Watson, May 27, 1892, Powderly MSS, Catholic University, Washington.

46. *SprRep*, October 12, 26, 1890.

47. *StPGW*, October 21, 1892; *AmN*, March 29, 1894; *Nation*, March 14, 1889; N. S. Shaler, "The Nature of the Negro," *Arena* 3 (December 1890): 34–35; "The Colored Vote in Mississippi," *HW*, August 22, 1891, p. 631.

48. Frank Parsons, "Political Movement of the Nineteenth Century," *Arena* 26 (September 1901): 268–73; W. D. McCrackan, "The Initiative in Switzerland," ibid., 7 (April 1893): 548–53; Robert Tyson, "Needed Political Reforms," ibid., 610–17; David Dudley Field, "Open Nominations and Free Elections," *NAR* 144 (April 1887): 328–29.

49. Speed Mosby, "Danger of Political Apathy," *NAR* 167 (October 1898): 502–4. On the emptiness of the machinery, see Wiebe, *Search for Order*, 222–23, and William Hemstreet, "The New Primary Law," *Arena* 28 (December 1902): 594–95.

50. *NYTr*, March 21, 1886; Ohio Constitutional Convention *Debates*, 1873, pp. 1842–43, 1868, 1875; *NYStan*, March 31, December 22, 1888; Edwards, "Gender in American Politics," 98, 295–302.

Chapter Fifteen

1. Hamlin Garland, "The Alliance Wedge in Congress," *Arena* 5 (March 1892): 457.
2. The story, with different emphases, is best told in Hicks, *Populist Revolt*; Goodwyn,

Democratic Promise; and McMath, *American Populism*. Goodwyn's account, which may have been the most influential in several generations, has a much weaker grasp of the heritage of insurgency than does McMath, and it shows a good deal less precision with the facts (outside of Texas) than do Hicks or various state studies.

3. Woodward, *Tom Watson*, 241–42; Korobkin, "Politics of Disfranchisement in Georgia," 33–35; Hair, *Bourbonism and Agrarian Protest*, 260–65.

4. R. Hal Williams, *Years of Decision*, 13, 19–20.

5. "The New States," *HW*, October 19, 1889, p. 826; *StLG-D*, November 9, 1888.

6. Kousser, *Shaping of Southern Politics*, 98–101, 111–14; Benjamin F. Hunter to John Sherman, August 11, 1890, V. S. Lusk to Sherman, July 19, 1890, and W. R. Albright to Sherman, July 12, 1890, Sherman MSS, LC; *Mobile Daily Register*, November 21, 1890; "The Outrage at Jackson," *HW*, February 18, 1888, p. 111; *CR*, 51st Cong., 1st sess., 804 (January 23, 1890). For similar violence in Arkansas, see Welch, "Violence and the Decline of Black Politics," 373–88.

7. H. H. Winn to William E. Chandler, March 6, 1890, Lyman Phelps to Chandler, March 13, 1890, M. A. Pledger to Chandler, February 4, 1889, M. W. Caldwell to Chandler, March 31, 1890, E. C. Wade to Chandler, June 10, 1890, and Abram S. Humphries to Chandler, February 26, 1890, ChanMSS (LC); Nils Haugen to John T. Hay, May 19, 1890, Haugen MSS.

8. Thomas M. Bayne to Matthew Quay, September 7, 1889, Quay MSS, LC; Robinson, *Thomas B. Reed*, 204–25; Stern, "Leadership and Formation of Policy," 75–80; Forgette, "Reed's Rules," 377–96.

9. *Nation*, February 26, 1891; "The Rules," *HW*, February 22, 1890, p. 134; "The Speaker's Victory," *HW*, March 1, 1890, p. 158; *Mobile Daily Register*, February 1, 1890; Commons, *Proportional Representation*, 52–56.

10. *Mobile Daily Register*, January 8, 1890; Robinson, *Thomas B. Reed*, 218; *Milan Exchange*, March 8, 1890.

11. Limbaugh, *Rocky Mountain Carpetbaggers*, 176; Gould, *Wyoming*, 114–20; "New States," *HW*, July 12, 1890, p. 535; *NYStan*, February 12, 1890; *CinEnq*, February 19, 1890.

12. Crofts, "Blair Bill," 256–63.

13. Thomas Brackett Reed, "The Federal Control of Elections," *NAR* 150 (June 1890): 672–74; Job Harrol to Leonidas C. Houk, July 18, 1890, Houk MSS, CMMHC.

14. Samuel Dibble to William A. Courtenay, July 1, 1890, Courtenay MSS, South Caroliniana Collection, University of South Carolina, Columbia; R. Hal Williams, *Years of Decision*, 31–32; Daniel W. Voorhees to John B. Stoll, February 14, 1890, Stoll MSS, Indiana State Library, Indianapolis; "The National Election Bill," *HW*, July 12, 1890, p. 534; *CR*, 51st Cong., 1st sess., 6934 (July 2, 1890).

15. *Baltimore American*, October 25, 28, November 2, 3, 4, 5, 6, 1890; Kousser, *Shaping of Southern Politics*, 113–14; *CinEnq*, February 18, 19, 20, 22, 26, 1890; *ClPD* October 9, 1890; Joseph B. Foraker to Daniel J. Ryan, March 29, 1890, Box 1, Folder 1, Ryan MSS, Ohio Historical Society, Columbus; W. S. Cappeller to Foraker, April 3, 1890, Foraker MSS, Cincinnati Historical Society, Cincinnati.

16. On New Hampshire, see *Manchester Daily Union*, November 26, December 9, 13, 16, 18, 20, 1890; *Nation*, November 27, 1890; Richardson, *William E. Chandler*, 421–24; Timothy L. Jenkins to William E. Chandler, November 18, 1890, and Paul Lang to Chandler, No-

vember 15, 1890, ChanMSS (NHHS); and *Concord Daily Monitor*, January 15, 1891. For New York, see Bass, *"I Am A Democrat,"* 191–99, and "'Stealing' a Legislature," *HW*, December 5, 1891, p. 958.

17. Kousser, *Shaping of Southern Politics*, 101, 116; *Milan Exchange*, August 9, 1890; Perman, *Struggle for Mastery*, 50–59; T. H. Baker to Leonidas C. Houk, August 8, 1890, and H. B. Lindsay to Houk, August 8, 1890, Houk MSS, CMMHC; "The New Mississippi Constitution," *HW*, September 13, 1890, p. 714; Perman, *Struggle for Mastery*, 70–90; Gordon, *Caste and Class*, 26–30; "E. G. D.," *NYT*, October 4, 1892.

18. *Waterbury Daily Republican*, November 14, 1890; Baney, "Yankees and the City," 149–54; *NYT*, September 4, 28, 1892.

19. Kleppner, "Voters and Parties," 55–67; Owens, "Patterns and Structure," 373–92; Kousser, "Towards 'Total Political History,'" 553.

20. Garland, "Alliance Wedge in Congress," 447–57; Annie L. Diggs, "The Farmers' Alliance and Some of Its Leaders," ibid., 5 (April 1892): 590–608; Annie L. Diggs, "The Women in the Alliance Movement," ibid., 6 (July 1892): 164–65; Thomas E. Watson, "Why the People's Party Should Elect the Next President," ibid., 6 (July 1892): 204.

21. Edward A. Oldham, "The Great Political Upheaval at the South," *Arena* 2 (October 1890): 632–33.

22. Weinstein, *Prelude to Populism*, 8–32; Hofstadter, *Age of Reform*, 70–81; Nugent, *Tolerant Populists*, 109–21.

23. Bromberg, "Pure Democracy," 435–42, 456–67, 484; Moore, "Agrarianism and Populism," 83–91; John B. Stoll address, February 23, 1891, Stoll MSS, Indiana State Library, Indianapolis; Kirwan, *Revolt of the Rednecks*, 87–91; Holmes, "Georgia Alliance Legislature," 514–15; Holmes, "Populism in Black Belt Georgia," 252–53; *Minneapolis Tribune*, October 4, 1890.

24. Goodwyn, *Democratic Promise*, 363–67; Argersinger, "No Rights on This Floor," 681–83; Fischer, "Rustic Rasputin," 225–39; Haywood, "Populist Humor," 34–37; Hair, *Bourbonism and Agrarian Protest*, 228; *NYS*, April 26, 28, 1894; *NYH*, September 5, 1892; *Philadelphia Press*, July 7, 1892.

25. C. W. Buckley to Robert McKee, January 12, 1892; A. H. Alston to McKee, July 7, 1891, McKee MSS, Alabama Department of Archives and History, Montgomery; "E. G. D.," *NYT*, October 3, 1892; Woodward, *Tom Watson*, 227–28.

26. *AmN*, April 19, May 31, June 28, November 8, 1894.

27. Richard J. Hinton, "The New Politics," *Arena* 11 (January 1895): 226; Goodwyn, *Democratic Promise*, 354–62; Hair, *Bourbonism and Agrarian Protest*, 252–55; *StPGW*, October 7, 28, 1892, August 4, 1893; Hans Nelson to Charles S. Brandborg, August 22, 24, 1890, E. B. Straub to Brandborg, July 31, 1890, and D. W. Hixson to Brandborg, March 7, 1891, Brandborg MSS, MHS; *AmN*, May 10, June 28, 1894.

28. Commons, *Proportional Representation*, 58–59; Webb, "Two-Party Politics," 185; S. H. Herrin to Thomas G. Jones, March 23, 1893, Jones MSS, Alabama Department of Archives and History, Montgomery; Argersinger, "To Disfranchise the People," 18–35; Argersinger, "'A Place on the Ballot,'" 290–300.

29. Hair, *Bourbonism and Agrarian Protest*, 260.

30. Robert McKee to Willis Brewer, August 7, 1892, McKee MSS, Alabama Department of

Archives and History, Montgomery; Hackney, *Populism to Progressivism*, 36; Gross, "Alabama Politics and the Negro," 207; J. C. Brooks to Thomas G. Jones, July 16, 1892, David M. Gold to Jones, July 16, 1892, and Chappell Cory to Jones, August 14, 1892, Jones MSS, Alabama Department of Archives and History, Montgomery.

31. Shaw, *Wool-Hat Boys*, 117; W. H. Hidell to Rebecca Felton, November 7, December 13, 1894, H. A. Scamp to W. H. Felton, November 9, 1894, W. W. Dudley to Rebecca Felton, December 26, 1895, and Rebecca Felton to Dudley, February 19, 1896, Felton Family MSS, University of Georgia Library, Athens.

32. Woodward, *Tom Watson*, 219–23; Holmes, "Georgia Alliance Legislature," 507; Korobkin, "Politics of Disfranchisement in Georgia," 20–38; Shaw, *Wool-Hat Boys*, 78–90, 109–10.

33. Kousser, *Shaping of Southern Politics*, 130–223.

34. *AmN*, April 12, 1894; Ostler, *Prairie Populism*, 72–133.

35. Ostler, *Prairie Populism*, 54–71, 154–74.

36. Argersinger, "Road to a Republican Waterloo," 462; Nugent, "How the Populists Lost in 1894," 252–53.

37. Towne, *William Stone*, 18–24; Hackney, *Populism to Progressivism*, 135–40; Williamson, *Florida Politics*, 180–81; Shaw, *Wool-Hat Boys*, 118–19, 134–35; Alwyn Barr, *Reconstruction to Reform*, 129, 164; Cotner, *Hogg*, 330; James Hogg to J. E. Downs, September 7, 1892, Hogg MSS, University of Texas Library, Austin.

38. Chrislock, "Politics of Protest in Minnesota," 134–35, 201–6; Cotner, *Hogg*, 344–45; Larson, "Populism in the Mountain West," 82; Acrea, "Wisconsin Reform Coalition, 1892 to 1900," 135–43.

39. Press, "Kansas Conflict," 323–28; Larson, "Populism in the Mountain West," 159–62; Simkins, *Pitchfork Ben Tillman*, 152–53, 232–33.

40. Frank, "Leviathan with Tentacles of Steel," 41–54.

41. Cherny, "Lawrence Goodwyn," 189–90; Cotner, *Hogg*, 432–33.

42. Argersinger, "No Rights on This Floor," 656–68, 688–89.

43. Clanton, *Kansas Populism*, 139–40; Argersinger, *Populism and Politics*, 288–89; *AmN*, July 5, 1894. For the difference between Union Labor Populists and mainstream-party Populists—between fusion-elected and straight-out elected Populists—see Argersinger, "Populists in Power," 90, 103–5.

44. Clanton, *Kansas Populism*, 140–46; Barton, "Party Switching," 458–66; *StPP-P*, October 9, 1890; *StPGW*, November 18, 1892.

45. Kirwan, *Revolt of the Rednecks*, 94, 96; *AmN*, July 5, 1894.

46. Argersinger, *Populism and Politics*, 138–44; Chrislock, "Politics of Protest," 131–37; *StPGW*, April 21, 1893; G. L. Stromberg to Charles S. Brandborg, February 21, 1893, A. O. Grigsby to Brandborg, May 15, 1893, R. J. Hall to Brandborg, December 1, 1892, E. H. Probtsfield to Brandborg, December 21, 1892, and Charles Canning to Brandborg, January 6, 1894, Brandborg MSS, MHS.

47. Hart, *Redeemers, Bourbons, and Populists*, 207–8; *AmN*, February 9, 1893, June 26, July 12, 1894; *StPGW*, August 22, 29, September 12, 1890, November 18, 1892, April 21, July 7, September 22, 1893; John S. Dore to Thomas V. Cator, December 3, 29, 1892, Cator MSS, SU.

48. For accounts with varying levels of sympathy for the mid-road movement, see Goodwyn, *Democratic Promise*, and Argersinger, *Populism and Politics*. For the fusionist side, see Nugent, *Tolerant Populists*.

49. W. A. Peffer, "The Passing of the People's Party," *NAR* 166 (January 1898): 16–19.

50. Hicks, *Populist Revolt*, 381–83; Wharton Barker to Luman H. Weller, June 22, 29, July 7, 1898, Weller MSS, SHSW.

51. Hicks, *Populist Revolt*, 383–87; Peterson, "People's Party of Kansas," 236–41; L. D. Reynolds to Luman H. Weller, June 30, 1898, A. W. C. Weeks to Weller, July 11, 1898, and Joseph A. Parker to Weller, April 20, 1899, Weller MSS, SHSW.

52. Jo A. Parker to Luman H. Weller, April 26, 1900, Weller MSS, SHSW.

53. Hicks, *Populist Revolt*, 397–400; Andrew Macomber to Luman H. Weller, September 25, October 3, 1900, R. M. Daniels to Weller, September 27, 1900, A. W. C. Weeks to Weller, September 18, October 2, 1900, O. Tyson to Weller, September 29, December 12, 1900, Charles R. Smith to Weller, September 23, 1900, Fred Hunt to Weller, September 25, 1900, and C. A. Wickes to Weller, October 12, 1900, Weller MSS, SHSW.

Coda

1. And seemed, as far as the House is concerned, is especially apt. In 1892, Democrats took 213 seats (59.8 percent), Republicans, 131, and Populists, 12. But the Democratic share of the vote was only 47.2 percent. Populists got 3.4 percent of the representatives for their 8.7 percent of the vote. Two years later, the same district system assured a disproportionate Republican sweep. Republicans got 48.4 percent of the vote and 68.8 percent of the House. Populists got 11.7 percent of the vote and only 2 percent of the representatives.

2. Commons, *Proportional Representation*, 57–58.

3. Kleppner, *Continuity and Change*, 71–76.

4. *Columbus Evening Dispatch*, November 5, 1916, p. 1.

5. Parish, "Great Kansas Legislative Imbroglio," 471–90.

6. See, most notably, Kousser, *Shaping of Southern Politics*; Hair, *Bourbonism and Agrarian Protest*; Argersinger, "To Disfranchise the People"; Argersinger, "Value of the Vote," 279–98; and Reynolds and McCormick, "Outlawing 'Treachery,'" 835–58.

BIBLIOGRAPHY

Manuscript Collections

Albany, New York
  New York State Library
    David Bennett Hill MSS
    David Bennett Hill MSS (Bixby Collection)
    Edwin D. Morgan MSS
    Horatio Seymour MSS
Athens, Georgia
  University of Georgia Library
    Rebecca Felton MSS
Austin, Texas
  University of Texas Library
    James Stephen Hogg MSS
Chapel Hill, North Carolina
  Southern Historical Collection, University of North Carolina
    Daniel M. Barringer MSS
Cincinnati, Ohio
  Cincinnati Historical Society
    Joseph Benson Foraker MSS
    Murat Halstead MSS
    Alexander Long MSS
Columbia, South Carolina
  South Caroliniana Collection, University of South Carolina
    William A. Courtenay MSS
    William H. Trescot MSS
Columbus, Ohio
  Ohio Historical Society
    Charles Foster Letter-Books
    Daniel J. Ryan MSS
    William Henry Smith MSS
Concord, New Hampshire
  New Hampshire Historical Society

Henry W. Blair MSS
William E. Chandler MSS
John H. George MSS
Mason W. Tappan MSS
Durham, North Carolina
    Duke University Library
        John E. Bryant MSS
Fremont, Ohio
    Rutherford B. Hayes Memorial Library
        William Claflin MSS
        A. L. Conger MSS
        Rutherford B. Hayes MSS
Indianapolis, Indiana
    Indiana State Library
        John B. Stoll MSS
        Lucius B. Swift MSS
Iowa City, Iowa
    State Historical Society of Iowa
        Jonathan P. Dolliver MSS
Ithaca, New York
    Cornell University
        Kernan Family MSS
Knoxville, Tennessee
    Calvin M. McClung Historical Collection, Knox County Public Library System
        Leonidas and John C. Houk MSS
Madison, Wisconsin
    State Historical Society of Wisconsin
        Wendell Anderson MSS
        James Rood Doolittle MSS
        Nils Haugen MSS
        Elisha W. Keyes MSS
        William F. Vilas MSS
        Luman H. Weller MSS
Montgomery, Alabama
    Alabama Department of Archives and History
        Thomas G. Jones MSS
        Robert McKee MSS
Montpelier, Vermont
    Vermont Historical Society
        Charles W. Willard MSS
Morganton, West Virginia
    West Virginia Collection, West Virginia University Library
        Ambler MSS
        Henry G. Davis MSS

        Stephen Benton Elkins MSS
        John W. Mason MSS
        Waitman T. Willey MSS
        William L. Wilson Diary
New Haven, Connecticut
    Sterling Memorial Library, Yale University
        Simeon Baldwin MSS
New York, New York
    Columbia University
        William R. Grace MSS
        F. W. Holls MSS
        Edward M. Shepard MSS
    New York Public Library
        Samuel J. Tilden MSS
        Timothy S. Williams MSS
Palo Alto, California
    Stanford University
        Thomas V. Cator MSS
        Stephen Mallory White MSS
Philadelphia, Pennsylvania
    The Historical Society of Pennsylvania
        Jay Cooke MSS
        William D. Kelley MSS
        Wayne MacVeagh MSS
        James Swank MSS
    Rare Book and Manuscript Library, University of Pennsylvania
        Samuel J. Randall MSS
St. Louis, Missouri
    Missouri Historical Society
        James O. Broadhead MSS
        William V. Byars MSS
        B. B. Cahoon MSS
St. Paul, Minnesota
    James J. Hill Library
        James J. Hill MSS
    Minnesota Historical Society
        Charles Brandborg MSS
        Henry A. Castle MSS
        Cushman Davis MSS
        Ignatius Donnelly MSS
        Knute Nelson MSS
        James A. Tawney MSS
San Marino, California
    Huntington Library

Thomas R. Bard MSS
Samuel L. M. Barlow MSS
Springfield, Illinois
Illinois State Historical Society
Joseph Fifer MSS
Washington, D.C.
Catholic University
Terence V. Powderly MSS
Library of Congress
William Allen MSS
Nathaniel P. Banks MSS
Thomas F. Bayard MSS
Wharton Barker MSS
James G. Blaine MSS
Breckinridge Family MSS
Benjamin F. Butler MSS
Frank Carpenter MSS
William E. Chandler MSS
Grover Cleveland MSS
Benjamin Harrison MSS
Thomas Jenckes MSS
Daniel S. Lamont MSS
John A. Logan MSS
Manton Marble MSS
Edward McPherson MSS
Matthew Stanley Quay MSS
Whitelaw Reid MSS
John Sherman MSS
John C. Spooner MSS
Alexander Stephens MSS
Elihu Washburne MSS
David A. Wells MSS
William C. Whitney MSS

Newspapers and Magazines of Opinion

Albany Evening Journal
Arena
Atchison (Kans.) Daily Champion
Atlanta Constitution
Auburn (N.Y.) Daily Advertiser
Augusta Chronicle
Austin Statesman
Baltimore American

Baltimore Sun
Bangor Commercial
Bangor Whig and Courier
Berlin (N.H.) Independent
Birmingham Age
Boston Evening Transcript
Boston Herald
Brooklyn Daily Eagle
Brunswick Telegraph
Buffalo Courier
Burlington (Iowa) Hawk-Eye
Burlington (Iowa) Saturday Evening Post
Canton (Ohio) Repository
Carson City (Nev.) Morning Appeal
Cazenovia (N.Y.) Republican
Charleston News & Courier
Chattanooga Daily Times
Chicago Daily News
Chicago Inter Ocean
Chicago Labor Enquirer
Chicago Times
Chicago Tribune
Cincinnati Commercial
Cincinnati Commercial Gazette
Cincinnati Enquirer
Cincinnati Gazette
Circleville (Ohio) Democrat & Watchman
Clarksville (Tenn.) Semi-Weekly Tobacco Leaf
Cleveland Plain Dealer
Concord (N.H.) Labor Reform Dispatch
Concord (N.H.) Monitor
Corpus Christi Caller
Crystal Springs (Miss.) Monitor
Davenport Daily Democrat
Des Moines Iowa State Register
Detroit Evening News
Detroit Free Press
Detroit Labor Leaf
Dubuque Herald
East Liverpool (Ohio) Potters' Gazette
Elmira (N.Y.) Weekly Advertiser
Evansville Courier
Frankfort (Ky.) Tri-Weekly Yeoman
Harper's Weekly

Hartford Daily Courant
Henderson (Tenn.) Reporter
Hocking (Ohio) Sentinel
Independent
American Nonconformist (Indianapolis)
Indianapolis Daily Sentinel
Indianapolis Journal
Indianapolis News
Irish World and American Industrial Liberator
Jackson Weekly Clarion
Jackson Clarion-Ledger
John Swinton's Paper
Journalist
Kansas City Times
Knights of Labor (Chicago)
Knoxville Journal
Laconia (N.H.) Democrat
Lewiston (Maine) Evening Journal
Lexington Morning Transcript
Little Rock Arkansas Gazette
Louisville Commercial
Louisville Courier-Journal
Manchester Union
Mechanicville (N.Y.) Era
Mechanicville (N.Y.) Mercury
Memphis Commercial Appeal
Memphis Daily Appeal
Meriden (Conn.) Daily Republican
Milan Exchange
Milwaukee Journal
Milwaukee News
Milwaukee Sentinel
Minneapolis Tribune
Nation
Newark Daily Advertiser
Newark Evening News
New Orleans Daily Picayune
New Orleans Times-Democrat
New York Evening Post
New York Herald
New York Standard
New York Sun
New York Telegraph
New York Times

New York Tribune
New York World
Norfolk Virginian
North American Review
Norwalk (Ohio) Daily Reflector
Omaha Daily Bee
Omaha Republican
Paducah Daily News
Philadelphia Inquirer
Philadelphia North American
Philadelphia Press
Philadelphia Public Ledger
Philadelphia Record
Philadelphia Weekly Times
Pittsburgh Post
Plattsburgh (N.Y.) Republican
Portland Daily Oregonian
Portland Eastern Argus
Poughkeepsie Daily Eagle
Puck
Racine Journal
Railway Age
Raleigh News & Observer
Raymond (Miss.) Hinds County Gazette
Reno Evening Gazette
St. Joseph (Mo.) Daily Gazette
St. Louis Globe-Democrat
St. Louis Post-Dispatch
St. Louis Missouri Republican
St. Paul Anti-Monopolist
St. Paul Daily Globe
St. Paul Dispatch
St. Paul Great West
St. Paul Pioneer
St. Paul Pioneer Press
Salem (Oreg.) Daily Statesman
San Francisco Alta California
San Francisco Chronicle
San Francisco Examiner
Sandusky (Ohio) Register
Springfield (Ohio) Globe-Republic
Springfield Illinois State Register
Springfield (Mass.) Republican
Tallahassee Floridian

Toledo Blade
Topeka Daily Capital
Kansas State Record (Topeka)
Trenton Daily State Gazette
Trenton Daily True American
Troy Daily Press
Washington Critic
Washington Post
Waterbury (Conn.) Daily Republican
Watertown (N.Y.) Daily Times
Wheeling Intelligencer
Wheeling Register
Wilmington Every Evening
Woodbury (Conn.) Constitution & Farmers' and Mechanics' Advertiser
Winona Daily Republican
Worcester Daily Spy
Xenia (Ohio) Republican
Zanesville (Ohio) Daily Courier

Books

Altschuler, Glenn C., and Stuart M. Blumin. *Rude Republic: Americans and Their Politics in the Nineteenth Century*. Princeton: Princeton University Press, 2000.

Anderson, Eric. *Race and Politics in North Carolina, 1872–1901: The Black Second*. Baton Rouge: Louisiana State University Press, 1981.

"Annus Domini, 1873–74–75, or, The Presidency of Horace Greeley by a Democratic Clairvoyant." New York: n.p., 1872.

Argersinger, Peter. *Populism and Politics: William Alfred Peffer and the People's Party*. Lexington: University Press of Kentucky, 1974.

Avey, Michael J. *The Demobilization of American Voters: A Comprehensive Theory of Voter Turnout*. Westport, Conn.: Greenwood Press, 1989.

Ayers, Edward L. *The Promise of the New South: Life after Reconstruction*. New York: Oxford University Press, 1992.

Baker, Jean H. *Affairs of Party: The Political Culture of Northern Democrats in the Mid-Nineteenth Century*. Ithaca: Cornell University Press, 1983.

Baker, Paula. *The Moral Frameworks of Public Life: Gender, Politics, and the State in Rural New York, 1870–1930*. New York: Oxford University Press, 1991.

Baker, Thomas Harrison. *The* Memphis Commercial Appeal: *The History of a Southern Newspaper*. Baton Rouge: Louisiana State University Press, 1971.

Baney, Terry Alan. *Yankees and the City: Struggling over Urban Representation in Connecticut, 1880 to World War I*. New York: Garland Publishing, Inc., 1993.

Barker, Charles Albro. *Henry George*. New York: Oxford University Press, 1955.

Barnes, James A. *John G. Carlisle, Financial Statesman*. New York: Dodd, Mead & Co., 1931.

Barnes, Kenneth C. *Who Killed John Clayton? Political Violence and the Emergence of the New South, 1861–1893*. Durham: Duke University Press, 1998.

Barr, Alwyn. *Reconstruction to Reform: Texas Politics, 1876–1906*. Austin: University of Texas Press, 1971.

Bass, Herbert J. *"I Am a Democrat": The Political Career of David B. Hill*. Syracuse: Syracuse University Press, 1961.

Baum, Dale. *The Civil War Party System: The Case of Massachusetts, 1848–1876*. Chapel Hill: University of North Carolina Press, 1984.

Bensel, Richard F. *Sectionalism and American Political Development, 1800–1980*. Madison: University of Wisconsin Press, 1984.

Bigelow, John, ed. *Letters and Literary Memorials of Samuel J. Tilden*. 2 vols. New York: Harper, 1908.

Biographical Cyclopedia and Portrait Gallery, with an Historical Sketch of the State of Ohio. Cincinnati: Western Biographical Publishing Co., 1884.

Blodgett, Geoffrey. *The Gentle Reformers: Massachusetts Democrats in the Cleveland Era*. Cambridge: Harvard University Press, 1966.

Bond, Bradley G. *Political Culture in the Nineteenth-Century South: Mississippi, 1830–1900*. Baton Rouge: Louisiana State University Press, 1995.

Brann, William Cowper. *The Complete Works of Brann, the Iconoclast*. 12 vols. New York: Brann Publisher, Inc., 1919.

Broehl, Wayne. *The Molly Maguires*. Cambridge: Harvard University Press, 1965.

Campbell, Ballard. *Representative Democracy: Public Policy and Midwestern Legislatures in the Late Nineteenth Century*. Cambridge: Harvard University Press, 1980.

Cartwright, Joseph H. *The Triumph of Jim Crow: Tennessee Race Relations in the 1880s*. Knoxville: University of Tennessee Press, 1976.

Carwardine, Richard J. *Evangelicals and Politics in Antebellum America*. New Haven: Yale University Press, 1993.

Chadbourne, Paul A., ed. *State of New York: The Public Service of the State of New York*. 3 vols. Boston: James R. Osgood & Co., 1882.

Christianson, Theodore. *Minnesota: The Land of Sky-Tinted Waters*. Chicago: American Historical Society, 1935.

Clague, Ewan. *The Bureau of Labor Statistics*. New York: Praeger, 1968.

Clanton, O. Gene. *Kansas Populism: Ideas and Men*. Lawrence: University Press of Kansas, 1969.

Clark, Thomas D. *The Southern Country Editor*. Gloucester, Mass.: Peter Smith, 1964.

Clubb, Jerome M., William Flanigan, and Nancy H. Zingale, eds., *Analyzing Electoral History: A Guide to the Study of American Voting Behavior*. Beverly Hill: Sage Publications, 1981.

Commons, John R. *History of Labour in the United States*. 2nd ed. 4 vols. New York: Macmillan, 1941.

———. *Proportional Representation*. 2nd ed. New York: Thomas Y. Crowell & Co., 1907.

Conrad, Will C., Kathleen F. Wilson, and Dale Wilson. The Milwaukee Journal: *The First Eighty Years*. Madison: University of Wisconsin Press, 1964.

Cooper, William F., Michael F. Holt, and John McCardell, eds. *A Master's Due: Essays in*

Honor of David Herbert Donald. Baton Rouge: Louisiana State University Press, 1985.

Cotner, Robert C. *James Stephen Hogg: A Biography*. Austin: University of Texas Press, 1959.

Cresswell, Stephen. *Multi-Party Politics in Mississippi, 1877–1902*. Jackson: University Press of Mississippi, 1995.

Current, Richard N. *Those Terrible Carpetbaggers*. New York: Oxford University Press, 1988.

Daniels, Josephus. *Tar-Heel Editor*. Chapel Hill: University of North Carolina Press, 1939.

Davis, Henry R. *Half a Century with the Providence Journal*. Providence, R.I.: The Journal Company, 1904.

Dawley, Alan. *Class and Community: The Industrial Revolution in Lynn*. Cambridge: Harvard University Press, 1976.

Debates and Proceedings of the Constitutional Convention of the State of California. 3 vols. Sacramento: State Printing Office, 1880.

Deverell, William. *Railroad Crossing: Californians and the Railroad, 1850–1916*. Berkeley: University of California Press, 1994.

Dobson, John M. *Politics in the Gilded Age: A New Perspective on Reform*. New York: Praeger, 1972.

Douglas, George H. *The Golden Age of the Newspaper*. Westport, Conn.: Greenwood Press, 1999.

Duis, Perry. *The Saloon: Public Drinking in Chicago and Boston, 1880–1920*. Urbana: University of Illinois Press, 1983.

Dunn, Arthur Wallace. *From Harrison to Harding: A Personal Narrative Covering a Third of a Century, 1888–1921*. 2 vols. New York: G. P. Putnam's Sons, 1922.

Dunn, Jacob Piatt. *History of Greater Indianapolis*. Chicago: Lewis Publishing Co., 1910.

Ellis, Franklin, and Samuel Evans. *History of Lancaster County, Pennsylvania, with Biographical Sketches of Many of Its Pioneers and Prominent Men*. Philadelphia: Everts & Peck, 1883.

Emery, Edwin. *The Press and America: An Interpretive History of the Mass Media*. 5th ed. Englewood Cliffs, N.J.: Prentice-Hall, Inc., 1984.

Fine, Sidney. *Laissez Faire and the General-Welfare State: A Study of Conflict in American Thought, 1865–1901*. Ann Arbor: University of Michigan Press, 1956.

Fink, Leon. *Workingmen's Democracy: The Knights of Labor and American Politics*. Urbana: University of Illinois Press, 1983.

Flick, Alexander C. *Samuel Jones Tilden: A Study in Political Sagacity*. New York: Dodd, Mead & Co., 1939.

Foner, Philip S. *History of the Labor Movement in the United States*. Vol 2. New York: International Publishers, 1955.

Fredman, L. E. *The Australian Ballot: The Story of an American Reform*. East Lansing: Michigan State University Press, 1968.

Frisch, Michael H., and Daniel J. Walkowitz, eds. *Working-Class America: Essays on Labor Community and American Society*. Urbana: University of Illinois, 1983.

Gentry, Claude. *Private John Allen — Gentleman — Statesman — Sage — Prophet*. Decatur, Ga.: Bowen Press, 1951.

Ginger, Ray. *Age of Excess: The United States from 1877 to 1914*. New York: Macmillan, 1965.

———. *Altgeld's America: The Lincoln Ideal versus Changing Realities*. New York: Funk & Wagnall's Co. 1958.

Going, Allen J. *Bourbon Democracy in Alabama, 1874 – 1890*. University: University of Alabama Press, 1951.

Goldberg, Michael L. *An Army of Women: Gender and Politics in Gilded Age Kansas*. Baltimore: Johns Hopkins University Press, 1997.

Goodwyn, Lawrence. *Democratic Promise: The Populist Moment in America*. New York: Oxford University Press, 1976.

Gordon, Fon L. *Caste and Class: The Black Experience in Arkansas, 1880 – 1920*. Athens: University of Georgia Press, 1995.

Gould, Lewis L. *Wyoming: A Political History, 1868 – 1896*. New Haven: Yale University Press, 1968.

Griffith, Louis Turner, and John Erwin Talmadge. *George Journalism, 1763 – 1950*. Athens: University of Georgia Press, 1951.

Grossman, Lawrence. *The Democratic Party and the Negro: Northern and National Politics, 1868 – 1892*. Urbana: University of Illinois Press, 1976.

Gyory, Andrew. *Closing the Gate: Race, Politics, and the Chinese Exclusion Act*. Chapel Hill: University of North Carolina Press, 1998.

Hackney, Sheldon. *Populism to Progressivism in Alabama*. Princeton: Princeton University Press, 1969.

Haferbecker, Gordon M. *Wisconsin Labor Laws*. Madison: University of Wisconsin Press, 1958.

Hair, William I. *Bourbonism and Agrarian Protest: Louisiana Politics, 1877 – 1900*. Baton Rouge: Louisiana State University Press, 1969.

Hamm, Richard F. *Shaping the Eighteenth Amendment: Temperance Reform, Legal Culture, and the Polity, 1880 – 1920*. Chapel Hill: University of North Carolina Press, 1995.

Hammack, David C. *Power and Society: Greater New York at the Turn of the Century*. New York: Columbia University Press, 1987.

Harris, Joseph P. *Registration of Voters in the United States*. Washington: Brookings Institute, 1929.

Hart, Jim Allee. *A History of the St. Louis Globe-Democrat*. Columbia: University of Missouri Press, 1961.

Hart, Roger L. *Redeemers, Bourbons, and Populists: Tennessee, 1870 – 1896*. Baton Rouge: Louisiana State University Press, 1975.

Haynes, Fred Emory. *James Baird Weaver*. Iowa City: State Historical Society, 1919.

Hicks, John D. *The Populist Revolt*. Minneapolis: University of Minnesota Press, 1931.

Hirsch, Mark D. *William C. Whitney: Modern Warwick*. New York: Dodd, Mead & Co., 1948.

Hirshson, Stanley. *Farewell to the Bloody Shirt: Northern Republicans and the Southern Negro, 1877 – 1893*. Bloomington: Indiana University Press, 1962.

Hoag, Clarence G., and George H. Hallett. *Proportional Representation*. New York: Macmillan, 1926.

Hofstadter, Richard. *The Age of Reform: From Bryan to F. D. R*. New York: Random House, 1955.

———. *The American Political Tradition and the Men Who Made It*. New York: Vintage, 1948.

———. *The Idea of a Party System: The Rise of Legitimate Opposition in the United States, 1780–1840*. Berkeley: University of California Press, 1969.

———. *The Paranoid Style in American Politics and Other Essays*. New York: Knopf, 1965.

Hogarty, Richard A. *Leon Abbett's New Jersey: The Emergence of the Modern Governor*. Philadelphia: American Philosophical Society, 2001.

Holt, Thomas. *Black over White: Negro Political Leadership in South Carolina during Reconstruction*. Urbana: University of Illinois Press, 1977.

Hoogenboom, Ari. *Outlawing the Spoils: A History of the Civil Service Reform Movement, 1865–1883*. Urbana: University of Illinois Press, 1968.

Howe, George F. *Chester A. Arthur: A Quarter-Century of Machine Politics*. New York: Dodd, Mead & Co., 1934.

Hurd, D. Hamilton, comp. *History of Fairfield County, Connecticut, with Illustrations and Biographical Sketches of its Prominent Men and Pioneers*. Philadelphia: J. W. Lewis & Co., 1881.

Hyman, Michael R. *The Anti-Redeemers: Hill Country Political Dissenters in the Lower South from Redemption to Populism*. Baton Rouge: Louisiana State University Press, 1990.

Issel, William, and Robert W. Cherny. *San Francisco, 1865–1932: Politics, Power, and Urban Development*. Berkeley: University of California Press, 1986.

Ivins, William M. *Machine Politics and Money in Elections in New York City*. New York: Arno Press, 1970.

Jensen, Richard. *The Winning of the Midwest: Social and Political Conflict, 1888–1896*. Chicago: University of Chicago Press, 1971.

Jewell, J. Grey. *Among Our Sailors*. New York: Harper, 1874.

Josephson, Matthew. *The Politicos, 1865–1896*. New York: Harcourt, Brace, 1938.

Juergens, George. *Joseph Pulitzer and the New York World*. Princeton: Princeton University Press, 1966.

Kantrowitz, Stephen. *Ben Tillman and the Reconstruction of White Supremacy*. Chapel Hill: University of North Carolina Press, 2000.

Kehl, James. *Boss Rule in the Gilded Age: Matt Quay of Pennsylvania*. Pittsburgh: University of Pittsburgh Press, 1981.

Keller, Morton. *Affairs of State: Public Life in Late-Nineteenth-Century America*. Cambridge: Belknap Press, 1977.

Kerr, K. Austin. *Organized for Prohibition: A New History of the Anti-Saloon League*. New Haven: Yale University Press, 1985.

Keyssar, Alexander. *The Right to Vote: The Contested History of Democracy in the United States*. New York: Basic Books, 2000.

Kirwan, Albert. *Revolt of the Rednecks: Mississippi Politics, 1876–1925*. Lexington: University of Kentucky Press, 1951.

Klein, Maury. *The Life and Legend of Jay Gould*. Baltimore: Johns Hopkins University Press, 1986.

Kleppner, Paul. *Continuity and Change in Electoral Politics, 1893–1928*. Westport, Conn.: Greenwood Press, 1987.

———. *The Cross of Culture: A Social Analysis of Midwestern Politics, 1850–1900*. New York: Free Press, 1970.

———. *The Third Electoral System, 1853–1892: Parties, Voters, and Political Cultures*. Chapel Hill: University of North Carolina Press, 1979.

———. *Who Voted? The Dynamics of Electoral Turnout, 1870–1980*. New York: Praeger, 1982.

Kornbluh, Mark Lawrence. *Why America Stopped Voting: The Decline of Participatory Democracy and the Emergence of Modern American Politics*. New York: New York University Press, 2000.

Kousser, J. Morgan. *The Shaping of Southern Politics: Suffrage Restriction and the Establishment of the One-Party South, 1880–1910*. New Haven: Yale University Press, 1974.

Kraditor, Aileen S. *The Ideas of the Woman Suffrage Movement, 1890–1920*. New York: Columbia University Press, 1965.

Lamar, Howard R. *Dakota Territory, 1861–1889*. New Haven: Yale University Press, 1956.

Lambert, Oscar Doane. *Stephen Benton Elkins*. Pittsburgh: University of Pittsburgh Press, 1955.

Larson, Robert W. *Populism in the Mountain West*. Albuquerque: University of New Mexico Press, 1986.

Lillard, Richard G. *Desert Challenge: An Interpretation of Nevada*. New York: Knopf, 1949.

Limbaugh, Ronald. *Rocky Mountain Carpetbaggers: Idaho's Territorial Governors, 1863–1890*. Moscow: University of Idaho Press, 1982.

Lipin, Lawrence M. *Producers, Proletarians, and Politicians: Worker and Party Politics in Evansville and New Albany, Indiana, 1850–87*. Urbana: University of Illinois Press, 1994.

Luce, Robert. *Legislative Problems: Development, Status, and Trend of the Treatment and Exercise of Lawmaking Powers*. Boston: Houghton Mifflin, 1935.

Luebke, Frederick C. *Immigrants and Politics: The Germans of Nebraska, 1880–1900*. Lincoln: University of Nebraska Press, 1969.

Magrath, Peter. *Morrison R. Waite: The Triumph of Character*. New York: Macmillan, 1963.

Marcus, Robert. *Grand Old Party: Political Structure in the Gilded Age, 1880–1896*. New York: Oxford University Press, 1971.

McCall, Samuel W. *The Life of Thomas Brackett Reed*. Boston: Houghton Mifflin, 1914.

McClure, Alexander K. *Old-Time Notes of Pennsylvania*. 2 vols. Philadelphia: John C. Winston Co., 1905.

McCormick, Richard L. *From Realignment to Reform: Political Change in New York State, 1893–1910*. Ithaca: Cornell University Press, 1986.

———. *The Party Period and Public Policy: American Politics from the Age of Jackson to the Progressive Era*. New York: Oxford University Press, 1986.

McFarland, Gerald. *Mugwumps, Morals, and Politics*. Amherst: University of Massachusetts Press, 1975.

McGerr, Michael E. *The Decline of Popular Politics: The American North, 1865–1928*. New York: Oxford University Press, 1986.

McKinney, Gordon B. *Southern Mountain Republicans, 1865–1900: Politics and the Appalachian Community*. Chapel Hill: University of North Carolina Press, 1978.

McKnight, David A. *The Electoral System of the United States. A Critical and Historical Exposition of its Fundamental Principles in the Constitution*. Philadelphia: J. B. Lippincott & Co., 1878.

McMath, Robert. *American Populism: A Social History, 1877–1898*. New York: Hill and Wang, 1993.

———. *Populist Vanguard: A History of the Southern Farmers' Alliance*. Chapel Hill: University of North Carolina Press, 1975.

McNall, Scott G. *The Road to Rebellion: Class Formation and Kansas Populism, 1865–1900*. Chicago: University of Chicago Press, 1988.

McPherson, Edward. *Hand-book of Politics for 1878*. Washington: Solomon's and Chapman, 1878.

———. *Hand-Book of Politics for 1880*. Washington: J. J. Chapman, 1880.

———. *Hand-Book of Politics for 1882*. Washington: J. J. Chapman, 1882.

Merrill, Horace Samuel. *Bourbon Democracy of the Middle West, 1865–1896*. Seattle: University of Washington Press, 1953.

———. *Bourbon Leader: Grover Cleveland and the Democratic Party*. Boston: Little, Brown and Co., 1957.

Miles, William, comp. *The People's Voice: An Annotated Bibliography of American Presidential Campaign Newspapers, 1828–1984*. Westport, Conn.: Greenwood Press, 1987.

Miller, Edward A. *Gullah Statesman: Robert Smalls from Slavery to Congress, 1839–1915*. Columbia: University of South Carolina Press, 1995.

Miller, George H. *Railroads and the Granger Laws*. Milwaukee: University of Wisconsin Press, 1971.

Montgomery, David. *Beyond Equality: Labor and the Radical Republicans, 1862–1872*. New York: Vintage, 1967.

Montgomery, Morton L., comp. *Historical and Biographical Annals of Berks County, Pennsylvania*. Chicago: J. H. Beers & Co., 1909.

Morgan, H. Wayne. *From Hayes to McKinley: National Party Politics, 1877–1896*. Syracuse: Syracuse University Press, 1969.

———, ed. *The Gilded Age*. Rev. ed. Syracuse: Syracuse University Press, 1970.

———. *William McKinley and His America*. Syracuse: Syracuse University Press, 1963.

Morgan, W. Scott. *History of the Wheel and Alliance and the Impending Revolution*. Fort Scott, Kans.: J. H. Rice & Sons, 1889.

Mott, Frank Luther. *American Journalism: A History of Newspapers in the United States Through 260 Years: 1690 to 1950*. New York: Macmillan, 1950.

Munroe, John A. *History of Delaware*. Newark: University of Delaware Press, 1979.

Myers, Gustavus. *The History of Tammany Hall*. New York: Boni & Liveright, 1917.

National Cyclopedia of American Biography. 63 vols. New York: James T. White & Co., 1897–.

Nevins, Allan. *Grover Cleveland: A Study in Courage.* New York: Dodd, Mead & Co., 1948.

Nevins, Allan, and Milton H. Thomas, eds., *Diary of George Templeton Strong.* 4 vols. New York: Macmillan, 1952.

Newman, Philip Charles. *The Labor Legislation of New Jersey.* Washington: American Council on Public Affairs, 1943.

Niven, John. *Salmon P. Chase: A Biography.* New York: Oxford University Press, 1995.

Nord, David Paul. *Communities of Journalism: A History of American Newspapers and Their Readers.* Urbana: University of Illinois Press, 2001.

Nugent, Walter K. *Money and American Society, 1865–1880.* New York: Free Press, 1968.

———. *The Tolerant Populists: Kansas Populism and Nativism.* Chicago: University of Chicago Press, 1963.

Olsen, Otto H. *Carpetbagger's Crusade: The Life of Albion Winegar Tourgee.* Baltimore: Johns Hopkins University Press, 1965.

Ostler, Jeffrey. *Prairie Populism: The Fate of Agrarian Radicalism in Kansas, Nebraska and Iowa, 1880–1892.* Lawrence: University Press of Kansas, 1993.

Ostrogorski, Moisei. *Democracy and the Organization of Political Parties.* 2 vols. New York: Macmillan, 1902.

Overacker, Louise. *Money in Elections.* New York: Macmillan, 1932.

Parker, George F. *Recollections of Grover Cleveland.* New York: Century Co., 1909.

Parsons, Stanley B. *The Populist Context: Rural versus Urban Power on a Great Plains Frontier.* Westport: Greenwood Press, 1973.

Peck, Henry L. *Twenty Years of the Republic, 1885–1905.* New York: Dodd, Mead & Co., 1919.

Perman, Michael. *Struggle for Mastery: Disfranchisement in the South, 1888–1908.* Chapel Hill: University of North Carolina, 2001.

Peskin, Allan. *Garfield: A Biography.* Kent, Ohio: Kent State University Press, 1978.

Polakoff, Keith Ian. *The Politics of Inertia: The Election of 1876 and the End of Reconstruction.* Baton Rouge: Louisiana State University Press, 1973.

Pollack, Norman. *The Populist Response to Industrial America.* Cambridge: Harvard University Press, 1962.

Pollock, James K. *Party Campaign Funds.* New York: Knopf, 1926.

Powderly, Terence V. *The Path I Trod: The Autobiography of Terence V. Powderly.* Edited by Harry J. Carman, Henry David, and Paul N. Guthrie. New York: Columbia University Press, 1940.

Reeves, Thomas C. *Gentleman Boss: The Life of Chester Alan Arthur.* New York: Knopf, 1975.

Reitano, Joanne. *The Tariff Question in the Gilded Age: The Great Debate of 1888.* University Park: Pennsylvania State University Press, 1994.

Reynolds, John F. *Testing Democracy: Electoral Reform and Progressive Behavior in New Jersey.* Chapel Hill: University of North Carolina Press, 1988.

Rice, Lawrence D. *The Negro in Texas, 1874–1900*. Baton Rouge: Louisiana State University Press, 1971.

Richardson, Leon B. *William E. Chandler, Republican*. New York: Dodd, Mead & Co., 1940.

Ridge, Martin. *Ignatius Donnelly: Portrait of a Politician*. Chicago: University of Chicago Press, 1962.

Ritchie, Donald. *Press Gallery: Congress and the Washington Correspondents*. Cambridge: Harvard University Press, 1992.

Robinson, William A. *Thomas B. Reed, Parliamentarian*. New York: Dodd, Mead & Co., 1930.

Ruoff, Henry W., comp. *Biographical and Portrait Cyclopedia of Schuylkill County, Pennsylvania, Comprising a Historical Sketch of the County*. By Samuel T. Wiley. Philadelphia: West & Co., 1893.

Russell, Charles E. *Bare Hands and Rock Walls: Some Recollections of a Side-Line Reformer*. New York: Scribner's, 1933.

Ryan, Mary P. *Women in Public: Between Banners and Ballots, 1825–1880*. Baltimore: Johns Hopkins University Press, 1990.

Sackett, William E. *Modern Battles of Trenton*. 2 vols. Trenton: J. L. Murphy, Printer, 1895, 1914.

Schudson, Michael. *Discovering the News: A Social History of American Newspapers*. New York: Basic Books, 1978.

Shank, Alan. *New Jersey Reapportionment Politics: Strategies and Tactics in the Legislative Process*. Rutherford, Pa.: Fairleigh Dickinson University Press, 1968.

Shank, Alan, and Ernest C. Roeck Jr. *New Jersey's Experience with General Assembly Districts, 1852–1893*. New Brunswick: Bureau of Government Research, Rutgers—the State University, 1966.

Shaw, Barton C. *The Wool-Hat Boys: Georgia's Populist Party*. Baton Rouge: Louisiana State University Press, 1984.

Shumsky, Neil Larry. *The Evolution of Political Protest and the Workingmen's Party of California*. Columbus: Ohio State University Press, 1991.

Silbey, Joel. *The American Political Nation, 1838–1893*. Stanford: Stanford University Press, 1991.

Simkins, Francis Butler. *Pitchfork Ben Tillman, South Carolinian*. Baton Rouge: Louisiana State University Press, 1944.

Siracusa, Carl. *A Mechanical People: Perceptions of the Industrial Order in Massachusetts, 1815–1880*. Middletown, Conn.: Wesleyan University Press, 1979.

Skowronek, Stephen. *Building a New American State: The Expansion of National Administrative Capacities*. Cambridge: Cambridge University Press, 1982.

Sproat, John G. *The Best Men: Liberal Reformers in the Gilded Age*. New York: Oxford University Press, 1968.

Staley, Eugene. *History of the Illinois State Federation of Labor*. Chicago: University of Chicago Press, 1930.

Stewart, James Brewer. *Wendell Phillips: Liberty's Hero*. Baton Rouge: Louisiana State University Press, 1986.

Summers, Festus P. *William L. Wilson and Tariff Reform*. New Brunswick: Rutgers University Press, 1953.

Summers, Mark W. *The Era of Good Stealings*. New York: Oxford University Press, 1993.

———. *The Press Gang: Newspapers and Politics, 1865–1878*. Chapel Hill: University of North Carolina Press, 1994.

———. *Rum, Romanism, and Rebellion: The Making of a President, 1884*. Chapel Hill: University of North Carolina Press, 2000.

Tarbell, Ida. *The Tariff in Our Times*. New York: Macmillan, 1912.

Taussig, F. W. *The Tariff History of the United States*, 8th rev. ed. New York: G. P. Putnam's Sons, 1931.

Taylor, Joe Gray. *Louisiana Reconstructed, 1863–1877*. Baton Rouge: Louisiana State University Press, 1974.

Towne, Ruth Warner. *Senator William Stone and the Politics of Compromise*. Port Washington, N.Y.: Kennikat Press, 1979.

Unger, Irwin. *The Greenback Era: A Social and Political History of American Finance, 1865–1879*. Princeton: Princeton University Press, 1964.

Uya, Okon Edet. *From Slavery to Public Service: Robert Smalls, 1839–1915*. New York: Oxford University Press, 1971.

Van Deusen, Glyndon. *Horace Greeley, Nineteenth-Century Crusader*. New York: Hill & Wang, 1953.

Van Dusen, Albert E. *Connecticut*. New York: Random House, 1961.

Villard, Oswald Garrison. *Fighting Years: Memoirs of a Liberal Editor*. New York: Harcourt, Brace, 1939.

Walters, Everett. *Joseph Benson Foraker: An Uncompromising Republican*. Columbus: Ohio History Press, 1948.

Weinstein, Allen. *Prelude to Populism: Origins of the Silver Issue, 1867–1878*. New Haven: Yale University Press, 1970.

Wendt, Lloyd. Chicago Tribune: *The Rise of a Great American Newspaper*. Chicago: Rand McNally & Company, 1979.

Werner, M. L. *Tammany Hall*. Garden City, N.Y.: Garden City Publishing Co., 1932.

West, Richard S. *Satire on Stone: The Political Cartoons of Joseph Keppler*. Urbana: University of Illinois Press, 1988.

White, Carlos. *Ecce Femina: An Attempt to Solve the Woman Question*. Boston: Lee and Shepard, 1870.

White, Leonard. *The Republican Era: A Study in Administrative History*. New York: Macmillan, 1958.

White, William Allen. *Masks in a Pageant*. New York: Macmillan, 1928.

Wiebe, Robert. *The Search for Order, 1877–1920*. New York: Hill and Wang, 1967.

Willey, George F., ed. *State Builders: An Illustrated Historical and Biographical Record of the State of New Hampshire at the Beginning of the Twentieth Century*. Manchester: New Hampshire Publishing Co., 1903.

Williams, Harold A. The Baltimore Sun, *1837–1987*. Baltimore: Johns Hopkins University Press, 1987.

Williams, John Alexander. *West Virginia and the Captains of Industry*. Morganton: West Virginia University Library, 1976.

Williams, R. Hal. *The Democratic Party and California Politics, 1880–1896*. Stanford: Stanford University Press, 1973.

———. *Years of Decision: American Politics in the 1890s*. New York: Knopf, 1978.

Williams, Wirt A., ed. *History of Bolivar County, Mississippi*. Jackson: Hederman Brothers, 1948.

Williamson, Edward C. *Florida Politics in the Gilded Age, 1877–1896*. Gainesville: University of Florida Press, 1976.

Wilson, Charles Reagan. *Baptized in Blood: The Religion of the Lost Cause, 1865–1920*. Athens: University of Georgia Press, 1980.

Woodward, C. Vann. *Origins of the New South, 1877–1913*. Baton Rouge: Louisiana State University Press, 1951.

———. *Reunion and Reaction: The Compromise of 1877 and the End of Reconstruction*. Boston: Little, Brown and Co., 1951.

———. *Tom Watson: Agrarian Rebel*. New York: Macmillan, 1938.

Wright, Henry C. *Bossism in Cincinnati*. Cincinnati: Privately published, 1905.

Wright, James Edward. *The Politics of Populism: Dissent in Colorado*. New Haven: Yale University Press, 1974.

Wynes, Charles E. *Race Relations in Virginia, 1870–1902*. Charlottesville: University of Virginia Press, 1961.

Yearley, Clifton K. *Enterprise and Anthracite: Economics and Democracy in Schuylkill County, 1820–1875*. Baltimore: Johns Hopkins University Press, 1961.

———. *The Money Machines: The Breakdown and Reform of Governmental and Party Finance in the North, 1860–1920*. Albany: State University of New York Press, 1970.

Scholarly Articles

Acrea, Kenneth. "The Wisconsin Reform Coalition, 1892 to 1900: La Follette's Rise to Power." *Wisconsin Magazine of History* 52 (Winter 1968–69): 117–31.

Ainsworth, Scott H., and John Anthony Maltese. "National Grange Influence on the Supreme Court Confirmation of Stanley Matthews." *Social Science History* 20 (Spring 1996): 41–62.

Altschuler, Glenn C., and Stuart M. Blumin. "Limits of Political Engagement in Antebellum America: A New Look at the Golden Age of Participatory Democracy." *Journal of American History* 84 (December 1997): 855–85.

Argersinger, Peter J. "New Perspectives on Election Fraud in the Gilded Age." *Political Science Quarterly* 100 (Winter 1985–86): 669–87.

———. "No Rights on This Floor: Third Parties and the Institutionalization of Congress." *Journal of Interdisciplinary History* 32 (Spring 1992): 655–90.

———. "'A Place on the Ballot': Fusion Politics and Anti-Fusion Laws." *American Historical Review* 85 (April 1980): 290–300.

———. "Populists in Power: Public Policy and Legislative Behavior." *Journal of Interdisciplinary History* 18 (Summer 1987): 81–106.

———. "Road to a Republican Waterloo: The Farmers' Alliance and the Election of 1890 in Kansas." *Kansas Historical Quarterly* 33 (Winter 1967): 443–69.

———. "To Disfranchise the People: The Iowa Ballot Law and the Election of 1897." *Mid-America* 63 (January 1981): 18–39.

———. "The Value of the Vote." *Journal of American History* 76 (September 1989): 59–90.

Asher, Robert. "Failure and Fulfillment: Agitation for Employers' Liability Legislation and the Origins of Workmen's Compensation in New York State, 1876–1910." *Labor History* 24 (Spring 1983): 198–222.

Baker, Paula. "The Culture of Politics in the Late Nineteenth Century: Community and Political Behavior in Rural New York." *Journal of Social History* 18 (Winter 1984): 167–94.

———. "The Domestication of Politics: Women and American Political Society, 1780–1920." *American Historical Review* 89 (1984): 620–48.

Barnes, Kenneth C. "Who Killed John M. Clayton? Political Violence in Conway County, Arkansas, in the 1880s." *Arkansas Historical Quarterly* 52 (Winter 1993): 371–404.

Barton, D. Scott. "Party Switching and Kansas Populism." *Historian* 52 (May 1990): 453–67.

Baumgardner, James L. "The 1888 Presidential Election: How Corrupt?" *Presidential Studies Quarterly* 14 (Summer 1984): 421–25.

Berthoff, Rowland. "The Social Order of the Anthracite Region, 1825–1902." *Pennsylvania Magazine of History and Biography* 89 (July 1965): 261–91.

Blodgett, Geoffrey. "The Mugwump Reputation, 1870 to the Present." *Journal of American History* 66 (March 1980): 867–87.

Boomhower, Ray. "'To Secure Honest Elections': Jacob Piatt Dunn, Jr., and the Reform of Indiana's Ballot." *Indiana Magazine of History* 90 (December 1994): 311–45.

Bridges, Amy. "Creating Cultures of Reform." *Studies in American Political Development* 8 (Spring 1994): 1–23.

Brundage, David. "The Producing Classes and the Saloon: Denver in the 1880s." *Labor History* 26 (Winter 1985): 40–48.

Burnham, Walter Dean. "Theory and Voting Research: Some Reflections on Converse's 'Change in the American Electorate.'" *American Political Science Review* 68 (September 1974): 1002–23.

———. "Those High Nineteenth-Century Turnouts: Fact or Fiction?" *Journal of Interdisciplinary History* 16 (Spring 1986): 613–44.

Burton, William L. "Wisconsin's First Railroad Commission: A Case Study in Apostasy." *Wisconsin Magazine of History* 45 (Spring 1962): 190–98.

Calhoun, Charles W. "Civil Religion and the Gilded Age Presidency: The Case of Benjamin Harrison." *Presidential Studies Quarterly* 23 (Fall 1993): 656–63.

———. "Political Economy in the Gilded Age: The Republican Party's Industrial Policy." *Journal of Policy History* 8, no. 3 (1996): 291–310.

Campbell, Ballard C. "Did Democracy Work? Prohibition in Late-Nineteenth-Century Iowa: A Test Case." *Journal of Interdisciplinary History* 8 (Summer 1977): 87–116.

Cherny, Robert W. "Lawrence Goodwyn and Nebraska Populism: A Review Essay." *Great Plains Quarterly* 1 (Summer 1981): 181–94.

Cosmas, Graham A. "The Democracy in Search of Issues: The Wisconsin Reform Party, 1873–1877." *Wisconsin Magazine of History* 46 (Winter 1962–63): 93–108.

Doolen, Richard M. "Pastor in Politics: The Congressional Career of the Reverend Gilbert De La Matyr." *Indiana Magazine of History* 68 (June 1972): 101–24.

Doyle, Don Harrison. "Social Theory and New Communities in Nineteenth-Century America." *Western Historical Quarterly* 8 (April 1977): 151–65.

Elkins, F. Clark. "The Agricultural Wheel: County Politics and Consolidation, 1884–1885." *Arkansas Historical Quarterly* 29 (Summer 1970): 152–75.

Ely, James W., Jr. "The Railroad Question Revisited: Chicago, Milwaukee & St. Paul Railway versus Minnesota and Constitutional Limits on State Regulations." *Great Plains Quarterly* 12 (Spring 1992): 121–34.

Fischer, Roger A. "Rustic Rasputin: William A. Peffer in Color Cartoon Art, 1891–1899." *Kansas History* 11 (Winter 1988–89): 222–39.

Forgette, Richard. "Reed's Rules and the Partisan Theory of Legislative Organizations." *Polity* 29 (1997): 375–96.

Formisano, Ronald P. "The 'Party Period' Revisited." *Journal of American History* 86 (June 1999): 93–120.

———. "Political Character, Antipartyism, and the Second Party System." *American Quarterly* 21 (Winter 1969): 683–709.

Frank, Thomas. "The Leviathan with Tentacles of Steel: Railroads in the Minds of Kansas Populists." *Western Historical Quarterly* 20 (February 1989): 37–54.

Giggie, John. "'Disband Him from the Church': African Americans and the Spiritual Politics of Disfranchisement in Post-Reconstruction Arkansas." *Arkansas Historical Quarterly* 60 (Autumn 2001): 245–64.

Gordon, Michael A. "The Labor Boycott in New York City, 1880–1886." *Labor History* 16 (Spring 1975): 185–204.

Hammarberg, Melvyn. "An Analysis of American Electoral Data." *Journal of Interdisciplinary History* 13 (Spring 1983): 629–52.

Haywood, C. Robert. "Populist Humor: The Fame of Their Own Effigy." *Kansas History* 16 (Spring 1993): 34–41.

Henningson, Berton E., Jr. "'Root Hog or Die': The Brothers of Freedom and the 1884 Arkansas Election." *Arkansas Historical Quarterly* 45 (Autumn 1986): 197–216.

Hinckley, Ted C. "The Politics of Sinophobia: Garfield, the Morey Letter, and the Presidential Election of 1880." *Ohio History* 89 (Autumn 1980): 381–99.

Holmes, William F. "The Georgia Alliance Legislature." *Georgia Historical Quarterly* 68 (Winter 1984): 479–515.

———. "Populism in Black Belt Georgia: Racial Dynamics in Taliaferro County Politics, 1890–1900." *Georgia Historical Quarterly* 83 (Summer 1999): 242–66.

———. "The Southern Farmers' Alliance: The Georgia Experience." *Georgia Historical Quarterly* 72 (Winter 1988): 627–52.

Holt, Michael F. "The Primacy of Party Reasserted." *Journal of American History* 86 (June 1999): 151–57.

House, Albert V. "The Democratic State Central Committee of Indiana in 1880: A Case Study in Party Tactics and Finance." *Indiana Magazine of History* 58 (September 1962): 179–210.

Howe, Daniel W. "The Evangelical Movement and Political Culture in the North during the Second Party System." *Journal of American History* 77 (March 1991): 1216–39.

Jacobs, James Henry. "The West Virginia Gubernatorial Contest, 1888–1890." *West Virginia History* 7 (April 1946): 159–220; (July 1946): 263–311.

Jensen, Richard. "The Religious and Occupational Roots of Party Identification: Illinois and Indiana in the 1870's." *Civil War History* 16 (December 1970): 325–43.

King, Ronald F. "Counting the Votes: South Carolina's Stolen Election of 1876." *Journal of Interdisciplinary History* 32 (Autumn 2001): 169–91.

Klebanow, Diana. "E. L. Godkin, the City, and Civic Responsibility." *New-York Historical Society Quarterly* 55 (January 1971): 52–71.

Kleppner, Paul. "Voters and Parties in the Western States, 1876–1900." *Western Historical Quarterly* 14 (January 1983): 49–68.

Kolbe, Richard L. "Culture, Political Parties and Voting Behavior: Schuylkill County." *Polity* 8 (Winter 1975): 243–52.

Kolesar, Robert J. "The Limits of Partisanship in Gilded Age Worcester: The Citizens Coalition." *Historical Journal of Massachusetts* 16 (January 1988): 94–106.

Korobkin, Russell. "The Politics of Disfranchisement in Georgia." *Georgia Historical Quarterly* 74 (Spring 1990): 20–58.

Kousser, J. Morgan. "Restoring Politics to Political History." *Journal of Interdisciplinary History* 12 (Spring 1982): 569–96.

——. "Towards 'Total Political History': A Rational Choice Program." *Journal of Interdisciplinary History* 20 (Spring 1990): 521–60.

Kruman, Marc W. "The Second Party System and the Transformation of Revolutionary Republicanism." *Journal of the Early Republic* 12 (Winter 1992): 509–37.

Larson, Robert W. "Populism in the Mountain West: A Mainstream Movement." *Western Historical Quarterly* 13 (April 1982): 143–64.

Lazerow, Jama. "'The Workingman's Hour': The 1886 Labor Uprising in Boston." *Labor History* 21 (Spring 1980): 200–220.

Leonard, Glen M. "Southwestern Boundaries and the Principles of Statemaking." *Western Historical Quarterly* 8 (January 1977): 39–53.

MacDonald, Wendell D. "The Early History of Labor Statistics in the United States." *Labor History* 13 (Spring 1972): 267–78.

Malin, James C. "The Democratic Party and Atchison: A Case Study, 1880." *Kansas Historical Quarterly* 28 (Summer 1962): 154–66.

Mayfield, Loomis. "Voting Fraud in Early-Twentieth-Century Pittsburgh." *Journal of Interdisciplinary History* 24 (Summer 1993): 59–84.

Mayo, Edward L. "Republicanism, Antipartyism, and Jacksonian Party Politics: A View from the Nation's Capital." *American Quarterly* 31 (Spring 1979): 3–20.

McCormick, Richard L., and John F. Reynolds. "Outlawing 'Treachery': Split Tickets and Ballot Laws in New York and New Jersey, 1880–1914." *Journal of American History* 72 (March 1986): 835–58.

McFarland, Gerald W., and Kazuto Oshio. "Civil War Military Service and Loyalty to the Republican Party: 1884." *Historical Journal of Massachusetts* 15 (June 1987): 169–74.

McFarlane, Larry A. "Nativism or Not? Perceptions of British Investment in Kansas, 1882–1901." *Great Plains Quarterly* 7 (Fall 1987): 232–43.

———. "Opposition to British Agricultural Investment in the Northern Plains States, 1884–1900." *Nebraska History* 67 (Summer 1986): 115–33.

McKinney, Gordon B. "The Politics of Protest: The Labor Reform and Greenback Parties in New Hampshire." *Historical New Hampshire* 36 (Summer/Fall 1981): 149–70.

Moneyhon, Carl H. "Black Politics in Arkansas during the Gilded Age, 1876–1900." *Arkansas Historical Quarterly* 44 (Autumn 1985): 222–45.

Moore, James Tice. "Agrarianism and Populism in Tennessee, 1886–1896: An Interpretative Overview." *Tennessee Historical Quarterly* 42 (Spring 1983): 76–94.

Nugent, Walter T. K. "How the Populists Lost in 1894." *Kansas Historical Quarterly* 31 (Autumn 1965): 245–55.

Oestreicher, Richard. "Socialism and the Knights of Labor in Detroit, 1877–1886." *Labor History* 22 (Winter 1981): 5–30.

Ostler, Jeffrey. "Why the Populist Party was Strong in Kansas and Nebraska but Weak in Iowa." *Western Historical Quarterly* 23 (November 1992): 451–74.

Owens, Kenneth N. "Patterns and Structure in Western Territorial Politics." *Western Historical Quarterly* 1 (October 1970): 373–92.

Paisley, Clifton. "The Political Wheelers and Arkansas' Election of 1888." *Arkansas Historical Quarterly* 25 (Spring 1966): 3–21.

Palermo, Patrick F. "The Rules of the Game: Local Republican Political Culture in the Gilded Age." *Historian* 47 (August 1985): 479–96.

Parish, Willam E. "The Great Kansas Legislative Imbroglio of 1893." *Journal of the West* 7 (October 1968): 471–90.

Peterson, John M. "The People's Party of Kansas: Campaigning in 1898." *Kansas History* 13 (Winter 1990–91): 235–58.

Press, Donald E. "Kansas Conflict: Populist versus Railroader in the 1890's." *Kansas Historical Quarterly* 43 (Autumn 1977): 319–33.

Reeves, Thomas C. "Chester A. Arthur and Campaign Assessments in the Election of 1880." *Historian* 31 (August 1969): 573–82.

Reynolds, John F. " 'The Silent Dollar': Vote Buying in New Jersey." *New Jersey History* (Fall–Winter 1980): 191–211.

Riker, William H. "Why Negative Campaigning Is Rational: The Rhetoric of the Ratification Campaign of 1787–1788." *Studies in American Political Development* 5 (Fall 1991): 224–70.

Rodgers, Thomas E. "Liberty, Will, and Violence: The Political Ideology of the Democrats of West-Central Indiana during the Civil War." *Indiana Magazine of History* 92 (June 1996): 133–59.

Scheirov, Richard. "Political Cultures and the Role of the State in Labor's Republic: The View from Chicago, 1848–1877." *Labor History* 32 (Summer 1991): 376–400.

Schuneman, R. Smith. "Art or Photography: A Question for Newspaper Editors of the 1890s." *Journalism Quarterly* 42 (Winter 1965): 43–52.

Stewart, Charles, III, and Barry R. Weingast. "Stacking the Senate, Changing the Nation: Republican Rotten Boroughs, Statehood Politics, and American Political Development." *Studies in American Political Development* 6 (Fall 1992): 223–71.

Treleven, Dale E. "Railroads, Elevators, and Grain Dealers: The Genesis of Antimonopolism in Milwaukee." *Wisconsin Magazine of History* 52 (Spring 1969): 205–22.

Vandal, Gilles. "The Policy of Violence in Caddo Parish, 1865–1884." *Louisiana History* 32 (Spring 1991): 159–82.

———. "Politics and Violence in Bourbon Louisiana: The Loreauville Riot of 1884 as a Case Study." *Louisiana History* 30 (Winter 1989): 23–42.

Voss-Hubbard, Mark. "The 'Third Party Tradition' Reconsidered: Third Parties and American Public Life, 1830–1900." *Journal of American History* 86 (June 1999): 121–50.

Watson, Harry L. "Humbug? Bah! Altschuler and Blumin and the Riddle of the Antebellum Electorate." *Journal of American History* 84 (December 1997): 886–93.

Welch, Melanie K. "Violence and the Decline of Black Politics in St. Francis County." *Arkansas Historical Quarterly* 60 (Autumn 2001): 360–93.

Wells, Merle. "Idaho's Season of Political Distress: An Unusual Path to Statehood." *Montana* 37 (Autumn 1987): 60–64.

Wertheim, Lewis J. "The Indianapolis Treason Trials, the Elections of 1864, and the Power of the Partisan Press." *Indiana Magazine of History* 85 (September 1989): 236–60.

White, W. Thomas. "A Gilded Age Businessman in Politics: James J. Hill, the Northwest, and the American Presidency, 1884–1912." *Pacific Historical Review* 57 (November 1988): 439–56.

———. "The War of the Railroad Kings: The Great Northern–Northern Pacific Rivalry in Montana, 1881–1896." In *Montana and the West: Essays in Honor of K. Ross Toole*, edited by Harry W. Fritz and Rex C. Myers, 37–54. Boulder, Colo.: Pruett Publishing Co., 1984.

Wyman, Roger E. "Wisconsin Ethnic Groups and the Election of 1890." *Wisconsin Magazine of History* 51 (Summer 1968): 269–943.

Unpublished Dissertations

Baney, Terry A. "Yankees and the City: Struggling over Urban Representation in Connecticut, 1880 to World War I." Ph.D. diss., University of Connecticut, 1989.

Boyd, John Alan. "Neutrality and Peace: Kentucky and the Secession Crisis of 1861." Ph.D. diss., University of Kentucky, 1999.

Brockman, John Martin. "Railroads, Radicals, and Democrats: A Study in Texas Politics, 1865–1900." Ph.D. diss., University of Texas at Austin, 1975.

Bromberg, Alan. "Pure Democracy and White Supremacy: The Redeemer Period in North Carolina, 1876–1894." Ph.D. diss., University of Virginia, 1977.

Chrislock, Carl H. "The Politics of Protest in Minnesota, 1890 to 1901: From Populism to Progressivism." Ph.D. diss., University of Minnesota, 1955.

Crofts, Daniel W. "The Blair Bill and the Elections Bill: The Congressional Aftermath to Reconstruction." Ph.D. diss., Yale University, 1968.

Edwards, Rebecca B. "Gender in American Politics, 1880–1900." Ph.D. diss., University of Virginia, 1995.

Ferguson, James S. "Agrarianism in Mississippi, 1871–1900." Ph.D. diss., University of North Carolina, 1952.

Fram, Steven J. "Purifying the Ballot? The Politics of Electoral Procedure in New York State, 1821–1871." M.A. thesis, Cornell University, 1983.

Gross, Jimmy Frank. "Alabama Politics and the Negro, 1874–1901." M.A. thesis, University of Georgia, 1970.

McDaniel, John E. "The Presidential Election of 1888." Ph.D. diss., University of Texas, 1970.

McHargue, Daniel S. "Appointments to the Supreme Court of the United States." Ph.D. diss., University of California at Los Angeles, 1949.

Petersen, Eric Falk. "Prelude to Progressivism: California Election Reform, 1870–1909." Ph.D. diss., University of California at Los Angeles, 1969.

Quay, William L. "Philadelphia Democrats: 1880–1910." Ph.D. diss., Lehigh University, 1969.

Rathegeber, Lewis R. "The Democratic Party in Pennsylvania, 1880–1896." Ph.D. diss., University of Pittsburgh, 1955.

Robbins, David Earl. "The Congressional Career of William Ralls Morrison." Ph.D. diss., University of Illinois, 1963.

Rogers, William W. "Agrarianism in Alabama, 1865–1896." Ph.D. diss., University of North Carolina at Chapel Hill, 1959.

Russell, Marvin F. "The Republican Party of Arkansas." Ph.D. diss., University of Arkansas, 1985.

Segraves, Joe T. "Arkansas Politics, 1874–1918." Ph.D. diss., University of Kentucky, 1973.

Stern, Clarence A. "Leadership and Formation of Policy within the Republican Party, 1889–1901." Ph.D. diss., University of Nebraska, 1958.

Thompson, George Hyman. "Leadership in Arkansas Reconstruction." Ph.D. diss., Columbia University, 1968.

Webb, Samuel L. "Two-Party Politics in the One-Party South: Alabama Hill Country, 1880–1920." Ph.D. diss., University of Arkansas, 1991.